Also by John Ralston Saul

NOVELS
The Birds of Prey
Baraka or The Lives, Fortunes,
  and Sacred Honor of Anthony Smith
The Next Best Thing
The Paradise Eater

ESSAYS
Voltaire's Bastards
The Doubter's Companion
The Unconscious Civilization

John Ralston Saul

REFLECTIONS OF A SIAMESE TWIN
CANADA AT THE END OF THE TWENTIETH CENTURY

VIKING

VIKING
Published by the Penguin Group
Penguin Books Canada Ltd, 10 Alcorn Avenue, Toronto, Ontario, Canada M4V 3B2
Penguin Books Ltd, 27 Wrights Lane, London W8 5TZ, England
Viking Penguin, a division of Penguin Books USA Inc., 375 Hudson Street, New
York, New York 10014, U.S.A.
Penguin Books Australia Ltd, Ringwood, Victoria, Australia
Penguin Books (NZ) Ltd, cnr Rosedale and Airborne Roads, Albany, Auckland
1310, New Zealand

Penguin Books Ltd, Registered Offices: Harmondsworth, Middlesex, England

First published 1997
10 9 8 7 6 5 4 3 2 1

Printed in the United States on acid free paper ∞

CANADIAN CATALOGUING IN PUBLICATION DATA

Saul, John Ralston, 1947–
    Reflections of a Siamese twin

ISBN 0-670-87099-4

1. Canada. I. Title

FC60.S38 1997   971   C96-930115-4
F1008.3.S38 1997

Visit Penguin Canada's web site at **www.penguin.ca**

To
the memory of my brother
Anthony

Ce fut un Vaisseau d'or, dont les flancs diaphanes
Révélaient des trésors que les marins profanes,
Dégoût, Haine et Névrose, entre eux ont disputés.

Émile Nelligan, Le Vaisseau d'or

An exposed ice surface often displays a dull, undifferentiated façade. The intricate crystalline structure can be revealed, however, by pouring a warm liquid over the ice.

Thomas Wharton, Icefields

Contents

Reflections of a Siamese Twin

PART I

MYTHOLOGY

"Comme si les grands principes se
rattachaient à nos plus intimes désirs."
François Charron, *La vie n'a pas de sens*

Victims of Mythology

1

CANADA, LIKE OTHER NATION-STATES, suffers from a contradiction between its public mythologies and its reality. Perhaps we suffer more than most. Perhaps the explanation is that, while all countries are complex, the central characteristic of the Canadian state is its complexity.

Mythology often turns into a denial of complexity. That can become its purpose.

On a good day it can provide relief from the endlessly contradictory burdens of reality. Mythology thus helps citizens to summon up enough energy to consider the public good—the good of the whole. And that simple act of consideration—of doubting—is an affirmation of their self-confidence as citizens. That self-confidence allows us to question how the public good might be served. In place of fear, and the certitude fear demands, we are able to question and to think.

On a bad day, mythology encourages the denial of reality. As if in a bank of fog, we stumble into illusion, which in turn produces an impression of relief or rather a state of delusion. In that atmosphere a rising undercurrent of fear creates that self-demeaning need for certitude. Absolute answers and ideologies prosper. These are asserted to be natural and inevitable. In this way mythology becomes not so much false as mystification.

And so it suddenly is rumoured or promised that prosperity is around the corner, the quarrelling will end, la fin des chicanes, inflation will be strangled along with unemployment, debts will be outlawed, duplication and overlap evaporate, efficiency reign, outsiders disappear. In such an atmosphere of certitudes the citizen

4   feels defenceless against the forces of superstition and the manipulation of false prophets.

Whatever their region or language or background, Canadians have no particular desire for mythologies gone wrong. Anglophones, francophones, Natives, Westerners, Maritimers, Northerners, new immigrants, whatever—none of us are more susceptible than the others to delusionary mythologies. And yet, our increasing inability to deal with our own reality suggests that we have somehow become the victims of mythology.

Mythologies gone wrong tend to turn on Heroics and victimization. Sometimes the Hero is also a victim. A martyr on behalf of a group. Sometimes this status of the Heroic victim is assumed by the whole collective. Suddenly we are dealing with or acting as if we are an Heroic, victimized people or region. All of this we have seen in the West, in Quebec, in Ontario.

The very act of brandishing slogans and flags, when done in the name of heroics or victimization, necessitates the identification of villains. Usually, in this careful society, those who require a villain also deny their need. And yet the concept is there, often in a code— a word or a phrase which believers understand to identify the enemy, unnameable because they are a race or a language group or believers in another religion.

This victim psychology has melted its way ever further into Canadian society. Scarcely a discussion goes on, between linguistic groups or regions or even within cities and towns, which is not a struggle between competing myths of victimization.

There is one other facet of public mythology. It involves specific qualities which are asserted or assumed. Often these are just good fun—harmless clichés. One group claims that it produces the best lovers, another appropriates the qualities of niceness or warmth or looks or food or courage or common sense or honesty. One claims the talent for making money. Another cares about others.

Why not? If it makes an individual or a group feel better about themselves and also fills the trough of social banter and self-congratulation, which we all seem to need, why not? There is nothing wrong with a bit of innocent comic relief. We know that, as the mythology of these specific qualities is approached, so it mysteriously recedes without damaging our convictions. However, if these appropriations of qualities are taken seriously, they quickly slip into assumptions about race or about loyalty versus betrayal or indeed salvation versus damnation. The asserted qualities of one become the unacceptable flaws of the other.

Like other western nations, we went down that road in the latter part of the last century and we have spent much of the twentieth century trying to rid ourselves of the resulting tics.

With hearts as brave as theirs,
With hopes as strong and high,
We'll ne'er disgrace
The honoured race
Whose deeds can never die.

This nineteenth-century "Song for Canada"—an apparently Anglo-Saxon Canada—isn't very different from the historian François-Xavier Garneau's "that which characterizes the French race above all others is this hidden force of cohesion and resistance, which guarantees national unity."[1]

Far worse was said on all sides and by well-known, well-educated people who should have known better. Pages can be and have been filled with these nineteenth-century mythological delusions. The word 'race' was then bandied about with the greatest of ease. It was shorthand for nationalism and national interests. The catastrophes that these assumptions would lead to in the twentieth century were still unknown.

That many of our intellectual and political leaders, from one end of the country to the other, went on talking that way beyond the middle of the twentieth century is quite another matter. Sensible, responsible people in the nineteenth and early-twentieth centuries knew that this sort of mystification of mythologies was dangerous, but didn't yet know how catastrophic it could be. Once that became clear, between the 1930s and the end of the Second World War, no room was left for naïveté on the subject of race. Those who continue to use the nineteenth-century formulae, or modern versions of them, do not deserve the respect which an attempt to understand their specific case would imply.

◄————————►

Whatever the situation, none of us believes that we live by myth alone. It's just that, during brief moments of excitement—when raging emotion is set loose, and often manipulated—we convince ourselves of what we don't really believe. Even these can be moments of healthy or harmless celebration or of necessary mourning.

But they can also turn into explosions of anger or despair, as if only unleashed mythology can permit their expression. And so the complexities of reality are funnelled and filtered down to the dangerous false clarity of mythological truth.

Clearly we cannot live without myth. Nor should we, any more than we can or should live without the various expressions of myth. We need a reasonable level of identity, nationalism, self-respect, pride and, for that matter, fantasy. But taken beyond the reasonable, these identification marks become the tools of deformed mythology and victimization. This is the territory not so much of mythology or even of false mythology, if such a concept can exist, but of mystification. Perhaps, to use an old term, this is fouled mythology. Suddenly the believers believe themselves to be alone in their sufferings and therefore in their rights. The *other*—the neighbour in another region, in the city, up north, speaking another language, of another colour—recedes ever further into the abstract meaningless typology of just that—the *other*. Too bad for him. Too bad for her. Too bad for them. They are merely the *other*.

Our difficulty is how to avoid myth being deformed into a negative force which breeds—among other things—a victim psychosis. If we fail, these shadowy simplifications will restrict and deform how we see ourselves and others. With that, we lose a great force— the ability to imagine what we might do if we embraced the complexity of our reality.

Not that reality is easy to seize. Myth, after all, is a marriage of the past and the present. And that past is itself wrapped up in a myriad myths. "The memory that we question," Saint-Denys Garneau wrote, "has heavily curtained windows." He was echoed a half-century later by bp Nichol:

the lack of substantial fact
makes history the memory of
an amnesiac

makes anything his
who works it with his hands

& such lies as we make myths
                                accepted
as planned.[2]

We cannot live without myth. But even a cursory glimpse through history suggests that more have died by it than have blossomed, once they become its servant.

Since the arrival of the nation-state only a few hundred years ago, most countries have tried to manage their real complexity by creating a manageable appearance of simplicity—a single language, a single culture, a single or dominant race. All of this has been dressed up in a centralized mythology. But these myths invariably required the real and prolonged use of state force. This violence has included

8   repeated wars against minorities, the forbidding of minority languages, the centralization of government and, of great importance, the writing of a centralized justificatory history.

The centralization of government has often been close to total—as in Britain and France—or clearly dominant, as in the United States. The force required to accomplish this state of being has created mythologies which could be described as enforced realities. With time, these become expressions of acquiescence by the various groups of citizens, who agree to forget what they once were. They don't necessarily forget everything, but usually enough to permit the enforced realities to function as if they were real.

Canada is no innocent in these matters. We have engaged in state violence against various minorities, particularly the Métis. We have attempted to forbid various languages in particular circumstances.

But most of this—by the standards of our friends and neighbours, the other nation-states—adds up to small potatoes. That hardly justifies what has been done. But none of it has come close to enforcing a reality which could produce a centralized mythology. In truth, none of those efforts have even been seriously aimed at producing the standard monolithic mythology of the other nation-states.

This is described by most federalists and anti-federalists alike as the failure of Canada. The failure to become like the others. To regularize a monolithic mythology. Some weep before the ever-retreating mirage of the unhyphenated Canadian. Others say its continued existence proves that the country is not real and cannot exist. For me, this failure to conform is in fact our greatest success. A proof of originality which we refuse to grasp as a positive.

In *Les Aurores montréales*, Monique Proulx's wonderful portrait of Montreal in the nineties, she talks of Canada as "un grand pays mou—a big soft country."[3] Soft because the classic nation-state is hard—hard in the force of its creation and its maintenance. Hard in the clarity of its enforced mythology. In the simple, monolithic model, the very concept of non-conformity is a simile for weakness. In general it is recuperated and reduced to a self-indulgent description of occasional, non-threatening non-conformity by individuals. Non-conformity becomes nothing more than personal particularities.

In the standard nation-state mythology of enforced reality, soft is unnatural and therefore not real. Big, soft and weak. But is this a fair definition of 'soft'? Perhaps the opposite is true.

Surely it is fear and a sense of inferiority which make a people require the defence of a monolithic, simplistic model. Was the violence required to enforce their mythology a sign of toughness, or the bravado of the insecure bully? Or did it simply reflect the determination of one group to dominate the others? And is softness not another word for self-confidence? Self-confident enough to live with complexity. Tough enough to assume complexity.

The essential characteristic of the Canadian public mythology is its complexity. To the extent that it denies the illusion of simplicity, it is a reasonable facsimile of reality. That makes it a revolutionary reversal of the standard nation-state myth. To accept our reality— the myth of complexity—is to live out of step with most other nations. It is an act of non-conformity.

My own sense is that the citizenry accept their non-conformity with some ease. They live it and so it makes sense. The élites, on the other hand, fret at being out of sync with élites in other countries, particularly those in the business and academic communities. But politicians also seem increasingly affected by a need to conform on some level perceived to be higher. It is an emotional or psychological problem. They don't want to feel out of step.

So long as Canada was a small, marginal place, more or less invisible on the world scene, the best of our élites embraced the originality of the project. And by élites I mean those who occupy any of the positions of responsibility in government or business or academia or public service. The growth of Canada and the growth of visible global models has triggered their inferiority complex. What we now call globalization, like it or not, is a great force for conformity. In this context the élites don't like not fitting in. They long to conform, each in their own way, to the old monolithic national models and the new monolithic international economic models.

"We have quietly accepted the disappearance of the past," writes the Swedish poet and novelist Kjell Espmark.[4] How can those who hold the various reins of power throughout society play their role if they are cut off from the reality of the society's past? I am not suggesting that they turn towards the past or act as its prisoners. But that reality and its mythology are always the key to the future.

Change may come at supersonic speeds and give the impression of anarchy all around us. But no matter how radical the forces of change, societies do not fly about in the air and transform themselves as if this were a matter of changing clothes. Those who successfully embrace change do so from the solid basis of what they are. Reality and a healthy mythology are the key to change.

Our élites have largely lost contact with our reality. They are so caught up in a need to conform that they have forgotten—perhaps wilfully forgotten—that the very originality of the Canadian experiment has always been to stay out of step with the norm. That's what makes it interesting. Not cliché patriotism, flag waving and simplistic emotional evocations.

What might be called Canada's moments of failure can usually be traced to those periods when we feel ourselves—or rather the élites feel themselves and so try to convince the population of the same— too insecure, too weak, too tired to carry the burden of an essentially complex nature. Then anglophones begin preaching unhyphenated Canadianism and francophones claim singularity as the key to survival. The models they reach for are imported, and are not intended to complement the local reality or improve it or strengthen it, but to replace or rather deny it.

This is the provincial, colonial mind at its most insecure. Social, cultural, educational and economic models from the Rome of the day are dragged back home as proof of sophistication. Local circumstances become embarrassing reminders to this élite that it is not really Roman. And so, in place of the classical weapons of enforced realities, the élites use their positions to engage in a modern form of violence. Their desire is to turn these models into mythologies divorced from reality.

How is this done? Practical memory is eliminated. The modern tools of communication become the tools of propaganda. And fear of the consequences of non-conformity is propagated.

During the 1995 referendum campaign, I personally could find only one sustained reference to the reality of our past. It was a particularly tortured version used by Jacques Parizeau in his speech introducing the referendum bill before the Quebec legislature. It called out for reply and correction, but none came. For the rest of the campaign Mr. Parizeau dropped all pretence of context.

As for the language used by Daniel Johnson, Jean Charest and Jean Chrétien, it was as if the country had popped out of an egg the day before, fully formed. And Lucien Bouchard's repeated references to the past referred only as far back as 1982. The statements made by the various provincial premiers—Frank McKenna, Mike Harris, Roy Romanow—were little more than cheap advertising copy filled with saccharine emotions, devoid of time and place.

Our future was debated and decided as if we had no past. No experience. Therefore no reality. And yet Canada is not a new country. In legal terms it is one of the oldest in the world. In constitutional terms it is one of a tiny handful of stable, long-lasting democracies.

As for the peculiar, non-conforming Canadian experiment, it is several centuries old. Elements were put in place very early on through European–Native treaties. The change of colonial regimes in 1763 was followed by seventy-nine years of groping in the direction of the final element to this triangular pact. It was formalized in 1842.

Louis-Hippolyte LaFontaine, standing in the legislature in Kingston, described this agreement as a binding handshake. His with Robert Baldwin. They were the original Siamese twins. But their handshake was far more than that. More than French Canada with English Canada. And more precisely that of the reformers on all sides—those whom we could today describe as the democrats, the decent men, the humanists—each with the other. "These relations have created not only mutual sympathies," LaFontaine said, "but moral obligations to which our honour alone imposes the imperative duty not to be found lacking." Moments before, Baldwin had spoken of a "union of hearts and of free born men." "The voluntary choice of a free people."[5]

That various schools of historians and politicians have sought out only the failures in this process, or concentrated on the wrongs done or the victories for their side, is another matter. I will come back to that later. But the intent of the handshake between Baldwin and LaFontaine, like that between Louis-Joseph Papineau and William Lyon Mackenzie or indeed between thousands of others less well known, was clear. The specific point here is the longevity of the experiment. And the complexity of it. This original triangle—because despite our prolonged denials, the Natives have always been part of the bargain—is like a multi-jointed box which can fold and unfold in many ways. Language, geography, experience, all change the way in which citizens see their situation and their role.

The result is a multitude of non-contradictory visions. This is a strength, not a weakness, so long as the memory of "moral obligation," "honour" and "imperative duty" to respect "the voluntary choice of a free people" is still there. What is difficult for us to remember is that this is not an invitation to introspection. Memory is at its least interesting when reduced to an evocation of past wrongs done by the *other*. The question is not, "How is the *other* treating me?" It is primarily an invocation to consider how we treat the *other*.

That is not easy when multitudes of mythologies tell each of us that
we are the aggrieved party.

Two centuries is a very long time in the history of any country. Perhaps this is because the typical nation-state asserts that it is the product of a natural and completed experiment. Civil wars, coups d'état, dictatorships, territories added by force, others lost, minorities digested against their will, minority cultures and languages eliminated; all of these are treated as minor accidents along the way. Accidents de parcours. They are quickly erased from the experience of the central mythology—the imposed reality. And so the state's idea of itself as a completed experiment is reasserted within a few decades of each disaster. The myth of natural permanency envelops and softens any real memory.

For Canadians, whatever their language or politics, the acceptance of complexity has meant the acceptance of a perpetually incomplete experiment. In such a myth, the link to reality is dependent on our maintenance of a whole series of equilibriums.

This idea of living with balance and doubt seems to have become more difficult as time has gone by. In part, I would put this down to a growing rift throughout western civilization—between reality and mythology. Our reality is corporatist, interest based, anti-democratic, determinist, and thus passive. As for mythology, it is increasingly a distraction, inflated and manipulated by the ever more sophisticated means of communication. This is mythology deformed into mystification.

A cynic might argue that the citizen is now manipulated with techniques first perfected in the 1930s by Hitler's film-maker, Leni Riefenstahl, in *Triumph of the Will*. She demonstrated how images, music and words could be detached from each other and so from reality. This in turn opened the door to highly efficient meaninglessness.

14   At its most banal this methodology has grown into that mass of words and images which constitute our daily propaganda; that is, our advertising, press releases, sound bites and personality pieces. But it is more than that. Suddenly emotion bereft of content is made so powerful that it obscures the mechanisms of reality; that is, of power.

That would be the cynic's interpretation. For myself, I would say that this new high-tech mythology has become the loser's consolation prize in the growing global structures of corporatism.

Why a consolation? Because insecurity and fear are the weapons of power in this mythology for losers. "Les murs lisses de la peur—the smooth and slippery walls of fear are the habitual refuge of the defeated."[6] That was how the great painter Paul-Émile Borduas put it.

But the mind-set of the defeated, whether it refers to a few thousand abandoned colonials on the banks of the St. Lawrence or to thirty million citizens in an enormous country, is precisely that—a state of mind. And that psychological state is lodged first and foremost in the minds of the élite, who fear and therefore propagate fear among the population as a justification for their own failures.

Borduas's formula succinctly describes the negative side of our mythology from its earliest days. To the extent that we are unable to accept and assume the complexity of our reality, so we are gripped by a fear of non-conformity. We are overcome by a desperate desire to present ourselves as a natural and completed experiment, monolithic, normal, just another one of the standard nation-states.

Jacques Godbout described this state of being in his novel *Les Têtes à Papineau*. The heroes are Siamese twins. They have one body, two heads and two separate but interrelated personalities. Together they are very interesting. Most people want them to be separated—to be normalized. Banalized. To become like other people. To give up their real non-conformity for perhaps a more self-indulgent, less demanding sort. Gradually they lose track of their sense that to be different is a positive. In the end they agree to be separated, and so conform to the norm.[7]

The insecurity we feel is constantly accentuated by our relations with the three countries who have played the central roles in our past and present—England, France and the United States. They are also the prime international models of violently imposed monolithic mythologies. In the case of Britain and France the result has produced a remarkably monolithic reality. We are descended from and have been dominated by countries which incarnate the completed experiment. Not only are these the least likely nations to admire the concept of the state as a perpetually incomplete experiment, my experience is that they don't actually understand the concept.

In the shadows of such powerful 'normalcy' it isn't surprising that we tend to mistake our strengths for weaknesses. Nor is it surprising that each element—anglophone, francophone, aboriginal and the great waves of immigration from around the world over the last hundred years—is so often seen by the other as an additional weakness in the quest for normalcy.

It has often seemed over the last few years as if public discourse in Canada bears no relationship to the reality lived by the citizenry. Variance has slipped into division. Fear, frustration, passivity and anger have grown as we focus on a mythological language which doesn't function in either English or French. The citizen can find no way into this false debate. The fact-driven and power-dependent élites are frightened by the citizenry and by the idea of non-corporatist participation. And the ever more deformed machinery of communications has indeed become a weapon for what the Counter-Reformation, four centuries ago, identified as propaganda.

In this atmosphere of insecurity and fear, mythology rarely functions as a practical tool of memory. Instead, it has become a tool to narrow and harden perceptions on all sides.

2 The Mythology of the Victim

THE VICTIMS OF VICTIMS ARE surely confused. What else can it mean when so many of us see ourselves as the party hard done by? How can we live in such a society? How can it function in such a clamour of competing inferiority complexes, particularly when so many of these are disguised as competing self-confidences?

> So in spite of ourselves . . .
> we spend our time denigrating people.
> it is fear
> moves me to say these things
> It was a country of pointless struggles.[1]

The professional victim is a professional innocent. As the one to whom things are done, the victim has no responsibility. This is a comfortable position of passivity. And, although it is difficult to give meaning to such a phrase, this is the classic description of a colonial mind-set—that of the passive victim. Not that there is necessarily any catastrophic level of actual victimization. But if this sense of victimization is kept at a level of repressed hysteria, then it becomes impossible to distinguish in any useful way between real cases of injustice and the psychotic state. In both cases it is the mind-set which will determine how each event will be interpreted. And in general it is easier to mobilize a sense of mistreatment over the mythological wrong than over the real.

Finally, it is the élites who find greatest comfort in such a situation. What those in positions of responsibility know is that a victim is an individual programmed to be afraid. Fear is thus the chief tool of colonial-minded leadership. In spreading fear among the citizenry, it could be said that the élites are exporting their own sense of being victims, which is another way of expressing their own fear that they are inferior.

Of course not everyone falls into the category of these attitudes. Much of this book is about the non-colonial élites. But the history of Canada is filled with waves of recurring insecurity among those who lead us. At the worst of times it is as if power is reserved for those who are crippled by their disbelief in their own worth and in that of the country they are responsible for.

The result is twofold. Changes can then easily be presented to the population as inevitable. And those who occupy the positions of power can do so without assuming the responsibility of power.

This state of mind now once again dominates Canadian public life. At the heart of Canadian leadership lies a need to blame. And blame can easily include expressions of craven admiration or acceptance. Toronto blames the United States. The West blames the East. Francophones blame anglophones. Northern Ontario blames Toronto. Newfoundland blames Quebec and, thanks to a separate issue, Quebec blames Newfoundland. The oil industry blames the consumer. Those with money, who want to keep it, blame those without, in need of help.

I could fill pages with this network of fear disguised as finger-pointing. But at the core of it is a refusal to assume responsibility. The victim does not do but is done to.

A recent book by respected Western intellectuals, *Western Visions*, summed up the past by worrying about "... where to begin a discussion of Western Canadian discontent.... the sheer number and range of grievances can make the task encyclopedic."[2] Of course, there have been and still are very real grievances. And a Western alienation has existed, difficult for everyone to deal with, from the nineteenth-century Métis wars to today.

18   The historian W.L. Morton wrote eloquently about that sense of alienation and described Louis Riel as the leader of the first of a line of Western reform movements. These would include important movements destined to change the whole of Canada, as well as charlatan movements feeding off the alienation. Still other groups were a mixture of the two extremes. The serious movements ranged from the famous Siege of Ottawa in 1910, with its Farmers' Platform, through the CCF, the early William Aberhart, the Progressives and the NDP. The charlatans or mixed bags have ranged from the later Social Credit to today's Reform party.

But the point here is the tone of this Western vision. It is a tidal wave of grievances which sweeps away the remarkable success of the West. Suddenly, the fact that the social contract in Canada— one of the real symbols of what Canada is—was invented and implemented largely from the prairies is not taken to be a matter of great importance. Yet even René Lévesque's social democracy began in Saskatchewan, before being carried to Ottawa and from there to Quebec politics. And somehow the remarkable economic success of much of the West is discounted. Only the failures and the errors matter.

Not that this stance of complaint damages daily life or weakens the region's great energy and creativity. However, it can't help but limit the region's possibilities and therefore those of Canada. After all, the substructure, the frame, the point of view, in other words the basic position, is a level of complaint which bears no relationship to reality and therefore reduces even the most successful of talented people to membership in a confederation of victims.

Indeed the meat of *Western Visions* goes on to undercut its own general assumptions. Having begun by setting in place the hard-done-by tone, these highly competent writers then edge back towards reality. This is what a society of victims expects from its discourse. First we weep, to demonstrate our basic shared assumptions, then we get on with the practicalities of the real world. But you do not escape your basic mythology with a mere rhetorical flip.

So long as you accept it and invoke it, your actions will be fed by it. And if your mythology denigrates you, you will be limited by it, whatever your talents.

The particular view of nationalism developed by Abbé Groulx was gathered up and reworked in the 1950s and 1960s by a group of intellectuals known as the Montreal School. Their sage was Maurice Séguin. Their principal mouthpiece was Michel Brunet.

Although Groulx is now rightly criticized for his social and racial attitudes, and although his arguments encouraged the idea of the victim, it must be said that his arguments about the Canadian experience in general had some depth. What he had to say was interesting, whatever your own politics. The Montreal School was quite another matter.

All they took from Groulx was the negative. The result was a victim psychosis in the extreme. It is now somehow assumed that the Montreal School is just the past. No longer relevant. But in fact their selective reworking of Groulx became the intellectual foundation of the current separatist/sovereigntist school.

This movement—indeed, the Parti Québécois itself—has within it two very different, often contradictory, parts. One is social democratic and reform oriented. The other comes from the Montreal School, which was conservative, in many ways reactionary, and was tied to the old clerical nationalism. I'll come back to this in detail, as well as to the terminology—separatist/indépendantist/sovereigntist. The point here is the importance of the victim mythology.

The Montreal School anchored their catastrophic view firmly in a highly selective editing and interpretation of the past. They set out to demonstrate that the shape and pattern of all that would follow had been cast in iron by a single determining event—the changeover of titular colonial powers. This, they insisted, was a conquest or rather the Conquest, always to be capitalized. "The first,"

20 said Brunet, "the great cause of our lack of a national sense, you could even say the only cause ... was the Conquest. ..." Séguin: "The moment they installed themselves in the valley of the Saint-Lawrence, English Canada fundamentally ruined the French colony."[3] The rest was inevitable. "Papineau's former lieutenants learnt with docility the difficult art of governing on the vigilant leash of their English colleagues ...", "... the pseudo-leaders of French Canadian society." "Once again they were the victims of history's evolution."[4] These are almost haphazard citations. There are hundreds more just like them.

Was there a conquest? Certainly Papineau didn't think so. He called it "the ceding of the country—la cession du pays." Nor did Philippe Aubert de Gaspé in one of the first and most important French-Canadian novels, Les Anciens Canadiens—"La Cession du Canada."[5]

Two sorts of people have always insisted on the idea of conquest. The first was the group Papineau described as "... those people who called themselves the conquerors of the country when they were merely the baggage train merchants..."[6] In other words, those anglophones (American colonials and on-the-make British immigrants) who tried to profit from a difficult situation by pumping themselves up as the new masters, in the hope of profiting from authority. They constituted themselves as the Château Clique. The second group were those in the francophone élite who supplemented their own authority by playing the victimization card. In other words, they argued that the catastrophic situation so limited the populace's possibilities that only this particular élite's methods could defend them.

They might be called not so much the nationalists (which is a perfectly responsible position) as the narrow or ideological nationalists. Or the victimization or masochist or isolationist nationalists. Perhaps the most accurate term is the negative nationalists.

The mind-set of both pro-conquest groups, anglophone and francophone, was and remains profoundly colonial. And both groups can be followed through our history down to today. Along the way they have burnt down parliament buildings, opposed the idea of democratic justice, tried to limit the other side's language, religion, rights. Today they can be found in the neo-conservative and negative-nationalist movements, just as they could in the equivalent groups two centuries ago. They continue to operate in opposition to the reformers and the positive nationalists.

But was there a conquest? Certainly there were some battles won and lost by varying sides. These were mainly skirmishes. There were a few real but small battles. There were a few casualties. And in the fallout over the next few years there were a few more deaths. By any standards of warfare, none of this amounted to much. There was then a European conference at which those British who made money out of fur in Canada came to an agreement with those French who made money out of sugar in the Caribbean islands. Had the French beaver lobby and the English sugar lobby been stronger, the treaty might have inverted the exchange of colonies. The colonial merchants in New York and Boston would have been annoyed, but they were always annoyed with London. The French colonial slave owners in the Caribbean would have been upset, but Versailles would have seen this as the inevitable tantrums of moneyed people. What was clear was that neither metropolitan power cared in the least for those who lived in the colonies.

This last sentence should not be misunderstood. I am not blaming either colonial power. Among those who live in colonies or ex-colonies, only those with a colonial mind-set have any expectation from the power at the centre of the empire. After all, our colonial empires, like all colonial empires before and after, existed solely for the purposes of the metropole. Why else should they exist? These purposes were primarily geopolitical and economic. Why should there be any other purposes? This narrow-based self-interest was both their great strength and, in the long run, their fatal flaw. They were therefore run and disposed of from those points of view.

That colonials living on those properties imagined themselves as humans with desires as important as those in the metropolitan centre was perfectly normal. That they expected the metropolitan centre to take this into account was perfectly romantic. That is the colonial mind-set—to imagine that the colony is a part of the living body of the metropole. It never is. It cannot be. It is not even an offspring of that body. At best it is an excrescence—because the essential relationship is commercial or military and strictly one way. The attempt to graft a human relationship on top results in a profound deformation. There is an appropriate Napoleonic political description: de la merde dans un bas de soie.

That ex-colonials should maintain illusions about their past relationship with London or Paris, or that those ex-colonials should reinvent themselves as colonials with dusted-off illusions about their current relationship with Washington, is a perversion of normalcy—a persistent colonial mentality. That this merely increases the indifference and even contempt in those centres is hardly surprising. The insistence on the maintenance of an illusory family relationship, where one limited only to political and financial interest existed and exists, is humiliating for those in the former/current colonies and embarrassing for the metropolitan centres.

This painfully romantic view of our relationships with France and England didn't really emerge until the second half of the nineteenth century. And interestingly enough the idea of the 'Conquest' appeared at the same time. French Canadians hadn't seriously entertained the thought that they were a conquered people until the romantic, nationalist historians began to insist on that idea seventy-five years after the event.[7] It rose in parallel with the Imperial nationalism of the British Empire. Both delusions reflected the growing pains of tiny colonies into an enormous complex country. But both were essentially irrelevant to what was happening in that society. They were the evocations of mythology detaching itself from reality. Jacques Godbout examined much of this confusion in his film *Le Sort de l'Amérique—America's Fate.*

I am not engaging here in an arcane discussion over a technical point. What we think about our origins determines what we believe about our current situation. And the Montreal School's approach to victim mythology is by no means out of our system.

In 1993, one of Quebec City's leading intellectuals published *The Genesis of Quebec Society*. Fernand Dumont, who died in 1997, was an intelligent, talented intellectual. And yet he regurgitated the entire victim scenario, almost as if Séguin and Brunet had dictated it to him from their graves. In the genesis of Quebec society there is "only a long resistance." Francophone federalists (throughout history) are inevitably described as traitors. ". . . the political yoke—le joug politique—could be felt until a short time ago. From the Conquest to the middle of the nineteenth century, England threatened the French Canadians with assimilation."[8]

Well actually, simple mathematics suggests that the "yoke" lasted 82 years. Since then we have built, not without crises, not without tensions, not unflawed, but increasingly firm levels of democracy. And that latter period has now lasted 155 years, which is not "a short time ago." In fact it has lasted twice as long as the period of the "yoke" which itself bears some examination. After all, this is a strong, unforgiving term. And yet the period in question was made up of both good days and bad days. It saw the growth of a French-Canadian middle class and 1791 brought the first elected legislature.

Besides, the period 1760 to 1842 was difficult everywhere in the west. The first reform bill didn't pass in England until 1832. And it gave the vote only to a well-to-do middle class. Not until 1867 did workers get the vote; farmers in 1884. Universal male suffrage came only in 1918. The principle of responsible government remained unclear in Britain until the second half of the nineteenth century. The Luddites were executed or deported in 1813. The Peterloo Massacre took place in 1819 in Manchester. There was constant violence over the nature of government. As for France, there was a brief violent fling with democracy in the 1790s; followed by violent dictatorship until 1830, when 504 were killed in the revolution;

followed by a non-violent dictatorship until 1848, when 1,500 were killed in the change of regime and 6,000 deported. At that point the whole of Europe went into a short period of hope which ended almost everywhere with repression. These same decades in the United States turned on low levels of franchise, a growing use of slavery and unimaginable levels of public corruption. William Lyon Mackenzie began by idealizing American democracy. His years of exile there, after the failure of 1837, left him horrified by it. Louis-Joseph Papineau spent most of his exile in Europe and so never had to measure his American ideal against reality. Those years were for Americans the lead-up to a massive civil war over the nature of power in the union. It was the first of those twentieth-century wars fought with a massacre strategy. Between 1861 and 1865, 620,000 American soldiers were killed by other American soldiers and much of the country laid waste.

Meanwhile, to the north, English and French Canadians were arguing verbally over the best structure for legislative government. In other words, what was happening in Lower Canada was not by any western standards a "yoke." Nor was it primarily racial or linguistic or religious. Those factors were not irrelevant. Of course there were racial and religious tensions and I'll come back to those events in more detail. But the struggle in question was fundamentally the same as was going on in Upper Canada—where the democratic forces were faced by the Family Compact—and in Nova Scotia under the divided leadership of Herbert Huntington and Joseph Howe.

In some ways the most original of the reform leaders was not Mackenzie or Papineau or Howe, but William Cooper, who led a pacific revolt in Prince Edward Island based on the withholding of rents. The landowners were the Island equivalent of the Château Clique or the Family Compact and land reform was the key to responsible government. Interestingly enough, it was precisely this issue which would eventually turn Papineau—a great landowner—into an enemy of reform and a pillar of what would become negative nationalism. During 1837 and 1838, Cooper's clever sedition caused him to be committed to the custody of the sergeant-at-arms of the P.E.I. assembly. In the 1838 election his party won control of the assembly, but London, on behalf of the absentee British landlords, went out of its way to destroy him by refusing to cooperate over land reform.

These small battles in small colonies were, in fact, identical to those going on in the rest of the western world. It was a battle for responsible government which gradually evolved towards an ever-wider democratic form.

It could be said that in the Maritimes and in Lower and Upper Canada the battle was won relatively fast and with relative ease compared with the disordered situations in Europe and south of the border. "We have made a conquest greater and more glorious," Wilfrid Laurier said in 1887, "than that of any territory. We have conquered our liberties . . ."[9] At that point France, Germany, Italy and Spain still had another seventy-five years ahead of coups d'état, civil wars and citizens slaughtering citizens before the essential democratic questions would be settled. As late as the early 1960s there were repeated coup attempts in France. And in the 1950s a whole sector of the American population was still excluded from any participation in their democracy by laws which, thanks to their Supreme Court, had installed an administrative form of slavery.

I am not making one of those inane arguments about which is the best country in the world. People live where they live and cheap xenophobia is just that. Nor am I suggesting some Canadian superiority which allowed us to avoid the disasters into which others fell. I am merely talking about context—a context which permitted us to produce a more complex social structure. You could call it a conscious use of geopolitics.

But the victim mythology, being a centripetal force, cannot register wider norms. In any case, the victim has an automatic mechanism for discounting all that is positive.

In Western Canada, for example, the mythology would have it

26   that it doesn't matter how rich the society has become. What matters is "... the wealth the region *might* have enjoyed had it not been for the intervention of the federal government."[10] And although LaFontaine, Cartier, Laurier and those who supported them might have thought they were doing something, it was an illusion. Séguin saw 1791 as just a British ruse. Nothing more than "... clever concessions to prepare the resignation and assimilation of French Canadians." A psychiatrist would probably say that Mr. Séguin had a persecution complex. "The capitulation of Vaudreuil (1760) led infallibly to the unconscious capitulation of LaFontaine."[11]

There is no escape from the arguments of victimology. No matter how well you do, you are betrayed by destiny, your unconscious or some other invisible force. No matter how rich you become, you could have been richer if only ... if only. ... No matter how much power you win, your victories were traps set to ruin you and force you to your knees. No matter how much good you do, some greater cause has been betrayed. Democracy, prosperity, the rule of law, social justice; these are mere shadows which cannot efface the mythological truth of the wrong being done to you. As always, when victimization and destiny are combined, the underlying theme is a contempt by the mythologizers for the intelligence of the citizen.

◄――――――►

All of us, it can't be denied, are victimized from time to time. But this is quite different from believing ourselves to be victims all the time. That is a state of mind, more often than not in large part unconscious. It is buried in our mythology. Or rather, this is deformed mythology—mythology become mystification. And the solutions proposed to this negative state almost invariably institutionalize precisely that same state of mind. This is the result of basing the solution on an assumption that the mythology is true. The solution to the problem instead formalizes the problem by theoretically defending against it. Listen carefully to the rhetoric of Western and Quebec alienation. It is filled with an assumption of the need to formalize that mythology, often precisely by asserting that it needs to be turned inside out.

Nonsense, many would reply. By getting at the root of the problem we eliminate it.

Not at all. By identifying the very origins of our civilization as being the problem, we can only root it out by eliminating the value of everything we have since done; in other words by effacing our experience, our past; in other words by eliminating ourselves. It isn't surprising that our existence is so often reduced by both sides to a few meaningless feel-good slogans. This is part of the explanation for the referenda discourse which floated about us in 1995 in an atmosphere devoid of a real past or present.

If all our problems lie in our origins, then the solution to everything can be reduced to a new pivotal moment in which we begin again. The mythological indignities of the past will not simply be eliminated. They will be washed away. Like babies, we will be reborn, fresh, new, clean, freed of all negative memories. It is not that reality will actually begin again. Rather this mythological rebirth is to resemble a re-found virginity. And from that it can be hoped that reality will somehow be affected.

In reality nothing is eliminated, neither on the level of the concrete nor the mythological. Instead, by entering into the pretence of rebirth we actually weaken ourselves.

Over the last decades we have seen wave after wave of high-quality, talented politicians and public servants severely handicapped in their ability to propose interesting policies by the ever-thickening walls of a mythological prison. The very illusion of possible rebirth itself becomes the completed prison. That is precisely why the ideologues of victimization insist so strongly that the root of all problems lies in the origins of the civilization. If you accept that premise you are in their hands forever.

◄――――►

Our most basic myth of victimization unites all regions, languages and classes. It is, in short, that Canada exists only because it did not wish to be American. In other words, that our existence is an artificial construct based entirely on a negative. That therefore there is no real purpose, content or agreement on a project. Our endless droning on about what it might be to be a Canadian was born with this fundamental assumption.

It is a negative idea of existence and can be found explicitly or implicitly in almost every historical description of our past. The threat from the south. The desire to be British. The desire to be French-speaking Catholics. Donald Creighton: "The ominous change which seemed to come over the United States during the civil war strengthened every force in British North America which was making for national union." "If they wished to survive . . .," well, they would have to come together.[12]

The 'not to be American' creation mythology contains a subsidiary myth: that the country is an artificial east–west construction which tries to deny the 'natural' north–south flow. The Montreal School couldn't have agreed more. "Canada was built against the United States." "In order to save its artificial separatism vis-à-vis the United States, English Canada had to erase the natural separatism of French Canada."[13]

This francophone role as the safeguard for English-Canadian survival created contradictory myths. One, that the creation of Canada also saved French Canadians from annexation and assimilation. But the ideological nationalists' interpretation was that Canada limited the development of Quebec's natural friendship with the United States. A whole sub-current of the negative-nationalist school saw and sees this north–south flow as natural and to be wished. From Papineau's calls for annexation to Bernard Landry's insistence that Quebec's real friends lie to the south, this has become the natural anti-myth of the other—that is, of the myth that Canada was built to avoid becoming American.

That by most accounts some half of the francophone population went to New England around the turn of the century and was promptly assimilated into the single language, single culture, all-or-nothing American mythology, and in this case reality, makes no dent on the logic of those who preach 'Quebec's natural friendship with the United States.' It isn't surprising. The two 'not to be American' creation myths feed off each other, not off any sense of reality. In both cases they eviscerate any belief that the civilization north of the border has a real reason to exist. What's more, the argument that Canada stands in the way of a natural virile north–south relationship can be heard as easily in Halifax or Vancouver or Calgary as it can in Quebec City, Montreal and Toronto. It is evoked with a petulant tone the way a child threatens to run away from home. 'I don't belong here. I'm too good for you. I could do better with the richer, better-looking, smarter people just down the way, who are, in any case, my spiritual if not natural parents.' The doctor could make more money, the director direct bigger films, the businessman do big business down there in the real world.

I will come back to this, but my own sense is that the American card is a denial of self which is filled with self-loathing. As such, it is not merely a suicidal act (like most victim myths), it is also profoundly untrue.

Not that there aren't concrete arguments which can be made for the north–south view of the continent. For a start, there is the role in the creation of Canada of the American threat during the 1860s. And there is the natural north–south economic flow. But are these circumstantial arguments or are they essential realities? Do they accurately reflect our experience?

I would say that they are circumstantial and that the natural flow is in fact east–west. What's more, it always was, long before the idea of confederation had been imagined, long before even the ceding of the country in 1762.

30   The difficulty which myths present is always the same. How are we to remember the past? In 1882, the French writer Ernest Renan spoke at the Sorbonne on "What is a nation?" One of Renan's points was that the terrible internal massacres which built the European nations made selective forgetfulness a key to their remaining nations. "To forget, and I would even say historical error, are an essential factor in the creation of a nation."[14] In other words, it was up to historians and written history to ensure that particularly unpalatable events were more or less left out or watered down or made palatable. Ask in France how many citizens were killed by other citizens in 1830, 1848, 1871, and you will find the numbers strangely absent. In 1944–45? Perhaps twenty thousand. Perhaps two hundred thousand. Who knows?

In 1996 the philosopher Charles Taylor commented at length on Renan's arguments. "It is necessary that many things be forgotten: the conflicts, even the crimes which divided our ancestors."[15]

But I wonder to what extent we choose that which is remembered versus that which is forgotten. Perhaps our duty is to remember everything, so long as our intelligence is devoted to giving balance and context to those memories. After all, the only real protection against the repetition of a barbaric or stupid act is a conscious recollection of the implications.

What often does happen would suggest that Renan was right, if only in a curious way. Often it seems that the worse the crime the less likely it is to leave traces of bitterness. It is the smaller acts of wrongdoing which take on a mythical life imbued with bitterness.

Renan talks of the prolonged brutality, extermination and terror used to unify France—few of those traces remain. One could say the same about many of the great crimes of the twentieth century—for example, the Holocaust and the legal murder which they called World War One. We try to remember. Constant intelligent efforts are made to ensure that we do remember. But strangely enough, even in these horribly extreme cases, the mythology is not one of victimology. The clarity of the wrong done seems to give the victim a sense of their just position. Perhaps it is this which in turn draws much of the poison from the wound.

Nothing which the outside world would consider a major crime has ever been committed in Canada. And yet we have had our tragic and clearly unacceptable moments. These are our real tragedies. The aboriginal community has suffered from endless acts of injustice, violence and dishonesty, including the trashing of treaties signed in good faith; the expulsion of the Acadians in 1755 was one of the most disturbing; and it was followed by a second internal expulsion in the 1780s; the persecution of the Métis was another; there was the legalized anti-Asian racism which culminated in the internment of the Japanese Canadians during the Second World War. "We are going down to the middle of the earth with pick-axe eyes," Joy Kogawa writes, "carried along by the momentum of the expulsion into the waiting wilderness." "We are the despised rendered voiceless...."[16] Here, as elsewhere in the world, it is interesting to note the low level of bitterness which these dreadful events have left behind.

Of course there have been hundreds of other unacceptable actions. As in the rest of the western world endemic anti-Semitism and a panoply of specific racisms plagued us from coast to coast in the first half of the century. The anti-Chinese head tax in British Columbia, Regulation 17 limiting French schooling in Ontario and the exclusion of the old Halifax black community are just three examples. Most of these and other prejudices have been beaten back into the shadows, where inevitably they still lurk. Again the levels of bitterness among the very real victims are surprisingly low.

But what about the palpable mistreatment of French Canadians inside Quebec? Surely that belongs on the list. The wrongs done were very real. But the context was also far more complicated. As the political scientist Jean-Pierre Derriennic puts it, "if you explain to an immigrant that French Canadians have also been second-class citizens, he goes off to look in the books. He discovers that the Saint-Lawrence valley has been governed since 1791, almost without interruption, by a State of Law which included an elected assembly."[17] In other words, you cannot compare the fate of those who once dominated in Canada—the aboriginals—with the state of the francophone community. Whatever its problems, the inheritance and the status of the latter is not a tragedy.

Its history is filled with positives and negatives and all of the interested parties have well-entrenched positions. Each has their list of wrongs. I would rather attempt to avoid the canonical approach, tipping my hat at appropriate moments as the stations of victimization are passed. That is, I would rather approach a complex problem with the dignity it deserves, and deal with it step by step throughout the book.

If simplifications are required, why not begin with what could be called the two great tragedies of Canada's first century? They began as political struggles and ended by infusing much of the mythological and real poison and bitterness into our society.

The first was the victory of the Ultramontane movement in Quebec and the second the victory of the Orange movement in Ontario. Each in its own way was a spearhead of intolerance and a manipulator of fear. The Ultramontanes took French Canada off a relatively normal track of political and social evolution. In many ways, the result was the loss of a century. The infection of healthy nationalism with a sectarianism that can still be felt in the negative nationalists was one of their accomplishments. The Orange movement provoked the Métis persecution, attacked francophone rights and caused Ontario also to lose close to a century of balanced evolution. Its infection of society can still be felt when unilingual movements or other reflections of prejudice break out.

It could be argued that these two racist, anti-democratic movements are the most important contributions made to Canadian political life by the mother countries. They invented and sent us organized philosophies which summarized their own internal battles and prejudices. These quickly took on lives of their own here and became the clear expression of the forces eager to destroy the moderate reformers. It follows that they were determined to destroy the positive, reforming anglophone–francophone alliance.

The Ultramontane movement came out of the French Revolution and represented the response of the reactionary part of the Catholic church to modernization. The Ultramontanes refused modernization and fought for church control over education and politics. The movement began to grow in Canada in the 1820s and its attitudes survived until the Quiet Revolution in 1960.

The Orange Order brought the prejudices and divisions of Ireland to Canada in an organized manner in 1830. It can be argued that it became a more moderate force as the century wore on and other more extreme groups appeared. But these new extremists were very much the children of Orange attitudes.

I am not talking here of an obscure past. These are the mechanisms of imported prejudices and they continue to function. If you examine the arguments, the vocabulary, the attitudes of the Reform party and the Parti Québécois, you quickly find yourself tripping over the arguments, vocabulary and attitudes of the Orange Order and the Ultramontane movement.

It could be said that D'Alton McCarthy and Monsignor Bourget, the ultimate key leaders of the two movements, are the dark figures of Canadian history. In C.G. Jung's terminology, they are the shadow side. They activated myths of the victim at precisely the moment when there was no justifiable reason to do so on either side. Although history is made neither by great men nor villains, for working purposes it could be said that they are the evil alter egos of the Siamese twins. It is they and their allies who have worked the obscure, abstract realms of mythology, defying reasonable comparisons and norms.

"I had no understanding," Arthur Buies wrote in 1867 in Quebec City, "how true it is that all the vices flow from ignorance." Ignorance, of course, is only marginally a matter of education or the lack of it. "When he could not understand a thing he straightway condemned it," was how L.M. Montgomery described that mind-set in

34   a town in northern Ontario. How curious that we should so suffer from the mind-set of a prisoner in this country "forever untouched," Bruce Hutchinson wrote, "unknown, beyond our grasp, breathing deep in the darkness and we hear its breath and are afraid." That is the force of mythology gone wrong. "To live in prison is to live without mirrors," Margaret Atwood puts it. "To live without mirrors is to live without the self." The conclusion is Milton Acorn's:

> I've tasted my blood too much
> to love what I was born to . . .
> I've tasted my blood too much
> to abide what I was born to.[18]

That is precisely the effect of mythological walls. And somehow, at least so far, modern communications have not helped. So far, as Harold Innis, the great philosopher of communications, saw it, they "have made understanding more difficult."[19] Communication without understanding is the new form of the negative nationalism promulgated by McCarthy and Bourget. The very mass of information and sounds flying around us creates unease, drives us into stubborn, ill-tempered passivity and makes it easier for the ideologues to work us with fear. To every attempt at balanced memory, we tend to reply with the bitter, often cynical assurance of the victim.

Imaginary Options

3

CONTAINED WITHIN EACH NEGATIVE myth lies an imaginary solution. That it is imaginary is the source of its charm. We caress ourselves with its promise. Sometimes we wrap ourselves in it as if it represented the life we already lead.

For a start, there is our self-eliminating creation myth: that we exist only in reaction to America. This can easily be turned into a positive. Since we are Canadian by negativism, we are positively American. For example, the 'natural' north–south flow makes us their greatest trading partner. We know them, they know us, each better than we and they know anyone else. We have, therefore, a *special relationship*.

And not just Canada as a whole. The Maritimes had, have a special relationship with New England. The old sailing-ship days are evoked. Nationalists in Quebec search back for old trading routes through New York. Bernard Landry talks of how much easier it is to do business south of the border, even though more than 90 per cent of Quebec companies that set up outside of Quebec do so in the rest of Canada. Businessmen in Ontario invoke their close U.S. relations, by which they usually mean they work for American companies. Albertans talk of their unity with the American west against the American and Canadian east. Again, the bedrock of this mythological unity is that a remarkably high percentage of the élites are American employees dependent on the sale of their natural resources for use south of the border. And, of course, British Columbia is California north, beneficiary of an intimate agreement on outlook with Seattle, Portland, San Francisco and Los Angeles. It isn't clear what this agreement might be. I've never heard anyone in those American cities mention it.

But what is a special relationship? The two words imply that each nation or corresponding region is willing to limit its self-interest in order to benefit the other. In other words, a special relationship is a very special friendship. But surely we would all know about these self-limitations on self-interest if they existed.

The reality is that nations rarely alter their self-interested actions for reasons that aren't related to power—that is, to dominance or dependence. In other words, the great powers don't have many special relationships. Canada does not have a special relationship with the United States any more than they do with us.

Trading goods with someone is not the basis of leverage let alone friendship. America has no exclusive need of our goods. Most of it they could get elsewhere. And what we have that they do need is bought in good part through companies they own. The real meaning of what we call 'free trade' agreements is that we have agreed to surrender any real power over the shape and use of that ownership. In other words, those agreements have little to do with freeing up trade and a great deal to do with removing the mechanisms of the citizens' power through their governments.

What about holidaying en masse in New England or Florida or California? A holiday is not a relationship. It's a holiday. The British flood into the south of Spain. Northern Europeans invade the south of France. No one pretends that there is a special relationship at play. One group wants sun, the other sells it.

The Roman Empire did not have special relationships any more than the British or French did. Great powers don't need them, except in so far as someone challenges them or occupies a space capable of affecting the great power.

For example, the United States has a limited special relationship with Germany, because the Bundesbank decides European monetary policy. And with France, to the extent that France challenges American cultural and military policy in Europe and foreign policy elsewhere. Britain rarely has even the hint of one, because its position vis-à-vis Washington is in general one of dependence. In other words, special relationships are about geopolitics. Between nations they usually take the form of an agreed stand-off or an agreement to act together. There are elements in the Canada–U.S. trade agreements which attempt to accomplish this—the arbitration panels. But Canada's general dependence is such that Washington simply ignores the results they don't like. If Canada wanted to have a real relationship with the United States, it would have to succeed at a very different international strategy which would lessen our dependence by developing with other countries long-term counterbalancing coalitions of interests capable of occupying real geopolitical space.

Instead, our attempts at independent action are so spasmodic and scattered that the effect is simply to annoy Washington, rather than to establish a recognizable relationship.

As for the regions, they have no cards to play except those of acquiescence. This is particularly true of the narrow nationalist governments in Quebec, who must build into their theory of independence the acquiescence of Washington. Which means that they must base the reality of any possible independence on their unquestioning acquiescence to Washington.

The Western victimization mythologies convert into assertions of self-creation. For example, British Columbia is its own creation. British Columbians have always had to make a special effort to remember that they are part of Canada.

Even recent histories keep coming back to what the historian Jean Barman calls British Columbia's ambivalence towards Canada. She quotes another historian, Keith Ralston, writing in 1982—"A settled community grew up on the Pacific coast and in the valleys and plateaus of the Western Cordillera which owed next to nothing

38 to any link with the Canadas, and practically everything to its oceanic ties to the rest of the world."[1]

Of course, the region is very different from the others, and why shouldn't it be? The more different the better. Each citizen and the citizenry as a whole have everything to gain from developing our particularities.

But no, British Columbia did not pop out of an egg. Wherever you drop into its history, the influences in and out are clear. And few of these influences support the contention of a little movement called Cascadia which today seeks to tie Vancouver closer to Seattle and Portland. B.C. did not, as they say, remain "tied economically and culturally to the rest of what was then a San Francisco-focused region"[2] after joining Confederation. Nor was that tie clear before they joined.

The colony in those early years did contain a prosperous group of Americans who remained relatively silent on public affairs. Their influence was limited to business. As for the anti-Canadian party of colonials, it was more or less the anti-reform party, in other words, the Western equivalent of the Family Compact and the Château Clique. The pro-Canada party stood for political-social reform and had a long-term economic view. The 'popped-out-of-an-egg' school of British Columbia history inevitably reduces joining Canada to an act of bribery. But if the economic advantage lay that way, then it did not lie to the south. So by their own argument the colony was not tied to a San Francisco-focused region. And the steady growth and prosperity of British Columbia proves that argument. Confederation did indeed pay off the debt, cancel road tolls and—thanks entirely to the determination of a French Canadian, Georges-Étienne Cartier—bring the railroad beyond the foothills over the mountains to the sea, thus making Vancouver the entrance and the exit to a continent, instead of just a regional city like Seattle. But Confederation also brought a much wider suffrage—the beginning of the long road to universal suffrage—and free public education. What's more, Confederation arrived under the impetus of all the interesting voices in the colony: Amor de Cosmos who had come from Nova Scotia, John Robson and Dr. I.W. Powell, both Canadian, and Dr. Robert Carrall from Cariboo. The intellectual and ethical forces in the province—the creative, progressive voices—were pro-Confederation.

The illusion of self-generating isolation turns its back on that very complexity which makes each region uncover its best. Take art as a small example. Emily Carr is the quintessential B.C. painter. For a long time she was more or less ignored at home. How did she become accepted for what she was?

Marius Barbeau, the great French-Canadian ethnologue, used his base at the National Museum in Ottawa to save much of what we know of Quebec folklore and Native folklore. He also had a particular interest in the Tsimshian people in B.C. Through this, he came to know about Emily Carr. Her painting, centred on the essential West Coast traditions—that is, of the Natives—struck few chords in the local white population. They were busy imitating irrelevant English imagery and rejecting any Native role in the land they wished to claim entirely for themselves.

In 1927 Barbeau convinced Eric Brown, at the National Gallery, to mount a show which hung the works of West Coast artists such as Carr along with Native art. To understand how revolutionary an idea this was, you have only to look at the scandal unleashed in the art world when in 1984 the Museum of Modern Art in New York hung a show demonstrating the links between "Primitivism" and twentieth-century painting, highlighting figures such as Picasso and Braque. Interestingly enough, the very idea of hanging art and artefacts together, suggesting an inclusive, animist approach towards art, may be a Canadian invention. In a sense this is a demonstration of our long-standing acceptance that place and humans are part of a continuing whole; as opposed to the rational view that humans must humble nature in order to reconstruct it in their own image. On November 9, 1848, Paul Kane opened "one of the first public one-man shows held in Canada" in the old City Hall, which still exists as part of the St. Lawrence Market in Toronto. He hung 240 oil and water-colour sketches along with the Native artefacts collected on his two-and-a-half-year trip across the continent.[3]

The 1927 Ottawa show was the turning point in Carr's career. On that trip, she met the Group of Seven, as recorded in her diary: "I wonder if these men feel as I do, that there is a common chord struck between us. . . . Oh, God, what have I seen? Where have I been? Something has spoken to the very soul of me, wonderful, mighty, not of this world. Chords way down in my being have been touched. Dumb notes have struck chords of wonderful tone. Something has called out of somewhere. Something in one is trying to answer."[4]

Of the seven, Lawren Harris in particular became her friend and supporter. In many ways he was the most exciting of the Group. He was also pure Ontario, of the tractor fortune. Over the years he kept encouraging her and buying her pictures. It wasn't until 1938 that Vancouver accepted her. In 1940, Harris settled in Vancouver where he became an artistic focal point. He played a role in the lives of many young artists, directly or indirectly. One was Arthur Erickson, whose genius would affect architecture across Canada.

Years later, a French-Canadian prime minister, an admirer of Erickson's work, would ensure that he built the Canadian embassy in Washington. In the courtyard of that embassy there is a massive carving by the Haida Bill Reid. These two remarkable objects—the building and the sculpture—are among the most important images of Canada abroad.

It was in good part Barbeau and Carr, and indirectly Harris, who brought the West Coast Native images into the Canadian imagination until they became central to the way Canadians saw themselves. And Erickson has had a key role in crystallizing this effect. What he concluded with the union of architecture and Haida sculpture in Washington, he had begun with his anthropological museum in Vancouver. Perhaps the final key event came from that same French-Canadian prime minister via Douglas Cardinal, the Métis architect from Manitoba, who built the Museum of Civilization in Hull. Its

Great Hall, which is the West Coast personified, has become one of the dominant and official images of the national capital.

All that this little dithyramb illustrates is how British Columbia's real mythology—its images, its buildings, its traditions, its sensibility—is caught up in a complex web with French Canadians, Prairie Métis, Torontonians and Ottawa civil servants. And this is only one example among thousands, even in the same domain of art. The role that Vancouver now plays in the careers of key contemporary painters, such as the Maritimer Mary Pratt and Attila Lukacs from Alberta, is a continuation of this web.

Sometimes the imaginary solution is tied even more firmly to the denial of context. For example, as our southern cities, in particular Toronto, have grown larger, so an urban mythology has developed which sees them as northern representatives of more southerly city-states. Thus Toronto and Montreal are somehow extensions or reflections of New York and Paris. This is the 'world-class' syndrome, the school of the aggressive inferiority complex. The only way in which this illusion can be made to work is if these cities are seen as their own reason for existence—self-defining, self-creating, self-justifying—cut off from the rest of their province.

This is a point of view which cuts across political and social lines. It cannot see what lies to the north as of any great relevance. Some will see it as vacation land. But the actual role of a city in a large territory and its relationship to this hinterland is lost in the desire to be New York North. That so little of the population lives outside of the cities somehow seems to discount the 95 per cent of the territory which does lie to the east and the west and the north. The desire to pretend that cities are free-standing city-states leads many within them to discount the role of nature in the mythology of the country as somehow outdated. Now that we've grown up, they seem to be saying, we can discard the relevance of our backyard.

This is one of the central urban Canadian imaginary solutions—that ours is not a northern country and that what comes with northernness is to be demeaned and disliked. The language surrounding winter, for example, has moved in the last quarter-century from one of acceptance, even pleasure, to one largely of dislike and suffering. The stock urban phrases greeting the arrival of snow are now negative. This can be seen as a frivolous delusion, but if your language refuses your physical reality, then your problems are serious.

Let me use an even more practical illustration. Public places in Scandinavia are equipped with enormous coat- and boot-check facilities. People can get in and out of theatres in seconds. In Canada there are sometimes no facilities at all. Often what there are, are closed. At best there is a modest infrastructure, as if we lived in some temperate climate where it rains from time to time. Vancouver aside, this is a curious form of self-denial. People are constantly stuffing large winter coats under seats or sitting with them over their knees for hours; anything to avoid the long coat-check queues.

If you take this minor sign of a temperate delusion and apply it to the essential infrastructure questions of the enormous territories lying to the north of our southern cities, you begin to understand why those in North Bay or Chicoutimi or Prince George so often feel hard done by.

◄——————►

Denial of context is one of the ways we try to compensate for a very real sense of alienation. On the prairies, for example, there is a tendency to assert that the present is the sum total of reality. Thus society is both what you see and what you experience in a direct way—it is reduced to the actual.

Actually that is hardly a description of a society, let alone of a civilization. If anything, this is a self-demeaning way to deny that you are part of a civilization—of any civilization.

A society is the totality of its experiences—seen, unseen, actual and remembered. To deny that is to step into the old European model of imposed mythologies.

The prairies are not a place recently opened up by a variety of European farmer/rancher settlers, some of whom then moved into resource exploitation. This view arbitrarily sets the parameters of the society at the arrival of my great-grandparents from Ontario, during the last quarter of the nineteenth century in Winnipeg, along with tens of thousands of others from Canada and the outside world, who then spread out across thousands of miles of plain. This arbitrarily truncates memory, experience, responsibility and imagination. What remains is a perpetually new, artificial idea of the society.

Yes, a certain aspect of prairie life is new to the place—the copycat European society. But the prairies are far more interesting than that, far more integrated into a long historic process. The fixing of self-invention in the late-nineteenth century is, of course, primarily aimed at denying relevance to the roles of Natives, French Canadians and Métis.

However hard those who win power try to eliminate the memory of those from whom they took it, the nature of a civilization remains tied inescapably to the effect of one era on another. Thus the French explorers were led through the West by the Natives, for whom this was home, a known place, a place in which they had found out how to live over centuries. The French were followed by the English. All of these explorations were simply adjustments of Native knowledge to serve European knowledge; a different view of need. The whole process was dependent on the concrete debt of the Europeans to the Natives.

Over the next two centuries a society developed based on the fur trade and on a further contract—both social and economic—between Europeans and Natives. The long-term role of this society, from the 1640s to the 1830s, has been eloquently described by the historian Gerald Friesen,[5] to say nothing of Harold Innis, perhaps Canada's greatest thinker. The West was 'opened up' over these two long centuries. The East–West movement of the country was settled in place. The essentially pacific relationship between the aboriginal and European civilizations was established. It's worth remembering that Pierre Gaultier de Varennes, Sieur de la Vérendrye, the man who solidified this process, was not merely some European explorer, but a Canadian born and bred. Between 1730 and 1749 he created a series of Native–French alliances. Alliances. These remain central parts of the treaty fabric and the political structure which define the shape and nature of Canada to this day. Note that his alliance with the Cree-Assiniboine-Ojibwa against the Dakota to the south was a key step in determining the East–West movement and in narrowing down where the as-yet-unimagined Canadian border would fall.

As Friesen points out, La Vérendrye's Native treaties brought ". . . relative peace in the western interior for most of the eighteenth century."[6] As for the nineteenth, it was a time when all of those patterns were further accentuated. If the Hudson's Bay Company was the dominant legal player, the Métis were the dominant society. The francophone and anglophone Métis population made up the vast majority of the total population. But more importantly, they represented the melding of the groups who had dominated Western society for two centuries. And their society was a further adjustment of how a civilization could function on the prairies—a true marriage of the Native and the European.

The result was a further solidification of the shape of the territory. The Battle of Grand Coteau in 1851, during which the Métis from the Red River Valley defeated the Sioux from further south for control of key buffalo hunting grounds, was a central event in this process—one of the defining Canadian battles and victories, without even the presence of any European apparatus. The Métis were defending a northern prairie society which would eventually evolve into Canada.

Indeed the Métis were, as W.L. Morton pointed out, the "one distinctly Western group of people."[7] In fact they were and are the living illustration of the triangular foundations of Canada: Native-francophone-anglophone. They dominated, settled, farmed and defended much of the prairies for close to a century. Their leaders are the great names of the West—Gabriel Dumont, Cuthbert Grant and, of course, Louis Riel.

The final stage in the formalization of the West was purely Canadian. As Morton put it, "the institutions of the Prairie West were Canadian institutions and . . . the people who worked those institutions and determined the political development of the West were in the overwhelming majority of Canadian birth and ancestry. . . ."[8] What's more, this continuity was there to be found in the active bilingual administration of the province until 1890—the administrative laws which still stand.

It was into this land, shaped by 250 years of treaties, battles, economic activity, cultural compromise and social habit, that my great-grandparents and a flood of others arrived in the latter part of the nineteenth century, very late in the day. Their way had been prepared by what can only be described as the reality of our civilization.

They spent the next quarter-century taking power and attempting to wipe away any memory of all that came before. Theirs was to be the creation myth. This is not to say that busting sod and living in huts and losing crops and fighting prairie fires and building cities and all the rest of that late-nineteenth-, early-twentieth-century experience was not a great adventure.

But, by trying to erase the past as a central factor in their own society, these newcomers condemned themselves to the victim mythology. To deny reality is to formalize marginality. Winning power does not authorize the elimination of context. To the extent that they rejected 250 years of reality, just because their particular group hadn't been present, so they rejected the reality of their own past as Westerners. They reduced their civilization precisely to the bias of inferiority proper to a group recently arrived and dependent on central Canada.

A well-balanced society is produced by each wave of dominant

forces assuming the full implications of the past. In practical terms
this may appear to require practical generosity towards the losers.
But it isn't generosity. It is the assumption of the full social contract
of the society by those with the power to shape it. In Western terms,
this begins with language rights, Métis rights and Native rights. If
this isn't done, the victors will have locked themselves into a self-
destructive conundrum of power and victimology.

Another imaginary solution to our negative myths requires a simple
change which will transform everything. Such a change usually has
profoundly religious properties. It is a lay version of the miraculous
event or of the victory of the just or is some combination of both.
These miraculous alterations will automatically simplify our lives
by eliminating the need to consider anything else as real.

For example, there is the constant cry from Ottawa circles for a
strong central government or a strong united Canada. What could
this mean? Canada has never had a strong central government in
any sense that could be understood by any other nation-state. During the two world wars more power did flow to the centre and
Ottawa did overstep its constitutional boundaries. But even so, the
mixing of these two phrases—a strong central government and a
strong united Canada—has always suggested the possibility of an
essentially unitary state. Not only that, by insisting on this fictitious
possibility, the eager centralists have simply handed ammunition to
the Parti Québécois, which can thus claim that it is fighting against
a powerful or potentially all-powerful central government.

Who wrote these words for Lucien Bouchard during the referendum campaign?:

A No means that Jean Chrétien can say to us, I want absolute
power over what happens in Quebec from now on, I want to be

master of Quebec's future, I want you to hand over to me the
French language, the culture of Quebec, I want you to hand
over employment, I want you to hand over all the policies
which shape the identity of Quebec. It is I, Jean Chrétien, who
from now on will decide for you. . . . We will be alone, dis-
armed, dispersed, divided, weakened . . . [9]

It would be easy to point out that this is drivel; that the laws and the
constitution render it fabulation; that it is pure fear-mongering; or
that, charitably, in the heat of a campaign many things are said on all
sides. But the important point is that the real authors of this paragraph—those who handed the ammunition to Mr. Bouchard so that
his words would appear to convey some reality—are the strategists
in Ottawa who constantly evoke the possibility of a strong central
government.

What makes their fabulation even more contemptible is that, for
twelve years now, the Mulroney and Chrétien governments, while
constantly evoking central power and national standards, have been
busy dismantling what central power there was and cannibalizing
the few national standards that existed. The result is that a powerful government, such as that in Quebec City, can still claim it is
powerless before Ottawa.

This is a double game of bravado in which the citizens are treated
by both sides as idiots. Ottawa and Quebec City are incapable of
admitting in public that an equilibrium does exist, even if both sides
find the equilibrium inadequate or unfair. That, behind the scenes,
a real discussion over continuing adjustment in that equilibrium
goes on every day is not the point. What matters is the use of the
public, through fear-mongering, in order to influence these back-
room negotiations. It is in this context that the 1996 program initiated by Heritage Minister Sheila Copps, to spend millions on
distributing flags, can be understood. Once you have removed all
content from the public debate and reduced it to the mythology of

48 promise, as illustrated by catch phrases, well, there isn't much room for debate. Waving flags becomes the sentence structure of mythological promise.

Not that flags don't have a certain role in society. They have always existed as rallying points in battles or marks of belonging to a community. Or, indeed, they are part of the pleasant expression of nationalism. But when they are used to replace reality, in place of ideas and purpose, to marshal unleashed emotions, then you know you are on the dangerous ground of deformed mythology, mystification and negative nationalism.

A few other phrases, in this case used by the PQ leadership, will illustrate the quasi-religious nature of these sorts of solutions. It was said repeatedly that a Yes vote would end the squabbling, bickering, petty quarrelling. A Yes would be la fin des chicanes. What's more, Quebecers would decide their future on their own. And 'English Canada' would be obliged to accept whatever they decided.

These are three interesting assertions. Pas de chicane dans ma cabane is the old phrase. 'No squabbling in my house.' This is the classic mother's order to fighting children. Go and play outside. It was a theme Lucien Bouchard and Jacques Parizeau came back to repeatedly in the twenty-six referendum speeches and press conferences I read.

Mr. Bouchard: "As for me, what I want is that we stop squabbling among ourselves. I want the petty quarrelling to stop." He worries that his son thinks "politics is quarrelling." That federalism is "bickering over power." "We have lost ourselves in constitutional bickering." "But why do we quarrel? Why? Because we are in a situation made for constant bickering."

The solution is to break up Canada.

That won't be done with bickering. Precisely because the aim of sovereignty is to bring the quarrelling to an end." "We will have solidarity on the aims, we'll all aim in the same direction, there will be no more bickering with those people in Ottawa... No, it's going to be just us—nous autres—making our decisions. That's beautiful isn't it?"[10]

Well, actually, what is suggested here is not beautiful. What he is doing is taking an old phrase about family bickering and applying it to the political process. But politics is about debate—about discussing differences; looking for compromises. The false-populists have always hated this process. Mike Harris hates it, just as the Italian politicians Gianfranco Fini and Silvio Berlusconi do. Just as the American neo-conservatives do. They promise, as the 1930s' corporatists promised, that they will bring public matters back to the intimacy of family and everyone will be in agreement on the aims and the directions. At the heart of their argument is disdain for the essential democratic function of citizens and their representatives caught up in endless debate. They say this is childish, a waste of our time.

La fin des chicanes has been, from its beginnings in the nineteenth century, one of the great anti-democratic themes of the corporatist movement. It reduces the citizenry to a limited role in deciding on how best they can be in solidarity. The state-initiated referendum has always been part of this logic. Stop the talk, we're going to decide, yes or no. At that point the citizen's role is to wave one flag or the other and cheer for one side of the simple question or the other. In other words, we are reduced to children. As for the serious matters of state, they will be decided by the representative interest groups around various tables. In this atmosphere, where each group knows what the interests of the other groups are, the emphasis can be kept on a type of solidarity which could best be described as smooth functioning. In that sense there is almost no difference between Mr. Harris's politics and Mr. Bouchard's.

But democracy isn't a simile for solidarity. It requires, above all, having enough confidence to enter into long debates and negotiations filled with disagreements and disinterest.

What about the second phrase—Quebecers will decide on their

own? It's a pretty idea. But no one decides anything on their own. Not if they live in a society. They live beside individuals, groups with whom they have long-standing relationships. Just as democracy is based on debate, so societies are based on the reality of all the people involved. You do not decide on your own because the person next to you is as real as you are and has as many emotions, ethics, children and needs, both spiritual and practical, as you do. When a society acts as a society, most matters are decided with as much care as possible for all the people concerned; which requires the involvement of those people.

That is why it is so difficult to make changes in the fundamental organization of societies. Because if it is done arbitrarily, the reverberations become uncontrollable and they reverberate on through history, often becoming worse and worse over the years, until some extreme event burns out the process and leaves a sort of dark, still water from which rebirth is sometimes possible. That is the meaning of the long-lived bitterness to be found on borders and between communities in Europe. Nothing is done alone. If it is, it is the beginning of an unpredictable, unfathomable series of events.

At some level—conscious or unconscious—both parties were perfectly aware of this during the 1995 referendum debate. And that explains the use of the third phrase: that 'English Canada' would have no choice but to accept whatever the other party decided. The national government's position that it would not negotiate in the case of a Yes victory was met by Mr. Bouchard's assertion that the Quebec government would force the Canadian government to negotiate: "The beauty of the situation is that we won't have to convince anyone, they will be forced to negotiate." "But, if they agree to a *partenariat* with us, it will be because they have been forced to do it. Because we will force them. . . ."[11]

Of course, neither side really means exactly what they say. But the rhetoric does mean something; above all that a Yes vote would be the end of debate and the beginning of les chicanes. That, after all, is one of the results of unleashing the uncontrollable reverberations which I described a moment ago.

What makes these phrases possible—the end of bickering, we'll decide on our own, they'll have to accept what we decide—is the reduction of the other person to merely the *other*. Categorization, typology. The English Canadian. English Canada. "Nous autres," in Mr. Bouchard's words, versus eux. Us against them.

Again and again during the referendum the complexity of Canada was reduced to this two-camp formula. Those outside Quebec were le Canada anglais. More often than not they were described as right-wing. To vote Yes was "to erect a dike which will protect us, in Quebec, from this invasion of the temptation of the right."[12] In a surprising return to the rhetoric of the Franco-German century of hatred and war, the phrase "l'autre côté de la rivière"—the other side of the river—was used repeatedly to describe where 'English Canada' lay. That Quebec is in the centre of Canada, not on one side of it, isn't the point. Nor that the Ottawa River is not the much-battled-over Rhine. Nor is it that one of Mr. Bouchard's first acts on taking power was to agree to the sort of anti-debt law which lies at the core of the American neo-conservative ideology being enacted by Mr. Harris.

What matters in such a situation is the reduction of the fellow citizen or even neighbour to an unknown *other*, across the river, fundamentally different from "nous autres." This facilitates the reduction of complex and interesting questions, containing real demands and grievances on both sides, to emotion and a Yes versus a No.

In all of this, the approach is very much like that of Mr. Harris, for whom those who disagree are automatically marginal to Ontario reality. They are rival interest groups, not citizens who disagree. And the corporatist idea of minimal debate and maximum action means interpreting a general election victory as if it were a referendum blank cheque. Changes are made rapidly in great multifaceted sweeps, making sensible debate impossible. Are you for or against? The citizen is again reduced to the emotive monosyllabic Yes versus No.

It wasn't until a few days before the 1995 referendum vote that Mr. Bouchard softened his vocabulary—as if realizing the implications of his rhetoric, should the Yes side win—and dropped into one speech a few sentences about "the neighbour with whom we have always lived."[13]

Again, my purpose here is not to accuse one person or another. The problem lies in our false expectations from mythology or rather our slippage into easy mystifications. This affects all of us, whatever our politics.

Take a minor comic example. In the spring of 1996, the stage and film genius Robert Lepage told a Swedish newspaper that English Canadians were the moneymakers, while French Canadians were the makers of culture. Perhaps he was thinking of himself versus the gold magnate Peter Munk. On the other hand, Laurent Beaudoin, the central force behind Bombardier, the most impressive industrial undertaking in Canada, is unlikely to agree. Nor would millions of people around the world who read Alice Munro, Robertson Davies, Michael Ondaatje and Margaret Atwood. For that matter, Robert Lepage himself wouldn't agree, since his first large public was in anglophone Canada. And it is there that he has found many key supporters for his work.

It was probably just one of those phrases thrown off by citizens struggling to deal with what others don't understand about who they are. In that sense we do miss the easy dominant mythologies which most countries have and to which people can pay lip service with an occasional nod in that direction. We are vaguely embarrassed by our lack of a facile discourse.

That our situation is unusual causes us to miss the role these myths usually play elsewhere. They are largely a steam-release device in societies with profound, real divisions. Put another way, they are face-saving mechanisms. America, for example, continues its fundamental battles over social organization, race, the nature of justice and fairness. Indeed the country is built upon the need for successive victories by one internal group over another—the colonist over the Native, the republican over the loyalist, the north over the south. In Britain and France great schisms of class and race lurk just beneath the surface, to say nothing of regional humiliations. Remarkable mythological unity deals with much of this tension.

Canada, on the other hand, suffers from an almost anarchic surface—a cacophony of mythologies, positive and negative, contradictory and often ridiculous. And this does make it difficult to express in a useful way those problems of maladjustment which do exist. After all, "the initial bias of prairie politics *was* the fact of political subordination in Confederation," as W.L. Morton put it.[14] And the difficulty of being a francophone in Canada and in North America is very real. The population numbers are real; as is the dominant sound of English on the continent. To be a francophone is to make an effort every day.

Few of these problems and others like them are now tied to concrete political structures. Most political structures are capable of change, for better and worse. The Canadian has more parts to it than most and so is capable of constant mutation. It's just that the myths and the public discourse seem to be immobile. As a result, they rarely relate to the reality of concrete changes. More than anything else these problems are tied to how we imagine ourselves. The playwright René-Daniel Dubois has put it in a way which could be applied to any group or area in the country: "What do you know about the pain of those who live among us? Because you cannot formulate it, you scorn it? You don't have the right to denigrate like that, without understanding the pain of a people who die in silence."[15]

Again, this silence is not the product of the cacophony of myths and is only in small part due to political structures. Above all, it is an expression of our psychological state.

In a curious way this is worsened, not eased, by the fact that beneath the disordered mythological surface there is relative agreement on the most important questions of society, race, justice, fairness and even language. That is why those who seek to create disagreement over things which matter, or who have no concept of a social contract, insist so on the importance of superficial deformed mythologies. This is as true of those who vaunt a common-sense revolution as of those obsessed by flag campaigns or by reducing societal relationships to "nous autres" versus those on the other side of the river.

The Quality of Solitude

4

BETWEEN SOLITUDE AND ISOLATION there is a great distance. Their reverberations make them opposites—one a positive, the other a negative. It is solitude which permits the individual to consider herself and her place and her life. Isolation is an impenetrable state which imprisons the individual and so removes the mirrors of reality necessary for self-examination. These same positives and negatives can equally apply to groups.

The dominant mythologies of most western countries confuse these two states. Solitude becomes a disloyal isolation. It is deviant behaviour, marginalized into eccentricity or anti-social behaviour, or trivialized into the false individualism of non-participation. The nation-state has largely devoted itself to structures of conformity; the citizen is isolated within.

It is only in the countries lying on the geographical margins—where the place itself carries a force of uncontrollability—that the concept of solitude has been built as a positive into the local mythology. This is as true of Canada as it is of Russia, Scandinavia and Australia. Yet, in Canada this positive is for some purposes turned into a negative—that is, solitude is confused with isolation.

The positive is to be found throughout our language, from Gatien Lapointe's "You are born alone and solitary, my country" to Glenn Gould's "The value of life comes from solitude." Pierre Morency ruminates on a guide obsessed by birds—What "had pushed this man towards such solitude? Social incompatibility? Broken love? Or simply the real attraction of the great forest?"[1] From the theme of Jacques Godbout's novel *Dragon Island*, to Tomson Highway's play

The Rez Sisters, to Thomas Wharton's novel *Icefields*, it is everywhere, in our daily conversation, in what we assume to be human qualities.

And yet what we take to be a positive is abruptly converted into a negative by a simple act of numerology. Solitude for one or many or all is a social strength. Solitude for two is a state of impossible isolation. The politicization of the positive turns it into a negative. And this goes far beyond the clichéd French–English two solitudes. That very concept causes each group—whether West or North—to claim as an unacceptable reality the incomprehension of isolation.

I would argue that much of the confusion between the two communities comes from the real weakening of the positive and the artificial strengthening of the negative. In other words, the real solitude, not just physical but mental, has been chipped away at over the last decades, creating a sense of false similarity to more controlled nation-states. And a sense of negative isolation has been exaggerated in order to play upon the resulting unease, offering a false compensation which insists that isolation is inevitable and therefore must be accepted.

But if you scrape away the false urbanity of the world-class school, you find that the virtue of solitude is still relatively healthy. And if you look dispassionately at the illusion of isolation, you find that it is interpenetration and shared sensibilities which seem to be inevitable.

The most satisfying of western mythological solutions is that of an imaginary country in which everyone knows everyone else, literally or figuratively. It is a dream in which family or neighbourhood society is miraculously inflated to include millions of people. This fantasy lay at the heart of nineteenth-century nationalism with its conviction that a nation was one race, one religion, one language, one figurative family. It is a static idea of the nation and is based on the manipulation of fear. In other words, only the family can protect you.

In the late-twentieth century, this idea has been actively picked up by the false populists, libertarians, neo-conservatives and proponents of direct democracy. At the same time, it continues to lurk in the unconscious of those who believe that certain impediments prevent groups from living together; for example, a range of mountains or a language separates them in some absolute way. Inversely, this same attitude leads people to believe that the only way for people to live together is in a fool's paradise waving flags, and swearing devotion to a few simple notions. The reduction of civilization to a few symbols will make everyone the same. Just as a few complicitous "nous autres" winks will efface social complexity. Or the city in which we live, because it is the biggest and the richest, will stand as the model for all citizens.

It would be foolish to deny that a gigantic territory, with a smallish population using two languages, complicates the practicalities of daily life in a political structure. This sort of situation requires a greater use of the imagination than a more standard situation. It demands of the citizenry a more open and active imagination, a more acute sensibility. It is not a situation for lazy minds and easy emotions.

But then the dynamic of a small country—for example, those in central Europe—carries with it a whole other set of tensions. There the apparent similarities of the dominant population accentuates the differences of the minorities in a negative way. And indeed, group atmosphere accentuates the difficulties of dealing with differences within the population. Non-conformity is easily treated as disloyalty. The history of theoretically homogeneous smaller countries has generally been as difficult and violent as those countries built upon complexity. Often it has been more so.

The Canadian reality is clearly complex and large. There is a need, every day, simply to accept our size, but more than that, to accept the uncontrollable nature of the land mass. Not to pretend it isn't there, as many of our urban dwellers now attempt to do, but to accept. This is as true on a regional basis as it is nationally.

Those who pretend otherwise are driven in part by the fears which such a reality subjects us to, fears lurking in the unconscious and fears intentionally provoked. The promise of emotional comfort, somehow tied to geographic comfort, is a great theme among false populists. But learning how to assume and in effect to enjoy the fear of this uncontrollability can also be a wonderful stimulus. In Brian Fawcett's phrase, "this is no world to make such beauty captive."[2]

The Franco-Manitobans look out over the prairies and call them le large—the open sea—as if they were living upon the shore. A few thousand kilometres away in nineteenth-century Upper Canada, Isabella Valancy Crawford imagined that distant space in the same way:

The sharp breath of the night arose
From the wide prairies in deep-struggling seas,
In rolling breakers, bursting to the sky.[3]

I am not suggesting that there is anything wrong with communities or individuals pulling in upon themselves as they look in every direction at the distances and differences. Nor am I suggesting the opposite—that a 'normal' country or a 'real' country is a place in which each individual must share a deep knowledge of life, one with the other, or that they must all lead similar ways of life or face the same challenges. What is the meaning of such differences? "It is only the truth of solitude," Leonard Cohen wrote.[4] Solitude: the privilege of a country placed on the margins.

The manic travelling habits of the late-twentieth century haven't changed the reality that the citizens of most countries spend most of their time in very limited areas. Much of our travelling relates to holidays—a time outside of all reality. For better or worse or neither, this is a Disneyland experience. And when these incubator movements are deducted, the picture is one of relative immobility. Italy is full of Italians who haven't been to Rome or have been once or twice—a honeymoon, on military service. People in the south of France go to Paris only occasionally for some specific reason. Most have never been or been once, a few twice. And what about going to Lille, the greatest city of the north-east? You would be hard-pressed to find people who have been, let alone know it, have friends or even acquaintances there. How many in Glasgow have been to Bristol? Yet Italy, France and Britain are small countries. And New Yorkers do not tour the various states, even as a patriotic duty.

For that matter, the people in Lac Saint-Jean have little experience of Quebec City, even less of Montreal. Why should they have more? They live somewhere else, just as people in Sudbury do. Farmers don't rush off their Saskatchewan land to inspect Prince George. The people of Saint John and St. John's don't dash back and forth as if there were no apostrophe.

It is an illusion to believe that countries are built on personally shared experiences. Usually it is the catastrophes that are shared—wars, floods and economic collapse. These disasters break the sedentary bonds and mix up the population as if in a cocktail shaker.

What is true is that a small élite travels endlessly—politicians, creative people, businessmen. If they are observant and committed, they will come to know the country and understand what makes it function. In Canada that élite is larger than average and travels more than in most other countries because the decentralized nature of power and the vitality of the regions means that you cannot do your job by sitting in one particular city. If anything, these élites need to travel even more.

Only in the clear light of false mythology is every citizen part of a united flag-waving family. Real countries are fragile constructs, more often than not the product of military or financial will. In a few cases a social vision lies in the country's origins, or at least emerges with time as the more unpleasant aspects of power are regularized. Canada is neither a military nor a financial construct, although there are elements of both. Nor was a great social vision clearly articulated at its origins. But within the complex arrangements of the original groups there were the elements of a social vision or what I would call a sensibility. One demonstration of its presence has been that each time attempts have been made to invoke military or financial imperatives—from conscription and the Winnipeg general strike to the War Measures Act and the trade deals—a great deal of harm has been done to the shared concept of the country's sensibility.

◄----------►

The logical prolongation of the one-family/one-country myth is that everyone else must belong to another family/country and live in another impenetrable solitude. Either you know people absolutely by some mysterious osmosis or you do not know them at all.

The meaning of Hugh MacLennan's title *Two Solitudes* was that differences were not prisons, merely complications which could be dealt with. In one of thousands of misstatings of this idea, Premier Bouchard told an American audience in 1996 that there was "a total lack of understanding between Quebec and English Canada."[5] In passing, his formulation of the families should be noted. The first, Quebec, was presented as a territory in which no differences existed; the second, English Canada, as a racial, linguistic group. In other words, the description was political rhetoric, not descriptive. But the point here is that on the same day that French-language newspapers were reporting this "incompréhension absolue"—June 4—they were also announcing the French-language radio dramatization of a Robertson Davies novel in translation which would play all summer. Also, the 25th Festival of New Cinema and Video in Montreal, they reported, would be opened by "three emblematic figures of modern film"[6]: a German, Wim Wenders, a Torontonian, Atom Egoyan, and a Montrealer, François Girard. Girard's career has been heavily marked by work done in both cities and in particular by his

32 Short Films about Glenn Gould—the mythological Toronto pianist. The other two hoped-for participants were the directors Robert Lepage and Denys Arcand, both of whom have an experience regularly linked to other parts of Canada. One of Arcand's films was an adaptation of *Unidentified Human Remains and the True Nature of Love*, by the Alberta playwright Brad Fraser.

What then is this "incompréhension absolue" on which the isolationists insist? The unusual presence of two major languages in a single country can create the illusion of unlinked worlds. And those in each language who wish to prove ignorance of the other as a statement of originality can more easily do so. But the flaunting of ignorance is not a particularly interesting characteristic in any situation.

The reality of the Canadian experience is that states of isolation, by the standards of an average country, do not exist. Differences exist as do arguments, sometimes serious arguments, prolonged stupidity on all sides and different concepts of how to proceed. All of this is relatively normal. In fact our ability to arrive at reasonable compromises over these problems, without seriously damaging one of the parties, would suggest that we have less difficulty breaking the barriers of isolation than do regions or groups in most other countries. Perhaps this is because we are used to the idea of solitude as a positive. That whole schools of historians and politicians have been devoted to proving "a total lack of understanding" does not change the reality of how we operate.

They may succeed in creating false barriers and in editing history to bolster their claims of ignorance. They may be well served by the mediocrity so persistent over the last decade among our political class that it damages our ability to handle large or complex political spheres. They may even succeed in so effectively selling the illusion of community-wide isolation that the country will come apart. After all, if there is a conviction in any particular group that it does not know another particular group, and that this is because it cannot know the *other*, then that *other* ceases to be made up of real people and needs not, therefore, be taken into consideration. In such an atmosphere—not of solitude but of isolation—the result is an artificially maintained ignorance which makes it easier to encourage misunderstanding. In such a situation, as Mikhail Lermontov put it in the first Russian novel, "the most fantastic of fairy tales can't escape the reproach of being meant as some personal insult."[7] But even if such a break-up should occur, the isolation of the solitudes will have been false.

To prove that these solitudes are actually a negative isolation, the arguer must first get over the hurdles of political experience and economic reality; that is, the practical structures of day-to-day society. If successful, he could then try to rest his case on the nature of culture and sensibility. He would try to show that unrelated cultures were involved, as well as contradictory sensibilities. Let me take an initial pass over this four-part theory of inevitable separation.

First, it involves ignoring more than three centuries of interwoven political activity; either that or editing them in order to leave only a trail of failures. But if such a catastrophic picture were accurate, the result today would resemble the Balkans, not the overly easy-going country which now exists. Let me touch on two key events.

The Rebellions of 1837 in Upper and Lower Canada are often presented as separate events. This permits the focus to be fixed on a racial interpretation of what happened in Lower Canada. In reality, William Lyon Mackenzie and Louis-Joseph Papineau were in contact with each other throughout the 1830s. Mackenzie went to Montreal to solidify relations in 1831. Their lieutenants were constantly meeting, carrying messages and letters back and forth. Their public resolutions usually contained supportive references to their Upper Canadian or Lower Canadian allies. They attempted to develop more or less coordinated strategies. I don't want to overstate this cooperation. After all, both reform parties were struggling in a vague and uncertain atmosphere. Their military strategies could only be shared in an ad hoc way since the whole situation was ad hoc.

Nevertheless they worked together and for a very good reason. Their causes were almost identical. Each was hoping to lead their respective new liberal middle classes and the farmers towards power over the false élite which clung to office as to a cash cow.

Papineau put it very clearly in the legislature in 1836: "They [the established élite] pretend to believe that our demands are the fruit of our different origins and of Catholicism, when it is obvious that the ranks of the liberals contain a majority of men of all beliefs and all origins. And what is the basis of their argument when you look at Upper Canada where there are few Catholics and almost everyone is of British origin, yet they denounce the same wrongs and demand the same reforms?"[8]

In their Declaration of July 31, 1837, the Reformers of the City of Toronto reiterated this point, as indeed it would be reiterated in meeting after meeting across the colony:

> Warmest thanks and admiration are due . . . to the Honourable Louis Joseph Papineau . . . and his compatriots . . . for their past uniform, manly and noble independence in favour of civil and religious liberty; and for their . . . opposition to the attempt of the British Government to violate their constitution without their consent, subvert the powers and privileges of their local parliament, and overawe them by coercive measures. . . . The Reformers of Upper Canada are called upon by every tie of feeling, interest and duty to make common cause with their fellow citizens of Lower Canada.[9]

One of the reasons the Upper Canada Rebellion went so badly was that Mackenzie launched the process precipitously when he received a plea for action from Papineau. A great deal is made of the military incompetence of the Upper Canada rebels versus the persistence, but nevertheless military incompetence, of those in

Lower Canada. But it is dangerous to discount one in so easy a manner. In some ways this is the result of history depending on an urban interpretation in which leadership is emphasized.

The leaders in both Upper and Lower Canada were urban. Papineau and Mackenzie were each, in their own way, catastrophic characters for a physical crisis. The rebel armies, however, were almost identical in that they were both dominated by poor farmers, dissatisfied, tough and perfectly capable of giving a good fight. The difference was that in Lower Canada the second level of leaders contained a few with military skills—Wolfred Nelson in particular— who got their chance to lead in battle.

In Upper Canada the two chosen leaders—who had ample military experience, more than Nelson and his friends—never made it to the battlefield. The first was killed just before the march on Toronto. The second arrived across country, too late to play a role.

The result was ridiculously disproportionate casualties—327 in Lower Canada versus 3 in Upper Canada and 12 hanged versus 2. But the numbers which more accurately describe the two movements were that approximately 1,000 were arrested in Lower Canada and 1,000 in Upper Canada. Indeed, while 58 were transported to Australia from Lower Canada, 93 were sent from Upper Canada.

A year after their respective catastrophes, both Mackenzie and Papineau were in exile and writing to each other, retracing where they had gone wrong. In reply to a letter from Mackenzie, Papineau wrote: "It is obvious that chance and uncontrollable accidents prevented the success of your attempt to take Toronto. Had you succeeded, the rest of Upper Canada would have followed. In that case, the movement would have taken a favourable turn for the Patriots in the two provinces."[10]

Three years later the next generation had taken over the push towards democracy. They were all men who had stood for the cause of reform in 1837. Some were moderates like Baldwin, who had been furious to find themselves squeezed between the rebels and the Family Compact. Others, like LaFontaine, had initially supported the rebellion. And still others—like the Lower Canada anglophone Wolfred Nelson—had fought to the end.

It is worth remembering that this was much more than a political coalition. LaFontaine and Baldwin, two youngish men in their mid-thirties, banded together for the first time in Kingston, where the legislature of the newly unified colonies was meeting, and became each other's closest friend for the rest of their lives. A small detail: Baldwin immediately began sending his two sons and two daughters, one after the other, to be educated in French in Quebec City. Long after both had left politics, they kept up a personal correspondence which is both moving and complicitous. LaFontaine, solid and practical, was often encouraging the romantic and rather fragile Baldwin, as much in personal as in public matters.

The ideologues of isolation deal with these and thousands of other political, indeed personal, relationships by ignoring them or talking of betrayals, failures, dupes and pawns. But what are these dismissals with the wave of a hand? Are they more than assertions which slip easily into historical *ad hominem* dressed up to sound like analysis? They don't reflect the political reality experienced by those who lived these relationships.

In the early 1840s Baldwin, LaFontaine and their allies put together a complex reforming coalition. What these francophones and anglophones drew from the events of 1837 was a realization which would shape the next century and a half. The principle which drew them together remains as true today as it was then: so long as the reformers stood alone in their respective regions, the anti-reform forces would always dominate. The only way they could build a reform majority was to do so together. The situation in Canada today—both national and provincial—is a perfect illustration of that conundrum. Today even those governments which call themselves Liberal or social-democrat are busy imposing anti-debt laws and closing down social infrastructures. Between the Liberals of Ottawa, the social-democrats of Quebec or the Conservatives of Ontario, it is difficult to identify more than differences of detail.

The coalition which Mackenzie–Papineau attempted and LaFontaine–Baldwin achieved is the key to the Canadian sensibility. Successful Canadian governments have always stood to the left of the political spectrum and, with a few particular exceptions, to the left of the provincial governments, the latter being more easily dominated by corporatist and narrow agendas. In practical terms this has usually meant hovering somewhere on the centre-left. And it has been as true of successful Conservative governments as of Liberal. Those who ignore this rule may win power for a term, a few for two mandates. But the damage they do to the national sensibility— as with Robert Borden and Brian Mulroney—will be felt for decades.

Let me restate this principle in *realpolitik* terms. No Canadian government has ever been defeated in a general election by a party running to its right. In other words, Canadians have never consciously voted for the choice of the right. Or, put another way, the idea of the right, as understood by each generation, has never been taken as a real option by Canadians.

This is not an attempt to idealize the more successful governments. Their failures and betrayals of principle are legion. Nor am I forgetting the middling, opportunistic governments more interested in dividing the spoils than in serving the public good. But politics is always a mixed bag and the whole picture must be examined, including where our national governments have stood in relation to those in the regions on major reform issues.

I am making a single point here. LaFontaine and Baldwin demonstrated that the only way reform movements could have a sustained impact was at a national level. And inversely, the only way Canada could be governed successfully was from the centre-left. If this could be maintained, the provinces would follow suit (as for example with Ontario from the mid-1950s on) or eventually be obliged to run to catch up (as with Quebec after 1960). Saskatchewan is the only exception to this rule, as it has sometimes led while the national government followed.

The obvious general point to draw is that Canadian politics has always been and remains an interwoven complexity. The subsidiary point is that the Mulroney and Chrétien governments, in attempting to govern from the centre-right, have undermined the essential political coalition which makes Canada work. The longer this trend continues, the more profound the damage will be and the more we will find that what looks like regional stress is really the return to power of the modern equivalent of the Family Compact and the Château Clique. In other words, the primary force for the argument of political isolation is not the existence of isolationist or neo-conservative or even selfish provincial governments. It is the existence of a government in Ottawa which refuses to govern from the left of the overall national spectrum.

This is why we have been well served for most of the country's existence by the presence in Ottawa of an opposition party to the left of the government. This presence reminds all of us on a daily basis of the shape of the political spectrum. This was as true of Henri Bourassa's embryo party as of the Progressives and the CCF.

One other key political factor is the extent to which those operating in one language know about the nature of the debate in the other. A celebration of aggressive intellectual stupidity—unilingualism—meant that in the first half of this century not nearly enough information moved back and forth between the two language groups. Different speeches were given in different communities. Events taking place in one language were simply not reported in the other.

This was not an absolute. The sophisticated and important roles of such bilingual politicians as Henri Bourassa and Brooke Claxton mustn't be ignored. But overall, there was a celebration of linguistic ignorance on both sides, although the greater part of the blame lay with the anglophones.

However, that period is long past. Politics and the coverage of politics takes place fairly effectively across the language barriers. The several million bilingual people in each of the communities means that, while the passage of information is not ideal, neither is it incidental.

As for the question of economics, it is straightforward. There has been a relatively constant pattern over three centuries and it was set in large part by the fur trade—competition, then coalition between anglophones and francophones. The disastrous decline in the role of francophone businessmen in the second half of the nineteenth century was followed by a sharp recovery in the middle of the twentieth. The reasons for that decline were not tied to an incompatibility between the two groups, but to specific ideological policies which I will come back to. And the initial political/economic bias, as W.L. Morton put it, which subordinated the West to Ontario and Quebec, has gradually been redesigned. Only the Maritimes have somehow not found an appropriate place in this system.

Today the economic interpenetration between all of the regions is extremely high, with Quebec the most successful in selling to the rest of Canada. In the 1990s much of the new growth in trade is taking place outside of the country, but that is precisely because the levels of internal regional interpenetration are so high. Many of the Canadian markets for Canadian products have been more or less saturated by the high levels of interprovincial trade.

The ownership patterns—foreign control excluded—represent a complex interwoven tapestry of activity. You have only to glimpse at a newspaper to discover that, for example, Quebec's leading agricultural cooperative has become Canada's largest dairy by taking over a major Ontario dairy.[11] You have only to get on one of the several planes per hour between Toronto and Montreal to sense the intimate nature of the economic relationship.

The only serious arguments for the existence of two negative, isolated solitudes must be based entirely in the cultural sphere. Of course there are also some embarrassingly soft assertions made about opposing sensibilities, but once removed from the cocoon of false rhetoric they evaporate. What do I mean by that? Imagine these assertions in the mouth of D'Alton McCarthy or Monsignor Bourget. If they seem appropriate on the shadow side, little more need be said.

What about the cultural question? The filter of two different languages certainly makes it easier to posit a lack of understanding, as if these cultures produced radically different messages.

But again, solitude is a positive theme throughout francophone and anglophone writing—a natural state of being and an advantage in such a large, marginal, northern country. It does not follow that solitude is a negative which prevents communication or common perceptions or actions or shared sensibilities.

Where did Hugh MacLennan pick up his literary theme of two religious/language communities working out how to live together if not from Philippe Aubert de Gaspé's *Les Anciens Canadiens*? Even the structure of the story and the relationships owe great debts to Gaspé's nineteenth-century novel. Was MacLennan conscious of this debt? If he wasn't, then the argument of creative interdependence is actually greater.

Some of what forms a culture is the product of experiences shared in the most intimate of ways. Much of it takes its shape on a far broader plane. A great deal of culture is born from sharing a situation or a place. The physical. "We can't change our geography," the Finnish president, Juho Paasikivi, said.[12] There is an almost identical Canadian phrase—we are prisoners of our geography. This idea is especially prevalent among people who live on the margins. Why? Because, in spite of intellectual claims to the contrary, not religion, not language, not race but place is the dominant feature of civilizations. It decides what people can do and how they will live.

In more temperate, central countries, the place is eventually dominated and so its role slips into the background. It is taken for granted, becomes decor. Out on the margins, place is never dominated because it cannot be, and so it takes on a conscious importance.

This is very clear in most countries existing on the margins. In Canada the message is confused because we have two language groups who are small percentages of the gigantic English-speaking empire and the large French-speaking empire. There is a constant

70   gnawing sense that language is our way into the heart of a great universal cultural truth. And, of course, it is important. Conventional wisdom has it that the linguistic isolation of francophones makes this anxiety especially important. Yet the presence of the heart of the English-speaking empire next door also creates an intense daily emotional crisis for anglophones.

The truth is that in a healthy society language is primarily a mechanism, not a religion; an important mechanism, a mechanism with properties of its own. And yet the differences within French, depending on place and experience, are so great as to constitute different languages in all except vocabulary and grammar. The same is true in English. It is not a matter of accent or cadence, but of meaning, of intent, of understanding. The context of the language and the way it is used are what make these differences. There is nothing wrong with this. To the contrary. While such differences complicate general understanding, these also constitute the deep roots of language; those which penetrate and permeate reality in a manner far more consequential than style. There are those who argue that style is far more important to French than to English. The history of the French language demonstrates clearly that this is not true. As with English, when style becomes the or even a determining factor, it is a sign that the language has slipped into the backwaters of scholasticism and lost its real powers of communication and imagination.

Without these real differences all you have left is the unreal language of academies or the surface language of propaganda. There is of course an international French, as there is English. But these banalized dialects generally require compromises which limit meaning.

There are people or texts which produce expressions of genius that pierce all differences. And that constitutes the international tentacles of culture within a single language. But again, most of the important creations usually break across the technical barrier of language. Beyond that, communication within the language empires and through translation is limited and deformed by the artificial structures maintained by the dominant players. To take an extreme example, a mediocre British police novel may circle the world thanks to British distribution empires. An anglophone Canadian police novel must be very good to do the same. We have no distribution systems of our own and rely on the interest and the taste of others.

So language is not a truth in itself nor is it, in the full sense of the word, a metaphor for culture. Superficial linguistic isolation may well be the result of economic imperatives or cultural geopolitics. In practical terms, those who understand what anglophone or francophone Canadians actually mean are far more likely to be found in the other language in Montreal or Halifax than in the same language in London or Paris. It is a troublesome, almost depressing thought, but it is the natural effect of experience and place. Or rather, it is the natural effect of the real meaning of languages.

Our shared sense of the physical comes back again and again in what we write. Louis Fréchette's images—

L'Inconnu trônait là dans sa grandeur première.
Splendide, et tacheté d'ombres et de lumière,
Comme un reptile immense au soleil engourdi,
Le vieux Meschacébé, vierge encore de servage
Dépliait ses anneaux de rivage en rivage. . . .

are those of E.J. Pratt—

This folded reptile was asleep or dead:
So motionless, she seemed stone dead—just seemed:
She was too old for death, too old for life . . .
Ice-ages had passed by and over her,
But these, for all their motion, had but sheared
Her spotty carboniferous hair or made
Her ridges stand out like the spikes of molochs.[13]

If you listen to Stan Rogers singing "North West Passage," you will hear the sensibility of Gilles Vigneault singing "Mon Pays" or of Ian and Sylvia singing "Four Strong Winds." In the aftermath of the October Crisis, Eli Mandel turned back, not surprisingly, to Vigneault's lines in order to express in English his own despair:

my country is not a country
                                but winter
rivers of ice
from St. Hubert terrible knives
run through the whiteness of my veins

politics pierce my heart
on a floor littered with history . . .[14]

The solitudes we live with are enormous and essentially healthy, but the concrete cultural interweaving which runs parallel to them is equally complex. For example, a great deal of our important literature is now translated both ways. We forget that this is a peculiarity of Canada.

The variety and size of the English-speaking universe has caused the two main publishing centres—New York and London—to translate less and less from other languages. The level of ignorance of what is happening in other languages is growing to a frightening degree. And the French-speaking world remains dominated by the publishing structures of Paris. These make an enormous effort to translate from every imaginable language. In other words, they make up for the smaller language pool by drawing others into it. However, the old colonial approach towards the rest of the French-speaking world still exists. Those literatures don't really interest the metropole, with a few exceptions which match its vision of itself. So the literatures least likely to be pushed by Paris, let alone pushed for translation out of French, are much of those which come from the francophonie.

Canada is thus one of the most interesting centres of English–French, French–English translation. Not that everything which should be translated is. Far from it. Instead there are waves of activity, which then peter out. During the last few decades there was first a drive from French into English, which is now largely over. It was followed by a drive in the other direction, which is still going on. Because we are so caught up in finding our place in our respective great language empires, we haven't pursued this advantage aggressively, especially on the international front. To reach out through a single language artery is fine and good. But it is also a very limited approach towards what makes up culture. The assumption that the language trail is all-important rips the guts out of real experience, whether it is the experience inside one of our communities or the larger shared experience. Some of the complexities of the relationships between culture and language can be found in a little book called *Dialogue in Translation*, a conversation between Anne Hébert and Frank Scott over the translation of Anne Hébert's poem "Tombeau des rois."[15] The foreword is by Northrop Frye, the master of the mythological roots of culture.

There are thousands of examples of these cultural cross-effects. Paul-Émile Borduas's career was built largely on shared aesthetic feelings in Toronto and Ottawa; feelings which translated into sales. When Marie Chouinard, a well-known nationalist, brings her modern dance company to sold-out houses in Toronto at the beginning of a pan-Canadian tour, I notice that most of her dancers are anglophones from outside of Quebec and are the products of a patchwork of trans-Canada dance experiences. Lise Bissonnette has tough things to say about Canada. She has given up on it. This won her the Bob Edwards Award—named after the great Western turn-of-the-century journalist—for outspoken honesty. I followed her to the same podium in Calgary a year later and everyone spoke of how moved they had been by her commitment; that is, her commitment to a cause they oppose. Indeed, the second public for her novels is anglophone Canada, not France or la francophonie. And when I speak in Quebec City or Chicoutimi, it seems to me that there is that same complicity—an understanding of what we mean which cuts through the formal divisions of political rhetoric.

My point is not a romantic one. These are merely scattered illustrations of how much effort is required to insist that our solitudes are negative and impenetrable.

So much of our sense of isolation is based upon affirmations of it by those who wish it to be so. This is not a question of politics or language. It is much the same on all sides of the political debate, which cannot be termed a debate since the intellectual alternatives offered by all sides—anglophone, francophone, East, West—are psychotic pessimism and infantile boosterism. Our own sense of self-loathing governs both positions, and, as Margaret Atwood pointed out in *Survival* two decades ago, it seems to require failure. This remains unchanged because it is the part of our mental make-up which we avoid examining.

Psychotic pessimism and infantile boosterism—is this unfair? We look around and find on all sides political leaders competing for the mantle to protect our culture or some aspect of it. This negative vocabulary—'protect'—suggests that they do not understand culture as a living force. Only a dead culture requires protection. Live culture requires a constant and aggressive strengthening of the structures which make creation and the production and delivery of creation a reasonable practicality. Culture is not heritage. The whole concept of heritage has grown over the last few years because it treats culture as something in the past—dead and boxable. Heritage is something which ideologies can use for appropriate purposes. It is controllable, non-threatening and malleable for those interested in isolating one culture from another.

Culture may contain some heritage, but above all it is alive and that heritage is tied to an uncontrollable continuity which is relevant to all aspects of society. And yet, when was the last time that a prime minister of Canada, or a premier of Quebec or Ontario or any other province, showed any sign of knowing what that culture was—the one they are so eager to protect? I haven't heard a prime minister since Trudeau cite an author or heard of one going to a theatre for other than official reasons. There hasn't been a national minister responsible for culture since Gérard Pelletier who seemed to read. The ministers of culture of the two largest provinces have been acultural at best. I repeat: at best. In many provinces the job is tacked onto the tourism or sports and recreation portfolio.

The only provincial minister of culture—from any province over a forty-year period—who comes to mind as a man or woman of culture was Georges-Émile Lapalme. I apologize if I've missed someone. Lapalme created the job in Quebec in the early sixties. He also invented much of the Quiet Revolution. He was quickly squeezed out of his job. There is no place in these governments for actual culture. What is required is culture as a manageable political slogan. Bob Rae is the one premier who actually dared show a sense of the culture of the society. But he named inept nonentities to the Cabinet position. (I won't even mention the Harris government.) As for those who declare that their mission is to save and protect culture—the Parti Québécois—their record during eight years of office was among the worst. And I have yet to hear the current premier mention a single Quebec writer. He is too busy telling us that he has read Proust. On his office wall is the complete Pléiade—the 'great books' of the metropole, defined by Paris and published on onion-skin paper in very small type. It is the sort of gesture you would expect from an insecure nineteenth-century colonial politician.

Never has the word culture been so regularly evoked. Never has there been so little evocation of culture as a reality at the centre of what we do. Why? In part because the politicization and bureaucratization of the concept has made those who wield power fear culture that is anything more than a slogan or a budget. Power, after all, is about control and enforced isolation. Culture is an uncontrollable, indefinable sea in which all of us swim.

There is a political obligation to address specific cultural policies.

But beyond that there is a need for power to be part of our social reality. And in large part that is cultural. What stops us from rewarding political debate which takes this reality into account? What are the sources of our aggressive public anti-intellectualism? It was not so true in earlier generations. John A. Macdonald and Wilfrid Laurier were ferocious readers. Go back to their speeches, Laurier's in particular. These were astonishing intellectual constructions. Baldwin and LaFontaine were in the same mould.

Read their appeals to the voters, mainly poor farmers with little education. These are complex, intellectual constructions, written without a hint of paternalism or cheap false populism. There is an unstated assumption that the citizen is capable of understanding the real argument—the argument itself—and need not be seduced by patriotic and emotional manipulation.

Baldwin wrote poetry, as did Georges-Étienne Cartier, Thomas D'Arcy McGee and Joseph Howe. None of it was particularly good, but it was the hobby of civilized men. They wrote a great deal of it, recited it enthusiastically in public, published it.

Much of what we are now experiencing is true throughout the west. The arrival of images which replace words, the false sense of urgency which the photo op and media clip create, the increasing sophistication of the marriage between entertainment and propaganda, which began in the 1930s, the professionalization of politics, the profoundly anti-cultural nature of management—all of these we share with others.

But beyond what is shared by all countries today, there are the underlying differences produced by each of our particular experiences. The Canadian experience has been relatively conscious and essentially intellectual. The originality and complexity of our idea of statehood, and our treatment of it as an ongoing experiment, would not have been possible had we embraced an anti-intellectual tradition. This is very different from the European experiences of change through noblesse oblige leadership or through the myth of blinding revolutionary clarity. And this is equally different from the dominant anti-intellectual populism—real and false—which has been central to American history.

What all of this suggests is that Canada's current acceptance of anti-intellectual false populism is a product of something more than the new global factors. So much of what we state about ourselves is governed by the perceptions of the victim—the victim who can take any circumstance and instinctively convert it into an appropriate loser's syndrome. Take our treatment of the seminal French-language poet Émile Nelligan. He is often described as a victim of the impossible attempts to reach across linguistic and community lines. His father was of Irish origins, his mother francophone. There was some tension between them, although it could hardly be called a failed marriage. Yet the mythology—even consecrated in an opera/musical—is that their failure contributed to Nelligan's insanity.

True, the father was opposed to the son becoming a poet, not a businessman. The question is: what ambitious middle-class Victorian father in what culture where in the western world did not take a similar position when faced by a similar situation? This is one of the most common artistic dramas of the period and was not primarily about language or community.

Montreal also contained a major exception to the rule. The greatest pre-modern Canadian painter—J.W. Morrice—faced a similar situation. In the end, his frustrated father went to ask the advice of the most powerful businessman in the city—Sir William Van Horne, who happened to be an amateur painter. Van Horne said the son should be sent off to Paris with a healthy allowance. Occasionally destiny is kind. Interestingly enough Morrice, like Nelligan, was not mentally stable and drank himself to death. It's worth remembering that so long as Nelligan's father was alive, the poet was given the best available care. When the father died, his son was transferred to the public ward of a mental institution.

Nelligan's schizophrenia, if that's what it was, struck at twenty, an age when it often first appears. We now know that this disease is the product of an imbalance in the brain. It has nothing to do with parents or unhappy versus happy childhoods. The miracle is that Nelligan was able to produce as much as he did.

The interesting point about language and community is that the first great modern francophone poet was in fact a product of the two communities and the two languages. But how did Nelligan see his own drama? That is, how did his art see it? Look at his great poem "The Ship of Gold." This golden galleon, this great ship of gold, its fabulous masts scraping the sky, sails across unknown seas, until a Siren draws it onto a treacherous reef where it is caught in a storm. In the disorder the crew fight over the riches and the ship sinks:

> She was a golden ship whose diaphanous hull
> Revealed treasures over which the blasphemous crew,
> Hatred, Disgust and Neurosis fought among themselves.

> What remains after the brief storm?
> What has the deserted ship of my heart become?
> Alas, it has sunk into the abyss of dreams!"[16]

It sounds very much as if Nelligan is condemning the arguments which divide his parents and, if you were making a political argument, you would have to say that he is condemning the arguments which divide communities. It sounds as if he is calling for cooperation. Or perhaps it is just a poem by a romantic, fragile young man. Still, he is clearly condemning the idea of solitudes turned into isolation. The ship of gold is his ideal, sailing the seas of non-conformity —the unknown seas. Who is the Siren calling it onto the rocks if not the self-loathing which makes so many on both sides need to believe in the inevitability of division?

In today's context, solitude as a quality is something that power fears. The manageable versus the unmanageable—these are the terms of debate which envelop the concept of power. Differences which complicate the options are to be feared. We are either to pretend they aren't there or to isolate ourselves from them. Debate is seen to be childish quarrelling—les chicanes. As Renaud Longchamps put it ironically:

> Na, Na, you scratch a sore
> It's mine! It's yours![17]

In such a context culture cannot be a complex living process which draws people and societies together because it is primarily seen as an instrument of power, a marriage of entertainment and propaganda, a defensive weapon, not a creative tool. In such a world sides are divided as follows: either the past is a prison and the future a promise of Disneyland; or the past is Disneyland and if we are not careful the future will be a prison.

The insistence that we live in isolation—in impenetrable solitudes—is a program of permanently maintained hysteria in which reality is to be feared. What's more, it simply isn't supported by the record of centuries of experience.

But let me take a step back from this question of positive versus negative solitudes to that of the old search for the source of human characteristics. We have moved from the inevitabilities of archetypes tied to destiny and gods, on to a single god who promised forgiveness and improvement, on to the promise of rational structures which will control our human impulses, and on to the psychoanalytic, which through an understanding of our early circumstances will allow us to control ourselves. Now, even that last liberating device lies discredited in part by its reliance on the very first step, that of archetypes and inevitability. The result in the late-twentieth century is a jumble of all that has come before—archetypes, destiny, religious puritanism, perfect rational models, waves of the uncontrolled unconscious. All come in the form of ideologies.

But in this jumble a single characteristic remains solidly in place. Bitterness. The bitterness of the one to whom things are done—the victim—is particularly strong when societies stagnate. It is there even in a healthy, balanced society; there, but of limited importance.

A responsible élite knows that this bitterness is always available to be used as a mechanism to increase power. Reach down, scratch it, agitate it, draw from each of us our most passive and self-destructive instincts; our latent self-loathing which can be turned against others with a bit of exploitative skill by those who set the public agenda. A responsible élite knows this and therefore does not use that power. They know that bitterness can unleash waves of emotion but can do nothing to build a society. It is a purely negative force. Indeed the principal responsibility of those with power is to avoid encouraging the negative forces which cannot help but exist.

What is particular about Canada is that the formal structure of politics is often based on the tension between those who avoid the lever of bitterness versus those who pull it rigorously as a means of getting and holding power.

As so often in history, passive self-destructive bitterness is presented as an aggressive sort of bravado which appears to be active and solution-oriented. Bravado is a classic characteristic of the victim mind-set.

The way out lies in a return to sources and thus to reality. The slight, the wrong, the weakness must all be placed in a fair picture of the whole. And in Canada that turns on the complexity of the positive, interwoven solitudes.

A Triangular Reality

5

WHAT IS IT THAT I HAVE BEEN describing over the last four chapters? An experienced country, even an old country, with long-established, stable patterns. Its strength—you might even say what makes it interesting—is its complexity; its refusal of the conforming, monolithic nineteenth-century nation-state model. That complexity has been constructed upon three deeply rooted pillars, three experiences—the aboriginal, the francophone and the anglophone. No matter how much each may deny the others at various times, each of their existences is dependent on the other two. This is what I mean by 'positive solitudes' as opposed to a negative state of isolation. Each of their independent beings has been interwoven with the other two over 450 years of continuous existence on the northern margins of the continent.

Such a tripartite foundation and experience does not exclude other individuals or groups. It doesn't exclude them from either early or contemporary history. The twentieth century in particular has been a demonstration of that. Smaller or more recently arrived groups therefore have nothing to gain by attempting to deny the three-legged foundation and the long experience. These merely set out the principal defining lines of the Canadian experience which—unlike those of most countries—permit an inclusive rather than an exclusive mythology.

Some might take these last two paragraphs for the ravings of a person who refuses to acknowledge current events or, worse still, those of a romantic. But in an era of courtierism and the worship of power, ideas are commonly discounted as romanticism. And current events, which have become our daily bread, are only the surface level of reality. Often they are a confusing illusion for which people pay dearly, because they take these events to be the signs of a deep, inevitable evolution.

History is far more stable than the evolutionists accept. Take the Russian experience of the last decade. The reporting of current affairs and the trumpeting of ideologues would suggest that we have witnessed the end of something deeply rooted in the society (communism) and that Russia has now moved on to a completely new experiment with democracy and the market-place. Calmer historians suggest that the Soviet regime was, in certain profound ways, not so very different from those of the earlier Russian tradition and that now Russian history is reasserting itself along even more traditional lines with the slow re-emergence of centralized autocratic power. As for romanticism, if it is to be found anywhere it is in the obsessional devotion to current affairs and ideology. The romantic approach is invariably built on a belief in some sort of end of history and the arrival of a hoped-for utopia. What I am suggesting is the exact opposite—the continuation of both history and complexity.

History, of course, is subject to particular interpretations. For example, even those who believe in the longevity of our experience tend to limit their attention to a few areas, such as French Canada. But as Glenn Gould pointed out, with Newfoundland's arrival in the fold in 1949, Canada gained four hundred years of additional history.[1] The patterns developed in the Maritimes, Ontario and even the West are equally old. Our error is to mistake the development of a sedentary society for the sign that civilization has begun. This is a European and American idea. The underlying force of Canadian society has never been sedentary; that is, it has never been tied to people settling down in a physically static pattern of life, whether rural or urban. The standard view of social evolution as a process moving from a nomadic to a sedentary structure simply doesn't apply to Canada. I will come back to this later on.

The experience of the Arctic is taken by many to be recent because the national government only brought about sedentary

Inuit settlements around 1960. The logic of northern life was indeed artificially changed at that point. But the relationship between the Arctic and the outside didn't begin in 1960. Since the seventeenth century outsiders—through the fur trade and yearly contingents of whalers—have been affected by and themselves had an effect on the north. Besides, the determining factor is not when the south imposed itself on the north, but whether the long-standing realities of the north continue to reign there or have an effect there, and whether the northern reality has had an effect on how Canada sees itself and acts. Just as we gained four hundred years of Newfoundland history, so we gained one thousand years of Inuit history.

There is another, technical view, which limits the importance of the Canadian experience by judging it according to standard concepts of institutional law. Thus, only in 1931 were a number of the questions of national autonomy dealt with by the Statute of Westminster. But one of the curious aspects of our complexity has been that constitutional details almost always lag years, decades, even multiple decades behind social reality. The legal fictions of western constitutional conventions have always had trouble adapting to the peculiarities of Canada. And the more we become obsessed by these conventions, the more trouble they cause us.

Constitutional expert Peter Russell points out that there is nothing in our constitutional past about founding peoples, and yet the concept is central to how Canadians see themselves.[2] Even those who energetically refute the idea confirm it by their very insistence. Russell puts this real mythology in large part down to the long and eloquent career of Henri Bourassa. Bourassa was an impressive exponent of the idea, but I believe it is buried deep in the full history of the country—in the way it was opened up and occupied; in the way century after century the waves of newly arrived immigrants adapted to the place and came to perceive the outside world; in the gradual unfolding of an idea of community which was specific to these experiences. The purpose of this chapter is to begin looking at the particularity of that idea.

Men like D'Alton McCarthy and Monsignor Bourget saw the Canadian experience as one of exclusive, contradictory rivalries. They
reached deep into that nineteenth-century idea of race in order to
imagine their isolations. But even if we were to go down the crazy
racial road of historical interpretation, the interwoven dependence
of the two groups would actually be accentuated. After all, in both
languages we were dealing in large measure not with English and
French, but with Scots and Irish, Bretons and Normans. In other
words, on both sides the origins were largely northern (Viking) and
Celtic. And on both sides these Celts were the descendants of the
losers in the wars waged by London and Paris for central control
and the elimination of both regional cultures and languages inside
Britain and France. There could be no more eloquent illustration of
the colonial mind-set than a bunch of Celts and Vikings in a distant
northern territory insulting each other as *les anglais* and *the French*
as if they were the descendants of the people who had subjected
and ruined them. But then racial interpretations always end up in
farce or black comedy.

Men like Fernand Dumont have insisted that no real intercourse
was possible because anglophones remained passively colonial for a
long time—"their concern for a Canadian identity came late. . . ."[3]
This sort of assertion can only be made by concentrating on the
anti-reform part of the colonial élites and by picking and choosing
among the political rhetoric of the day.

After all, during the major battles of the War of 1812–14 in Upper
Canada, the make-up of the forces—one-third settlers, one-third
aboriginals, one-third British troops—was a clear expression of how
the society functioned. Robert Baldwin, returning early in 1837 from
his first trip abroad—a political negotiation in London—wrote in
his journal: "On the morning of Thursday, 9th of February was again
in Upper Canada, my own, my native land . . ."[4] In May 1841, taking
the oaths of office for the first time as an executive counsellor, he

refused the oath of supremacy. He could not accept that any foreign prelate—in this case English—had authority in Canada.

In 1843, Baldwin was under attack in parliament from the supporters of the Family Compact who had put down the 1837 Rebellion and had now organized themselves into the party of the King's loyal subjects, that is to say, they opposed responsible government. Within the decade, their current of thought would burn down the Parliament Buildings and call for American annexation. As the decades rolled by its inheritors would fight against francophone language rights, demand conscription, oppose most acts of national independence, oppose the fair language policies of the 1970s and, in the 1980s, returning to their earlier position, drive forward economic policies aimed at the integration of Canada into American structures. In 1843 their tactic was to question Baldwin's loyalty to the Crown. What Fernand Dumont might have noted was that LaFontaine's friend did not fall into easy rhetorical protestations of devotion to the motherland and the Crown. Instead, he replied—"I am a Canadian by birth, education and by feeling and I am proud in that avowal. Canada contains all I possess in the world—all that is dear to me. . . . My [only desire] is to see measures calculated to advance the interests of my native country."[5]

Later in the century, when the Orangists and a newly flush, craven colonial élite were throwing their political weight around, John A. Macdonald carefully secreted just enough empire verbiage to hold the right wing of his party in place. But his actions, his instructions during international negotiations and his letters to ministers and representatives abroad all made clear how he imagined Canada—an independent, parallel kingdom. The great journalist J.W. Dafoe, whose personal experience stretched from Macdonald, through Laurier to King, described Macdonald's view as "much closer to the British Commonwealth of Nations, which ultimately emerged," than to the view of the Imperialists.[6] And indeed that had been the portrait of the future Confederation he put forward at the Quebec Conference in 1864.

Thomas D'Arcy McGee, who was often the clearest and most eloquent of the Confederationists, put their view in the House on April 8, 1868. It was his last speech, late on the evening which ended with his assassination—"I speak here not as the representative of any race, or of any Province, but as thoroughly and emphatically a Canadian, ready and bound to recognize the claims, if any, of my Canadian fellow subjects, from the farthest east to the farthest west...."[7]

The naïve or disingenuous views on this subject of the Montreal School and its inheritors, such as Dumont, are based on ignoring whatever didn't suit their argument. For example, the clear and influential language with which the Group of Seven surrounded their painting, anchored as it was in place and in a vision of the society and the public good, is ignored. But the mediocre rantings of a colonial and persistently unsuccessful political voice such as Arthur Meighen's would be highlighted.

Much of the blame for this idea of a late rise in consciousness among anglophones belongs to a number of its own leading intellectuals, who persisted in reaching back into English or American history for explanations of how anglophones acted. Donald Creighton's idealization of the British model was not very different, at a mythological level, from Abbé Groulx's idealization of France's role in New France. Even George Grant, who rightly described Macdonald's economic nationalism as Gaullist long before Gaullism existed, felt obligated to trace the anglophone sense of the common good back to English traditions.[8] At the same time, francophone reformers were tracing their own impetus back to the post–World War Two Catholic left in France.

My own sense is that the Canadian concept of the common good is very much a product of local experience. The economic and infrastructure construction policies developed by Cartier and Macdonald were revolutionary for their time. These two men invented what we identified after the last World War as the model of a mixed economy, combining social democracy with market forces. What we call Gaullism was really Cartier–Macdonaldism. Not only have Canadian approaches to their internal situation been largely the product of local experience, the threats to the equilibrium these try to produce invariably come from successive waves of international ideology. That is as true today as it was in 1917 or 1943.

Another barrier to intercourse between the solitudes is the constant insistence from narrow nationalist circles that leading francophones in Ottawa have been irrelevant there. Somehow credit is rarely registered for the key role they have played in fashioning the shape of the whole. In other words, francophones are quite rightly conscious of the role anglophones have played in shaping Canada, although the Montreal School and its inheritors would see this as largely negative. On the other hand, there is almost no conscious acceptance of the extent to which the anglophones have embraced a construction of Canada built around the views and power of francophones.

Two simple examples. It was Laurier who, at a series of Imperial Conferences in London, killed the whole idea of organized imperial power. Today his position seems self-evident. Then, however, he was dealing with the most powerful empire in the world, flushed with its success and its eternal destiny. Laurier frustrated them with enormous sophistication. What's more, he did it at a time when there was another option on the table—a sort of formalized international imperialism, not unlike some of the models proposed today by the United States. This was an option subscribed to by most people at the core of this empire and in the other dominions. It was the sort of model already being imposed inside the other, smaller empires, such as the French, German and American. In order to understand how original and difficult to carry out the Laurier strategy was, you have only to equate the situation with Canada's position during the FTA and NAFTA negotiations and multiply the stakes by ten. In effect, Laurier's categoric though elegant refusal was the first step in the shutting down of the British Empire and, with it, of all the other nineteenth-century empires.

The Imperial model of the turn of the century seemed so real to many that fifteen years later Robert Borden would foolishly sacrifice his premiership, and come close to sacrificing the country, to the Empire 'ideal' during World War One. With hindsight we see to what an extent Laurier was right. Borden's imperial experiment remains as an unfortunate, even tragic aberration.

However, the point here is that Laurier led Canada in a specific direction away from what appeared to be self-evident. Canada— anglophone and francophone—supported his originality in election after election, as he carried out these policies.

Let me add to this a second example, less revolutionary but nevertheless important. It was Ernest Lapointe who, between 1926 and 1930, played the key Canadian role in the negotiations which led to the Statute of Westminster. In a sense, he finished what Macdonald and Laurier had begun.

The idea of a triangular foundation may be difficult for many to accept because there is still little conviction anywhere that the role of aboriginals has been a central factor in the shaping of Canada. The betrayal by the anglophones and francophones of their fundamental commitments to Natives is taken to have eliminated the original pillar of the society. The gradual return of aboriginal influence, from the 1970s on, is often interpreted as a legal oddity or as a phenomenon of guilt or charity or as the annoying appearance of yet another interest group. Surely not. Surely it is the logic of history painfully kicking back into gear.

Certainly the extent to which the original aboriginal role was slowly turned into a negative is remarkable. Step by step the Natives were erased from conscious argument as avowable ancestors for individuals, let alone for a nation. Their status declined, via legal transformations, from that of allies to that of minors during the nineteenth century, and to that of wards in the early part of this century. Government policy was intended, in Duncan Campbell Scott's words, to cause them to "disappear as a separate and distinct people."[9] Scott wrote not as a leading poet, but as the senior civil servant charged with carrying out this policy.

John Norquay was a highly successful premier of Manitoba for a decade in the late-nineteenth century. His success was welcomed in part because he was a Métis. His arrival in power somehow re-established a sense of normalcy after the confusion of the Métis wars. An anglophone Métis, he was supported by the francophone Métis and the Franco-Manitobans. Norquay represented all the forces which had created Manitoba and his success reasserted their relevance. Some sixty years later, in 1947, a plaque was unveiled in his honour in the legislature. His descendants were furious that it referred to his Métis origins, which they denied.[10] There were exceptions to this refusal of a complex past. Peter Lougheed, for example, has always made a point of his paternal grandmother, Belle, being Métis. She was part of the early Western élite and married a young lawyer who would become Senator James Lougheed.

But self-denial was the more common attitude and it spread throughout Canada. The late-nineteenth century's unfortunate love affair with race meant that much of the twentieth has been spent denying all racial mixtures. Some English-language historians, such as the American Francis Parkman, wrote as if French-Canadian stock had been weakened by mixing their blood with that of the Natives. In a sense replying, Abbé Groulx would write: "It is enough for our pride to have the blood of France in our veins and to have no other."[11] As proof, he claimed that a study of 2,226,232 marriage records, over a period of two centuries, had uncovered only 94 to Natives, none of whom had left descendants!

With hindsight, we can mock all of these nonsensical arguments as the natural product of an age obsessed with the purity of race. But they also help us to understand why the Métis were consistently ignored by all sides.

As for the Natives, Duncan Campbell Scott eventually recognized that they would not be assimilated. Not that that had any effect on a hundred years of persistent governmental delegitimization, which led to the social disaster that is only now—grudgingly and slowly—being addressed. It is important to recognize formally the failure of assimilation. That is the first step towards dealing with the consequences of past actions. Grand Chief John Kelly put it this way to a Royal Commission in the 1970s: "We have proved that we will not be assimilated. We have demonstrated that our culture has a viability that cannot be suppressed."[12]

But what was not assimilated, in spite of truly impossible conditions, must have been unassimilable and thus it must always have been present. I do not mean present as a suffering people reduced to humiliating poverty—although this was a large part of the concrete reality—but present as a central element in the Canadian imagination and even the Canadian reality. In spite of social catastrophe, the Native community remained and remains the foundation it has always been. Although aboriginals as a reality were eliminated for a long time from the social project and the social contract, what they represented in the line of our experience and our attitudes largely remains. As Stan Dragland argues, the dominant culture will "feed on and extend its power by absorbing the vitality . . . of the other."[13] This represents both a compliment and a tragedy. It means that the Native role as the original pillar of our triangular foundation has continued to strengthen over the last century—in spite of superficial impressions to the contrary—because of our dependence on the place they occupy in the Canadian collective unconscious.

Many of the catastrophic social problems remain, but the aboriginals are emerging from this bleeding process with a new wave of vitality: a new, expanding élite and a growing population. West of Ontario, they and the Métis are on their way to making up high percentages of the population—perhaps as much as 30 per cent in Saskatchewan. And in the north an Inuit government is in the making. In the western half of the north, the Dene will remain key.[14] The population numbers are small, but the territory in question throughout the country, particularly from B.C. right across to Quebec and throughout the north, contains the elements of real power; that is, natural resources.

To get an accurate picture of what is happening, you must search out the long view rather than the little close-ups of modern analysis and current affairs. These close-ups are often limited to mechanisms such as new technologies and economic fashion. They miss completely the force of what Tolstoy described as the great waves of history, in which tides flow in, then recede, then return with great force.

From the middle of the sixteenth century to the middle of the nineteenth, the Natives were in a superior or equal position to the European immigrants. The twelve thousand or so whalers and fishermen—Basque, French, English, Portuguese—who came every year to the east coast in the 1570s were dependent on Montagnais, Algonquin and Iroquois support and advice. Contemporaries recorded that Natives were "ready to assist them with great labour and patience . . . an ingenious and tractable people."[15] The European dependence was so great, and Native superiority so obvious, that in French military settlements, for example, the officers worried about the assimilation of their men.[16] This was not merely the superiority of a civilization adapted to the place. These soldiers, fishermen and fur traders felt more at home in Native society than in their own.

Every inch of penetration westwards by first the francophones and then the anglophones was dependent on Native support for guidance, food, tactics and negotiation. Over the centuries a series of battles won singlehandedly by or with the support of northern tribes or Métis gradually shaped what would become Canada.

In that sense, the French colonial/Native alliances eventually dovetailed into the English colonial/Native alliances. In the long run, their assumptions about the Native–European relationship were the same. They differed however from those adopted in the new republic to the south.

As a result, the geographic lines established slowly over the centuries in New France were consolidated on a westward line, thanks in large part to the genius of the Mohawk leader Joseph Brant in the late-eighteenth century. They were further consolidated in the early-nineteenth century by chiefs such as Tecumseh and John Norton, who had succeeded Brant as the leader of the Loyalist Natives on the Grand River. Then, as the century wore on, these lines were stretched ever farther west by the military genius of the Métis. The Battle of Grand Coteau was just one example of the strategy they had evolved: mixing Native and European methods. From a military point of view they dominated the prairies for almost a century, until defeated at Batoche.

I use the word genius repeatedly to clarify just how remarkable these contributions were. Brant was complex and contradictory, but he was also one of the few effective leaders on the Loyalist side. Without him the northern line during the American revolution would probably not have held. In every description we have, you sense how superior his intelligence and skills were to those of the mediocre colonial figures who stood in his way. Polyglot, original and dangerous on the battlefield, he was persistent, even annoying (a strength) in councils, whether those of the Native alliances or of the Court in London. And he was confident that, though his civilization was in danger, it could be saved by building new alliances and learning new skills. The key was that he saw his civilization as a central player in the future of North America. And, yes, behind the patriotic mythology, Tecumseh actually was a remarkable leader and tactician. And, yes, Big Bear, given a weak and difficult hand to play, played it with a long-term skill matched by few Canadian politicians. And without John Norton and the Mohawks from Brant's settlement, the Battle of Queenston Heights would probably have been lost, leaving the American army time to establish itself on the Canadian side of the Niagara River and thus probably changing the direction of the war.[17]

And, yes, the Métis military methods are among the few original contributions of Canadians to this second oldest of professions. It had all the marks of sophisticated modern guerrilla warfare. And in spite of the final Métis defeat, their approach was absorbed into a certain Canadian approach towards action. This is hardly to be found in formal military training, but it came out, for example, in the fighter pilots of World War One, and gradually emerged in the expeditionary force as it was increasingly allowed to organize its own tactics.

The master of guerrilla strategy was the great Métis buffalo hunter Gabriel Dumont, whose role is constantly overshadowed in modern history by the political martyrdom of Louis Riel. But Dumont was a much more original and authentic figure, operating free of the classic European conventions of religion and text which so limited Riel in his actions. Dumont was the real Métis leader, the man who had more or less led them for decades and in the process dominated prairie culture. He was the leading hunter and a remarkable political-military strategist. The philosopher George Woodcock alone has written about Dumont in a way which makes it possible to understand him as a far more important figure than many of the anglophone and francophone politicians over whom we dote.[18] Dumont was seduced by the urban, legalistic talents of Riel, and felt powerless before his messianic religious force. Had he resisted these and remained true to Métis strategy, he would have been perfectly capable of drawing Ottawa's little formal army on and on, across the terrain, until negotiation became inevitable. But Riel's more 'respectable' and 'clarified' European approach destabilized the careful, complex balance of the Métis.

Even during the period of Native and Métis decline which followed, the atmosphere in Canada remained one of alliances not conquest. That's why, in the 1870s, the American government spent $20 million a year conquering the Plains Indians, while the Canadian government was spending less than $400,000 a year on the Mounted Police.[19] The Canadian approach was filled with hypocrisy, but it was about a great deal more than hypocrisy. It reflected the underlying structures of the long-term relationship. Indeed, one of the principal roles of the police was to protect the Natives against the waves of invasive settlers who did not understand or want to understand that relationship.

In Rudy Wiebe's fictionalized biography of Big Bear, the aging chief defended himself with these words at his trial following the Métis uprising:

> This land belonged to me. When I had it I never needed your flour and pork. . . . Before many of you were born I ran buffalo over this place where you have put this building, and white men ate the meat I gave them. I gave them my hand as a brother; I was free, and the smallest Person in the band was as free as I because the Master of life had given us our place on the earth and that was enough for us. But you have taken our inheritance, and our strength. The land is torn up, black with fires, and empty. *You have done this.* And there is nothing left now but you must help us.[20]

The point of this litany of Native and Métis events and names is that anglophones and francophones, for more than a century now, have attempted to rewrite the past. Some of us concentrate on a strict, two-culture deal; others deny even that, as if each successive group, by its simple arrival, wiped the national slate clean so that all would begin again on a different footing. Worse still, dressing ourselves in outrage or guilt, we often try to make use of the aboriginal social crisis without recognizing the reality of the aboriginal role.

Gabriel Dumont, when he returned from his exile and was brought to Montreal by Riel's supporters, found that their interest was not in the Métis or their Western culture, but in Honoré Mercier's re-election and how they could use his presence to aid this

with evocations of the martyrdom of Riel. Dumont's public statement that the priests had betrayed the Métis during the revolt was
not what the politicians required—to the contrary. He left rather
than be used as a political tool in a provincial election.[21] This is not
so very different from the use which some federalists are attempting
to make today of Native dissatisfaction with the current Quebec
government's policy to break up Canada. As with the Métis and the
West, the Native position today exists on its own terms, not merely
as a useful tactical weapon for others. And because it is a real dissatisfaction, it also represents a real dissent from PQ policy, not
something which can be reduced to or characterized as federal
scheming or Native narrow self-interest.

It isn't surprising in such an atmosphere that many of us have
looked with a mixture of pity and satisfaction at the difficulty Native
culture has had dealing with such European habits as alcohol. We
observe these problems as if failure on this front were a fundamental human failure. We forget that we ourselves have done no better
at dealing with the introduction of a Native ceremonial stimulant—
tobacco—but have had great difficulty not succumbing to the full
effects of its addictive and destructive force.[22]

Concentrating on the difficulties Natives have had adjusting to
European structures is just another way for us to deny the triangular nature of our society. And it is essential to identify that denial,
because it is above all a form of self-denial. This is an important
part of the colonial mind-set which makes it impossible for us to
accept where we are and what we are, except in the narrowest of
highly predictable terms. In other words, if we can't consciously
accept our experience, then we are resigning ourselves to a confused state of delusion.

It isn't surprising that we fall easily into childlike protests over
who has treated the Natives best—Ottawa or the provinces? Anglophones or francophones? These questions are irrelevant. They are
also profoundly paternalistic. Given the chance, we have all treated

them badly. That which matters in our relationship exists at quite a different level—that of the legitimate inheritance of a relationship now 450 years old.

Instead, we continue to debate superficially about cultural or contractual relationships. For example, there is bitterness in various quarters over whether the Natives have chosen to communicate with governments in English or French, and whether they look to Ottawa or Quebec City or Victoria. These are paternalistic debates which are still structured for a parent–child relationship. It would be more interesting to ask how best the Natives feel they can re-assume their role as an essential element in an arrangement which has now lasted almost half a millennium.

It seems that although the Ottawa relationship remains fraught with paternalism, it nevertheless contains those essential elements of legitimacy which stretch back to the early-sixteenth century. The Natives are therefore determined to maintain that relationship. On the other hand, what we might call corporate bodies—that is, interest-based structures—seem to most effectively convey their point of view through provincial governments. At that level they can be relatively certain that the manifest destiny of economic interests will be expressed without more complex issues of the common good interfering. Their attitudes haven't changed much in a hundred years, nor have they fundamentally weakened, as their resurgence in Ontario under the Harris government has demonstrated. The question they ask is still the same—how much will it cost to get the Natives out of the way?

Parti Québécois governments, stung by Native disinterest in their separation project, insist that the James Bay deal was the best ever given to Natives anywhere in Canada by any level of government. But the point is not one of giving or taking. The question is: was the James Bay deal the first of a new-style admission of Native inclusion in the essential social project? Or was it the last of the old-style buying-off of Natives who stand in the way of anglophone–francophone economic projects? However generous or ungenerous the James Bay contract, it was clearly conceived in the old style. The PQ insistence that it will give the Natives of northern Quebec more or less whatever self-rule they wish is, again, more an offer to set them aside *with dignity* if they will tacitly accept the government's separation project. In that sense it reconstitutes almost exactly the context of the reservation treaties of the nineteenth century.

God knows that there has been little to admire in Ottawa's approach towards Native affairs. Yet, in this forest of betrayals, hypocrisy and paternalism, we can now see the growth of a new style—or rather of a halting acceptance of some sort of return to the original status of triangular interdependence. This can be found in Ottawa's support for the Arctic Council and in the Nunavut negotiations, out of which the Inuit will emerge with a structure of power that works within society as a whole. It is the acceptance of Native relevance to the project of Canadian society which could constitute some acceptance, little and late, of the fundamental roots of our experience.

Whatever there is to be said on the subject of the decentralization versus the centralization of various governmental powers, Natives do not belong as pawns in this debate. The handing-off of Native affairs to provinces is not a victory for decentralization or provincial rights. Nor is it a reassertion of the terms of the BNA Act. It removes the role of the Native from the heart of the long-term social contract of what was conceived as a northern nation and so demotes that role to a mere regional interest-based contract. In other words, it represents the reduction of an essential element in our social contract to little more than a commercial contract; the reduction of a fiduciary relationship to a commercial relationship. To the extent that Ottawa does this, it is giving in to the sort of corporatist interests which did so much damage in the nineteenth and early-twentieth centuries and is guilty of a fundamental social betrayal.

98   Let me put this in even more general terms. The triangular nature of
our society was first built over a period of some three centuries,
during which francophones and anglophones were either dependent on the Natives for survival and advancement or were engaged
in an alliance of equals with the Natives. This was followed by a
century and a half—the last 150 years—of anglophone–francophone
domination.

In historical terms the second period has lasted only half the
length of the first, and in many ways is already coming to an end.
When you consider the periods of time involved, it becomes easier
to understand Stan Dragland's idea that the dominant party in a
society must try to absorb the vitality of the other. Early in the last
century Robert Baldwin twice wrote long poems glorifying Tecumseh. His intent was neither good nor evil. He was integrating his
own mythology into a longer, more fundamental experience. The
man who was himself moving towards a battle against established
power naturally wrote of the slain Tecumseh:

> But now all gastly, wan and pale
> Low on the field he lies
> Nor hears a wife's loud plaintive wail
> Nor hears a nation's cries.[23]

He was evoking a certain view of the curiously symbiotic tension
between Natives and colonials. A few years before, the Indian
Commissioner had written to Joseph Brant, asking one of those
questions filled with European assumptions of superiority: "Is civilization favourable to human happiness?" Brant threw it back in
his face:

> The question is not whether a degree of refinement is con-
> ducive to the happiness, but whether you or the natives of this
> land have obtained this happy medium.... I am obliged to give
> my opinion in favour of mine own people. In the government

you call civilized, the happiness of the people is constantly sacrificed to the splendour of empires. Hence your codes of criminal and civil laws have their origin; hence your dungeons and prisons. I will not enlarge on an idea so singular in civilized life. Among us we have no prisons. . . .[24]

In 1970 Grand Chief John Kelly put this in a more inclusive way— ". . . as the years go by, the circle of the Ojibway gets bigger and bigger. Canadians of all colours and religion are entering that circle. You might feel that you have roots somewhere else, but in reality, you are right here with us."[25]

Some who read these quotes will reject their use as romantic politicizing. Some varieties of nationalists will feel, as they always do, that the evocation of the Natives is merely the introduction of a competitor to their own vision of national exclusivity and inevitability. Others will find that the complexity and therefore added tensions which such an approach assume are unliveable and therefore unrealistic. My own view, as I have been setting it out in these chapters, is that complexity is the nature of the Canadian experience. Not to embrace it is to enter into self-denial. And the assumption of our internal tensions is precisely what differentiates our experience from the standard monolithic nineteenth-century national model. As for accusations of romanticism, that is a classic shot from those who assert their own narrow view as hard-headed realism.

Consider instead the extent to which the international environmental movement has found its origins within Canada. Four examples: Maurice Strong, a Manitoban, who is in many ways the father of the movement; Greenpeace, the most persistently aggressive of guerrilla fighters, from British Columbia; David Suzuki, who spent part of his childhood in a Canadian internment camp and has brought the scientist's eye to the aid of the public good; and the Nobel Prize–winning chemist John Polanyi, who came to Canada as a young man and has devoted much of his life to combating the dangers of nuclear weapons. Of course, we also have our fair share

100   of activists on the other side—the clear-cutters and polluters; the executives of masculine assertion through physical destruction. But blind self-interest and aggressive self-reassurance exist everywhere. What is interesting and original is the ease with which the environmental movement appeared and appeared to be a normal phenomenon in this particular country. Grand Chief John Kelly's 1970 declaration of inclusion went on: "I do not know if you feel the throbbing of the land in your chest. . . ."

Environmentalism is a contemporary face—often presented in rational or romantic garb—of the all-inclusive animism which Europeans found here when they arrived and with which they lived for a good three centuries before actively trying to erase it. What they erased were many of the superficial signs. The thing itself had already penetrated their own culture.

Obviously there are other factors which explain environmentalism. Some of them are related to social animism, such as living with a massive uncontrollable nature.

I am neither limiting nor idealizing the role of Native culture any more than that of the francophone and anglophone immigrants. Had these elements come together farther south in more temperate, controllable circumstances, the result would probably have been very different. Instead, the deeply rooted relationships which have developed over four and a half centuries are based upon the sort of interdependence and compromise which you would expect in a nation built on the geographic margins of a continent.

The North American Nation

6

THE IDEA OF THE NATION-STATE—a European idea—is one of domination. The nation conquers within and it conquers without, in so far as abutting nations will permit. Domination is essential because it permits a monolithic expression of the nation's purpose—its manifest destiny. We tend to call that an identity or a culture.

What must the nation conquer? It must conquer the unknown, the uncontrolled, in order to fully express its purpose. Frontiers must be conquered and thereby converted into borders. The physical frontiers will be transmogrified into the sacred borders of destiny. But there are many other sorts of frontiers to be tackled—the linguistic, cultural and economic. All of these can and must, it seems, become borders. The greatest challenge is the frontier of the imagination. The more our imagination is bordered, the more we fit the classic description of 'a people.' This is because in the frontiers of the imagination are lodged our doubts about identity. The classic nation-state seeks to eliminate these in the name of unity or loyalty or *realpolitik*.

The idea of the conquered frontier is therefore central to that of the European nation-state. Multifaceted borders provide the reassurance of belonging. They do this by imposing multifaceted limitations.

Finally, the emergence of the European nation-state is closely tied to that of rationality and thus of organization. The frontier is feared because it is uncontrollable and therefore unorganizable. Only the elimination of the frontier will make it possible to structure the nation-state. In rational mythology man is a conquering force which brings the irrational forces of nature to their knees, breaks them

102 down into essential elements and reassembles those elements in a manner useful to humans—that is, a rational manner. The place and what it contains is thus utilitarian. Once harnessed, the purpose of the place can be unleashed to help civilization assume its destiny. In the logic of the nation-state—the internal logic—all that is done for this civilization is inevitable.

Now, there is a very curious affectation, dear to Canadians, that they are more European than the Americans to our south. Britain is included in this Europe. There is an even more curious affectation dear to Americans that they are proper to the American continent and therefore essentially different from Europeans. Both these mythologies seem to involve confusing the superficial aspects of a civilization for that which drives it. We allow the political, social and economic compromise which Europe as a whole is in the process of constructing to wipe out our memory of the European idea of the nation. We forget about two thousand years of European wars—both civil and external—in order to assure ourselves that Europe represents a meaningful parentage for this country, built over half a millennium of relative peace on the northern margins of North America. This causes us to compare the nature of our social order and the similarities in our social policies—tattered as they now are—with those of Europe, and then to oppose them to the exclusivity and violence of the American system.

I would argue the exact opposite. Canada is profoundly un-European. Its attitudes and policies are largely the product of local circumstances, in part because we have constructed a country on the margins of western civilization. Those circumstances moved us away from the European model of the monolithic frontier-conquering nation-state. It was a model which could not work here. The United States, on the other hand, is the natural prolongation of the European idea. It is the European state personified. It has become what France, Germany,

England and Spain dreamt they might become if only they had had the space. For centuries they fought each other in the desperate hope that they could conquer the necessary territory to fulfil their rational, nation-state dream.

What I am saying is neither a compliment nor an insult, merely an attempt at clarification. From the first moments of its birth, the United States embraced the full rationality of the nation-state project as it had been unfolding from Machiavelli to Cromwell and Richelieu and on into the eighteenth century. The American formula, which so distrusted both power and the citizenry that it imposed a web of legal strait-jackets on its own mechanism of action, is perfectly Hobbesian. The proclamation of its ideals sums up the Enlightenment ideal. Its sense of a manifest destiny which justifies sweeping away any and all obstacles is a straight evocation of the European tradition.

Consider the American idea of the frontier. I don't mean the evocation delivered through Hollywood entertainment and political rhetoric. The real frontier was there to be conquered—to be eliminated. As a result, it existed for a remarkably short period of time—approximately twenty years—before the whole continent became part of the bordered nation-state. The Natives were often described as enemies, which was classical European terminology for obstacles to a manifest destiny. The $20 million a year, which I have already cited as being spent annually on the war of the American army against the Natives, is merely the practical evocation of a standard European approach. The conquering of a frontier usually includes the elimination of rival cultures.

Canada fulfils none of the criteria I have been describing. It is not, nor was it ever, a rational project. The contradictions within the process—the regional, linguistic and cultural differences—have largely been accepted as characteristics of the nation rather than obstacles to its creation. The idea of the conquering within and without, on behalf of a particular manifest destiny, has never been seriously proposed or accepted as a mainstream approach to

104 nation-building. Universal ideals are therefore not proclaimed as if they were personal property of the particular civilization. We fail all the Hobbesian tests of legal strait-jackets intended to impose self-control.

The key to our non-European nature lies in our relationship to the frontier. It is not there to be conquered for the simple reason that it cannot be conquered. Most of us throughout the developed world are now agreed that the idea of conquering and redirecting nature is a flawed one. Nevertheless it lies at the heart of the European idea and of its American child.

The Canadian particularity is tied to constructing a nation in a place where there can be no serious pretension of human domination. The best—or rather the worst—we can do is pretend that most of the country doesn't exist and that we are somehow here by accident.

The overall result of what I have been describing has been the development of two very different models in North America—one a conquering, European model; the other a more complex accommodation with place and circumstance. These separate trends were already highly developed by the middle of the eighteenth century. The European view was clear in the French colonial ruling class who came and went and used the colony as a source of income. They carefully limited what the local economy could do, in order to maintain control over its markets and raw materials. To the south, the more favourable geographic and climatic conditions allowed the development of a European-style expectation of domination among the permanent élites. The growth of slavery is one illustration of those rational expectations.

The Canadiens, by contrast, had survived in large part by compromising with the place—with the Native population and with the demanding requirements of a society which was dominated by the difficult place in which it was found. They had come to terms with the contrast between their formal civilization and the reality of living with a dominant Native population in a place where cooperation was rewarded over domination.

They weren't alone in their approach. To their south, a whole section of the British colonial population had come to much the same conclusion. Instead of transporting a conquering myth with them, they seemed to find great freedom or release in rejecting the rational view. They saw themselves more as a bridge between the civilization they had escaped and the one they were discovering. They saw nature not as an enemy to be conquered but as a new form of life of which they were a part.

The most famous of these new Americans was Sir William Johnson, who died as the American revolt began. For decades he had been the British government's chief representative to the aboriginals. But more than that, he was a man who took pleasure in confusing the two cultures. He was as happy painted and dressed in Native clothes, fighting at their side, as he was playing the colonial squire. His wife, Molly Brant, came from one of the most important Mohawk families. She had always played a role in Johnson's politicking and after his death she emerged as one of the most powerful Natives during the American war. Johnson's young brother-in-law, Joseph Brant, along with Johnson's son, led the only successful forces against the revolt. They all shared the opinion which Johnson had repeatedly expressed—that receiving justice for the Natives at colonial hands was an "utter impossibility." He had seen the "encroachment of the ambitious in America" as inevitable if power over new lands were not kept out of colonial hands.[1]

He was referring, even before it had been formalized, to the growing sense of manifest destiny among the new European-style élite which was rapidly taking form. This included Colonel George Washington, who was speculating in land on territory which lay within legally protected Native territory. With time, the new republic's attitude towards the aboriginals would come to resemble that of the Spaniards. The reality of whoever stood in their way would be abstracted into theories of nationhood, which conveyed absolute rights upon the 'nationalists' and erased those of the 'dissidents.'

On the other hand, the complexity of the mythology embraced by men like William Johnson has not been conveyed to us, except as amusing marginalia. Instead, we have been left with simplistic messages from history. We remember Canadiens abandoned to their fate but loyal to their European origins; and Loyalists who stood by their king and so brought yet more European attitudes north with them.

The reality was quite different. In New France the authorities had held back on the creation of even the most local of government institutions. There were, as Allan Greer points out in his remarkable analysis of democracy and its origins in Canada, no printing presses and no municipal governments. With the arrival of British government, printing presses appeared but not municipal government, let alone anything at a higher level. Quebec and Montreal were two hundred years old before they got town councils and Toronto had to wait until 1834.[2] Nevertheless, Greer shows that "forms of local public life were firmly in place right across British North America" among francophones and anglophones. They "either created their own customs and institutions" or adapted whatever was imposed on them by the authorities. Thus community religious structures were collective and "fiercely self assertive" among francophone Catholics. Protestant congregations played the same role for anglophone Protestants. This was the advantage to be drawn from isolation and governmental indifference. It is worth noting to what extent the patriots of Lower and Upper Canada in 1837 came from rural areas, where their sense of themselves was not softened by the proximity of colonial government. Much later, these local religious structures, both Catholic and Protestant, would be recuperated by the respective negative nationalists. But by then the reform movements had taken on a form of their own and become more or less the enemy of the various churches.

Of course, all Loyalists did not resemble William Johnson or Joseph Brant. They were a mixed bag, from idealists and animists through public servants and frightened minorities to opportunists and criminals. But many did come because they had a radically different view of life on this continent from that proclaimed by the

European-style revolutionaries. They were people who had come to terms with the complex, contradictory, even incomplete nature of their new home. They didn't identify with the myth either of domination or of a monolithic civilization. The idea of the unconquerable frontier actually attracted them. Without knowing it, they shared this world view with the Canadiens.

What I am describing, bit by bit, is their very original view of the nation-state. You could call this the more authentic American nation-state, as opposed to the European model to our south. You could call it the model of the marginal or frontier or northern nation-state. And indeed there are similar attitudes to be found in much of Scandinavia and even Russia. Given the uncontrollable nature of the place, this was a model which was not intended to achieve the sort of static state implicit in the mythology of domination. This is a nation conceived as existing in permanent motion; more a sensibility than an ambition.

Such an approach would probably have been untenable in a richer, more temperate zone. But the circumstances of defeat pushed the anglophones northward where they found another population which had already come to similar conclusions. You might say that in the north William Johnson's myth of the old world freed by the uncontrollable nature of the new could progress on its own terms, driven now by geographic and climatic necessity.

In place of abstract theories of nationhood, a much more practical approach towards place and partnership emerged. The single most important element of this progress was the impossibility of domination over nature or society. The marginality imposed by climate was a specific constant reminder that progress would in general be built on alliances and interdependence. These circumstances placed animism at the heart of culture. It was a concrete animism, very different from the Rousseauian, romantic view of nature under control which was emerging to the south.

What is interesting about the non-European view which emerged in Canada is that it was shared from the beginning by most of those people living on those northern margins—the Natives, the French Canadians and the refugee American colonials. In other words, neither anglophone nor francophone Canada was built—as so many of the European-inspired intellectual schools insisted—on the negative force of anti-Americanism and inspiration from across the Atlantic, but on a positive acceptance of place and society as expressions of complexity.

It was three-quarters of a century before the force of monolithic, conquering, European nationalism began to make itself seriously felt in Canada. The Orange and the Ultramontane movements were filled with the triumphalist spirit of national truth. And like all movements of this sort, they drew everyone's eye towards 'the people.' At first glance this seems to be a healthy phenomenon. But what really happens in such circumstances is that the eye becomes so fixated on the self that context is eliminated. Place is eliminated. The particularity of experience is eliminated. Any memory not useful to the advancement of the 'truth' is eliminated. Other religions, languages and groups fade from focus except as cardboard cut-outs. Suddenly there is no real *other*. 'The people,' it turns out, are not the people, but an abstraction. The citizen's sense of reality is thus undermined.

What results is an odd sort of selfishness which justifies forgetting everything I have just listed. It becomes impossible to weigh sensibly our various assertions of victimization and exclusive originality. We can't see that they are only manifestations of the old European nation-state idea, with its need of a central—that is, monolithic—mythology, itself based on an assumption of domination.

As this sort of nationalism grew in the nineteenth century, so did the myths of the Mother Countries. Curiously enough, the real role of these countries was then receding into the past (France) and shrinking (England). But the growing attempts to deform Canada in order to 'normalize' it required an active mythological role for the mothers. An active force within the francophone and anglophone élites—both intellectual and political—began to assert that we died and lived according to the availability of our mother's generous breasts. They insisted we were needy offspring. For example, if French Canadians had been conquered, well then their tragic victimization had to be based on the loss of France's leadership and nourishment. This meant forgetting the suffocating political and economic policies which the metropole had enforced. More importantly, it meant that the narrow nationalist school would have to base its idea of manifest destiny on a consistent underrating of the accomplishments of French-Canadian society. As for the rhetorical credit increasingly given to English justice, English organization, English everything, it masked the reality of what the intelligent and engaged political élites were doing. To take a small example, the success of the Mounted Police in the West was not an accomplishment of British administrative methods, but the practical application of the more restrained, cooperative Canadian approach, which had been developing since the eighteenth century, if not before.

Men like Papineau, Nelson, Mackenzie, LaFontaine, Dr. Baldwin and Robert Baldwin, Denis Benjamin Viger and Egerton Ryerson would have been amazed, or rather horrified, by the growth of such a toadying mythology. It rolled on into the twentieth century and is still with us, just under the surface, because the historians who set in place the arguments we have today were infatuated by the illusion of the essential mother-country role. Perhaps the best-known example of an historian unable to imagine a Canada outside of the English mould is Donald Creighton in the 1950s. But, as I have already mentioned, even George Grant, in his perfectly justifiable critique of the Canadian élites, continually fell back on the assertion that the Canadian idea of the common good stood in opposition to American liberalism and was born of a certain "... tradition of British Conservatism ..."[3] Actually the Canadian reform movements of the 1820s to 1840s came out of local rural conditions and the development of a local idea of moderate reform. This was the product of a permanent state of cooperation and compromise between the groups present in the various colonies. There wasn't a shred of

British tradition in this evolution and most certainly not of British Conservative tradition.

At the same time that anglophone intellectuals were inventing Canada's English roots, men like Maurice Séguin and Michel Brunet were weeping intellectual tears over the loss, long before, of their "protector and wet nurse," those who had first "humanized" the wilderness, those who "stood behind the colonials to protect them militarily, to colonize them with their men, their institutions, their capital. . . ."[4] That the metropole had strangled immigration and refused institutions and that the metropolitan élites had extracted rather than invested capital and sailed back to France without a glance over their shoulders at the lost colonial market-place was ignored.

This romanticism on both sides allowed leading anglophone intellectuals to characterize French-Canadian society as church-ridden and backward, while leading francophone intellectuals like Brunet would accuse "British Canada" of "suffering from a profound spiritual poverty."[5]

Such mutually comic stylizations of 'the other side' were only worsened by the appearance of phrases such as "peace, order and good government" in the Constitution of 1867. These fed the idea that Canada was a country in the full European tradition of law and administration. To the south the myth of unchained individualism suggested their society was somehow the opposite—an unleashing of human energy in a new continent.

But, of course, the United States was, from its origins, the very model of a society built on law and structure, for better and worse. On the other hand, most of the essential Canadian conventions—such as those between groups and communities—were based on largely unwritten agreements. This technical looseness has produced some catastrophes, but in general it is an approach which has seemed to encourage an ongoing process of moderate reform.

Let me put this in more general terms. The dominant system of power in the west has been Platonist—a system which functions on highly developed levels of structure and law. This is the school of pure rationality and fear of the undefined—fear of doubt. The minority system has been Socratic or humanist. It is interested in doubt and not overwhelmed by the Platonist-Hobbesian desperate need to tie things down. The Platonists finish inevitably in a highly written or scholastic society. The Socratic approach has room for complexity and for the oral. Of course, no nation belongs absolutely to one or the other. Elements of both the Socratic and the Platonist as well as the tensions between them can be found in all western societies. But most of these countries are clearly of Platonist inspiration. What makes Canada interesting is the extent to which it has been, from the beginning, of Socratic inspiration. It is not a matter of conscious or unconscious inspiration. What I am referring to is the road chosen. Whether the society which chose is even aware of the various intellectual traditions is neither here nor there. These are simply the two patterns into which western societies have tended to fall.

Though flawed, the early relationships between Native, francophone and anglophone are illustrations of a Socratic approach. The unfolding of the Lower Canada–Upper Canada arrangement is an even clearer indication.

"It is in the interests of the Reformers of the two provinces," LaFontaine wrote to his electors in 1840, "to meet each other on the legislative terrain in the spirit of peace, union, friendship and fraternity. Unity of action is more necessary then ever." Baldwin pledged to him that they would work together to obtain "Justice *upon precisely the same footing* in *every* particular as *ourselves*." He believed that it was Responsible Government "coupled with that forbearance, moderation and firmness on the part of the people which, so long as it compromises no great principle, affords the best assurance of the possession of fitness for the exercise of political power."

The governor and the Montreal élite physically prevented LaFontaine's election in Terrebonne. So Baldwin, who had won two seats, stepped down in the fourth riding of York, the countryside running north of Toronto from Uxbridge to Lake Simcoe, and wrote to his electors there, calling on the population of small farmers to choose LaFontaine in his place. It will be a "substantial pledge of our sympathy with our Lower Canada friends and form the bond of union between us." Baldwin had to go on leading the reform forces in the legislature, so his father took his place during the by-election. The great, old Dr. Baldwin was in many ways the founder of the responsible government movement. He was weak and in poor health, but when LaFontaine arrived from Montreal, the doctor took him up north and they canvassed the rural riding side by side. Each time LaFontaine gave a speech, the doctor introduced him. The farmers liked the message of a reform coalition, took to LaFontaine and elected him in a landslide. A year later, Robert Baldwin was defeated and LaFontaine successfully put him up for election in Rimouski, where the same message was embraced by the voters.

LaFontaine stood in the legislature in Kingston for the first time in 1842, to continue the argument begun in his letter of two years before to his electors. He spoke, of course, in French because the law forbidding its use had simply been ignored by the anglophone and francophone reform majority from the beginning of the Union. Indeed the first Speaker of the unified Parliament of Canada was a French-Canadian reformer, Austin Cuvillier. "The Act of Union," LaFontaine said, "in the mind of its author, was intended to crush the francophone population; but he made a mistake, because the method employed didn't evolve as expected. The mass of the two populations of Upper and Lower Canada have common interests and they will work out how to get on together."[6]

There is an interesting Inuit concept which reflects the reformer's approach. *Isuma* is a human quality—"a kind of intelligence that includes knowledge of one's responsibilities towards society," is how the writer and film-maker Kevin McMahon puts it.[7] *Isuma* grows with time and needs—as do people—to be constantly nurtured. Reality never permits us to establish such an ideal social tension. But what I am describing here is intent, and what is attempted.

In a way this is what Nellie McClung, who led the battle for the women's right to vote, called "the fair deal."[8] Seeking the fair deal was her vision of what the country should make possible.

However flawed the application of "the fair deal" or *isuma* or "the common interests" might be, it is a process which helps us to understand the humanism at the core of the early Canadian devotion to moderate reform. This was how they adjusted to reality.

It is moderation which makes the reforms possible, even normal. Such a careful approach on both sides infuriates the ideologues and those devoted to the clarity of the European model. Accusations which convert care into weakness, compromise into betrayal and moderation into a boring characteristic have dogged the Canadian model from its beginnings. When, for example, Mackenzie King responded to the discontent in the West in the 1920s with a careful openness—"We must have regard for all shades and all parts of the country, and any policy that is extreme we must avoid"—his opponents were infuriated, as were the interest groups and the ideologues.[9]

But moderate, careful attempts at equilibrium, which are central to democracy as an expression of humanism, do not in any way suggest anything but the most radical, even violent—intellectual and, if necessary, physical—rejection of that which destroys moderation.

The middle way is neither soft nor easy. It is the most difficult of roads, because it is the most fragile and is exposed to easy attack. The ways of ideology and absolute answers, the monolithic view of the nation-state, the dominant centralized view of culture—all of these are filled with bravado. The corporatism which so dominates today has nothing but contempt for a complex middle road. But then corporatism is the logical partner of simplistic nationalism. Together they are the modern expression of the old Platonist model.

Any examination of which of these models is boring, which exciting, reveals the exact opposite of what bravado promises. Tolstoy put it best in his story "Father Sergius": "When he banished doubt, he also banished desire."[10] Power has always been a stand-in for desire.

114   In the old European monolithic model of the nation-state, desire
        becomes central to the mythological relationship between those who
        have power and the citizenry. A great deal is made of the potency of
        the powerful. No country escapes this phenomenon, but the intro-
        duction of complexity and doubt into the model of the state is also a
        way to introduce an idea of desire which reduces the craven aspects.

        It is interesting to note for example the conscious decision of the
        authorities from the very beginning of the Union to avoid the use of
        state violence. Of course, it has been used, but I am talking about
        relativity. In 1849, when the élite of Montreal rioted and burnt
        down the Parliament Buildings, LaFontaine as premier and Bald-
        win as *de facto* deputy premier went out of their way not to use state
        force. They knew that the pendulum of violence, if set on a great arc,
        would then swing back and forth, from extreme to extreme, as it did
        in so many nation-states where the cultural project was the domi-
        nation of a single force. Such a situation in Canada would make it
        impossible to maintain the course of moderate reform. They knew
        that it would eventually shatter the alliance of the reformers of
        Lower and Upper Canada. They somehow understood instinctively
        what we now know from experience—that serving the public good
        in Canada would be based on restraint and moderation. Whenever
        we have done anything in the name of ideology, it has worked
        against that public interest and left deep wounds.

        That is why the Métis rebellion and the Ontario language edu-
        cation law of 1912 and the internment of the Japanese Canadians
        and the Padlock Law and the Asbestos Strike and the War Mea-
        sures Act hang around our necks like albatrosses that no telling of
        the story will let drop away. The clarity of these and a few other vio-
        lent acts become overwhelming in our imagination. They were
        small acts by international standards, but by our own standards
        they were enormous.

        It is worth going back again to the example of LaFontaine and
        Baldwin. There is no bravado. No matter how unfairly they are
        treated, their response is never one of personal affront. It is impossible

not to be struck by their moderate personal ambition. Their perception of public life is one of ideas and the implementation of those ideas. They see the nation-state as a sensibility much more than an interest. They both walked away from power at the height of their careers. It was said of LaFontaine that, "As disinterest made the man, he couldn't understand the existence of personal interest in others."[11] As for Baldwin, he left office in June 1851. During his resignation speech he wept uncontrollably, with the prime minister—LaFontaine—and the other francophones and anglophones weeping around him. He left on a matter of principle when others would have clung to their place.

Their project was not at its core one of bringing together races or even languages—although they firmly established language and group rights. Rather it was a non-ideological idea of equilibrium and shared sensibility. Yes, it would draw groups together in order to protect them. But by drawing them together on far more than issues of self-interest, it would be possible to move beyond them to an idea of the public interest.

There is no question but that the result was and remains a very peculiar sort of nation-state. You might describe it as a long-standing experiment which has rejected the nineteenth-century truisms. The very idea of accepting that unconquered frontiers—social as much as geographic—are a stimulus of healthy tension is enough to make the society interesting. The refusal of the monolithic is a remarkable expression of social progress.

When writing about Harold Innis and Marshall McLuhan and the interpretation of history, Graeme Patterson argues that "discontinuity" is a "unifying technique" in all sorts of modern activities.[12] Picasso and James Joyce are two masters of unity through discontinuity. So are Innis and McLuhan. The leadership role which these and other Canadian thinkers have played in unravelling modern communications takes on a certain logic when you consider the influence on them of a country built on a curious sort of union through discontinuity.

116   In a way this was the real question raised by Jacques Godbout in *Les Têtes à Papineau*. Together his Siamese-twin heroes are complex, interesting, contradictory, original. Separate them and they become like everyone else. Normalcy has its attractions. Its comforts. "It's for your own good!" said the doctor. "One can't spend one's life half this and half that. . . . Gentlemen, you are nothing more than half-men."[13] Of course, with normalcy you lose the disadvantages of McLuhan's "discontinuity." You also lose its advantages. You join the majority school of the monolithic nation-state, providing your geographic reality permits it. The one question Godbout didn't raise was the rate of mortality in operations to separate Siamese twins. It is very rare for both to live. Sometimes one survives. Usually neither.

PART II

SOME MYTHOLOGICAL PROPOSITIONS

"minus these coincidences
what is the world trying to tell me?"
bp Nichol, *Continental Trance*

Deformed mythologies and mystification produce
a determination to become a victim,
to embrace repressed hysteria,
to believe that life is not being American,
to chant that all good things flow north–south,
to have sexual fantasies involving special relationships
    with empires,
to deny that ours is a northern state
and so on
and so on.

And yet,
the reality remains that
complexity is Canada's central characteristic,
a non-conforming, particular idea of a nation-state,
polytheistic by nature,
a permanently incomplete experiment,
built on a triangular foundation,
to produce an American phenomenon
versus the European republic to our south,
and other strange
peculiarities.

What then are the mythologies which reflect this reality?

Ideas over Facts

7

"The facts are too overwhelming to be denied or even struggled against—except by something stronger than a fact: an idea!"[1]

ANDRÉ LAURENDEAU RECORDED with approval this piece of testimony heard in Winnipeg. It was 1964 and he was travelling the country as co-chair of the Bilingualism and Biculturalism Commission. The fact in question was the proximity of the United States and all that that implied, given the standard geopolitical interpretations of a country's 'situation.' But the sentence might just as accurately have referred to the absence of a dominant, monolithic culture in Canada or to the astonishing and—in the conventional, factual sense—impossible geography of the country. For that matter, it might have referred to any number of the characteristics of the Canadian condition.

Laurendeau's acceptance, that an idea could in practical terms be stronger than facts, is not an expression of sentiment or emotion or dreaming or even of an aspiration. All of these imponderables do exist in each of us and, providing they don't dominate our actions, are necessary, even positive elements. But an idea is quite another matter. It is something solid; far more solid than the squalid little herds of facts so often marshalled to justify what is presented as the inevitable.

Canada either is an idea or does not exist. It either is an intellectual undertaking or it is little more than a resource-rich vacuum lying in the buffer zone just to the north of the great empire. And despite protestations to the contrary, that vacuum would be as vacuous in British Columbia, Alberta and Quebec as in the Maritimes or Ontario.

At each stage in our political development the idea has been clear, even if only in a nascent form. The union of francophone and anglophone reformers in 1841 was not a mere political manoeuvre. And

122 none of them saw it as such. Even the opponents opposed precisely because it did represent an idea of how to organize social relationships—that is, it represented an idea of a society. It was an original, inclusive and long-term idea imagined by men who could think well beyond the fractious daily dramas of two small and backward colonies. The same could be said for some of the breakthroughs in Nova Scotia and Prince Edward Island.

The practical ideas surrounding public education, property ownership, a widely based franchise, a multilingual, multi-denominational society were unprecedented in the west. The idea of creating a nation as a mechanism for reform, as opposed to a military or economic or tribal reason, was even more original. In a sense, these nineteenth-century activists were inventing what many other countries wouldn't arrive at until halfway through the twentieth century—a middle-class society in which social democracy would mix public and private forces. This was unrelated to the negative idea of the 'bourgeois' society which the Europeans were then struggling with.

I say unprecedented, in spite of the great enfolding myth of originality which floats, as it always has, up from the south. Remarkable though the American ideal was and is, it was, as I have said, not so much original as the logical continuation of the European experiment. As such it continued the assumptions of a class-based society. The American leap from thirteen colonies to a new European idea of the nation was remarkable and yet predictable. The concept of the Lower and Upper Canadian reformers in 1841 was a leap into the imagination.

No one had attempted such a thing elsewhere. It was neither predictable nor inevitable. It was a new idea about social relationships and—looking at the American and European nations as they struggle today to adapt to their suddenly more complex societies—it was an astonishingly modern idea.

We tend to miss the dimensions of this originality because of the

close relationship in Canada between theory and practice. Throughout the west we are used to ideas being presented as great abstractions filled with the promise of a perfectible future world. In other
words, we are used to ideals being presented as if they were ideas—
which is like ideologies being presented as if they were ideas. For
example, the American ideal—from its very beginning—contained,
indeed survived upon, slavery. Yet this didn't seem to matter. The
ideal was untouched. After all, in political philosophy an idea is
often presented as a promise for the future. It then dons a great
mythological robe which embraces that future, while unconscionable acts are done under its folds.

The Lower and Upper Canadian reformers lived in such marginal societies that there was little temptation—let alone possibility—to go down that grandiose route. Ideas might be original and
designed to evolve over the long term, but they were to be applied
immediately or they could not exist.

Those in search of purer intellectual excitement might gaze envi-
ously at larger societies where wonderful ideals could be presented
as ideas, however undermined they might be by reality. From their
point of view the Canadian experiment wasn't even an idea. It was
merely a matter of practicalities. Indeed, if you gaze through the
close-up focus of the cynic, every action can be interpreted as low-
level political manoeuvring.

But draw back and examine the shape of these practicalities.
Compare them with the concrete conventions accepted elsewhere.
You quickly see the ideas. What's more, you see their originality.

In 1867 the reformers managed to step away from what were by
then relatively sophisticated party strait-jackets, in order to think
about the larger interest. When you read the lengthy interventions
of Cartier and Macdonald, it is clear that their idea of the public
good was a continuation of the reform coalition of 1841.

Curiously enough, Confederation has been described by various
political groups as a small *c* conservative project. The opponents—

124 Antoine-Aimé Dorion, Joseph Howe and others—of course had
their arguments, some of them perfectly valid. But for the most part
theirs was the static, fearful position. None of the key players—not
Cartier, Macdonald, Brown, McGee or Tupper—were small *c* conservatives. They all had an original and long-term idea of their
undertaking. They were closely linked to ideas of social equality.
Just as Baldwin had taken steps towards universal public education
and LaFontaine had fought against those Seigneurial Rights which
Papineau supported, so Tupper and Cartier were closely tied to the
drive for universal public education. Cartier's distrust and dislike
of the church's rising power led him to take a series of initiatives in
the direction of government-led and government-inspired education. These were eventually swept away by the Ultramontane grip
on politics and nationalism.

Invariably the sign that we are drifting into trouble is that we abandon the concept of a country of rather unusual ideas and embrace
instead the facts of power. Suddenly everything is seen through the
myopic eye of the simpleton's *realpolitik*. That was what happened in
1914–18, and indeed that has been happening with ever greater
speed for the last decade. The failure of élites is important in any
country. It is particularly important in a country which has been
built upon the development of non-conforming ideas in marginal
geography with a small population.

What we have experienced over the last decade has been a rush
to conformity among our élites. As they have embraced the rise of
corporatism in the west, so they have accepted the simultaneous
revival of the rather inane absolutes of nineteenth-century economic
theory. These theories of trade, globalization and so on are claimed
to be fact-based. The result has been a false conformity to a false
universal reality.

"Where was the spirit broken," one of Monique Proulx's characters asks, "at what precise instant did her life swerve towards the
disaster of banality?"[2] Laurendeau ruminated on "the need for conformity" which Canadians, like everyone else, feel. But it is precisely
because Canada is an experiment that it can only develop by
rewarding non-conformity.

And one of the central non-conforming ideas of Canada is that its
principal creative decisions have not been driven by economics.
Neither 1841 nor 1867 was an economic scenario. Both led to economic difficulties. In fact, they involved backs being turned on economic imperatives in order to concentrate on political, community
and social imperatives. That economic plans were subsequently put
in place was hardly surprising. But neither those plans nor the
expectation of them drove the agenda. The same was true of Laurier
refusing the Empire Pact. After all, the received wisdom of the
day—to which the other dominions and colonies tended to sub-
scribe—was that the empire route was the road of prosperity. And
the gradual creation of social programming from Mackenzie King on
constantly came in the face of opposing market-place arguments.

Economics was always perceived as a tool of society; something
to be conceived in light of society's choices about itself. With the
arrival of Brian Mulroney this delicate balance was reversed and we
slipped into following empire trends. The provinces—Ontario and
Quebec in particular—have accepted this reversal. They have even
played a role in pushing Canada down the conventional route.

In the process of embracing these absolutes we have forgotten
the originality of our experiment. "The middle road is the only one
that does not lead to Rome," Arnold Schönberg said. But our élites
are in a conforming mind-set and they dream of Rome along with
dozens of other similar élites elsewhere. The middle way is the most
difficult. It requires the constant use of the mind, the expending of
energy to not do as the facts dictate.

The burden of originality doesn't lessen with time. No doubt

126 Canadians, and in particular their élites, feel the burden of holding themselves apart in order to deal with a different idea of what a country can be. And so they have slunk into the universal mould. Even so, whatever short-term comforts conformity brings, there is nothing to be gained by dressing in other people's clothes.

A Country of
Minorities

8

IT IS DIFFICULT TO THINK OF another country—except perhaps Australia—so consistently populated by the abandoned and the
defeated. The Natives feel themselves the victims of both the anglophones and the francophones; the francophones of the anglophones;
the anglophones of the Americans just across the border and yet present twenty-four hours a day; the waves of religious minorities, poor,
persecuted, exiled and excluded, who have emigrated here each feel
to some extent the victim of those who have come before. Often they
have felt this with good reason as we have treated them, having let
them in, with all the conventional prejudices of the day. That we have
gradually, over the last few decades, concentrated increasingly on rich
immigrants is an anomaly in our history.

The idea of a country in which three large minorities cooperate so
as to constitute the founding majority and to which dozens more
minorities are then joined, often through at least partial membership
in one of the original groups, amounts to conceiving the idea of a
nation of minorities.

Once ten thousand French settlers had arrived they were,
through various political and religious restrictions imposed by Paris,
effectively denied further immigrants. So eventually they found
themselves abandoned at the level of sixty thousand men, women
and children. The population which had been stagnant for years
exploded with the change of government and continued to grow.
Whatever the cultural problems, the social effects of the Treaty of
Paris were apparently positive. A small bourgeoisie came quite
quickly into being, and within thirty years the population was
showing great aggressivity in public affairs. In other words, the

shock of the change, which had turned them into internal refugees, had somehow produced or released a vibrant community. One of the unusual—by the normal standards of competing empires—advantages of this internal refugee status was that they didn't lose their land.

Only twenty years after that changeover, refugees began straggling across the border, fleeing the lost war in the American colonies. There were seventy thousand of them, and perhaps twenty-five thousand Natives. A few of these exiles were prosperous. Some were charlatans. But most had lost everything. They were refugees as we now understand the word—political and economic at the same time. And most were refugees for the second time, because they were the minorities within the American colonies. These Scots, Irish, religious minorities, blacks and others had always been close to the Crown because they felt they needed protection against the colonial majority in the thirteen colonies and its élites. They brought with them to Canada the energy and aggressivity of the loser.

The bringing together of these destabilized francophones and anglophones is generally told through the focus of political-power battles won and lost, language and religious differences, as if it were all part of a slow and methodical process filled with portentous intent. In reality, twenty years is the flickering of an eye, and the two communities, thrown together in this anarchic moment, had all the psychic similarities of refugees and exiles—people to whom things have been done without them being able to control or even affect events.

The Natives would gradually be made to fit into this pattern of internal refugees. And other groups would soon begin arriving to complicate the argument over which minority was most hard done by. But the pattern of minorities was set, as was that of refugees. In 1992 the United Nations said Canada was home to 570,000 refugees; 100,000 more than the United States, six times more than Britain, three times more than France. In the developed world, only Germany had taken more, largely the result of the Soviet Bloc collapsing next door. In other words, we don't only take millionaires.

With three founding minorities and dozens more added on, it is obvious that the European nineteenth-century project of, as Bismarck put it, "sorting out the tribes" could never be undertaken. That didn't stop the Orange Order and the Ultramontanes from trying. But it was always nonsense. And this impossibility of clarifying the minorities continues to bedevil the narrow nationalists on all sides. It keeps getting in the way of their obsessions with an unhyphenated Canada or a pure laine Quebec—or whatever their particular desire for simplicity and clarity and certainty happens to be called. It gets in the way because they are missing the point. Since the eighteenth century Canada has functioned as a confusion of minorities major and minor. That is what the country is.

None of which means that life is equally easy or difficult for each minority. It is much more difficult for the Natives than for the others. In many ways it is more difficult to be a francophone than anglophone. But it is important not to draw the wrong conclusion from that reality. Very few anglophones think of themselves as belonging to a majority. They think of themselves as a minority faced by the United States. And even within this country, the political and regional differences have meant that anglophones very rarely manage to get together as a group. This is just as well and it has happened only three or four times in our history.

The lesson Europe eventually learnt was that the tribes can never be made pure enough. There will always be some jarring minority in the way. What makes Canada interesting is that it was built upon the assumption that a jarring note was a positive thing.

The Halifax poet George Elliott Clarke writes eloquently about this complexity even within minorities: "Canada is an assembly point for all African peoples both Old World (Africa) and New (North and South America)." This also means Loyalists, soldiers in the War of 1812–14, refugees through the underground railway and, more recently, people coming from the old British Empire and the French, feeding into one or the other of the linguistic communities, or indeed straddling both. "The variegated composition of

130   the African-Canadian community frustrates trans-ethnic, trans-linguistic communication. Hence, no truly 'national school' of African-Canadian literature has been created, nor will we ever see one." But his reaction is not to mourn the impossibility of a monolithic school. "I confess that I prefer the eccentric, the perverse, the Gothic attitude that Canada inspires in many artists."[1]

I remember a photograph in Toronto's archives, showing a group of Scandinavian immigrants being taught the "Duties of the Citizen" in Larchwood, Ontario, 1913. They are grouped in front of a blackboard on which is written:

Duties of the Citizen
1. Understand our Government
2. Take active part in politics
3. Assist all good causes
4. Lessen intemperance
5. Work for others

I could ridicule this image with endless stories of prejudice and exclusion. But the point is that the general assumption attached to immigration was an expectation that the immigrant would quickly join in the social process, which was democratic and cooperative. The primary duty was participation not patriotism. This is very different from the Grandfather Law used to exclude immigrants from the citizen's role in the United States and from the common nineteenth-century vision of an immigrant being miraculously transmogrified into a different being—an American, for example, or a Frenchman or an Englishman.

In a recent study on twins, the author pointed out the complications of the situation. "We think we know who we are. We struggle to build our characters through experience; we make ourselves unique by determining what we like, what we don't like, and what we stand for. . . . But what if, in spite of all the differences, we and the *Other* arrive at the same place? Isn't there a sense of loss? A loss not only of identity but of purpose? We are left wondering not only *who* we are but *why* we are who we are."[2]

That is precisely what makes a country of minorities interesting. It is the doubt, the questioning, the uncertainty which is there to keep us focused on the idea of the society rather than slipping into the old nationalist certitudes.

9 Poverty

"Thou barren waste; unprofitable strand,
Where hemlocks brood on unproductive land...."
Standish O'Grady, *The Emigrant—Winter in Lower Canada*

IN THE SECOND HALF OF THE twentieth century, Canada managed to produce a social equilibrium which, whatever its flaws, has been admired as remarkably successful. As the century wore on, so this equilibrium began to come apart, as in other western countries. The reigning orthodoxy has it that our loss of prosperity is the result of interfering with natural economic forces. Therefore the solution to the problem is to let free those natural forces.

What this misses is that social equilibrium and economic prosperity are not actually the same thing. In the case of Canada, the latter has been very much the product of the former—that is, economic prosperity grew out of social equilibrium. Why? In large part because Canada is essentially a poor country. Yes, it has some good farmland and lots of natural resources. But the exploitation of natural resources does not tend to produce a stable, balanced economy. To the contrary. Commodity markets were and are subject to incessant devastating swings. This sort of economy almost invariably produces an extreme social divide between a few rich and many poor. As for land, our climate severely limits its value. Of course, there is more to our economy than natural resources and agriculture. However, for industrial activity and the new high-tech industries, Canada is geographically on the edge of the developed nations and lacks a critical density of population, both characteristics necessary for industrial success. The question of density is even central to the high-tech field, which needs a large, educated population to generate research and development and to consume the products.

That Canada managed to turn its unfavourable circumstances into a positive situation—one of the most prosperous of societies—

was dependent on its ability to recognize and come to terms with the essential poverty of this place. Such poverty, combined with the energy of the refugee population and the absence of effective élites capable of enforcing a subservient social order, produced an early egalitarianism. Most people were rural and had land. That meant most men had the vote from very early in the nineteenth century. So the roots of practising democracy are deeper here than in most of the western nations. What's more, the simple feat of survival in this difficult northern place meant favouring cooperation over competition. I'm not simply referring to the old barn-building bee. What was needed was far more than cooperation for a few decades, just long enough to turn the frontier into a settled area. Canada exists in a permanent state of marginality which from the beginning was as true of the cities as of the countryside.

This early egalitarianism, marked by an individualism which was understood to mean cooperate or perish, was the key to turning Canada from a place of poverty into one of reasonable social equilibrium; or at least one in search of a reasonable social equilibrium. Those are the roots of the astonishing levels of government involvement in the economy every step of the way, from the early land settlements and railway building on. The Red Toryism which George Grant wrote of grew not out of English conservatism, but of Canadian poverty.

In his "Address to the Electors of Terrebonne," LaFontaine argued in favour of the Lower Canada/Upper Canada coalition of reformers in the name of that egalitarianism.

> The only way in which [the authorities] can prevent us from succeeding is by destroying the social equality which is the distinctive characteristic as much of the population of Upper Canada as of Lower Canada. This social equality must necessarily bring our political liberty.... No privileged caste can exist in Canada beyond and above the mass of its inhabitants.[1]

134   It would be decades before the political leadership found ways of making this egalitarian poverty work. The levels of hardship should never be underestimated. Jean-Baptiste Meilleur, the first superintendent of Lower Canada education, "underline[d] with insistence the poverty of the people"[2] in his 1843 report to the government. The statistics on immigration versus emigration show that from 1861 to 1901 Canada was losing more than it was gaining—often close to twice as much. And until 1941 there was still a heavy emigration. It could be said that those who stayed were, at least in part, those ready to come to terms with the situation.[3]

This question of systemic poverty always makes me think of the explorer David Thompson, halfway up the Black River with two Native companions. In a comedy of errors their canoe overturned and everything was lost in a waterfall, except for the canoe itself, an axe, a gun and a small tent. They were dressed in a single layer of light clothing and it was the early black-fly season. "We had no time to lose . . . we divided the small tent into three pieces to wrap round ourselves, as a defence against the flies in the day and something to keep us from the cold at night."

The most obvious tent to be spread around in Canada was education—public universal education. It began in Prince Edward Island in 1852, when the first solid reform government passed the Free Education Act. This seems to have been a conscious attempt to give leasehold farmers the ability to deal with the owners. Nova Scotia had been working in the same direction and Charles Tupper eventually led the way. Lower and Upper Canada, as so often, were engaged in similar struggles. Politicians like LaFontaine and Cartier, with the support of superintendents of education like Meilleur and Pierre-Joseph-Olivier Chauveau, fought against the Ultramontane movement, while politicians like Baldwin, with the support of Egerton Ryerson, fought against Bishop Strachan and the Anglican desire for an élite-based education. That Ryerson won while Meilleur and Chauveau were defeated would slow French Canada's ability to deal with systemic poverty.

It's worth taking note in passing of the Trinity yell—Trinity being the Anglican college founded in Toronto by Bishop Strachan as a last intervention when his view of education had been rejected by Upper Canada:

> We are the salt of the earth
> So give ear to us
> No new ideas shall ever come near to us
> Orthodox, Catholic, crammed with divinity
> Damn the Dissenters
> Hurray for old Trinity.

As the actual history of the college shows, Strachan's attitudes failed to take hold even in his own college and the cry remains only as something resembling an ironic football chant in a college known for intellectual questioning.

It's also worth noting that Tupper, like Ryerson, like Meilleur, sought out the elements relevant to their systems not in England, where the class system dominated education, and not in France, where the church still dominated, but in places like Prussia, Holland, Scotland, Switzerland, Massachusetts and New York. There the ideas of universal education had made the greatest progress. This was long before the American systems would decline back into the English model of unbridled opportunity, with money and influence giving itself the best schools by creating a large private sector, leaving the underfunded public schools for everyone else.

Throughout the Canadian colonies the principal opposition to free universal education came from the élites who would have to finance it through taxes. They portrayed it as everything from authoritarian (i.e., Prussian) to communistic. Emily Carr wrote of how English settlers in Victoria took a generation and a half to stop sending their children to private schools and accept the Canadian public schools.[4]

The success of the public system could be seen at the turn of the century. Out of a population of five million, one million were in school. Only seven thousand were in university. Eighty-three per cent of the population could read and write. In Toronto alone, there were 150 publications.[5] The Canadian answer to systemic poverty was constructed first and foremost on a successful public education system.

This was bolstered by continual government intervention in the economy at all levels. We tend now to run all western mixed economies together as if they have been part of exactly the same process for the last 150 years. But government intervention in Canada became a core policy in the third quarter of the nineteenth century, when most other western nations were still caught up in the dream of the self-regulating market-place, competition, the invisible hand, free trade and other dreams of the early to mid-industrial revolution. Canada couldn't afford such romanticism.

The third element in the Canadian answer was the redistribution of wealth. By the turn of the century this had already moved beyond the traditional liberal and social-democratic ideas—of redistribution among individuals—to that of regional redistribution. Prairie protestors were calling for "nation-wide calculations of income" and "nation-wide redistribution of wealth."[6] It was an idea which was eventually formalized as Transfer Payments, a remarkably original approach towards governing a federal state in which some regions were richer, others poorer. It was becoming clear to those thinking about the public good and struggling to serve it that, left to its own devices, particularly in a resource-based economy, the market-place would tend to accentuate rather than minimize these differences.

These three elements—public education, government intervention in both social and economic structures, and transfer payments—allowed us to build prosperity on the foundations of systemic poverty. A number of other countries existing on the margins—the Scandinavians are the most common example—went down not dissimilar routes. And it was on the basis of the social equilibrium created by these policies that the business sector was able to blossom.

This is the principal difficulty which Canada has with the sweeping absolute economic truths we have imported and accepted over the last decade. In order for market forces to be accepted as the great leader, all physical realities must be taken to be the same. The only variables relate to becoming competitive and specialized. But this is an astonishingly abstract theory. In fact, delusion would be a better word than theory. All physical realities are not the same, nor can they respond to circumstances in the same way. The new truth tries to obscure this stubborn reality by assigning blame to those who can't keep up. Indeed, the whole theory of a single economic model for all circumstances isn't even good capitalist theory. It is essentially a derivative of very old-fashioned turn-of-the-century management methodology in which content is treated as interchangeable filler for the ideal management form.

The history of Canada bears no relationship to these economic theories. Of course there are always moments when belts must be tightened or when some economic factor such as debt must be concentrated on. But these are the details of ongoing management. They aren't meant to be the driving force of civilization. To believe that you can re-launch the Canadian social equilibrium by embracing romantic universal economic theories is to undermine precisely what the society is built upon. This is one of the reasons why the cutbacks of the last decades and the opening up to monolithic economic forces has produced more poverty than prosperity. These policies are a romantic and highly abstract denial of concrete experience.

Neither materialism nor utilitarianism has ever been central to this society. The two central founding agreements—the LaFontaine–Baldwin handshake and 1867—were not driven by economics. If anything, they involved economic sacrifice. In the late 1840s we were in a deep depression brought on by British free-trade policies. With a single, unified voice the economic élite of Montreal—that is, the dominant economic élite of Canada—called for annexation by the United States as the only road to prosperity. The population of Lower and Upper Canada—anglophone and francophone—ignored them. They seemed to understand that—as Harold Innis noted—"materialism is the auxiliary doctrine of every tyranny." Even the building of the railroad was not primarily an economic act. Had economics been the driving force we would have saved ourselves time and money by going the American route. And Laurier's refusal of the Empire Pact was in part a refusal of an economic life-insurance policy.

It is hard to digest these arguments today. Everything has changed, we tell ourselves, as if somehow economic interest has transformed itself over the last century to become more intelligent or more suited to leading a society. Somehow we have become too sophisticated to continue on the principles which built the country.

But what precisely does our new sophistication consist of? In what way are we thinking at a more complex level about how a country functions than that of LaFontaine, Baldwin, Cartier, Macdonald, Laurier? I read their speeches and arguments. I read the arguments we are offered today by Messrs. Chrétien, Martin, Bouchard, Harris, Klein, Tobin. I do not detect an intellectual progress. I notice a net regression in sophisticated analysis and the virtual disappearance of intellectual discourse. In its place are simplistic formulae, emotional manipulation and a slavish adherence to the most banal economic clichés of our day.

We are now in the grip of a corporatism which makes very effective use of the new means of communication. This allows materialism and utilitarianism to be presented as romantic, noble, courageous, masculine, intelligent, fun and, in complete contradiction with all of the preceding, as inevitable. Innis put it that "The shell and pea game of the country fair has been magnified and elevated to a universal level."[7] Today that country-fair game is called consumption and globalization.

Anti-Heroism

10

> "Napoleon would have been a nobody here."
> George Bowering, *A Short Sad Book*[1]

THAT LINE MIGHT HAVE BEEN written by Saint-Denys Garneau. It is difficult to think of a country where the modern idea of the Hero is less celebrated. This is not to say that thousands of people haven't acted in an heroic manner, in wars and out of wars. The hero of the heroic action has nothing to do with modern Hero worship. And it must be said that, even when it comes to the hero of the heroic act, Canadians are willing to show respect, but little more. They are nervous that anything more might slip into that other thing.

George Woodcock examined this phenomenon in his biography of Gabriel Dumont. "The pattern is clear. Canadians distrust heroes, partly because heroism is always a kind of imposition; the hero is dominating us by his strength, by his brute courage, and we have become suspicious of such qualities."[2] He puts this down to the sense that "we see ourselves generally imposed upon," an idea which Margaret Atwood first explained and which any number of francophone writers would echo in their own way. Arthur Buies, for example: "Egotism pushes us to false glory and there is scarcely a hero of the people who is not at the same time the jailer of another."[3]

All of this is sensible and probably true, but I wonder if our reaction to Heroes doesn't go beyond the idea of sufferance. After all, that is something we share with many other countries and they have more often than not adopted a classic attitude towards heroism. Many throw themselves into Hero worship as the solution to sufferance. Heroic nationalism with Heroic leadership and Heroic martyrdom are rather common among those who feel put upon.

As Woodcock points out, we do actually identify easily with martyrs. But even then this is rarely an Heroic identification. Perhaps it's because we like to think of ourselves as martyrs. Perhaps we simply find it an easier relationship to assume since the Hero, being dead, is less able to impose himself on us.

Whether they are alive or dead, our aversion to Heroes seems to come from something else. After all, how could a country built on ideas not conquest, a place of three dominant minorities and many others, a poor place which evolved, thanks to a sense of individualism as cooperation, embrace the worship of Heroes?

The very form of the country is an anti-Utopia. That is what makes it interesting. And Hero worship is dependent on a willingness to believe in Utopias; to believe in the perfect place which has never and will never exist. The utopian ideal is the original form of ideology. Most countries slide between the unreasonable belief that a utopian form is possible and a realization that the utopian quest is exclusionary and catastrophic for real societies. But various phenomena—the illusion of racial unity or of cultural unity or a dominant historic mythology—lead some people to believe that fulfilment—le salut—can only come by embracing one or more of these false unities. From time to time the combination of utopian leaders and favourable circumstances pushes a perfect solution to the fore. The result is usually disastrous.

Canada has never embraced these illusions of unity. The effect of trying to impose one—as various leaders have tried and continue to try to do—is merely to convert complexity into division. To suggest on the other hand that Canada is not a real country because it lacks the illusion of unity is to evoke the Heroic vision. I would say that it isn't worth preserving Canada if it can be reduced to a utopian ideal.

Let me go back for a moment to our peculiar attitudes towards war. These have seemed to divide us—francophone versus anglophone, but also rural versus urban. In spite of this we have sent unusually high per-capita levels of soldiers to fight, with not equal but reasonable representation from all language and regional groups, and they have fought as well as or better than others.

And yet, once the propaganda and excitement has died down, virtually no heroic literature is produced. A great deal is written, much of it of very high quality, and it isn't exactly an anti-war literature. Again, Canadians lack the easy romanticism of being able to pretend that something which has always existed is likely to disappear. On the other hand this literature contains a curiously consistent internal line—it is anti-heroic. Heroic acts are admitted to, but invariably put down to accident or misadventure.

The doctor based on Norman Bethune, in Hugh MacLennan's *The Watch That Ends the Night*, admits that he won his Military Medal after a suicidal charge, having caught the clap in his first sexual experience. He was actually trying to kill himself. "For committing murder because I'd caught the clap, I was called a hero."

In a scene eerily similar to that in *War and Peace*, when Napoleon decorates one of the Tsar's soldiers, Robertson Davies's main character in *Fifth Business* finds himself staring into the eyes of George V as the king pins a Victoria Cross onto his chest. "Here am I, I reflected, being decorated as a hero, and in the eyes of everybody here I am indeed a hero; but I know that my heroic act was rather a dirty job I did when I was dreadfully frightened. I could just as easily have muddled it and been ingloriously killed. But it doesn't much matter because people seem to need heroes; so long as I don't lose sight of the truth, it might as well be me as anyone else."

The same atmosphere can be found in Colin McDougall's novel *Execution* or Timothy Findley's *The Wars* or Farley Mowat's memoirs, *My Father's Son: Memories of War and Peace*, or Kevin Major's dramatization of the massacre of the Newfoundland Regiment in *No Man's Land* or Oakland Ross' *Guerilla Beach*, with its contemporary Latin American war stories.

142   Jacques Brault's wonderful—

> They say you died for our Honour   they say
> and stroke their sagging belly they say that you
> died for Peace   they say   and suck on their cigar
> long like a barrel

might be put down to an anti-war atmosphere in Quebec, except what then do you do with a Westerner like Nellie McClung, feminist leader, friend and supporter of Mackenzie King, who wrote—

> Oh! her sunny-hearted lad! So full of love and tenderness and pity, so full of ambition and high resolves and noble impulses, he is dead—dead already—and in his place stands "private 355," a man of hate, a man of blood!

And what do you do then with most of the pictures painted by Canada's official war artists during the First World War?

There were some traditional heroic canvases, but nothing more anti-war was produced by any writer than F.H. Varley's pictures "The Sunken Road" and "For What?" with their corpses, not like fallen heroes but like clods of mud, indistinguishable from the heaving landscape. Or there was A.Y. Jackson's dark, ironic picture of seared tree trunks, water-filled craters and mud. He called it "A Copse, Evening." Varley wrote home of the effect the war was having on him. "You must see … the dead on the field, freakishly mutilated—headless, legless, stomachless, a perfect body and a passive face and a broken empty skull—see your own countrymen, unidentified, thrown into a cart."

The dominant Canadian war images were not those of the heroic school. The general image produced by the official war art came from that of the Group of Seven and David Milne and was profoundly anti-heroic. Emily Carr recounts Lawren Harris lecturing in the years after the war "about the churches and their smugness, and of mothers offering their sons as sacrifices, and the hideous propaganda of politics and commerce exploiting war with greed and money for their gods while we stupidly, indolently, sit blindfolded, swallowing the dop ladled out to us. . . ."[4] The Group of Seven may have been a nationalist school. But it was not nationalism of the old school. It was not about race or Heroes.

In truth, there seems to be no heroic war literature and in general little heroic war culture, at any rate of a quality which could survive the propaganda drive of the moment. Even those who were eager to fight or to send others to fight have shown no interest in the classical representation of glory.

◄──────►

And yet various nationalist schools of historians and politicians have attempted to introduce a taste for great men. Abbé Groulx was full of the glories of great men, as in his own way was Donald Creighton. But it didn't catch on. For example, the number of biographies of public figures has shrunk over the last few decades to virtual non-existence. And those that are written are rarely hagiographies.

This frustrates experts in communication who would prefer to find a taste for advanced personality worship in the population. You can see this in the desperate reworking of hockey over the last years. There have always been great players, and they have had something of the heroic about them. But both they and the public have seen the game for what it is—a profoundly cooperative experience. The great teams have been just that, teams. They also have a few great individual players.

The needs of commerce in an era dominated by the Heroic Hollywood entertainment myth have endlessly twisted the game to look and sound like an undertaking of great players who, incidentally, play for good teams. Still, you can feel that Canadian audiences are only marginally interested in this Heroic approach to the game. They watch it as they know it is played at its best—a flying, rough, corps de ballet.

This is probably because every Canadian male has played hockey at some age or ends up believing he has. The game has thus become one of those basic physical mythologies which reveal and reflect the larger myths. If Canadians are anti-heroic, they will treat their basic game as anti-heroic and team-oriented. You can see the forces which now control the professional level of the game struggling with, or rather against, these attitudes. Their conforming commercial attitudes require a game of Heroes and goals. Canadian audiences persist in an interest in how the game is played.

Among the same experts in communications there is a constant moaning about our lack of heroes and leaders in public affairs. Pierre Trudeau, the most personally successful politician in Quebec and throughout Canada since Laurier, refused to play by these new rules and instead based his popularity on a relatively abrupt and intellectually direct public manner. He broke all the formulae of Heroic communications, while men like Jean Chrétien, Preston Manning and Lucien Bouchard are each in their own way obedient to those rules.

Even so, the citizenry seem to have withdrawn even farther into their shell, as if wary of such public figures, while leaving a surface impression of acquiescence. They have become increasingly indecipherable, perhaps loyal to the view laid out by George Frederick Cameron, in the middle of the nineteenth century.

I am not of those fierce, wild wills,
    Albeit from loins of warlike line,
    To wreck laws human and divine
Alike, that on a million ills
    I might erect one sacred shrine . . .[5]

The Coureur de bois–
Habitant Tension

11

THIS IDEA OF THE TENSION BETWEEN a society of constant movement versus one so fixed in place as to be static is made difficult by its apparent simplicity. All sorts of people are ready to feel insulted the moment it is mentioned. Professional historians rush forward—quite rightly—to point out that things were much more complicated than that, in fact that this tension never really existed, in fact in practical historic terms the same men were often both traders and sedentary, forest men and farmers, depending on the season and the state of their economic fortunes.

But this is in part my point. The tension I'm referring to was not some short-term division particular to New France or to nineteenth-century Quebec. Nor did it divide society into two opposing groups. Rather it was and remains a tension central to the functioning of Canada. It was and is to be found in the country as a whole, the provinces, the towns, indeed in each individual. It could be redefined as the tension between a society of movement and a sedentary one.

While this sort of opposition exists to some extent in most societies, the Canadian phenomenon is quite different. Both movement and sedentariness are necessary, but to the extent that the balance slips towards the sedentary in Canada, so the country loses all sense of itself and begins to pull apart. To the extent that it is in movement—and I mean emotionally and intellectually, mythologically as much as physically—it comes alive and is able to make something of its complexity.

The sedentary, the habitant, carries the sense of being rooted, eternal, fixed in place. Humans have always liked this illusion of belonging to something eternal, of a mythological physical comfort blending into the pretence of immortality. And certainly the fear settlers felt when they came here was in part the fear of arriving in an uncontrolled, perhaps uncontrollable place. Oliver Goldsmith described all of this early in the nineteenth century:

> When, looking round, the lonely settler sees
> His home amid a wilderness of trees:
> How sinks his heart in those deep solitudes,
> Where not a voice upon his ear intrudes;
> Where solemn silence all the waste pervades,
> Heightening the horror of its gloomy shades. . . .

And just as Goldsmith's fear was aimed at the promise of pastoral comfort, so that was the approach Gilles Vigneault took in the preamble to the 1995 law leading up to the last referendum:

> And now comes the time of harvest in the fields of history. At last the time has come to gather in that which four hundred years of women and men and courage sowed for us, rooted in the earth and continually turned over.[1]

Of course, Vigneault has the peculiar talent of expressing both sides of the tension. Many of his songs are so much part of the idea of movement—of the coureur de bois ethic—that, while he wrote them as credos of Quebec nationalism, they were immediately picked up across the country as being directed to the sensibility, for example, of Westerners. The singer/poet whom Vigneault most resembles is an anglophone, the Nova Scotian Stan Rogers. He evoked exactly the same tension—the joy and pain of movement and the freedom that comes with it, versus the warmth and comfort or pain of the sedentary existence. Even the tone which holds these two opposing sides together is almost identical in the two men. Rogers's melancholic, deep-rooted songs about putting "another season's promise in the ground" come up against his own discomforting, stirring themes, "North West Passage" in particular—

Tracing one warm line
Through a land so Wild and savage.[2]

This formless distance, with lines drawn through it, almost like the Aboriginal song-lines, not surprisingly brings out fear in most people. It often strikes those with power more severely than the rest of us. Formlessness, distance, the uncontrollable. Power, even in the most responsible of hands, can't help but be to some extent about control. Jacques Parizeau's moment of revelation, during which he saw in a flash that Canada couldn't work, came not surprisingly on a train when, as a senior Quebec civil servant, he was crossing the country on his way to a national meeting being held in the West. His explanations of the event have the feel about them of a European-American sedentariness, not so very different from that expressed by Edward Blake, the Liberal leader of the Opposition in Ottawa, 125 years ago. He was horrified by the idea of building a railroad "over that sea of mountains." "The country's wealth, its millions after millions squandered—Lost in the gorges of the Fraser." You can sense Blake's habitant care—"His soul as clean as surf," was how E.J. Pratt put it. "No one could equal him in probing cupboards, / Or sweeping floors and dusting shelves."[3] It is almost as if you can hear Blake in the voice of the modern habitant—the technocrat—worried about management and who will have which power.

The exact opposite was what Alfred DesRochers wrote about, beginning, "I am a fallen son of a race of supermen."

... And I dream of going, as my ancestors went;
I hear—crying within me—the unlimited white space,
Across which they ran, illuminated in the blast of a hurricane,
And like them I loathe the constraints of masters.[4]

I don't want to create the impression that this tension is just another way of talking about a constitutional crisis. In a sense, the narrow-nationalist discourse does build on the sedentary—an illusion when you look at the historic movement of francophones. But you can find the same tension throughout society. For example, Canada is the developed country most dependent on trade—that is, on movement and on the constant energy that movement requires. It has been like that from the beginning. Visions of history have been developed around these great movements of resources—the staples theory, for example.

Whatever the explanation, economic survival here has been based on movement, internal and external. In other developed countries— the United States in particular—exports are almost the jam, the extra spread on top of a more or less self-sufficient economy. Most other small nations are tucked in among countries of varying sizes and much of their trade, while necessary, has a predictable, almost sedentary aspect to it.

This at first glance is an explanation for our eagerness to tie ourselves tightly into economic integration treaties with the United States. We call them free-trade treaties to suggest that they are indeed part of our need to increase movement. Except they had and have almost nothing to do with trade as such, since our tariffs at the time of signing were already below 5 per cent and disappearing. When you look closer, you find they are more accurately treaties created to please the sedentary—the managerial technocracy of the large corporations. These are treaties designed principally to facilitate dependence on a single, dominant market. In other words, they offer the population in general a solution of apparent comfort, with all the accompanying seigneurial disadvantages. It requires an enormous application of false naïveté not to understand that, if your economy is dependent on trade and your sales to a single market rise to over 80 per cent of the total, then you have placed yourself in a passive, dependent position, not an active, creative one. You have not launched yourself into free trade, but rather have locked yourself into a sedentary box and given the key to someone else.

For those politicians, deputy ministers and corporate executives who have forgotten, a quick visit to a first-year university course in economics or political science will remind them that, in any market-place, dependence on a single source, whether for buying or for selling, is a weakness not a strength. To go out of your way to consciously accentuate this imbalance is irresponsible. It re-creates, on a societal level, the status of the habitant. The passivity imposed translates into an inability to develop or maintain such things as social policies, if they do not fit in with the pattern set by the dominant player.

The job of the functioning élites in such a situation is to concen-trate on counterbalancing the imbalance. It isn't enough for the quantity of trade to grow. The context in which that trade takes place can turn it into a tool of poverty or of inertia as easily as of prosperity. We see now in Canada that, although our trade grows incessantly, somehow it does not bring wealth, either through employment or new economic creation. And what wealth it does bring is not spreading out through society. This is typical of societies which develop dependent economies. Rather like narrow national-ism, these sorts of trade agreements are bravado sedentarism— grand declarations of bullish competitiveness, even of courage and toughness, to distract us while the real mechanisms of power are dealt away.

◄┈┈┈┈┈►

I was thinking about these contradictions the other day, flying from Vancouver to Toronto. It is odd how much difficulty we now have dealing with this tension between movement and sedentarism, although most of us act as if we still recognize it. I was chatting with a Montreal francophone in the next seat. Both of us were exhausted. He was going on to Quebec City the next day and then to Toronto the day after that. He made an ironic comment about us crossing the endless country "dans un gigantesque cigare volant" and I looked down at the prairies in late April—that time of still death, the snow gone and the land frozen under ice at the end of the day, reverberating in the low sun, as it stretched out a thousand kilometres, all mauve running to purple. Six months later the land would be golden waves, like some great sensual, luminous, eternal beast.

And I remembered that in 1994, at the end of an international gathering of writers in Quebec City at almost the same time of year, a group of us were walking through the streets of the lower town on our way to the festival's closing performance in the theatre of the Museum of Civilization. It was cold and windy and snowing lightly. For some reason none of us had coats. Outside the museum we paused, our eyes drawn upwards by tens of thousands of Canada geese arriving in gigantic formations from the east and the west and the south, all converging on the same unmarked magic point in the centre of the St. Lawrence, then wheeling in great density, like grand armies, onto one of those song-lines, north-east towards the Isle-aux-grues, where they would pause before continuing north.

We all stared, hypnotized—Gaston Miron, the nationalist poet; René-Daniel Dubois, the playwright who would criticize the Yes position during the referendum; Pierre Morency, André Ricard and other francophones; along with Matt Cohen from Toronto and a mix of writers from Europe and other parts of the world. It was one of those scenes we have all read about in which early settlers look up and the sky is, literally, filled with birds. Miron began one of his wonderful theatrical improvisations, explaining to the outsiders what was happening. Every year at exactly the same moment, the geese converged and wheeled with an accuracy that would have amazed any eighteenth-century field marshal. Miron's performance and the scene above made me think of Don McKay's oration *Birding, or desire*:

> All night huge flocks of Whistling Swans
> are whistling milky ways across our dreams, the chaste
> idea of arctic.[5]

After a while the non-Canadians began to shuffle uncomfortably in the wind and slipped their way inside. We stood for a moment longer in the dying light.

In truth there was nothing to be explained to the visitors. It wasn't about birds or migration. It certainly wasn't about folklore or even the worship of nature in the conscious environmentalist way. I suppose it had something to do with that great force of movement—a marriage of freedom and necessity—that you can feel in the north. Force, energy, effort, constant effort.

Certainly none of us, poets, playwrights and novelists, standing about in the lower town of Quebec City, were DesRochers's supermen, any more than were any of those flying across the country with me in a gigantic cigar. Nor could any of us have understood the fatigue of those who, one or two or more centuries earlier, began crossing the land or learning how to live upon it in one place. But we were part of that continual movement; what Michael Ondaatje has called "... the preoccupying image of figures permanently travelling, portaging their past.... We are all still arriving. From the *filles du Roi* to Dionne Brand's new Canadians is a miniscule step."[6]

That idea of movement and new arrival brings out fears not only in Quebec francophones, but in all those who have come before and are settled elsewhere in the country. It would be naïve to pretend that arrival and movement doesn't create problems. But seen as part of an ongoing process, properly treated and balanced with ideas of stability, it is a great force, even in Quebec where the education system now deals better with immigration.

In any case, this fear has never really been tied to population statistics. It has always been with us. We arrive here from somewhere else and quickly feel the need to pretend that we have always been wherever we are, doing what we do, and so claim the right to transform the place into our own image. The sedentary is tied to ideas of stable families, religion, whether churches or nation-based, and a middle-class obsession with self. All of these are necessary and

152 probably inevitable. It is the classic western—more precisely, European—view of how a society works.

The whole idea of the coureur de bois is quite different. It turns on an acceptance of place—of human integration into the place. Not the simple rational idea of fences and fields and countryside, but of humans as part of the place itself. And because that place is on the edge, that is, on the northern edge of the continent, where it is impossible to organize society according to the classical ideas of rational sedentarism, so the people and their society, like the place, cannot help but be in constant motion. In truth, all places are in constant motion, but in many places the circumstances make it possible to deny this.

The differences between hockey and baseball illustrate the two poles. These are national games because they are appropriate to their respective civilizations. Hockey is about constant and, if well played, unpredictable movement. Baseball is fundamentally static, with regular rational explosions, almost like a game of chess made linear. When baseball is at its best these explosions are filled with brilliant calculation. It is the perfect game for the ultimate European society which sees civilization as a controlled space in which disorder is replaced by risk.

Hockey at its best conveys a sense of competing instincts applied to the fluidity of the rink. Wayne Gretzky, at the height of his talents, moved across the ice as if there were unfixed patterns which he could sense before others, or even himself, and somehow could identify their fleeting manifestations. The tension in hockey—the sometimes unbearable levels of emotional and physical energy—is tied to the ability of one team to impose imaginary flowing patterns on the other.

Jacques Godbout describes the tension clearly in *Salut Galarneau!* The hero builds a wall around his house and won't come out, until at last, bored by his sedentary existence, drawn by entreaties from the outside, he climbs over the wall and finds a life of movement to be normal.

Alexander Mackenzie wrote of the early coureurs de bois he had known in the fur trade—". . . they became so attached to the Indian mode of life, that they lost all relish for their habits and native homes." Needless to say he saw this as a decline. ". . . it requires much less time for a civilized people to deviate into the manners and customs of savage life, than for savages to rise into a state of civilization." The same words could have come from a priest in a rural village.

Somehow the obvious hadn't struck him. That the men he pitied had simply found this new way of life better than that offered by what he called civilization. Or, the situation not being as clear as he suggested, that a society in a great complex northern space might require a new sort of social balance. Or that the tension he deplored, as if it were a short-term problem in those territories which would become Canada, had in reality been set in place here long before his experience of it, even before the modern nation-state had consolidated in Europe; that it had preceded the wars of religion and the enforced domination by England and France over Scotland, Ireland, Brittany and Provence.

The habitant approach, taken as the model for such a society, simply denies a pattern which has been with us since the first Europeans arrived in Canada. This may be a society of immigrants, but its basic patterns are endemic and not importations to be constantly mirrored by those who arrive.

Or, of course, it could simply be that, like Lermontov in the Caucasus, the coureur de bois had found a curious "temple of liberty," full of poverty and labour but where nature was "stronger in relief than that of mortal heroes."[7]

12 East–West

THE NATURAL FLOW IN CANADA IS east–west. Received wisdom has it that this east–west flow was the artificial creation of nineteenth-century central government initiatives, such as the railroad and the Nation Policy. But that argument reduces history to little more than mechanisms and economics. It would be more accurate to say that those policies gave a nineteenth-century form to something which already existed.

Let me put it another way. It is possible through massive governmental intervention to force a social-political-economic flow as important as the one discussed here onto a completely different path. But if that requires ignoring the elements of reality—the desires of the population, the nature of the borders, the various regional forces, the historic patterns—then the result will be failure, poverty, disorder and discontent. These elements of reality are not simply a banal current-affairs snapshot of where power lies at a given moment. Indeed those snapshots may themselves be artificial impositions or simply options for which other choices exist.

A refusal to come to terms with the fundamental forces driving or struggling within a country or ready to impose themselves upon it from without is an ideological act which will finish as ideology invariably does. Those are the penalties of pretending that reality is an illusion.

Governments are most successful in altering the social-political-economic flow within a country when several real possibilities already exist within the constraints of reality. Policies can then be developed to favour one over the others. Some may be more difficult to achieve, but that is a matter of tactical skill not strategic impossibility. Social structures, for example, can be encouraged into different patterns.

The Canadian government intervened in the twentieth century to favour a more balanced social structure, which seemed to reflect the tendencies already driving within the society, even though these ran against the more class-based approach south of the border. In other words, we were faced by a choice over the meaning of individualism. Did it mean opportunity or a combination of opportunity and results? The Canadian government favoured the latter. That this combination put limits on the possibilities attached to both opportunity and results was merely an expression of the more cooperative tradition of egalitarianism in Canada.

But let me go back to the larger question of the natural flow in North America. This is one of those ultimate questions which must encompass everything—economics of course, culture, ideas, ways of life. If the natural flow were indeed north–south, it would be hard to explain how Canada comes to have one of the oldest constitutions in the world and a relatively successful social structure. The country may have political problems, but these don't resemble the implosions of an ideological illusion.

Nevertheless, in this north–south theory there is apparently a centre to the continent, presumably with ever-increasing extremes towards the north, at the end of which the flow bounces off a northern wall back to the extreme south. The same reverberation effect must exist somewhere in the south. The Arctic Sea is apparently the clear wall off which these flows bounce. To the south the barrier is a little less clear.

You will note that this is not a centripetal argument. The centre in this case is a horizontal line running east–west somewhere south of the Canada–U.S. border. Everything runs up and down through it.

This is odd, because the poles of power inside the United States —with the exceptional particularity of Chicago—lie in the east and the west. In other words, the theory seems to be that if you are an

156   American most things will run more or less east–west. But if you are
a Canadian, they must run north–south.

This would suggest that our theory is based not on geography or
history or even serious economics, but on political prejudice and a
colonial psychosis. That the people most likely to advance the
north–south argument belong to the right wing in anglophone
Canada and the PQ in francophone Canada rounds out the psychosis argument nicely.

But there are other peculiarities attached to this view. For example,
one of the very few interesting international initiatives—perhaps the
only—undertaken by Ottawa over the last decade has been its leadership role in the creation of the Arctic Council. It took seven years
of diplomatic pushing for this to come into being, with all the countries bordering on the Arctic Sea as members and its headquarters in
Ottawa. The importance of the Inuit populations and of environmental questions have been built into the centre of the structure.

Most of the resistance to this body came from Washington, which
feared it would have a weak position on the Council, given America's small role in the Arctic. In other words, the natural, inevitable,
uncontrollable north–south flow is natural, inevitable, etc., only as
far as the northern coast of the continent's mainland. Then, for reasons somewhat hard to grasp, it comes to an abrupt end, so that
the east–west flow which governs the United States can be reasserted as an east–west sweep across the Arctic Sea. Curiously
enough this change in direction of natural forces comes just in time
to cut Canada off from its Arctic Islands and from any natural relationship with the Russian north.

Would it be churlish to point out that this dogma of Canada's
necessary submission to a natural north–south flow seems to lack a
bit of internal logic? It doesn't even meet the rather low-level standards of rational argument.

Perhaps I'm being unnecessarily pedantic. After all, natural forces
don't require logic or explanation. Like all mystical phenomena,
they carry the revealed truth. Their very existence is a proof of truth.

Or perhaps we are dealing with an artistic phenomenon. It could be argued, for example, that the north–south theory is a late-blossoming expression of surrealism.

In any case, the reaction of the Canadian political and economic élites to the Arctic Council initiative has been to ignore it. They are willing to believe in a north–south flow, so long as it doesn't continue across the Arctic Sea. As Paul Painchaud of Laval University puts it—"We have so long neglected the only international and regional system to which we really belong: the circumpolar system."[1] This represents a fundamental failure of our élites. And, even in practical economic terms, that's too bad, because Russia lies just on the other side. And its serious northern economic and environmental problems offer a remarkable opening for Canadian expertise.

It is as if what those obsessed by natural free-market flows—the neo-conservatives, Ralph Klein, Bernard Landry, the Business Council on National Issues—actually mean is that we are the north and our interest should therefore be to the south, even if it means turning our backs on the reality of our own northernness. It is as if north–south actually means south with us sitting as a detail on the northern tip; as if to think in a northern manner would involve too active an approach towards opportunity or, worse still, would involve thinking of yourself as being at the centre of an opportunity, instead of being a passive beneficiary on the edge. For most of our élite, the north–south argument is a passive expression of their desire for a life of reaction not action.

This idea that we live at the tip of a northern extreme is rarely discussed in a sensible manner. What does it mean? We're not discussing a cake. The north may be white part of the year but its role is not that of the icing.

Nor is the north limited to the Arctic or the Barrens or the north of our bigger provinces or even the land just to the north of our southern cities. Remember that until the Western provinces were created, that territory was called the North-West. The whole country—even those southern extremes of British Columbia and Ontario, which by

158   virtue of their role in our society are appendages of the rest—is northern. That's why the rural idyll, so powerful in Europe and the United States, scarcely exists in Canada, even in farming areas, with the possible exception of Prince Edward Island. The country's vocation, practical existence, strengths and weaknesses all come from the reality of the place. That is, our destiny is tied to the territory of which we are custodians—that is, the northern half of the continent.

We almost never engage in calm, open discussion of this reality because the implications would be too embarrassing. They would gradually focus on the failure of an élite to function.

Apparently we are to imagine ourselves as the upper fringe of something which takes place elsewhere. This is why the levels of American ownership, and its implications, have for some time been rarely discussed and to all intents and purposes are now never discussed. These are at levels unprecedented for a western country—officially some 25 per cent of the economy, which is five times that of most developed countries. However, that statistic is dependent on using a measuring stick—the share ownership level of what constitutes ownership—set naïvely high, as if it took 51 per cent of the shares to control a company. In most cases of wide-spread public-share ownership, 20 per cent is more than enough to give that control. The real figure of effective foreign ownership is thus probably closer to 50 per cent.

Since the artificial enforcement of a north–south economic structure through the FTA and NAFTA, this figure has been growing at unprecedented rates. Statistics Canada: "the foreign controlled share of corporate revenues earned in Canada rose by more than a full percentage point to 29.8%" in 1995.[2] Quebec is a slight exception to these statistics because of its quantity of locally owned small to medium-sized companies. At one level that is an advantage. At another it is central to the province's economic problems—and to Canada's as a whole—because the revenue growth for the larger foreign-owned companies is three times that of the smaller Canadian-owned firms. Ineffective though the large corporations tend to be in real capitalist terms, they control the shape and direction of the economy and so profit from it without an appropriate contribution to real growth, new thinking and real risk.

Of course there are exceptions to this rule. Some of the large corporations do their share or more than their share of risk-taking and new thinking. And some subsidiaries find ways to act as if they were not subsidiaries. Nevertheless there are three practical problems tied to such high levels of foreign ownership. Subsidiaries tend to be passive. The result is a loss of initiative and real growth needed to bring wealth to Canada. And our trade surplus in goods and services must be enormous in order to make up for the growing drain of profits sent home to foreign owners. Our élites are eager to talk to us of the disastrous drain of interest paid on foreign debts. They are careful to avoid the subject of the disastrous drain through ownership patterns of the profits earned in Canada. Both have the same effect of bleeding capital out of the economy.

To suggest publicly that any of these realities constitutes a problem is said to be a sign of anti-Americanism or nationalist protectionism or old-fashioned socialism or indeed of general old-fashionedness in a new global economy. Why such an aggressive refusal even to discuss calmly an identifiable anomaly? Why such *ad hominem*? In the rules of classic rhetoric, this sort of response is a tactic consciously used to avoid the other side's exposing a real weakness.

A reasonable interpretation of this situation might be that our élites have failed to understand the nature of the responsibility incumbent upon those with power. In short, they are failing to do their job as businessmen, economists or political leaders. They have difficulty with this idea because responsibility is something which seems to come into effect only as you approach the centre of the north–south flow. They see themselves as a passive force on the fringes of reality. The marginal dreamer believes that to assume responsibility would be risky and therefore irresponsible. And so, what would be unacceptable in any other developed country, they consider normal.

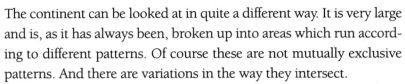

The continent can be looked at in quite a different way. It is very large and is, as it has always been, broken up into areas which run according to different patterns. Of course these are not mutually exclusive patterns. And there are variations in the way they intersect.

The United States has traditionally moved in two swaths east to west—one across the southern American states, the other across the north. Canada does the same in a single swath. It did so long before the Europeans arrived. The geography determined part of the pattern. This physical state has produced massive political-economic east–west explanations—Harold Innis's staples theory for a start. And there is Donald Creighton's Laurentian theme—". . . the St. Lawrence is the one great river system that leads from the Atlantic seaboard to the heart of the continent of North America. . . . The river has inspired a generation of Canadians to build a great territorial empire, both commercial and political, in the western interior of the continent."[3]

But again, such long-lived, complex patterns are not the product of one or two mechanistic factors. There are any number of related elements. Perhaps the most important is the simple reality or logic of living in the north. It has always been quite different from that farther south. As I have already discussed, different tribes, with different assumptions about how life could and should be lived, created a soft east–west border long before the French–English struggle began. And the old pattern was merely confirmed by the new immigrant invaders as they advanced across the continent with aboriginal help.

La Vérendrye, in 1734 on Lake Winnipeg, allied himself with the Cree and the Assiniboine, which meant the Dakota would be his enemy,[4] just as Champlain more than a hundred years before had allied himself with the Huron and Montagnais, making the Iroquois his enemy. In fact you can see the whole east–west story unfold, as in a prophecy understood by none of the participants, when Champlain on his first visit in 1603, without knowing where he really was or what lay ahead, allied himself with the Etchemins, Montagnais and Algonquins at Tadoussac. The Hurons were in turn their allies, and so on. When he came back in 1608 he reconfirmed the alliances and went to war on their behalf.

The shape of Canada was decided that first summer, on a beach at low tide straight across the Saguenay from Tadoussac, when Champlain went by small boat to join a Native feast. As so often in this country, the site is unmarked. You get to it through a farmer's property and the beach lies probably more or less as it was, unless the river has changed the configuration over four centuries. It is the sort of place which is good for nothing except watching the sun rise or structuring half a continent.

What formalized the modern east–west flow of Canada had only very late in the day to do with government-led economic initiatives coming out of Ottawa. It was set in place by Indian alliances with the French and the French Canadians in the seventeenth and eighteenth centuries, and with the English coming from even farther north later in the seventeenth and on into the eighteenth. And these alliances were based on an acceptance of the northern nature of the place and all that that would imply.

Later on, economists would pin down the common features of the north—in a utilitarian manner—by concentrating on commerce. The north was furs and logs. But most of the economists had little to say about the logic of a northern experience, or the expectations it permits or prevents. Yet these are quite particular. To point out that there were 4,736 lynchings of blacks in the United States between 1882 and 1962 is neither to judge that nation nor to suggest that blacks did not suffer from racism in Canada. It is a number which simply highlights how different the experience was running east to west across the southern part of the continent.[5] On the other hand it is interesting to note that ten of the thirteen American states which do not have the death penalty run either immediately along the Canadian border or on the border of another state which also doesn't have it and is itself on the Canadian border.[6] In a very inexact way this suggests a different political experience in the north. I suppose you could say it suggests that the border was drawn a little too far north and that those states might have comfortably fitted into the Canadian pattern. Indeed the voting patterns in those states tend to resemble those in Canada, not those in the rest of the United States.

The east–west movement opened with the ports on one coast and thousands of kilometres later reopened on the other. The east–west idea is not about limited ends rebounding to a centre. Whatever Toronto or Montreal may think of themselves as centres, the east–west flow has always been one of continual movement. In Newfoundland the whole society faces the sea, not the land, not the Rock. Its imagination and what riches it has have been fed from the water. Halifax, at its height, functioned as one of the two doors into and out of the interior. In periods of poverty it sends its own people on to the West.

> They're Calgary roughnecks from Hermitage Bay. . . .
> In the taverns of Edmonton fishermen shout.[7]

The tragedy of Maritimers and Quebecers having to send their people on down the line after three hundred years in the same area is not something central Canadians and Westerners spend a lot of time trying to understand.

But the great double door which opened onto the West was Montreal. The city's wealth, its growth, its remarkable culture came, from its days as a village and the birth of the fur trade all the way up to today, out of the role it played as the entrance to all that lay farther west. Montrealers talk of holidaying in Maine or Florida, but their city was built on the proceeds of reaching westward to northern Ontario and the prairies and Vancouver. This was true of the great staple trading businesses, of banking, of much of the manufacturing; but also of ideas and concepts. We have become used to creative figures who combine stage and dance exporting their ideas from Montreal and Quebec City to the world, just as anglophone writers from Toronto and other cities do. But francophone thinking on politics, economics and society in general has been exported almost solely on this east–west line, and is responsible for much of the imagining of how the rest of Canada would function. There isn't much sign of this intellectual force having any impact on a north–south axis, any more than I've noticed any particular effect of the Toronto political, economic and social intellect on New York or that of Vancouver on Los Angeles.

In spite of Montreal's crisis, some of the east–west dynamism remains today. Companies like Bombardier are now as important to Toronto as to Montreal. And for all the protests that Quebec was left out of the final reformulating of the constitution, its affairs and concerns still dominate the east–west national debate. However much the West protests about the power of the centre, it talks about Quebec. Newspapers devote a great deal of space covering the province in detail, so that anglophones actually know quite a bit about what is happening there, from politics to culture. *The Globe and Mail* has five permanent correspondents. This is not a very convincing solitude.

On the other hand, Quebec papers maintain no reporters beyond Ottawa. This is said to demonstrate a lack of shared activity and a lack of interest. But there is enormous real shared activity—political, social and economic. The absence of francophone reporters from Quebec anywhere beyond Ottawa—with the exception of French-language CBC—is therefore more a denial of reality than reality itself. The francophone élites read English-language papers in detail and the press rely heavily on news services. Radio-Canada makes an effort to fill the gap. And there is a relatively high level of bilingualism, at any rate in the Montreal area. On the other hand, it can't be denied that by refusing to cover the rest of Canada directly, the élites who do read the English-language press impose an artificial isolation on those who do not. And this has a limiting effect on the ability of the anglophone provinces to explain themselves to francophones. It is a situation which represents not so much a lack of east–west interest as an artificial political limitation.

In more utilitarian areas such as agriculture, the east–west system remains more or less as important as it has always been. One example: the prosperity of Quebec dairy farmers turns on an agreement that B.C. farmers will produce less than their population quota in order to drink Quebec milk. More precisely, Quebec holds 48 per cent of the national quota for industrial milk. That is not unfair. That's as it should be in an east–west system.

But Montreal's crisis today comes in large part from its loss of a three-hundred-year-old vocation—the vocation which took it from the status of a small village to that of the country's leading city for more than a century. This loss came through no particular fault of its own. To the contrary. Its ability to deal with languages and different communities makes it potentially a city of our times. Nor was its vocation lost because of the need to deal over the last forty years with the unreasonable domination of a small anglo community in the business sector or the imbalance in social conditions. These could have been handled—however uncooperative the players in the 1960s and 1970s—without destroying the city's role. These problems were not even, at heart, a matter of economics, but of political options.

That ever since 1976 there have been respites of a few years between the political crises which hit Montreal does not ease the situation. People are not like dogs. They have a different quality of memory. They can see ahead. They know that a two-year truce is nothing more than that. And so the energy and investment go elsewhere. Even the francophone economic leadership are gradually moving their investments elsewhere because they don't accept the situation. A few festivals and a few international organizations are not a replacement for the vocation which made Montreal a great city and the *de facto* capital of Canada. In fact the extent to which the city is now dependent on what are essentially marginal activities demonstrates the depth of the crisis.

It is remarkable to look at the manner in which, from the early 1600s, small groups of men leapfrogged westward into the unknown. These were great strategic leaps of the imagination; not careful tactical ploys. In 1615 Champlain, following the lead of Étienne Brûlé five years before, led a party of fifteen francophones and a Huron escort out of the tiny village of Quebec in a remarkable leap 1,500 kilometres to Huronia. He paddled up the St. Lawrence, past what would be Montreal and on up the Ottawa, past the site of the future capital, named through a French corruption of an Indian word. In our desire to denigrate politics we talk today of the place as artificial and out of the way. Whatever the problems of its politics, Ottawa was never out of the way. It was a long-standing Native settlement, in good part because it was placed at a strategic point on what had always been and would continue to be the great river highway to the north and the west, delivering first fur, then lumber back the other way. Champlain went on up the Ottawa to the Mattawa, down it to Lake Nipissing, across it to the rivière des Français, down it to Georgian Bay. Thirty-five portages, many several kilometres long, plus fifty patches of rapids to be negotiated. Then down the coast of the bay through thirty thousand islands to the kingdom of Huronia on the southern shore where the soil was rich.

As for that coast, it has changed little over the centuries. It is too rough, too poor; most of it exposed rock, twisted and tortured, in pink, black and grey. They say it is the oldest exposed rock in the world. The violence of its beauty became one of the great inspirations of the Group of Seven. In the late-nineteenth century the trees were cut, the mass of gigantic fish removed as through a sieve, all in one of those fast-grab, quick-profit sweeps. Money came and went in a few decades, and the population with it. The trees have now grown back and the great archipelago sits—a few cottages here and there, usually without electricity—much as Champlain first saw it.

On Frying Pan Island, out near the main channel where the water is almost always difficult, there is a monument:

Samuel de Champlain

by

Canoe

1615

"As for me, I labour always

to prepare a way for those

willing to follow it."

Even now it is moving, eerie, to imagine him, there with his Huron allies almost four centuries ago, their canoes pulled up in this little natural harbour a few metres away, a small protection for one night from la mer douce—the fresh water sea—as he called it, wondering where this great leap would drop him and whether he would be able to leap back east by a completely different route.

Having led the way into the Great Lakes, Champlain would be followed by others leaping onward in three different directions—west, north-west, where they would eventually collide with the English, and south down the Mississippi. This last was the only real failure, because the Americans, expanding westward, would make that line impossible to hold. The continent runs east–west, not north–south.

Interestingly enough, the narrow or negative nationalist schools have most often celebrated precisely this failure on the Mississippi, as if it had been a triumph. This seems to be an expression of their north–south obsession. It is as if they are desperate for anything which might demonstrate a link to the great American empire—even a defeat—as opposed to the broad reality of the history of which they are actually a central part.

◄——————►

The real drive was west and north-west, jumping off le large, as the Manitoban Métis call it, into the sea of the prairies and on to the port of exit-entry on the Pacific coast.

When the railway did come in the late-nineteenth century, it was merely a conversion of the age-old east–west waterway transport route into modern mechanics. At that point, a north–south commercial route might have been easier. But it would be a mistake—of the sort typically found in ideologues, particularly those seduced by utilitarian logic—to conclude that facility equals destiny and that therefore the conversion of the waterways into railroads was an artificial aberration which temporarily cheated some universal, all powerful, commercial logic. To the contrary. The eradication of centuries of social, political, military and economic flow, because of a temporary technological facility in another direction, would have been an aberration. Only a century later we can see that that facility has been bypassed by new technologies—planes, communication networks—which can serve the east–west flow as easily as any other without any particular mechanical acrobatics. Indeed, they can do it more easily than at any other time in our four centuries of evolution, providing there is a social will to continue developing a particular idea of society.

We spend little time thinking about the effect on the whole of Canada of Vancouver as one of the key points of east–west transit—westward, on from the city across the Pacific and eastward off the ocean, through the city and on into the country.

Vancouver has never been a wall, in spite of its flawed racial record. It has, from its beginning, been an active point of transit, not simply for goods, but for immigration from Asia. After all, the most important of east–west and west–east movements is not commercial, but human. And after the human comes ideas, social structures and politics. And from all of this comes travel. Because of the city's role as one of the great opening doors to human movement, its schools have always had to struggle—as they do today—with balancing normal education alongside language and other basic training for the children of immigrants. It is the city where Canada first succeeds or fails in its old idea, going back to Baldwin and Egerton Ryerson, that the citizen is created in the public-school system.

Vancouver has been key to Canadians imagining themselves, not simply as a Pacific nation, but as people with a particular approach to issues. As Gerald Friesen points out, there were at least six hundred Canadian missionaries in China during the 1920s.[8] Our early recognition of China came out of that. Most of our China hands of the postwar period, right up through the 1970s, were sons of those missionaries. Our early wheat sales and our ethical confusion today are all outgrowths of that long-standing reach across the Pacific.

What does this mean in practical terms? The western provinces export less southward—just over half—than does the rest of Canada. And a quarter of the West's exports continue straight on west to the other side of the ocean.[9] That quarter is continuing to grow.

As for the east–west movement over the whole continent, John Helliwell has recently done a study of trade patterns in the context of population densities and distances.[10] He finds—despite our external trade being concentrated on the United States—that internal east–west trade remains the dominant factor. Quebec in particular succeeds at—or is reliant on—the east–west versus north–south flow; in part because of centuries of established east–west commercial movement, in part because of the facilitating aspects of French being one of the national languages. More than half of Canada's total trade was east–west in 1989. Given our small population this represents a high penetration and so the percentage has been dropping. But what Helliwell finds is that the east–west trade in services—that is, the more sophisticated commodities of modern exchange—has not been slipping. It continues to run two to three times the value of north–south exchanges.

This is only economics, but the persistence in east–west services, despite the artificial reorganization of the economy to attempt to force it onto a north–south pattern, tells us about something beyond economics. Harold Innis's great work was to carry the idea of physical communications on into that of the "communication of ideas."[11] How, over time, have the ideas of civilizations been carried? How have civilizations imagined themselves? In part through the physical means of transport—the rivers, the communication devices. Marshall McLuhan described how Innis investigated "the trade routes of the mind."[12]

When I talk of Canada's originality lying in its idea of what a country could be, a non-linear country, I am exploiting that Innisian concept—that idea of a country of the imagination, a country imagined in permanent movement, leapfrogging as the coureur de bois mentality did, down the river, then leapfrogging with the ideas of a northern complex nation, more inclusive than exclusive, running over great distances east to west.

It is interesting to think about what infuriates—or is it frustrates and insults?—many francophones and anglophones about the artificial imposition of the north–south flow over the last few years. One of the elements is the curious alliance of right-wing economists and businessmen, anglophone and francophone, with the Parti Québécois in order to bring it about. Perhaps more upsetting is how their alliance demonstrated to what an extent their idea of what a nation should be is static. It sits like a heavy, passive denial of the growth of a few tiny poverty-stricken colonial pockets of internal and external refugees, Native, francophone and anglophone, surviving on the northern half of North America, into a remarkably successful middle-class society. And it denies the successful growth of sixty thousand poor French colonials into eight million francophones within a society which, whatever its flaws, with its good periods and bad periods over the last century and a half, has on

170   balance encouraged the expansion of that phenomenon. And there
seems to be no understanding that an impossibly fragile little economy on the northern margins has slowly been turned, through our
east–west structures, into one strong enough to belong, in however
fragile a manner, to the Group of 7 economic leaders.

In this north–south assertion, all accomplishments of the past
are denied. We spring from the earth, victorious children of a new
truth, freed apparently from centuries of failure, from generations of
parents who must have been failures, from centuries of leaders who
can only have been mediocre failures.

Like all denials of a real past, this forces us to embrace self-
loathing and enter into the mind-set of the craven. But above all it
is a self-indulgent, self-congratulatory denial of the movement of
ideas and of the imagination through which Canada grew over four
centuries on an east–west axis.

Practical Metaphysics 13

CANADA WAS BUILT OVER A CENTURY and a half through eight dramatic strategic acts. The key word is strategy. Not tactics. Not the practicalities we deal with on most days. Strategy is about marrying ideas and capabilities with intuition and daring. It depends on finding the point of pivot which converts the apparently impossible into something reasonably possible. Most good strategic generals—there haven't been many—would admit in private that what all of this amounts to is a sort of practical metaphysics.

In a sense you could say that these strategic acts are demonstrations of the characteristics I keep coming back to—that Canada is above all an idea of what a country could be, a place of the imagination; that it is based on the dominance of constant movement, the strategist's first tool; that in spite of a recurring desire to find outside inspirations, it is very much its own invention.

← →

But where did this concept come from, of building a country through great strategic acts? How did Joseph Howe, the provincial secretary of the little colony of Nova Scotia, come to say, in 1850:

> It is the first duty of a government to take the front rank in every noble enterprise, to be in advance of the social, political and industrial energies, which they have undertaken to lead.

Howe, the great Nova Scotia journalist, politician, colonial minister, anti-Confederation crusader, Canadian Cabinet minister, epitomizes the Canadian idea of individualism as a search for balance between opportunity and results. This is not the American idea that freedom equals opportunity, however imprisoning the results may be for those who fail to reach the starry heights. Nor is it the European idea that raison d'état must normally dominate, because it will be in the long-term interests of the individual's freedom.

In Canada, the restrictions of northern poverty, low population density and difficult geography have meant that great individual initiative will always be needed, but so will great public initiative.

Howe epitomizes this balance for two reasons. There were many combative journalists in the nineteenth century, but his successful personal defence against libel charges in 1835 made him the father of freedom of speech and of freedom of the press in Canada. He had attacked the honesty and fairness of the magistrates and the police. They in turn had tried to ruin him via criminal libel charges. What made his defence so important was that his original attack on the justice system was not a secondary cause in the battle for responsible government. It was a personal attempt to exercise both freedom of speech and of the press, to do so directly, as any citizen might.

There are those who argue the technical point that Howe's victory didn't change the unacceptable law and therefore he did not establish free speech or a free press.[1] But that is to miss the point. Howe set the standard which we are still struggling to attain or maintain.

In defending himself with a remarkable six-and-a-half-hour speech Howe both heightened the sense of his cause and heightened the risk of personal ruin. "If I wished to be tried by your sympathies," he pointed out, there were a number of ways he could appeal to them—their knowledge of his personal life, his reputation. But he refused the personalization of sympathy. "My public life is before you." And as a journalist, "the only questions I ask myself are, What is right? What is just? What is for the public good?"

And yet this clear idea of the citizen's individualism did not make him a libertarian or a nineteenth-century laissez-faire liberal. As

soon as he held government office, he used his power and the public purse to advance great projects which he believed were in the
public interest. His cause in the 1850s was a railroad, and he
advanced it with effectiveness and without corruption.

Indeed, Canada was built from its very beginnings on the belief
that public leadership in the economy and on social issues would be
as effective and cheap as anything done by the private sector. In all
probability it would be more effective and cheaper because the state
could concentrate on longer-term goals than the market-place, with
its recurrent instability. In most cases our experience has been that
if the goals are truly long-term and advance into untried areas, the
private sector will be unwilling and unable to do it unless the government takes the lead or holds their financial hand. That was the
case with railroads in Nova Scotia in the early 1850s.

What was in question, however, was not primarily economics.
The very idea of long-term goals is beyond economics. What was in
question was an idea of society—an idea of social, cultural and
political relationships. And the practicalities of life being what they
are, these relationships would require economic action. In a sense
that is what McLuhan was talking about when he said that Harold
Innis at the end of his life "shifted his attention from the trade-routes
of the external world to the trade routes of the mind."[2] The communication of ideas means the communication of how a society
might construct itself.

The building of the national railroad, for example, is invariably
presented as an heroic act—an act of physical heroism and political
determination. This is because we find it easier to concentrate on
the concrete. And John A. Macdonald was an apparently practical
politician who invited that kind of interpretation. But if you concentrate instead on Georges-Étienne Cartier, the real force behind
the idea, you find a manic poet driven by enormous dreams. Macdonald was not without these, but his style was more colloquial—he
hid his goals in the minutiae of political survival and jocular asides.

Cartier understood the full meaning of the national railroad; that

174   is, its many implications. In a single remarkable strategic act, he would deny the Americans their dream of North American control.[3] And his challenge to British Columbia's negotiators, that they must demand a railway right to the shore of the Pacific, was actually a challenge to himself and to the country to demonstrate that it had the energy and the desire to exist. At that point Cartier had no idea how it would or could be done, physically or financially. It was a great creative idea—an act of invention—in the sense that a scientist understands a discovery before proving that it is there.

Canadians, in a curious psychological twist, tend to deny that there is anything very dramatic in our way of doing things. It has suited the colonial, conforming side of our minds to present ourselves as careful, nice and pedantic. We prefer to describe our past not through great strategic gestures, but through constitutional wrangling and the slow process of building. These are accurate memories in that they did take place. But constitutions are merely that. Most countries have had dozens of them. Some of the most beautiful of these documents have somehow allowed slavery or done nothing to prevent state violence. Some places have never bothered to have one at all. An obsession with constitutions is an obsession with form over content—with the control of powers as opposed to thinking about the intent of powers. We need these instruments, and wrangling will inevitably take place. But this is not history; it is the minutiae of history.

As for recalling the slow building process, this version of the past is not all bad. It encourages us to be careful about details and careful not to engage in the sort of international bravura which in reality we cannot back up. Canadian participation in the two world wars is usually presented as the most daring of our actions in this slow building process. For many these were great acts of self-affirmation, yet also acts of bravura which, in taking us too far, brought on the disasters of the conscription crises. They are therefore constant reminders of the need to be careful.

But however noble the participation of the hundreds of thousands of individuals who went over to fight, it is very odd to treat Canada's participation in these wars as the creative acts necessary to building the country. To see them as central and necessary stations on our road to nationhood is to take an astonishingly baroque, Christian view that sacrificial blood-letting is the only road to salvation or manhood. This is not an attitude towards war which Sun Tzu, the greatest of strategists, would have understood. He would have said that to treat war as a necessary step in coming of age was an act of criminal incompetence.

◄――――――►

As for the real construction of the country, it has been anything but careful or bravura. The LaFontaine–Baldwin handshake in 1842 was the first strategic act and it was the opposite of either the timid or the careless. It was a sudden and unexpected reconception of how the two colonies might be governed. Power was to be gained and held—not on the basis of geographic interest, but on that of ideas and principles shared across geographic divides. The reformers had suddenly understood that their society could only be constructed in a humanist mode—which was capable of including a multifaceted culture and two languages—if francophone and anglophone reformers cooperated with each other, rather than with the anti-reform groups within their own religious-linguistic group.

This approach had nothing to do with the common nineteenth-century obsession with sacred nationhood based on monolithic convergences. Nor was it a late manifestation of eighteenth-century ideals. It was a strange, almost off-the-wall marriage of reform principles with an open, complex idea of society and community. However strange and original, the LaFontaine–Baldwin handshake would give the centre and centre-left a hold on national power which has remained in place for most of the last 155 years.

The wisdom of this coalition of ideas can be seen today when it has been at least temporarily ripped apart on the formal political

176   front by the federal incursion of the fatally flawed coalition of the Parti Québécois. I say fatally flawed because, whatever its laudatory strengths, its core is not ideas or principles or a complex idea of community, but nineteenth-century nationalism. That is something which has always been based on a central rallying cry, such as religion or language or race. Throughout the western world these cries have often been effective precisely because they do appeal to a very real fear or threat felt by the population. However, they are dependent on a temporary suspension of all real differences within society; in other words, differences over ideas and principles.

Of course, all political movements are coalitions. But the PQ englobes important groups ranging from the old hard right to the social-democrats. Like all nineteenth-century movements, their constant call for the temporary suspension of real differences in the name of the sacred cause shared by all gradually becomes their real and permanent view of society. Unity for the cause becomes the party's central theme. This faith in unity is then preached to the population: unity before the enemy. Such an approach almost invariably turns up traitors. A traitor is anyone within the defined community who doesn't accept that unity is sacred. Unity is the classic call of all ideological movements.

But the concept of placing unity above the expression of real differences invariably favours the anti-reform elements. Take the small example of André Joli-Coeur, the Quebec City lawyer and leading PQ member, who agreed in the summer of 1997 to more or less represent Quebec's position in the Supreme Court case on the legalities of a unilateral declaration of independence. The Quebec government had been boycotting the case, which was their right. And they were understandably upset that a PQ member had broken ranks in this way.

Whatever one may think of the case itself, what was interesting about Mr. Joli-Coeur's move was the reaction of the provincial minister of intergovernmental affairs. The minister denied any attempt to intimidate lawyers from taking part and then, without drawing breath, attempted straight intimidation: "We didn't ban anything; we didn't use any constraints; we simply said that, considering the position of the government of Quebec, a lawyer from Quebec who accepted the mandate to be a friend of the Court would discredit himself in the eyes of the legal community in Quebec."[4] All of this in the name of unity for the cause.

The result over the long term is a strange conundrum. The PQ and the Bloc take left-of-centre stands on several issues, yet the effect of their monolithic view of loyalty is to undermine public debate and so facilitate the cause of those against reform politics. The threat issued by Minister of Intergovernmental Affairs Brassard would have fitted nicely into the mouth of Sir Allan MacNab, defending the Family Compact in the 1840s.

The effect of the existence of such a strong nineteenth-century-style coalition in Canadian politics in the late-twentieth century has been to push politics in Ottawa and Quebec City towards the right. The arrival of the Reform party, a curiously similar coalition, even though its policies are clearly on the right, has accentuated the move. If the other provinces had not already been headed in that direction, it would have been difficult for them to resist.

In spite of all this, the LaFontaine–Baldwin concept of power—exercised on the basis of ideas and principles shared across geographic divides in cohabitation with a complex culture—has not been disproved or destroyed. If anything, the conformity and banality of current politics are there to remind us to what extent the original coalition was appropriate and necessary.

The descent of Cartier, Macdonald and the other Canadians on the Maritime premiers at the Charlottetown Conference in 1864 was the second key strategic dash. It was the sort of bold action rarely seen in constitutional negotiations anywhere. And it produced Confederation.

The national railroad was the third. With a single intellectual sweep, it converted the traditional water routes east–west into a modern mechanical route. At the same time, it solidified the border with the United States over thousands of lightly inhabited kilometres.

The fourth was the National Policy—this time entirely Macdonald's creation, as Cartier was dead. It is usually described in terms of protectionism versus free trade; or central Canadian industrialization and Western dependency. Yes, Montreal, Toronto and their hinterlands grew rich on the National Policy. It turned Quebec into an urban society decades before the nationalist historians got around to rewriting their rural myths. But the West also grew. And the overall effect of Macdonald's strategic advance was to create a context in which this poor, disparate, northern country, which had been losing more through emigration every year than it gained through immigration, could function as a society more or less on its own terms.

Strategy isn't about eternity. It is about creating major opportunities. If the West is largely rich today, it is because the National Policy provided a context for its growth from a few people on rolling unbroken prairies and scarcely penetrated mountains to a modern society ready to challenge the old centres of power on every front.

The next move was Laurier's. You have the land—millions of acres. Fill it. Fill it or someone will take it from you. Nature abhors a vacuum. As do rival powers sitting across borders. And so the immigration flood began. It was Clifford Sifton's idea. He and Laurier made it happen. They knew they were creating an unmanageable situation. But strategy isn't about management. They had enough confidence in the society that was building itself that they could afford to take the risk. A great deal of time would later be spent on the elements that went wrong; on the incidents of racism; on the language crises. But as a strategy it was successful and it carried Canadian society on to a whole other stage.

Laurier's refusal to go along with London's great empire strategies, late in the nineteenth century and through the first decade of the twentieth, is the odd man out on this list. It was more a refusal of action than an aggressive action. At first glance it might be categorized as an act of high defensive tactics. But then Sun Tzu, who was the first and remains the most important military analyst, identified strategic genius at its greatest as the ability to win without engaging. Laurier's refusal to engage, and the skill with which he refused, made it possible for the country to go on creating itself.

The next wave began slowly, before gathering speed. Analysts are constantly seeking the points of influence which led to the creation of a social-democratic structure in the northern half of the American continent, while to the south of the border the United States chose to go in a very different direction. These analysts keep coming back to the role of English liberalism or Disraeli conservatism or the French Catholic reform movement or those of the American agrarian reformers. But note that these were either marginal movements of reform in their own countries or led to seriously divided societies, as in Britain.

The strategic advance towards an inclusive societal structure in Canada came with the growth of a conscious belief that the best way to deal with a fundamentally poor northern country was to accentuate the middle-class standard. In other words, it was not an advancement of the classic socialist dichotomy of favouring the working class over the few rich. Rather it imagined the conversion of the whole into a middle class. From early on it became clear that this could only be done if wealth were moved around, not simply within society, but in great blocks of money redistributed by the central government across the continent.

This process of understanding began in the last years of Laurier's premiership. He found himself faced by the social anger which the growing inequalities of an unbridled market-place were provoking. The farmers on the prairies drove home how unacceptable this imbalance was as the prime minister made his tour across the West, shortly before losing power in 1911.

It was in political opposition that the idea first grew. By January

180 1919, just before his death, Laurier was calling not simply for
stronger unions, but for worker participation in the shaping of
industry. "Labour has looked upon capital as a master and capital
has regarded labour as a servant. In such relations as these there
should be neither master nor servant, but equality, equality of right
and co-operation in administration.... [D]emocratize the Government of industry so as to give to the workers and consumers a larger
share in the government of industry."[5]

Mackenzie King's arrival in power in the 1920s coincided with
the consolidation of the socialist movement and the appearance of
agrarian reform movements which culminated with the Progressive
party. The existence of all these groups changed the cultural balance, and the concept of social reform began to move slowly forward. The foreign models on offer gave no obvious guidance. The
left in America was increasingly marginalized. In Europe, Germany,
Italy, Spain, France and other countries were experiencing an
unbroken rise of the right, with any victories of the left simply provoking a more violent schism in the society. And Britain's approach
was based on divisions which still hamper their society today.

Under Mackenzie King a strategy was never permitted to look
like a strategy. Sun Tzu would have approved. Whatever the appear-
ances, one was gradually taking form. For a long time its timidity
caused it to run behind the desires of the society.

> ... c'est l'usine
> Où chaque jour, aux doigts crocheteurs des machines,
> Ils laissent un lambeau palpitant de leur coeur.[6]

The ideas were pushed forward a bit faster, a bit at a time, by men
like the young Vincent Massey and Brooke Claxton. Long-term
thinking, provoked by the Depression and then the Second World
War, gave the ideas of social reform another shove forward. In general the provinces resisted and so slowed the process still further. On
the other hand, the CCF created a constant threat of punishment at

the polls for governments which persisted in inaction. And their arrival in power in Saskatchewan gave impetus to what until then had resembled tactics more than strategy.

With Pearson and Trudeau social equilibrium clearly became a strategy and the provinces gradually gathered up enough courage to fall into line. Quebec, which had been held the furthest back by the negative-nationalist policies of Maurice Duplessis, made a sudden leap. Georges-Émile Lapalme—"I hear the voices of those today who reproach us with having thrown them into a world in disequilibrium."[7] He was the Liberal leader of the Opposition in Quebec who struggled with great intelligence against the provincial blockage. "Ottawa," he lamented, "alone of all the Canadian governments, was thinking about what to do in the postwar period."[8] In spite of his qualities, Lapalme was denied power. However, following on what Ottawa had done or proposed, he conceived what would be called the Quiet Revolution. Jean Lesage replaced Lapalme and became the official father of the Revolution, but Lapalme was the strategist of this astonishing dash to catch up with the rest of the country.

The eighth strategic move was begun by Lester Pearson and largely put in place by Pierre Trudeau: the Official Languages Act, the immersion schooling initiative, the public-service hiring programs to reflect the reality of the country. These and the dozens of other initiatives which accompanied them had the simple effect of formalizing what had been intended and had existed at the time of LaFontaine–Baldwin and Macdonald–Cartier. Under circumstances and pressures that I will discuss later, this fair balance had slipped away bit by bit over the first half of the twentieth century. In a sense Pearson and Trudeau reaffirmed the original understanding.

Many, with reason, will not forget the interim period in which the original handshake was in part forgotten. Each conveniently forgets that there was fault on both sides. Others believe history is a one-way street and the past irrelevant when it comes to power. They can't accept the idea that there are continuing agreements which constitute legitimacy.

Whatever the interpretation of all these events, the reality is that they constitute an integrated continuation. We have pursued an internal logic in which the first and each succeeding step remains present in what follows.

These eight strategic leaps—the reformers' alliance, the Maritime dash, the railroad, the National Policy, the immigration flood, the refusal of imperial engagement, the social revolution, the cultural engagement—actually fit one into the other like a preplanned campaign. Of course they weren't preplanned. But from the LaFontaine–Baldwin handshake to the Pearson–Trudeau cultural policies, each of these advances has been a continuation of the same idea of a new sort of individualism—that is, one in which opportunity is balanced by results. In other words, they have all been ideas in search of an equilibrium between an individualism of unstructured risk and an individualism of the public good. But what I am describing is not simply a compromise between two extremes. The practical metaphysics of the Canadian approach have all been designed and executed with the particularities of a poor northern nation in mind.

Over the last decade, as repeated attempts to carry the country off this course have been initiated, the common refrain has been—"Surely a country isn't a railroad?" "Surely a country can't be reduced to social programs?"—as if the strategic acts I have been describing were above all utilitarian mechanisms.

Of course a country is neither a railroad nor a medical program. But then these questions have been structured as answers, in the mediaeval scholastic tradition. The real question surrounding strategic acts relates not to concrete policies, but to the intent of those policies. What is the political and national concept of which they are the sequential practical manifestations? The social policies of the 1960s, 1970s and 1980s were the intended inheritors of the LaFontaine–Baldwin handshake and of Cartier's railroad concept. They are part of the continuing flow of the country. All eight are, each in its own way, expressions of how the country imagines itself. They are the practical metaphysics of the national imagination.

What about the intent of those who seek to dismantle what is in place? Any fool can dismantle. What is their proposed continuation of the flow? The neo-conservatives, the corporatist public-relations spokespeople, the mediocre leadership seem to be suggesting that a nation is advertising jargon, chants, flags, sports events and other feel-good aspects of cheap patriotism. Somewhere, just under the use of these tools, lingers the idea of deformed nationalism, that if you have to ask you will never know, because a nation is blood and self-interest.

Certainly that was the message of the Mulroney years. Concrete policies were put in place which blocked the flow of interlocking ideas stretching to us from LaFontaine and Baldwin. These were replaced by a barrage of distracting patriotic paraphernalia to help us forget that a nation is created on ideas and intent. Nothing has happened under the Chrétien government to stop this destructive denial of self. Indeed, the provinces have almost unanimously slid back into their role as the Cassandras of the public good. The difference is that they now have the dominant role in public policy.

They claim, along with the general purveyors of received wisdom, that governments can no longer "take the front rank in every noble enterprise." But they do not suggest what they *can* do as the representatives of the citizens and therefore of the public interest. They protest that Ottawa has cut transfer payments. This is true and it certainly puts the Maritime provinces in a difficult spot. But the richer provinces are in a position, if they believe in the public good as defined and developed over 150 years, to take on the responsibility of raising the necessary money. Instead, even an NDP government in as prosperous a province as British Columbia every year

184   cuts the per capita amounts put to the education of children. Everywhere class sizes are sliding up into the thirties, whatever the official limitations stipulate. And Ontario and Quebec, like Alberta, are cutting into Medicare in a manner which demonstrates that these governments do not understand the contract—social, political and economic—on which the country was built.

Animism

14

WHAT COULD IT POSSIBLY MEAN to say that Canada is an animist country?

This simple word has always provoked horror in the western heart, as if it were the ultimate denial of our various abstract ideologies—whether of the religious or political variety. The very hint of animism destabilizes the rational defences attached to these ideologies, because they are invariably structured on an idea of exclusion.

Ideologies are designed for selected humans, who have been mysteriously chosen as the beneficiaries of a universal architecture aimed at the establishment of a paradise in heaven or on earth. These are not real mysteries, but rather assertions which produce large truths, invariably involving gods or market-places or races or some other central force. As for non-humans—the animals, plants, rocks, water, natural forces—they are the instruments of the chosen because they are dumb, dumber, inert and are thus destined to be controlled.

It may sound as if I am slipping into some sort of environmentalist argument. And no doubt this new movement has revived some elements of animism. But environmentalism on its own can also turn easily into determinism—in other words, into another ideology. Animism is the opposite of a goal-oriented idea of social order.[1] And it is not principally about nature. Nor is it necessarily the description of a religion most commonly found among what Europeans might call Native peoples or hill tribes.

Animism is simply an inclusive idea of the planet; a non-determinist view. It is inclusive because it sees everything as alive and interrelated. In that sense it is a beehive of causal relationships.

Anthropologists now tend to avoid the term because it became identified inside their corporation with nineteenth-century studies of what they identified as 'primitive societies.' Animism was therefore a primitive religion. The preferred term today is Native spiritualism. But that has all the flaws of the European rational approach. First it reduces western religions to spiritualism, which is usually one of their more superficial characteristics, rather than their core. In the Christian context, we hear 'spiritualism' to mean superstition. And by adding on the word 'Native' it is suggested that animism is somehow a Native version of Christian superstition. Images of 'primitive' people limiting their actions because there is a spirit in a rock spring into our imaginations.

Wittgenstein offers a good example of the standard view of animism—"Could one imagine a stone having consciousness?" To do so would be "image-mongering." But his question misses the point. Or rather it is itself word-mongering. We all now understand the rudimentaries of atoms. We accept that a stone, cut from its place and exposed, changes. It may harden or rot, darken or bleach. The dynamics have been changed. The choice is therefore not between us and them, between an inert mass and one having signs of human consciousness. It is worth going back to the great discussions of animism in the nineteenth century. Perhaps the best-known writer on the subject, E.B. Tylor, put it that animism "embodies the very essence of spiritualistic, as opposed to materialistic philosophy"; that the essential division was that between animism and materialism.[2] Note: the spiritualistic used in this way, as the opposite of materialism, is clearly not something you reduce to spirits.

Were he alive and writing today, Tylor might have added that the essence of science is a defence of animism, which is why over the last two centuries scientific progress has continually undermined the abstract, intellectual form of the western religions that set man apart. Tylor would probably also say that there is an essential division between science and materialism. The point is that the essential divisions are not between the intelligent and the dumb. Or between the animate and the inanimate. If everything is in some way alive then everything contains a form of intelligence. You might call it a form of existence.

Different societies will deal with this reality in different ways. Those who have long lived with the sense that they dominate the space they occupy will develop ideas about their relationship to that place quite different from those who do not dominate. The former will tend to deny any animist view and the latter to accept it as normal. That doesn't mean they are expecting to have an interesting conversation with a rock.

To the extent that the materialistic or rational societies do manage to integrate animism, they will transform it into something else; something designed to confirm the special human mission. Ancestor worship—common in traditional animist societies—will be condemned, but it will be replaced by Hero worship, which in the century following the death of God has become to all intents and purposes a religion. Heroes, we have come to believe, lead us and form our societies. Without them—without leaders—we are lost. In fact western dependence on Hero worship far outstrips in importance that on ancestor worship elsewhere.

And since nature continues to exist in even the most dominating of societies, it is redefined as a place of romantic escape. The pastoral poetry of the seventeenth century, filled with shepherds and shepherdesses, turns into Rousseau's romantic view of nature as an indulgent park. And that in turn became Walden Pond in the middle of the nineteenth century:

> ... I lived alone, in the woods, a mile from any neighbour, in a house which I had built myself, on the shore of Walden Pond ... and earned my living by the labour of my hands only.

Note that for Thoreau to be alone in the woods is to be a mile from your neighbours.

In October I went a-graping to the river meadows and loaded myself with clusters more precious for their beauty and fragrance than for food. . . . It was very exciting at that season to roam the then boundless chestnut woods. . . . Everyone looks at his wood-pile with a kind of affection.

Thoreau's return to the forest was pure pastoralism—a two-year romp in a Rousseauian garden. "This is a delicious evening when the whole body is one sense and imbibes delight through every pore. I go and come with a strange liberty in Nature, a part of herself."[3]

In Manitoba's boreal forest there are twenty species of black flies and twenty of mosquitoes. As the great Estonian poet Jaan Kaplinski puts it, "The mosquitoes dictate the form of my writing. . . . I would like to think a little. To find associations, metaphors. But the mosquitoes will not allow it."[4] Or more precisely, an eighty-five-year-old White Spruce will be eighteen inches across in southern Canada. As you move north, kilometre by kilometre, it will shrink until at last it is only two inches across on the edge of the Barrens. Each one of those kilometres northward from the border or the Great Lakes or the St. Lawrence represents the elimination of various species which cannot grow or survive at that latitude.

The view of place in northern countries is not that of domination or sustained romanticism. What cannot be dominated must be part of an ongoing coalition. If nature is "without bounds," as August Strindberg put it, then we are involved as part of it. Pastoral poetry makes no sense there. Instead, George Bowering writes, "We all grow out of the ground and that is the way we grow." Or Joy Kogawa—"We are the silences that speak from stone." Or Kaplinski—"The wind does not blow. The wind is the process of blowing itself." Or Anne Hébert—"Je suis la terre et l'eau, tu ne me passeras pas à gué mon ami, mon ami.—I am the water and the earth, you will not cross over me, as over the shallows of a river, my friend, my friend." Or Al Purdy—"I think the land knows we are here." Or Gatien Lapointe—"This land is without measure, / This figure without memory. / . . . I

am nothing but a clump of root-filled earth." Or Gwendolyn Mac-
Ewen—"This land like a mirage turns you inward, / And you become
a forest in a furtive lake."[5]

As you read through Canadian poetry and literature—whether in
French or English—it is literally constructed of animist language.
Whether the scene is wilderness, countryside or city changes nothing in this. The city exists as a live body, just as it does in Russian
writing. Or in Swedish. Kjell Espmark in *Hatred* looks at society
through the eyes of an assassinated prime minister. In the days
before he is killed, the leader feels "subsidences in the ground, the
sound of ice breaking up."[6]

The place is never the background. It is a leading character and
the humans unfold in images which include the whole. No matter
how urban the inspiration, place remains omnipresent, even when,
as in Ivan Goncharov's novel *Oblomov*, the character scarcely leaves
his bed.

There is an argument common in Quebec that anglophones are
obsessed by the physical while francophones are more interested
in language, are more European. Any reading through the texts
shows that this just isn't so. In any case, animism isn't about the
physical. It is about context and inclusion. Anne Hébert's context,
like Alice Munro's, includes the place. It does not use the place, it is
of it. Besides, the Russians and the Scandinavians—the northern
Europeans—have this same relationship to place.

The Quebec argument is quite understandable, even if not
accurate. It was originally a reaction among liberal intellectuals
against the dominance of narrow religious nationalism which built
itself on the myth of a rural paradise. Le terroir. The earth was the
touchstone.

But the agrarian dream of the Ultramontane school and their
inheritors, such as Abbé Groulx and the Montreal School, was
Rousseauian romanticism. The earth was static and pastoral. Le terroir was the opposite of an animist substance. It was about belonging and controlling and excluding.

190   What is more, I am not using animism here as a simile for nature. As Rudy Wiebe puts it, the idea of north is not "simply a variation on nature and wilderness."[7] Louis-Edmond Hamelin, in *Canadian Nordicity*, has written at length about the role of perception:

> A country is not merely the result of ecological factors, it is more or less the fruit of a way of thinking, whether this is expressed or not, exact or not, politicized or not. . . . By this process we create images, the impact of which can overwhelm even those of the clearly identified physical realities.

Hamelin talks of nordicity as a condition in which climate, bio-geography, geography and psychology are weighted in order to establish the degree of northernness of a location. It is as much about an approach to the place as the place itself.[8] While Hamelin is talking about a farther north which few Canadians have seen, let alone lived in, his arguments can be applied to the much more general concept of the northern half of the continent.

Being in the north is a central factor in our animism. It is not simply a geographic option—one among many in which humans may choose to live. Nor is it a mere progression beyond what lies farther south. It is a condition in and of itself, one which makes it impossible to turn away for more than brief periods from an animist approach to our existence.

This is not to minimize the role that Native animism has played in the approach of our society. Europe has the clear memory of its animist roots in the Greek myths. But the memory is so distant and intellectualized that those roots are no longer perceived as having been animist. In Canada, only a little over a century ago, those same myths were alive and well in the indigenous cultures. When Duncan Campbell Scott was writing his Native-filled poetry and taking part as a civil servant in the undermining of that civilization early in the twentieth century, he was dealing with people whose "material and spiritual lives were not severed."[9] Today that culture is still very much alive.

As a result our situation has produced a peculiar and difficult meeting between an extremely sophisticated animism more or less unbroken in history and an almost unconscious animism re-adopted and readapted by those of us who have arrived from places where it had been reduced to the vague reminder of a distant past. That there has been a meeting and that some sort of marriage has resulted is what pours out of our literature and our painting. "The disturbing thrilling awareness is that there really is a world out-side of language which, creatures of language ourselves, we trans-late with difficulty."[10] Our creativity has been a constant reworking of that difficulty.

◄ ┈┈┈┈┈ ►

In 1936 the anthropologist Diamond Jenness had a series of con-versations with a seventy-five-year-old religious figure called Pierre, in Katzie, a Coast Salish village about forty kilometres from Van-couver on the Fraser River.[11] He was a well-known medicine man, widely respected and considered effective. Jenness convinced him to recount all that he knew about Salish beliefs. As well, Pierre described at length the process by which he had become a healer.

At one level the beliefs could be seen as just another complex, highly sophisticated set of myths running parallel to Christian mythology. What differentiates them, however, is the remarkable integration between the elements. All of the animals and fish were originally humans, as were the principal sites which marked their movements up and down the coast. In a sense this centres every-thing on humans. In another sense, since everything is human, humans are part of everything. They are not separate or above.

The Sockeye salmon are humans who live down the coast and change into fish during certain months. As a result the Salish let

192   some of the schools swim by and throw the bones of the first fish eaten back into the water to reconstitute as fish. An environmentalist would call this selective fishing a very sensible management program. But it isn't management. It's a relationship. For this reason there is a great deal of talk in Salish mythology about the vitality of a human or a species or an object and how it might be transmitted from one to another. Perhaps Wittgenstein would have had less trouble with the concept of the vitality of a stone rather than troubling himself over its possible consciousness. As for Pierre's training as a healer, it was a lengthy cleansing process during which he survived in nature alone under the most extreme conditions. Thoreau would not have approved. And what with the lack of "graping" and of affectionate wood piles, he would probably not have survived. There is also a complex idea about guardian spirits which—unlike the Christian idea of imposing saints—turns on individuals preparing themselves, again through a cleansing period in solitude which actually resembles the western Christian traditions of fasting and meditation. The meditation takes the form of "wandering in lonely places" and praying in solitude.[12]

The overwhelming message contained in what Pierre recounted was that there are uncounted centres of power in things.[13] This is an idea which science now insists is accurate. From an animist point of view, westerners, by seeing everything in their own terms, have betrayed a lack of imagination.

It was George Grant's view that we, the immigrants, could have no real relationship with this animism—"When we go into the Rockies we may have the sense that gods are there. But if so they cannot manifest themselves to us as ours."[14] But what sort of manifestation would we require? A rational, structured manifestation, accompanied by theological texts and footnotes and the music of a magnificat rolling through the valleys?

It seems to me that these gods, whatever they are, have been manifesting themselves in our society for a long time. A world outside of

language is precisely what we find in Robert Lepage and in Gilles
Maheu of Carbone 14. And why has the Jungian movement been so
strong in Canada, with Robertson Davies as its great writer?

> ... no self-deceiving folly and no meddlesome compassion, but
> a humble awareness of the Great Justice and the Great Mercy
> whenever they choose to make themselves known.

There are hints of Christian language here. But no, it is essentially animist. In *Fifth Business*, Mary Dempster brings the hero's
brother back to life in a way which would have made more sense to
Pierre the healer than to your modern churchman, let alone to most
medical specialists. She resembles the healer in Hugh MacLennan's
The Watch That Ends the Night. Pierre Morency's meditation on the
Great Heron could have been written by Pierre, the Salish religious
figure—"To possess the Great Heron would be to become the Great
Heron, even better: a clump of reeds, a still branch, a reflection of
minerals." As could Don McKay's meditation on the same theme,
which begins—

> What I remember
> about the Great Blue Heron that rose
> Like its   name over the marsh. . . .

As could the scenes in Paul Quarrington's *King Leary*, when the
monks teach hockey to their reform-school boys by instructing
them to become a specific animal. As could the description of the
famous affair in Marian Engel's *Bear*.

Engel's creation of an emotional, erotic relationship between a
human and a bear only touched the logical edge of animism. In
a sense, if humans are part of the whole, then they are engaged in a
continuous emotional, erotic relationship with their place. Writing
of Montreal, Claude Gauvreau put it gently:

The river spread out her body of a rich woman dressed in the
     Orient, and the stocky city reflected his love on her.
The city lay his new jewel on the river's throat, a jewel of flesh.
The lover shuddered, and the flesh mutely took his place
     in an iridescent furrow of her multiple breasts.

This sort of integration between human and place can be found throughout northern literature. The Swedish writer Kerstin Ekman filled her novel *Blackwater* with the earth and the forest in constant human mutation—"[T]he ground had dried to dead flesh in the body of the landscape." "The greenery was obscene." The heroine saw it as "bushy pubic hair."

There is nothing new about this. Isabella Valancy Crawford, young and proper in the nineteenth-century urban world of southern Ontario, wrote what A.J.M. Smith called "geographical animism." But it was much more than geographical. It was physical in the full sense that animism can imagine. For example, there is her wonderfully dirty poem, "The Lily Bed":

His cedar paddle, scented, red,
He thrust down through the lily bed;

Cloaked in a golden pause he lay,
Locked in the arms of the placid bay.

Trembled alone his bark canoe
As shocks of bursting lilies flew

Thro' the still crystal of the tide,
And smote the frail boat's birchen side . . .

All lily-locked, all lily-locked,
His light bark in the blossoms rocked.

Their cool lips round the sharp prow sang,
Their soft clasp to the frail sides sprang...

With golden hand she grasped the mane
Of a red cloud on her azure plain....

They swayed the high, dark trees, and low
Swept the locked lilies to and fro.

With cedar paddle, scented, red,
He pushed out from the lily bed.[15]

But all I have done in these last few pages, some might say, is offer literary examples, as if they told us something about reality. They do. Western civilizations express themselves accurately through their literatures, particularly when they do so with such insistence, in such quantities, in both languages, across the regions and across the distance of time. It is part of the Canadian paradox that in order to do this we have had to work to make our language communicate what lies beyond language; and above all, what lies beyond style.

When Big Bear is offered land to settle his people in one static place, Rudy Wiebe has him reply—"Who can receive land? From whom would he receive it?"[16] The sense that land is not simply owned has had an effect, ever since the European arrival, on our concept of the public good. Of course, we haven't embraced the Native ideas of non-ownership; that, for example, intimacy and attachment gave a man rights over land, but not exclusive rights. Or there is the more aggressive idea in the north that humans are owned by the land and not vice versa.[17] But there has been an almost unconscious attempt in Canada to marry these animist ideas to the European. An "intermingling of place and person," in Sharon Butala's words. And this has come about more as a natural reaction to the place and what it demands of those who live in it, than by any

196 compromise over social models. "Nature has reinvented us," David Young writes.[18]

That reinvention has been central to our ability to advance a small, poor society by conceptual leaps. I have talked about a society of ideas. That these have not been of the calculated sort, but have bred in an atmosphere of movement and communication, is tied to animism. Yet over the last decade we have slipped increasingly into a predictable, mechanistic, measuring view of our society. In other words we have increasingly conformed to the standard western abstraction of civilization as something which aggressively eliminates all hints of the animistic. The more we have done this, the more it has seemed impossible to engage in original initiatives here; strategic initiatives which have some relationship to the place. With this 'normalization,' the very idea of Canada has become increasingly impossible.

The Animistic Image

15

IT IS WORTH CONSIDERING THE Native and Métis trappers—
among the toughest men society had to offer—who went off on
their long absences in the woods among the black flies dressed in
delicately embroidered leather clothes. Pink was usually the dominant colour, flowers the continuing theme. With undyed deer or
moose or caribou skins as background, such masses of embroidery
stood out as a fine and civilized cover for a man. This silk decoration
was in common use until the 1920s. Today an urban man will be
more likely to wear something shapeless and artless in order to suggest that he is tough—jeans for example—but will spend his time in
the tame and static surroundings of an office and a gym.

The Ojibwa and Cree have no word for art, let alone art for art's
sake. Yet they have always had a great deal of it—some decorative,
some more clearly driven by what we would call the imagination or
creativity. Marius Barbeau, at the Toronto opening of the famous
1928 show combining West Coast Native objects and contemporary
art, explained that "Carving, painting, singing, dramatic art and
social standing in the community were all part of each other ... art
was not a luxury to those people; it was the most vital necessity in
life, next to food."[1]

The separation between art and society, or rather the arts and
place, is not so old as we pretend in the west. However, it reached
its extreme point in the late-nineteenth century with the arrival of
the art for art's sake movement. At the same time, impressionists,
symbolists and post-impressionists were fighting back. And in this
century what is often called modernism reached out to the sculptures of animist people—principally in Africa, but also in North

198   America and the Pacific Islands—in search of forces which would help them to break away from the static destiny of the European arts. After all, the arts, once separated from an animist sense of place, became profoundly static. That is the European inheritance.

Now the curious thing is that Canadians and other northerners, by the very nature of their surroundings, were already in the position that the modernists were seeking. What prevented these northerners from seeing their situation in such simple terms was their need to feed even the most animistic of creative impulses through the intellectual conduits of European art. By 'need' I mean the need they felt. This is the provincial or colonial reasoning of those who live on the margins.

And so a reading of the theoretical sources of Swedish, Norwegian, Danish, Russian and Canadian artists over the last 125 years is a ceaseless series of references to France and other European centres. Even Roald Nasgaard's *The Mystic North*—the most complete and imaginative attempt to define the place of northern painting as a school or a movement stretching all around the top of the globe— was rooted in the symbolism and post-impressions of western Europe. And yet, at the same time, he writes of the northerners' ability, unmatched elsewhere, "to re-establish contact with the primal sources of experience."[2]

It is to the European references that the critics and art historians keep coming back. But when you look at the paintings of Edvard Munch, Karl Nordström, Akseli Gallen-Kallela, August Strindberg, James Wilson Morrice, Lawren Harris, Paul-Émile Borduas, Jean-Paul Riopelle, you don't find those sources on the canvas.

Of course in the technical sense the universal elements are there. There is no such thing as a national technique. Technical influences fly about and painters take what they need from them. More often than not they then produce art which bears no resemblance to its technical origins. The need, in spite of this, to find resemblance is what the poet A.J.M. Smith described as colonialism—". . . a spirit that looks elsewhere for its standards of excellence." But in these northern countries the colonialism isn't particularly apparent on the good canvases, so it isn't of great importance.

What can be seen on these canvases are the relationships between the northern painters. "I paint not what I see but what I saw," was Edvard Munch's motto. But what had he seen? What had they seen? Whatever it was, they did not do so through the filtered lens of rational, controlled pastoralism. Their lens was much more complex because it was permanently out of control, out of focus. "How nature is torn asunder; what disorder! Where is the architectonic or painterly unity that makes the landscape of the south, with its clear and serene lines, so seductive to artists? Where is the classical line? Not here."[3]

Many people have written about the links between northern images; mainly they refer to the Group of Seven and the influence of a Scandinavian show seen by Lawren Harris and J.E.H. MacDonald in Buffalo in 1913. In part this created a technical connection, in part a connection of intent. But shared animism in our images goes well beyond a conscious or concrete connection. When you walk through galleries of Scandinavian nineteenth- and twentieth-century art or even Russian art, your eye continually falls on similarities with the Canadian. This is more a family of intent and effect than of technical evolution. The colours, intensities of colours, particular uses and combinations of colours are continually familiar. Ivan Aguéli seems to have understood North Africa in the same terms as James Wilson Morrice. Karl Nordström is sometimes reminiscent of Morrice, sometimes of the early A.Y. Jackson; Richard Bergh of Tom Thomson. There is one painting of Nordström's I keep coming back to—*Varbergs fäste*—because of its remarkable marriage of geometry and wild colours. If it were hung in a gallery of twentieth-century Canadian painting, most of us passing by would assume that it belonged there. There is the family portrait by Edvard Munch in the Thiel Gallery in Stockholm for which I can think of no other artistic relation than the paintings of Jean-Paul Lemieux. At the same time, the blocks of colour and the light in his portrait of Nietzsche,

or in *Förtvivian*, make you think of Lawren Harris. August Strind-
berg's strange non-abstract abstracts in search of an artistic family
have the same feel as much of Jean-Paul Riopelle's work. The Dane
Jens Willumsen was doing something quite different from Paterson
Ewen, yet the effect is similar, as is that, today, of the Norwegian,
Frans Widerberg.

Curiously enough, when Canadians or Scandinavians talk about
their painting they often fall into an embarrassed tone over
chronology. The feeling is that in order to qualify as creators rather
than imitators, those late-nineteenth-, early-twentieth-century
painters should have been painting their pictures a decade or two
earlier. This attitude tells us just how deeply the technocratic spirit
has penetrated the arts. After all, images are not about competition. First is not best. The order of appearance is only relevant in an
anthropological sense. The point of northern painting is not its
place in a calendar of international events, along with Grand Prix
races and high-jump records. Art does not require a definition of
purpose, but if it did, the place to begin might be the search for
ways to express *not* the north, but the northern sensibility through
a northern eye.

To worry about a few decades one way or the other is to reduce
images to fashion. Rembrandt was old-fashioned in his time, as was
J.S. Bach, as was Tolstoy. And technical analysis is not what matters.
An obsession with chronology causes the art historian to miss what
is really happening.

There is also a certain embarrassment in northern countries
about the importance of landscape in these paintings. After all,
abstract though they are, even Borduas and Riopelle are pure landscape painters. Borduas's 'evacuation of all intent' was a political
approach, not one which could control what we can see in his
painting.

What isn't clear is why this should be a problem. The last century has been dominated, throughout the west, by various forms of
landscape, from Cézanne to Picasso. Embarrassment over subject

matter is pure provincialism. A sunflower field in Provence is somehow acceptable landscape, as are the hills around Aix, but there is
something wrong with images drawn from the north.

If you put aside the particularities of place, what you find is that
all of these artists who share the western tradition, from the north to
the south, were searching for tools to break the pure-art stranglehold on the European image. It was almost inevitable that this struggle would lead towards the image as an animist object. And so,
however hidden in abstraction or mathematical theory, one of the
central highways of modernism has been landscape. If anything,
the European schools have been more locked into the conventions
of landscape as pastoralism than the northern schools. Karl Nordström, for example, found Gauguin's paintings too decorative—
"ornamental simplicity and clarity for its own sake, for decorative
purposes alone."[4]

Even portraits and realism have sought to integrate the human
into the whole. You can see the northern approach to this when you
look at the paintings of the Dane Vilhelm Hammershoi. It is as if he
were the father of magic realism. You can find Alex Colville in his
Five Portraits and Christopher Pratt in his remarkable *Dust Dancing
in the Rays of Sun*, an internal scene looking out. The simple idea of
a world seen from inside through windows is repeated endlessly in
northern images. In Attila Lukacs there is, of course, some continuation of German expressionism. But above all he expresses the
force you are more likely to find in Russian sculptors like Ossip
Zadkine or the Lithuanian Jacques Lipchitz.

What strikes me repeatedly when I look at these northern images
is the unexpected combination of flamboyance and toughness—the
trapper decked out in embroidery. There is no hint of the prettiness
of the impressionists. There is rarely a sense of permanency, of the
static. It is all uncertainty and tension. Rather than celebrating the
intellectual, it is buried in the force of movement and colour. One of
the great challenges of European modernism was to break the
bounds of perspective, of surface, of gravity, in an attempt to see

what we fully see instead of the superficial conventions of mere sight. The northern images broke all of those bounds, but in a completely different way; a more direct manner because the illusion of those bounds was not so easily maintained in an animist culture. You can see Emily Carr doing this in exactly the same way as Edvard Munch: for example, in her *Scorned as Timber* and *Beloved of the Sky* and his *The Sun II*.

What also strikes me is how rarely American images are part of this school. Their impressionists are more pastoral, pretty, still, static, even than the Europeans. Thomas Dewing, Theodore Robinson and Maurice Prendergast are filled with the celebration of comfort— whether warm interiors or pastoral exteriors. These are not interiors looking outside. These are the interior as a warm belly of civilization. What could be more still, less threatening and more controlled than a Winslow Homer? Two pictures stay in my mind—*A Woman Walking in the Mountains* and a ship seen from *The Lee Shore*. The waves pound, the woman walks and all is calm and well with the world. There is none of the uncertainty that you might find even in a Morrice, such as *Village Street, West Indies*, with the earth in movement, a pedestrian apparently struggling against its movement. Or compare the stillness, the frozen, static mystery of Edward Hopper's urban American scenes with those of Lawren Harris's houses in Toronto, Halifax and Glace Bay, where the land is alive and heaving, the houses mere temporary structures, unnatural outgrowths.

Harris's Glace Bay painting is among the most important Canadian statements on social justice, ranking for eloquence with Laurier's speeches on the Métis Rebellion. And yet he gets to that impact not through an intellectual structure or intent, but via what I can only see as an animist image or object. What are these miners' houses? The hills to which they clasp seem to have heaved up. Are these tombstones planted on top of them? Deformed plants? Extensions of the rock? What you sense is that the inhabitants have been turned into victims, not of the earth but of whatever has caused them to live in this way. It is a portrait of animist integration deformed into something destructive for humans and for the earth.

David Milne was an admirer of the American Maurice Prendergast. Yet Prendergast is filled with that frozen quality of Puvis de Chavannes or even the romanticism of Eugène Boudin, while Milne's deceptive simplicity and minimalism is filled with a tension which makes perfect sense next to a Paterson Ewen. That same frozen, static quality of Prendergast is there in Andy Warhol—the art of the ironic microscope. It is easy to imagine him as the star courtier in some royal palace in the late-seventeenth, early-eighteenth centuries, amusing and disturbing everyone with his images and his antics. The Ontario painter Greg Curnoe, on the other hand, would have been a flop at court. He had that uncontrolled quality you find so often in northern images.

The very choice of terms—the American 'hyper' versus 'magic' realism—tells us a great deal about American art as a European continuation and Canadian as a peculiar, northern phenomenon on the margins of western civilization. Why magic? Because these are not examinations; not hyper microscopic blow-ups. They are animist objects. Magic is not really the adjective. It is the noun. These paintings have nothing to do with realism, while the hyper realists have everything to do with it.

Of course I have chosen examples to suit my argument and there are exceptions on all sides. Mark Rothko and Willem de Kooning could hardly be called static. There is the turn-of-the-century American black painter Henry Tanner, who displays a force and freedom which is perhaps that of the outsider. Or there is the pure outsider, Albert Ryder, who painted with the force of the naïve.

But these and a few others are the exceptions to the American sensibility. Walk through a retrospective collection of American art. You will be surprised by the controlled, European atmosphere. George Bingham's *The Jolly Flatboatmen* is an important nineteenth-century painting. And it is one of the most convincing demonstrations of a European atmosphere. In the 1870s a barge is making its way down a great river, wilderness on both banks. And yet the shore is soft and welcoming, while the boatmen pose on the flat roof of their craft like sedentary European peasants. One of them is dancing in the centre of the boat; dancing in an Heroic, controlled manner. They could be at a village fête.

None of what I am saying is either a compliment or a criticism. Bingham, like Hopper, like Warhol, shows us how America sees and has always seen itself—as both a rational continuation of Europe and as the new centre of that continuity.

The Canadian sensibility is that of the edge, the unknown, the uncontrolled. In the art this produces there is an assumption— sometimes consciously political, sometimes unconsciously creative, sometimes both—that place and art are the same thing; not place in the common, physical sense, but place in the sense of the whole, the animist idea of borderless inclusion.

What's more, you can see this sensibility filtering down through the artists. Morrice said he would only paint winter in Canada because the autumn was too pretty and the summer too green. That fear of prettiness, of European pastoralism, is there from the first of our great painters. The Group of Seven are his inheritors. They solve the problem of prettiness. But Lemieux also inherits from him an idea of the light, and of reality as something floating and borderless. Put any of his winter portraits beside Morrice's *Return from School*.

Somehow the World War One experience of Varley and Jackson reinforced the un-European strain in the painters of their time. It seemed to explode the idea of humans being apart and entrusted with a mission. Varley's *The Sunken Road* is truly one of the best pictures we have produced. Heroism is erased, dead soldiers are already part of the earth, there is no shape or meaning to what has happened. The blasted landscape of the war prepared these painters, from Varley to Milne, to look at their own landscape without artifice. Or perhaps it only confirmed their view of what they already saw.

J.E.H. MacDonald's *The Elements* appeared in 1916. Men are seen camping on rocks by the water in Georgian Bay. Yet it is the same picture in many ways as *The Sunken Road*. The men, the rocks, the clouds are one. There is no separateness of the men from the elements, no sense of a possible control. Or when you look, one after the other, at MacDonald's *Tangled Garden* or *The Wild River*, then Riopelle's *Pavane* or *Untitled, 1947* in the National Gallery, they suddenly appear to be explanations for each other. If there is one other painter Riopelle brings to mind, it is Emily Carr at her most delirious, with the forest swirling about as if it were a tornado's funnel, sucking the viewer up into some animist nirvana. These are not the relationships of formalized art history. And yet they are there. Look at a Morrice winter scene, one of Harris's geometrical portraits of the force of nature and a late minimalist Borduas, for example his *3 + 4 + 1* in the National Gallery. There seems to be a line running directly from one to the other.

Barker Fairley wrote of Varley's war pictures, "They are executed in an impersonal way, neither laboured or mannered," and of Jackson's as "detached and excessively scrupulous."[5] In a way this set the tone for everything that followed. Animism is neither romantic nor a matter of style. I'm sure Borduas would have been happy with these descriptions himself.

Throughout this century the energy of creativity has bounced back and forth from Montreal to Toronto. Morrice to the Group of Seven to Les Automatistes, and Borduas to the Painters Eleven. Borduas's impact on Jack Bush and others in the latter group was only in part painting. They produced a manifesto which purposively echoed Borduas's *Refus global*. Even Curnoe claimed some influence from Borduas. All the time, their politics were both aggressive and yet careful. They didn't want to be used by narrow interests.

"Artistic expression is a spirit, not a method, a pursuit, not a settled goal, an instinct, not a body of rules...." Group of Seven Catalogue, 1922 Exhibition.

"Break permanently with the customs of society, dissociate yourself from its utilitarian values. Refuse to live knowingly beneath the level of our spiritual and physical potential...." Borduas, *Refus global*.

At first glance these declarations of independence might be confused with the classic act of disassociation from reality so common in the pure-art movements and the accompanying ideas of élitism— 'this is pure art, we do it for art's sake and expect few to understand us.' But that was the position of those who refused the idea of place: the Empire painters, anglophone and francophone. Those were the people who, in the guise of universalism, sought the core of their inspiration in the old capitals and saw art as destined for an élite.

"Until an artistic elite is formed, it is useless, I believe, to speak of art in our country. The public isn't interested... we are striving to form an elite ready and willing to take an interest in art and artists." Fernand Préfontaine, 1918, in *Le Nigog*.[6]

At the same time, the Group of Seven were declaring their project to be purposively populist, which is why today's Empire-obsessed élites still have trouble simply accepting what they accomplished. Yet the Group's attitude was exactly that of Borduas in his *Refus global*:

I am convinced that where I can recognize myself in my most intimate self, the most particular, millions of others will also recognize themselves if they follow exactly where I have gone. And I maintain the hope that it will suffice for them to know my paintings well enough in order to recognize in these that same resonance.

This could be a Jungian explanation of archetypes. It is the perfect evocation of animism as an inclusive sensibility. The particular is a reflection of the whole.

In 1950, Borduas set about creating nine small wooden sculptures, "une sorte de géographie mythique."[7] They were simple and abstract. Each one was eventually named after a country. The image of the 'United States' evoked power and sport, 'France' was extremely abstract and evoked a mythic flame of liberty. The others were more erotic, particularly 'Canada' and 'Russia.' They were phallic symbols. The most purely erotic was Canada. And it had two heads. A Siamese twin.

"A beauty of dissonance" was the way A.J.M. Smith described the peculiar manner in which Canadians relate to their place. "This is the beauty of strength broken by strength..."[8] But perhaps the best description is given by Michael Ondaatje on the subject of Paterson Ewen's pictures. Or are they constructions? Ewen called them "inner phenomenon." Ondaatje says they are "great metaphors of the heavens." They produce "an indelible sense of precariousness.... Viewer and painter are too far into the form for comfort ... a remarkable recreation of power ... a vision of nature beyond the human ego."[9] This is a description of the painting as animist object and could be applied as easily to Borduas or Curnoe, the Group of Seven or James Wilson Morrice.

16 Oral over Written

"IT IS A LAND AFTER DANTE'S HEART," the painter J.E.H. MacDonald said, when he first went north of Lake Superior.[1] Was he referring to an idea of hell or paradise or both? In either case, Dante had seized on the idea of our full, eternal destiny being one with the earth. After all, his narrator hadn't popped off to heaven to meet the dead.

Underlying what Dante wrote was his conviction that he was creating an oral tool or weapon for society. It was written, but only in order to capture and enrich with poetic form the people's language. His was at heart an oral undertaking.

From the midst of our law- and technocracy-driven society it would be hard to argue that the oral dominates in Canada, thus making us the exception to the western rule. The written dominates everywhere in the developed world. It dominates to such an extent that our current difficulties come in part from what amounts to a scholastic blockage of our ability to think, debate and act. As I've said elsewhere, the word scholastic is taken here in its mediaeval sense of knowledge being used, by those who have it, to block rather than to advance society.

At the heart of the western tradition there is a tension between the oral and the written. The oral at its best is a force of creativity and change; at its worst, one of disorder. The written at its worst is a force of control, even repression; at its best, of stability and responsible organization. Power shifts with time from one to the other and then back again, usually for longer periods to the written. And then for shorter, liberating periods to the oral.

Different societies have different relationships to the oral/written tension. It is in this spectrum of relationships that Canada seems to fall outside of the norm of western societies.

Some countries have literally constructed themselves through the written. France is perhaps the purest example of this. When you stand back from the delightful mythology of sacred borders enclosing a romantic civilization of individualists, great generals and cheeses, you find seven hundred years of careful legal and regulatory construction, to say nothing of enforcement. No society has been more successfully converted into an administrative reality. And most of this has been a textual accomplishment, beginning with *La Grande Ordonnance* of Saint Louis (Louis IX) in 1254. It excluded the use of Langue d'oc in matters of public administration, which included such things as buying and selling property. In other words, the king gave a legal monopoly to the dialect of the north (langue d'oïl) over that of the south (langue d'oc). His decree was unlikely to be understood by the southerners if issued in langue d'oïl and to write the law in langue d'oc would have been an admission of its political intent. It was therefore drawn up in Latin, the ultimate language of organization. The centralizing effect of this measure favoured Francien, the dialect of the Paris region, over the other, northern variations. So without taking the political risk of forbidding the southern tongue, the king destroyed it by denying it any utility. This same obsession with structuring society through written texts has led the French through fourteen constitutions in two centuries. And the period from Napoleon on has seen a remarkable 'deconstruction' of the old concept of a society in order to reconstruct it on the basis of carefully defined élites, each formed in its own Grande École. With this came a highly centralized and methodical approach towards what all children would be taught. And from the first official dictionary in the seventeenth century, the language itself has been subjected to increasing forces of formalization. Today that written formality and its increasing separation from the oral has become French's greatest weakness as an international tool of communication.

England, in spite of its self-perpetuating myth of itself as a place of common sense and no constitution, has taken almost as stringent a written approach as France. From the Magna Carta on, a textual and centralized society has been developed until, under Margaret Thatcher, Britain actually overtook France as the most centralized of western countries. Through this period, using the same written tools as France, rival languages and dialects on the British Isles were virtually eliminated. The principal factor that has saved English from a scholastic island prison has been the development of rival Englishes elsewhere, more important or as important as the original. To understand how carefully defined and regulated language is in British society, you have only to look at its Draconian libel laws, the most discouraging in the developed world.

As for the United States, it defined itself into existence through a series of texts. Wonderful texts. Beautiful texts. But the revolution of free men was first a scholastic exercise and the strength of that scholasticism can be seen every day as that nation attempts to live within the textual boundaries it set itself two centuries ago. If it is a country of lawyers and legal wrangles, that is because it is one of the most written societies to have existed.

The Canadian relationship to the oral/written tension is relatively different. This is a country built much more through the oral, some of which can be put down to the factors I have been discussing in the two preceding chapters. The survival of the animist involves what lies beyond language, but it also favours the oral—the imagination of existence rather than the defined method of existing. Our northern, marginal status legitimizes the oral. Glenn Gould, in his verbal symphony *The Idea of North*, seemed to be saying that the north is an oral idea. That is part of what Louis-Edmond Hamelin has been saying about nordicity. It is a great deal more than climate. It is an attitude, a form of social relationships.

The most obvious element in this orality is the aboriginal community, which remains as one of the three pillars on which the society was originally constructed. If much of the aboriginal culture has been taken into the larger new complex culture, then the oral must have come with it.

Take the example of Meech Lake and the manner in which it was killed by Elijah Harper, silent, with a feather. We have become so used to seeing ourselves as victims that we all—on all sides—interpreted this event from the point of view of our own mythological martyrdom.

Almost every political party, federal and provincial, from the prime ministers and Cabinets all the way down, saw their will being thwarted. They had decided. They had announced their decision and put their jobs on the line. Instead, the quasi-totality of the political élite was humiliated. Many of their careers were effectively destroyed. Francophones in Quebec, even though they weren't particularly excited by the package, saw its collapse as a personal humiliation, as did the many anglophones across the country who had supported it. And the anglophones who opposed it felt not triumph but a curious embarrassment, even humiliation, before the evident reality—they could not say they had won, because their cause had not been expressed as a noble or even worthwhile option. There had only been silence and a feather. Some patted themselves on the back with the notion that the Natives had somehow taken revenge for their treatment in Quebec or indeed their treatment in the whole of Canada. And in this sense it was a curious celebration of self-humiliation.

But none of us were really listening to what Mr. Harper was saying. He and his friends weren't trying to humiliate heads of governments or francophones. Nor were they trying to help anglophones engage in an act of ritual self-humiliation. He wasn't thinking about any of us. He was reacting to what Natives saw as the ultimate aggression of a textual society. In Stan Dragland's words—"These people whose culture is characterized by the spoken word have been rendered voiceless in determinations about their own affairs."[2] They saw a highly utilitarian and textual re-division of the states' powers which, in leaving them out, left them behind.

It is difficult for those who felt themselves wounded by what happened to stand back and see this much larger and in western terms curious duel between the assembled, structured forces of the written and the disassembled forces of the oral.

Since francophones were those who felt most targeted by what happened, let me put it in a larger context. What Harper did was in many ways a long-delayed reply to the loss of the Riel Rebellion. It would be pushing the argument a bit to say it was Riel's revenge since, as George Woodcock put it, "like many defenders [Riel] did not belong to what he defended... he was trying to impose the theories and visions of a man trained in a classical college" onto an essentially oral society, whether Métis or Native.[3] However, it would be reasonable to say that Harper's refusal was the Native and Métis reply to their humiliation in the nineteenth century and to the gradual marginalization of their civilization. If it was aimed at anyone or anything, it was aimed at the central power in Ottawa.

I can hear serious, worthwhile people saying, 'But this is vague speculation. The practical reality is that the death of Meech has undermined the country.' Perhaps. No doubt. Perhaps the country won't survive. But the easy response to a crisis is to see it only in close-ups and assume, each of us, that we are the aggrieved, injured party. Those are the requirements of the current-affairs approach. The more interesting reaction would be to attempt to stand back in order to see what really happened.

But what about Premier Clyde Wells of Newfoundland? Well, his opposition was of the most predictable, rational sort and of little real interest. He was even more scholastic than those he fought.

On the other hand, the province he was speaking for is the last which can still pretend to an authentic oral society. It is also the province which, after the Native community, feels the most left out of the Canadian social contract. In other words, those who feel most left out are most likely to block the way in moments of crisis. Why? Because that is the only moment when they have the power to make themselves heard. On the other hand, it is hard to think of an inter-vention more inappropriate to the Rock than that of Clyde Wells.

What was astonishing about the whole affair was the seeming inability of the assembled Canadian élites to do anything about Harper's opposition. What could they have done? Let me put it this way: I can't think of another western country in which the written, structured élites would not have imposed their will by one means or another.

There are two reasons they didn't. The first was the blustering, irresponsible—and for a prime minister, almost criminal—phrase that Brian Mulroney let loose at the key moment. "A roll of the dice," he said, was how he played the negotiations. All of those who were against the project, but had laid their beliefs aside because they had been told it was in the national interest, suddenly felt manipulated and indeed humiliated. If there was a structural way past Harper, the will to find it and use it was destroyed by the then–prime min-ister's intervention. The visceral loathing which so many Canadi-ans have for Mulroney was activated and formalized in good part by that phrase. There is nothing more devastating for a citizen in a democracy than to discover that the person to whom she has given power has contempt for her.

The second reason the élites did not try to impose their will involves a wider, more distant interpretation. Ours has always been a society in which the oral carries its weight and in this crisis it found its way to the strategic pivot of public affairs. In effect, Meech was a reminder that the important events and debates in Canada's past have not revolved around textual debates and interpretations. Our constitutional obsession of the last few decades is an historical aberration when seen in the line of Canada's development.

I am not defending Jean Chrétien's view that governments should get on with business and forget the abstract questions. After all, government is not a super public-relations firm for the private sec-tor. The public interest reaches far beyond simple commerce and in

214   a complex democracy like ours it is only if the greater interest is
well served that the economy will be well served.

In any case, constitutional reform is not a great abstract question. It has little or nothing to do with the social contract or the
public good. An obsession with constitutional reform is scholasticism at its most written. That's not to suggest that changes are never
useful. From time to time they are. But utility is the test. To invest
constitutions and constitutional changes with mystic importance is
a peculiar way of avoiding real debates over the social contract.

It is interesting to note that for a century our constitution
remained very much in the background. After all, it was domiciled
elsewhere. Some important judicial interpretations were made over
that period, but in reality the society grew accustomed to imagining
itself without the presence of its central legal document. This is one
of the factors that kept the force of the oral in place at a time when
elsewhere it was being eliminated.

A practical sign of that orality came in the run-up to the repatri-
ation of the constitution in 1982. The provinces challenged the federal government's right to act unilaterally. The Supreme Court
replied that, while Ottawa could legally do so, that act would lack
legitimacy. And so the government backed away from doing so. The
difference between legality and legitimacy in constitutional affairs is
in good part the difference between the written and the oral.

What I am suggesting is that constitutional obsessions will invariably work to the disadvantage of those who pursue them because
the logic of the country does not respond to haggling over clauses.
That this creates certain legalistic problems is obvious. But you cannot turn a constitution, which for more than a century has been a
rather malleable how-to instruction booklet, into a mythical abstraction of the ideal state, when the country was developed on the basis
that it didn't need or want to be tied to a Bible-like text.

◄-------►

A sign of this difference is the role that public debate has played in giving the country direction. The nineteenth century was a time of debate everywhere in the west, but as the century advanced, the structures of power grew stronger and the public formulation of ideas retreated to a marginal role.

Yet in Canada Laurier became party leader and prime minister at the end of the century in large part through four astonishing speeches, filled with political philosophy, ethics, history and an idea of the public good. Two were given in French, two in English. The first, in Quebec City in 1877, was his defence and definition of modern liberalism. The second was in Montreal before fifty thousand people on November 22, 1885. They were there to protest the hanging of Riel.

The other lead speaker was Honoré Mercier, who would build his governmental coalition out of this crisis and become premier in just over a year. Mercier was a seductive speaker, but it was in the style of the classic nineteenth-century nationalist demagogue—great emotional flourishes, a world divided into good and evil where martyrs struggled against opponents who, by virtue of their opposition, were traitors; where the only solution was solidarity. Traitors and solidarity are still the two great themes of this school.

Laurier on the other hand came at the tragedy of the North West as a crisis of the public good—the greater good that everyone could and should share. His condemnation of the federal Conservative francophone ministers was on that level, not one of demonization or of racial division. And then, because his position was based on the ethics and understanding of responsibility proper to a social contract, he was able to move well beyond blame and recrimination to place himself in the centre of the ethical standards he demanded from the government—

Had I been on the banks of the Saskatchewan, I also would have taken up my rifle.—Si j'avais été sur les bords de la Saskatchewan, j'aurais, moi aussi, épaulé mon fusil...[4]

216   Laurier was the leading Opposition francophone in Ottawa. He was almost challenging the authorities to charge him with sedition.

The House was recessed. When it reconvened there was a debate on the Rebellion. Laurier waited until the end, then late on the evening of March 16, 1880, he rose to give a speech no one in his own party wanted him to give. He spoke for two hours. It remains, unless something has escaped me, the finest speech given in either French or English in Canada. He built his condemnation of the government's "judicial murder" on all of the ideas, standards and traditions which responsible governments claim for themselves.

> Rebellion is always an evil, it is always an offence against the positive law of a nation; it is not always a moral crime.

And the paragraph which cannot be repeated enough—

> What is hateful is not rebellion but the despotism which induces that rebellion; what is hateful are not rebels but the men who, having the enjoyment of power, do not discharge the duties of power; they are the men who, having the power to redress wrongs, refuse to listen to the petitions that are sent to them; they are the men who, when they are asked for a loaf, give a stone.

Then he turned the idea of loyalty on its conventional head by invoking the supremacy of the public good over the interests of the state.

> Loyalty must be reciprocal. It is not enough for the subject to be loyal to the Crown; the Crown must also be loyal to the subject.

> Have the Government been loyal to these half-breeds? If they had been loyal to the half-breeds no such trouble would have occurred. But the Government has not been loyal to the laws.

Had they taken as much pains to do right, as they have taken to
punish wrong...

Our prisons are full of men who, despairing ever to get justice
by peace, sought to obtain it by war, who despairing of ever
being treated like freemen, took their lives in their hands, rather
than be treated as slaves.[5]

Toronto's Orange newspapers dared him to repeat his defence of
Riel in Ontario. His party and friends discouraged him. There were
threats of violence, but the Young Liberals asked him to come. An
enormous crowd turned out in the Agricultural Pavilion on the 10th
of December, including a large contingent of those who had dared
him to come to Toronto. Perhaps the tension and expectation of
this first entry into the eye of the storm set him slightly off balance.
The speech was a bit heavy, but it was more than enough—

When we find a government ill-treating a poor people, simply
because they are poor and ignorant, we must ourselves feel that
injury and injustice.... It is the duty of all citizens to resist this
violation and to fight freely with all the means that the constitution places in our hands.[6]

The opponents scarcely managed a heckle. His triumph was not
just that of a successful evening. What he had done was demonstrate that it was possible to draw people together, by rising to the
values they hardly seemed to realize they shared, rather than seeking power through the divisions of race or religion. More precisely,
he proved himself a possible prime minister by the courage and
intelligence with which he defended the Métis before those who
opposed them.

218   I'm not suggesting that the oral tradition is the normal road to power in Canada. Rather, my point is that much of the shaping of the country has taken place outside the mechanisms of power, through ideas pressed forward in public debate. Power itself seems to have been slightly less important than elsewhere, perhaps because of the complex system of a highly decentralized country. As no one government can dominate, there is space left for a public debate which can sway a citizenry spread across different regions and even sway the uncoordinated governments.

And so William Lyon Mackenzie and Louis-Joseph Papineau were primarily tribunes, not men of power. Thomas D'Arcy McGee, George Brown, Joseph Howe, Henri Bourassa, J.S. Woodsworth, Tommy Douglas, Georges-Émile Lapalme, to name only a few, were tribunes. They weren't demagogues. They were men who thought out loud in public. Their language did more to shape the country than most ministers, indeed than many prime ministers.

Some of them were independent journalists who used their papers as podiums, printed yet in the oral tradition. J.W. Dafoe in Winnipeg and the wonderful Bob Edwards in Calgary understood what Mackenzie and Howe and Bourassa had understood—that thinking out loud is half the job; the other half is relentless criticism.

Mackenzie saw words as "efficient weapons" to be put into "the hands of free men." Defending himself against a charge of libel brought by the Family Compact in 1831, he replied—

If all false quotations and false opinions are improper, then all discussion, either in this House or through the Press must also be improper, for one set of opinions must be wrong. And if none but true opinions can be given or quoted by either party, then there can be no argument.

Censure of government causes inquiry and produces discontent among the people, and this discontent is the only means

known to me of removing the defects of a vicious government
and inducing the rulers to remedy the abuses.[7]

As William Kilbourn put it, Mackenzie was "the most unselfish of idealists; he was a born muckraker and scandal-monger."[8] That is precisely the job of the oral critic. The aim of most libel laws is to prevent criticism by drawing it through the formalized mechanisms of a highly written society.

But the creative influence of these tribunes went far beyond their critical talents. If there was a real father to Pierre Trudeau's Official Languages Act and to the immersion schooling system, it was Henri Bourassa. Joseph Howe sowed the seeds of provincial power long before Oliver Mowat and Honoré Mercier began to exercise it. J.W. Dafoe was at the heart of the strategies to distance Canada from the Empire. And the social net in Canada is the child of J.S. Woodsworth and his friends more than of any government. They created the debate which helped the citizenry to imagine that such policies were possible.

This oral phenomenon is not simply the creature of politics. For example, management is the everyday religion of our time. It is one of the most scholastic of exercises, revolving as it does around structural control and rhetoric. As a science of methodology it has accentuated precisely what needs to be avoided in administration. Two of the world's leading centres for thinking about the flaws of management, working within the religion but against the scholastic, are in Montreal under the leadership of Alain Chanlat, at the Hautes Études commerciales, and Henry Mintzberg, at McGill's business school. Their approach is one which leads towards the humanist, the informal or flexible. It belongs to the oral tradition.

This is less surprising when you consider that the leading western

220 thinkers on modern communications—Harold Innis and Marshall McLuhan—were centred only a few hundred miles away at the University of Toronto, and that they were examining the tension between the oral and the written in the context of new technology. Indeed, George Grant, pessimist though he was, walked down the same path. And Northrop Frye was seeking within the great texts meanings which escaped mere text.

Perhaps the strangest of all these intellectual phenomena was the role played by one of the leading modern anarchists, George Woodcock, living in Vancouver. He devoted the second half of his life to such things as the Métis question and the shape of modern Canadian literature. Anarchism, by its very refusal of conventional structure, is in part an oral phenomenon. It was Woodcock who took the debate over the Métis Rebellion beyond the martyrdom of Riel. He did it by concentrating on Gabriel Dumont, the Métis's Métis, a paragon of action and of oral culture; in many ways an anarchist's dream.

Seen from this perspective, the Rebellion was less about an heroic martyr and more about what Woodcock called a failure of Canadian democracy.

For the truest democracy is not that in which the majority imposes its will on all minorities. It is surely that in which minorities are allowed to flourish, even at some expense to the patience of the majority.[9]

Woodcock played an important role in bringing this conception back to the centre of Canadian public life. Somehow he also found in Canadian writing the contradictions which could interest an anarchist's mind: the regional contrasts, the languages, the oral. He became one of the Western voices putting intellectual flesh on the ideas of decentralization, helping to take it beyond resentment and power bargaining. The point is that there aren't many places where applied anarchism could have a serious and long-term effect.

But then this is the same society that was able to digest much of

Marius Barbeau's idea about the importance of traditional oral cultures. Some in Quebec were understandably concerned that his approach might give comfort to the static, nationalist religion of Le terroir. But with time they saw that Barbeau's argument was quite different. He was evoking these earlier oral cultures as a way through to the modern.

In that sense it isn't surprising that this is one of the few developed countries where poetry remains an important factor. It isn't important by its sales. But poetry continues to play a central role in how our literature functions. The quantity and size of public readings are an illustration of this. What is this role? Why are poets— from Anne Hébert and Leonard Cohen through Margaret Atwood and Michael Ondaatje—still at the core of our imagination? I can only think it is because ours is an essentially oral culture.

17 An Idea of Balance

THE ABILITY TO ASSUME COMPLEXITY is a great strength. You could call it the ability to deal with reality. All nine of the mythologies I have been discussing turn on the complexity of Canadian society.

No doubt this situation creates a problem—emotional, intellectual, political, practical—for those unable to accept the cards which have been dealt us. I have a certain sympathy for them. After all, the purpose of the standard nation-state mythology throughout the west has almost always been to achieve a sense of both unity and belonging through the illusion of simplicity. Indeed the central drive of these organisms has been to transform complex realities into real simplicities through centralization, the eradication of distracting cultural and linguistic strands and the dominance of a heavily written code, whether legal or social, supported by factual structures which confirm the existence of the nation. The intended effect of all of this is to create a mythology which could be described as a modern lay religion or a national ideology.

It may sound as if I am describing the nation-state at its worst—Nazi Germany, for example. Not at all. If we look coolly at the history of the west, over the last two centuries in particular, we find a number of factors cohabiting as best they can. The mythology of the nation-state has evolved more or less as described. Fortunately other factors, such as the rise of modern democracy, have often softened the unforgiving edges of these single-focus mythologies.

Canada has been by no means excluded from these monolithic dreams. After all, if this approach has been so important in the west, it is in part because it also represents a great strength—that of concentration. The surface is romantic, the underpinnings utilitarian. The psychological drive is fear dressed up as pride.

We have had our fair share of movements which attempt to impose the remedy of simplicity upon us. D'Alton McCarthy and Honoré Mercier firing volleys of self-righteous indignation at each other across communities is a good example. They were intelligent, intellectually sophisticated men and so they wrapped their mono-lithic visions in legal and philosophical robes. They actively denied they were appealing to race or prejudice or even to the fears which one group might have of the other. Their respective dreams of unity just happened to be built on mono-cultures with one religion, one language and, in nineteenth-century terms, one race. All they were arguing for, they would say, was the historic imperative of a real nation. Since then the inheritors of their views have repeatedly encouraged us—and continue to do so—in the dream of the standard nineteenth-century monolithic nation-state myth.

Complexity demands a very different sort of strength. It is much less comfortable. It demands more of the citizen. It is the more Socratic position, as against that structured Platonist certainty to which most of us have become accustomed. It is a calmer, more discreet form of mythology because it cannot flash simple answers and definitions. It depends more on the relationship between citizens than on the assertion that the citizenry are united on the essential but unstated questions. These are unstated because they are unstatable, except as heart-warming mythologies.

The assumption of complexity is a search for balance between different elements; not eradication or domination of one over the others, but a continuing struggle to develop and maintain some sort of equilibrium. That this myth exists at all in Canada comes in part from the needs of a northern society—a society living on the geographical and political margins. It is also a habit taken from a long, relatively stable coexistence with the Natives. It is important to keep on repeating that for much of that time the Natives' real standard of living or quality of living was higher than that of the European immigrants. That relationship did not end in a defeat of one by the other and the eradication of the loser's myths and social values. Rather there was a betrayal of trust; that is, of an agreement which was legal. Even more important, that agreement was the product of centuries of cohabitation. But the effect of these slow and relatively recent acts of bad faith was to allow much of the Native culture to be integrated, almost by sublimation. Our superficial European triumphalism simply ignored the aberrations which Canadian society was calmly accepting.

The construction of this society by two large minorities with two languages and more or less two religions; the sense that everyone was an internal or external refugee; the distrust of the Heroic gesture, which was a natural outcome of living with complexity; the sense of constant movement, somehow inevitable and necessary in a society seeking stability over great distances; the curious middle-class cooperation or socialism, which was invented in the nineteenth century by this small population living in relatively poor conditions, in order to deal with the complexity of their situation—all of these factors and more led to an idea of egalitarianism rather than populism.

The American idea that egalitarianism is opportunity not result, as Seymour Martin Lipset has described it in *American Exceptionalism*,[1] could have little relevance here. In fact, their idea is not so much egalitarianism as populism. This contains some very real positive qualities and strengths. But it comes in a form particularly susceptible to false populism and class differences.

The experience of Canadians over the last four centuries has developed the idea of individualism as a balance between opportunity and result. If we are now losing track of that difficult idea it is because the relative success of our balanced egalitarianism has created enough widely spread wealth to fool us into believing that we are a naturally rich country, like our neighbour. The immediate effect of imitating their model—as we have increasingly done—has been the rapid return of the sorts of endemic poverty we worked so long and hard to lessen.

The irony at this moment, when our élites in particular have grown tired of the Canadian condition, is that the élites of many other nations in the west have found their old mythological tools to be no longer very effective. These seem to have slipped inexplicably out of their hands into those of a new, strong mythological simplicity—the economy.

Suddenly people with responsibilities are saying *globalization*, the way they used to say *homeland* and once said *heaven*. The market-place is evoked with the tones of racial purity. They sing the praises of competition—of their forceful ability to compete—the way they once sang those of their national language. And the salesmen of trade have taken up the old nationalist military vocabulary. Glory and courage are their stock-in-trade. Each of them is tougher and smarter than the other. Heads of government now cheer on traders the way they once cheered on generals. The practical impact is just as mixed. At least this is a less bloody form of self-indulgence. But it is still built on mythological simplicity, not on the complexities of reality, that is, of society.

The Canadian élites—anglophone and francophone, centralist, federalist, decentralist, sovereigntist, separatist—have taken up the new chorus. For the first time since the world wars they have been allowed to chant and believe in childlike mythological dreams along with their colleagues in other countries. They have been able to talk and act as if the complexity of the place, of which they are an élite, does not exist. And that to all intents and purposes the place itself does not exist as a society with the particularities of a long experience. In tune with this global chorus they have also taken up the new relatively harmless nationalism, which could better be described as a communications strategy. The citizen is treated as something between a sports fan and a consumer who is subjected to repeated barrages of public-relations campaigns. This is

226   the nationalism of warm and fuzzy feelings and it accompanies the new globally minded élite.

But the irony, I repeat, is that the élites of the other nations are finding that their own simplicity myths no longer function. The reassuring vapour these once emitted has been dispersed by the force of economic rhetoric. The result is not so much clarity as an inadvertent mythological void.

It could be argued that a more realistic view of the nation-state has begun to settle into the citizenry of many western states. This is a citizenry which is annoyed, confused, insulted and uncertain of how to protect the structures of the public good they struggled so long to put in place. Abruptly the national élites seem to prefer playing another game in which the public good is subjected to what they say are larger truths. All of these turn out to be either pedantically utilitarian or highly romantic. The utilitarian involves the reduction of society to self-interest. The romantic involves the selling of economic mythology as a new universal religion.

In other words, the citizen in the west is struggling for the first time in a long while with a view of reality which is pervasively complex.

Canadians have the good fortune always to have existed on that plateau of complexity. We built our country on the acceptance of it. It is a sign of just how out of sync and essentially colonial our élites are that, at precisely the moment when those in other countries are beginning to see reality in our way, we are abandoning our own intellectual terrain in order to grab onto the sort of myths which they are discarding. But then the provincial and colonial state of mind always leaps to pick up what the empires discard.

Mythologies—not mystifications—are essential to the existence of any society. The great truths of ideology, filled as they are with inevitabilities and unrelated as they are to the realities of any place, can only hold sway for short, intense periods before their own failures cause them to peter out.

In the meantime the outlines of our mythologies are still in place.

This remains a society centred on complexity. It is so much part of our history that it colours every aspect of our lives and all of our attitudes. The difficulty is not whether our myths remain true or applicable, but whether we can find ways to apply them.

And so, while our élites increasingly give themselves over to their myths of globalization—or are these mystifications?—the citizenry seem to be withdrawing into a state of sullen non-cooperation. Why? Because they are repeatedly told that the mythologies, and indeed the realities, by which they built the country can no longer function.

Sullen non-cooperation is a curious tool often used by frustrated populations. It can take the form of growing cynicism or of scepticism, of disengagement, of loss of interest in public affairs. None of this is necessarily a sign of passivity. These are also expressions of active doubting.

The question now is of what this doubt consists. Are people questioning their own realities and the mythologies which express those realities? Or are they doubting their élites' protestations of global inevitabilities and of all being for the best? Are they wondering what they can do about these people on whom they have conferred power in so many domains, but who use that power to dismiss the relevance of the society's experience and memory? After all, the dismissal of honest mythologies is an indication that those who hold power do not wish to assume the responsibility which comes with it.

PART III

OF REALITY AND ILLUSION, THE NATURAL AND THE UNNATURAL, THE POSITIVE AND THE NEGATIVE

"Too many times married men think they're still single"
Tomson Highway, *Dry Lips Oughta Move to Kapuskasing*

An Existential Moment   18

THE UNEXPECTED MEETING AT AN intersection between a human being and reality does not necessarily produce an act of courage or intelligence or wisdom. It may. But an existential act is not by definition a moment of glory. Above all, it is a meeting, though even that we may deny.

As for reality, it is relatively easy to erase, at least from our consciousness. We can turn and run or close our eyes and pretend nothing is happening or, if our mythologies are so deformed that they bear no relationship to our experience, well, we can simply pretend that what is taking place is not at all what it appears. Rather it is something quite different, which happens to suit our myth of reality.

In any case, the existential moment is unexpected, always unexpected. That's why we prepare for it. Soldiers are trained precisely in order that, when the moment comes, they may act automatically, as if the unexpected were expected. Failing that, most of them, most of us, being sensible people, would dive into a ditch. Most of their lives, politicians are preparing for that one moment of glory or disaster, when all will be possible or all will collapse. What will they say, indeed do, if and when it comes?

All of us prepare in various ways for whatever we believe our moment might be. We rarely prepare for the right meeting and, even if we do, the reality of it when it appears is still, somehow, unexpected.

The existential act is thus not even a moment of truth. To believe that it is would imply that those involved were prepared to take on responsibility for the truth. Rather it is a moment when we reveal ourselves to ourselves, even if we are careful to deny it. And we reveal ourselves to history, even though a thick application of mythology may erase all memory of the event or so transform it that the original fades away like an illusion.

Late on the morning of October 27, 1996, in downtown Montreal, 150,000 people or more did not assemble on a square. I draw this conclusion because if this event is mentioned to anglophones an embarrassed, almost confused, silence follows. And if you mention it to francophones they tend to look away and blurt out that they're not interested. These are odd reactions, both of them, given that this gathering, had it taken place, would have been the largest political rally in four centuries of Canadian history.

In a way it's a pity that it didn't, because examining the event as a surprisingly real illusion I can't help finding all the signs of a remarkable revelation. We revealed ourselves to ourselves and the reality of it was so unsatisfactory that everything was done to transform or deny the moment.

To begin with there were the appalling speeches. I choose the adjective deliberately. There was something so empty and out of sync with reality in everything said that day by the three leaders of the No forces on the podium and the two leaders of the Yes forces from the sidelines that a citizen couldn't help being filled with bewilderment or despair.

There was a phrase in Mr. Chrétien's speech which perhaps explained why he and Mr. Bouchard and the others on both sides indulged in either the fluffiest of nationalist rhetoric or wounding attacks on the intentions of the citizenry. "This is not the day of the political class... it is your day, the citizens...." What this seemed to mean was that, since they weren't talking to their own class, the politicians would act as if they were talking to young children. The federalist leaders stood in the centre of the city where much of Canadian history was written and much of the country conceived and organized, yet managed to give speeches that would have worked as well in Pittsburgh at a Shriners' convention.

A few hundred metres off to their right, Canadian democracy had been firmly established in 1849 thanks to the pact between LaFontaine and Baldwin and their determination not to give in to the violence of the anti-democratic élites. The house in which Georges-Étienne Cartier planned how the largest communication system in the world would reach the Pacific stands a bit farther away in the same direction. Not far behind the podium, Champlain passed on his way up the river to open the centre of the country. Somewhere just before them, a hundred metres one way or the other, Jacques Cartier had climbed the little mountain and called it Mount Royal. The statue of Laurier, who more than anyone was responsible for the settling and organizing of the Western provinces, stood just across the crowd in front of them. And yet all the leaders could do was speak about emotion and love, as if quoting from greeting cards in a vacuum; as if nothing real had happened for four centuries. In A.M. Klein's words,

Enter Politico and p.d.q.—
To tell you what a lovely land is ours.[1]

Jean Charest's airy references to children and to flags blowing in the wind, and his calls for the crowd to chant No! No! as if at a football game, were perhaps the most offensive. Jean Chrétien and Daniel Johnson were simply awkward and pedantic.

But what was striking was not the irrelevant or insulting style, it was the absence of content. These three men seemed to have forgotten that the citizenry are perfectly capable of listening to complex arguments about public policy. Perhaps this wasn't the moment for great complexity, but there are, after all, many stations of oratory between obscurity and drivel. There is a long history of Canadian leaders talking intelligently and emotionally at the same time to large crowds of citizens. After all, Papineau didn't have any trouble making himself understood with complex, sophisticated arguments, nor did LaFontaine, nor Georges-Étienne Cartier nor Laurier nor Henri Bourassa nor Ernest Lapointe nor Pierre Trudeau. Perhaps the reason those earlier leaders made the effort was that the citizenry are more likely to be persuaded if spoken to in an intelligent manner.

The three young women who spoke on October 27 interspersed between our three current politicians seemed far more conscious of what is expected when 150,000 people come together and millions are listening through television and radio. The citizens have gathered neither to worship their leaders nor to be condescended to. They are hoping to hear, from those with responsibility, something which might help them, the citizens, to understand the situation and to act. They are expecting to be addressed as if they were the source of legitimacy and not just a crowd susceptible to easy emotions. They are assuming that their leaders will enunciate clearly the sort of arguments the citizen will feel comfortable assuming and using. Instead, they were subjected to cheap patriotism.

The one interesting image of the day came from Mélanie Pressault, the first student to speak. She managed to evoke her age group in an honest way. In a manner which went well beyond economics, she spoke of the costs of breaking up a country: "As in any divorce, it is the young who suffer most."

The night before, Lucien Bouchard had already set the level for the next day with his attack on the citizens who would take part— "des cupidons un peu intéressés—self-interested cupids." He then moved on to more sinister images. "Blushing suitors who are going to tell us they love us on cheap tickets." "When Quebec is on its knees, they don't say that they love it. They say it when Quebec is getting ready to stand up." These images of wartime military oppression and of resistance movements were carried further by Jacques Parizeau who, on camera, called upon Montrealers to remain calm before the equivalent of an invasion. Surely there was a hint of irony in his words. Mr. Parizeau can usually be counted on for a tone which lies somewhere between irony and sarcasm. In any case, both Mr. Bouchard and Mr. Parizeau were talking to the citizenry as if they were fools. Or as Laurier put it—"It's easy to raise prejudices."[2] And one of the primary responsibilities of those who hold positions of power is not to do so.

Even on the subject of how many and who were there, mythology quickly took over. The Yes forces kept insisting that there had been a disappointing 35,000, even though the police confirmed the 150,000 estimate. And the crowd, they still repeat, was made up mainly of anglophones who had come in on free tickets. As for the others, Mr. Bouchard said at his press conference the same afternoon—"a very great number were paid to come."[3]

I must confess that I wasn't. I didn't even have a cheap ticket. Apparently there were only a few. It was more a PR stunt by the transportation companies than a reality. I went out onto the square with two francophone friends several hours before the event began. We were curious to see what the crowd would be like and so spent our time wandering through it as it grew. My impression was that approximately two out of three were francophones. And many of the anglophones were Montrealers. Most people seemed to arrive in couples or small groups, as if they were locals or people who had found their own way there, as I had. There were, of course, non-Quebecers. Mr. Bouchard's number for them was 15,000. It was probably close to the truth. Suppose it was 30,000. That would still represent a small percentage of the crowd.

But why would the organizers of the Yes campaign have made such a fuss about these people? They continue to speak as if they are bitter about it. Yet they have insisted that the rally backfired and cost the No side votes. They have done this so insistently that even those who were there are now confused as to whether they did the right thing.

My sense is that their presence disturbed the illusion proper to referenda—the illusion that a pure decision is being taken in a closed system where everything is accounted for. All the parameters are so clearly defined that the complexity of human society has been erased. As a result, there is a growing suspension of disbelief, at first reluctant, then willing, until people begin to believe that a mere Yes or No will provide a clear answer and solve all the problems.

The argument that Quebecers must decide their future for themselves has elements of truth in it. But the formulation of the idea, or rather the formalization of it, erased all context. It took the very vague idea of two solitudes in order to convert healthy differences into an impenetrable wall, put the idea of a thick geographical border around it, and with the snap of mythological fingers erase all surrounding realities. Everyone on the other side of the river was abruptly eliminated, even though many other people would be just as affected by the vote as Quebecers themselves.

I am not referring here to banks and corporations which, as constituted interest groups, can be counted on to defend their own interests and will usually do so in a ham-handed ominous way. Everything they say is not necessarily wrong, but democratic debate is not their strong suit. The people I am referring to, who would be just as affected by the vote as Quebecers, are those who live in other provinces. They are the *other*. They are as real as a fellow-citizen can be, and are therefore likely to have strong opinions on the subject at hand. As their lives would be profoundly changed by any Quebec decision, they are likely to want to be heard.

In that sense, it doesn't really matter whether the presence of non-Quebecers at the rally won or lost votes. At least they indicated that the barriers of the referendum system were artificial. "Just look at my face," goes the Gordon Lightfoot song, "when you tell me goodbye."[4] They did more to destroy the PQ's strategy than any of the federalist leaders. What was that strategy? Create an illusion of isolation so that the reality of the *other* will be suspended. For how long? Long enough to get the lobster into the trap.

But why did the federal leaders play along with this illusion? For the same reason that they talked to the 150,000 citizens as if they were children. Because they also had a strategy, which also was based on a suspension of reality. What was their strategy? First, prevent the intervention of any uncontrolled non-expert—i.e., the citizenry. They might do more harm than good. This is a very corporatist view, in which democracy is seen as a situation to be managed because the citizens represent a threat of disorder. Second, pretend nothing is happening and it won't. Neither of these elements flatters the intelligence of Quebecers. Nor does it flatter that of their fellow-citizens in the other nine provinces.

You could see how far we had drifted into unreality when, a few days before the imaginary gathering in Montreal, Mr. Chrétien and Mr. Bouchard addressed the nation. What did they say? Almost nothing. Mr. Chrétien fell back on solemn warnings that a Yes meant Quebecers "would no longer enjoy the rights and privileges associated with Canadian citizenship." He specified the passport and the dollar, hardly an edifying capsule portrait of a country. But it was a continuation of the insecurity argument, the argument of fear. And Mr. Bouchard threw back his own version of a fear campaign by holding up a newspaper front page on which Mr. Chrétien was called a traitor. A few months later, when Mr. Trudeau called Mr. Bouchard a traitor, the latter flew into a tizzy of mortification, saying a word like that should never be used in public discourse. He seemed to be arguing that there was an ethical difference between writing a word in a newspaper and holding up the same written word on television.

But, again, a referendum by definition quickly descends into these mechanisms of fear. Referenda have nothing to do with persuading people because they are aimed not at understanding or debate or participation, but at a definitive one-syllable word. Again Laurier is helpful, this time on persuasion:

> It is therefore perfectly normal to change the opinion of the
> elector, by reasoning with him and by all the other means of

persuasion, but never by intimidation. In fact, persuasion changes the elector's conviction, intimidation doesn't."[5]

It isn't difficult to understand how these two sides fell into intimidation, just as they did into rival claims of love. In politics, love and intimidation are the same thing. They have nothing to do with democracy or persuasion. It was the PQ's original position that they had a monopoly on love. "Nous autres," as Mr. Bouchard would say, are a single indivisible group, a real group. The federal position from the beginning of the campaign was one of intimidation—'vote Yes and you will be poor.' At no time did they manage to evoke any sense of how Canada worked or what it was or what it was built upon.

In a sense this was a logical outcome of the gradual tendency over the last decade to put the Canadian agenda solely in economic terms. This has meant increasingly that Canada is defined by the business community.

There is nothing wrong with business. But it has nothing to do with defining the public good in a democracy, let alone defining a democratic nation-state. For a start, the business community is not capable of giving democratic leadership. Its talents lie elsewhere—in the short-term, self-interested, profit-oriented world of the market-place. The tendency to see the state through business eyes has been just as strong at the provincial level and in particular in Alberta, Ontario and Quebec. There, as in Ottawa, as in the other provinces, it is a sign of advanced corporatism.

What then would you expect commercial managers to do if given the job of defending a country? They quote numbers, talk trade and threaten. They throw out large figures which suggest that some sort of paradise or disaster is just around the corner, as if they were bulls or bears playing the market and we, the citizens, were buying and selling stocks and shares. Of course, these methods are common in business management and market competition. There is nothing wrong with them in that context. Ideas, ethics, community, public debate, citizen participation—these are not of central concern in a business atmosphere.

And so Ottawa bullied and threatened the citizenry with imminent economic woes, forgetting that Canada was not a creation of economic self-interest, nor was that its primary reason for continued existence. There was therefore no reason to expect Quebecers to react any more positively to these threats than other Canadians would.

In following this logic the federal government placed themselves to the right of centre on the political spectrum, an atypical position from which to defend Canada; one which in the past has never borne long-term fruit. And in doing this, they vacated the more humanist position in the debate, leaving it for the PQ to occupy unchallenged and with little real justification.

As the Quebec government's actions in the year following the referendum have revealed, its left-of-centre position was rhetorical and not an expression of real intent. Even a small attention to detail would have shown that this would be so. For example, there were Lucien Bouchard's constant references during the referendum to the forces of the market-place making it inevitable that the rump of Canada would sign a partnership agreement.

But the federalists, in their desperate desire to occupy the corporatist and market-place terrain, were unable to deal with the illusions of the other side. They never talked about the reality of the east–west economic system and Quebec's central place in it, because they were mesmerized by NAFTA, north–south and global trade. They were so busy threatening catastrophe that they forgot to talk about Quebec's success in this national system—a system which seems to work particularly well for them. They were so caught up in low-level corporatist arguments promoting efficiency that they never dared deal with Canada's real strengths which lie in its complexity. They were and are terrified by the idea of an overlap in services involving the two levels of government and so couldn't argue that this overlap—especially in the area of culture—has been an advantage not a disadvantage. True, it may cost a few dollars more, but the citizen gains power and gets a choice. They were so busy talking about a 'strong and unified' Canada—a meaningless phrase—that they never dealt with the reality of Canadian decentralization. They never took up the question of the European model, which Lucien Bouchard evoked as the system to be aimed for after Canada had been broken up. After all, Europe already has more rigorous internal social and political rules than Canada. In many areas, to go the European route would mean greater centralization than we currently have.

They were so eager to sound lean and mean that they let the PQ get away continually with presenting Quebec's social programs as the most generous and advanced in the country; proof, they said, that Quebec was a social-democratic island which needed independence in order to protect its politics against the neo-conservatism of the anglophones. In fact Quebec, which a few years ago stood within the top half of the Canadian provinces when it came to per-capita spending on social programs, has slipped down to the seventh position, ahead only of Newfoundland, Nova Scotia and New Brunswick.[6] Even the gross slashing of Messrs. Harris and Klein does not seem to have changed that situation, because Quebec has made the same sorts of cuts. In other words, Ottawa didn't even think of standing up for higher levels of social equality, which has been the historic federal position, because they have been so eager to slip away from it.

Nor did they talk of the effects of a decision to break up the country on other Canadians, particularly Maritimers. It was as if the federal government acquiesced in the PQ's central strategic illusion: that Quebecers were interested only in themselves. Like any other group, if their élites constantly speak to them in a context of isolation as if this were normal, Quebecers will tend to judge the situation in isolation. If, as a result, some voters chose within the logic of such an atmosphere, the fault lies with the federalists, whose obligation it was to demonstrate how false the isolation argument was.

The federalist leaders didn't even deal with the most basic contradictions in the PQ's historical argument. For example, on the first page of the law preparing the *Déclaration de souveraineté*, Mr. Parizeau's government talked of the conquest of 1760. A few lines on, it declared that in 1791—only thirty-one years later—Quebec had "installed one of the first parliamentary democracies in the world."[7] Well, if Quebec was free to install one of the first parliamentary democracies in the world, it can't have been much of a conquest. In fact it sounds like the beginnings of a relatively healthy social structure.

The federalist leaders were unable to talk about that social structure because they were too busy advancing precisely those economic forces which would weaken it. They made no attempt to explain that, from the beginning, the idea of Canada had been to move beyond the narrow, unitary concept of nineteenth-century nationalism towards an equilibrium between groups and cultures. The very idea of Canada as a new idea of a nation was never evoked.

And so the Quebec voters took what they were hearing for what it was—an insult—and turned to the more attractive mythology of the other side. But that mythology was built on the brittle terrain of love; a terrain on which you are either one of the beloved or a traitor.

Again the lack of room for democratic debate in a referendum left very few options for the citizenry—No or Yes, utilitarian threats or emotional threats.

The two versions of nationalism were reduced to financial or emotional hold-ups. Your money or your love. These are "the smooth and slippery walls of fear" that Borduas wrote of. Fear of the economic unknown versus fear of standing out in a group where unity and loyalty to "nous autres" was presented as the essential quality, as if the citizen were one of Ionesco's rhinoceros.

And so when those citizens—inside and outside Quebec—who had refused the PQ myth finally lost patience with the inept, bullying representation of the country made by Ottawa, the business community and the provincial Liberals, they quite naturally turned to the only other available position. They also began invoking the tyranny of love, in this case for Canada. October 27 thus became a day of rival emotions. Nothing could be more unsatisfactory in public affairs, nothing more unforgiving than rival emotional claims on the same territory involving the same people. Before you knew it, citizens were being ridiculed for their motives by political leaders such as Mr. Bouchard. And, as in an essay by Vaclav Havel, events which were witnessed by many simply did not happen or were transformed into something else.

◄——————►

You could sense another kind of frustration in the crowd that day— a sort of frustration I had noticed throughout the campaign on all sides, in and out of Quebec. It was as if the citizenry were having increasing difficulty dealing with their élites and with the political choices presented to them.

The 150,000 could be criticized for a day of simple emotions and flag-waving, as could the crowds at most of Lucien Bouchard's rallies. But that is an easy blow to land. It is precisely the sort you would expect from the professional courtiers on both sides who believe they have the answers and do not believe the citizenry have anything concrete to contribute except their vote. And in the tradition of the self-fulfilling prophecy, they organize public education and public debate in a way which makes it difficult for individuals to find the language or the opportunity to participate. It is as if the citizens find themselves denuded of the tools of practical memory which would help them to deal in a sophisticated manner with issues of public importance.

Suddenly we are beginning to pay for the weakness in our historical and political education. We know about it. We also know that there is little political will-power to act.

Ken Osborne in Winnipeg has endlessly demonstrated how the

teaching of history has been undermined throughout the anglophone provinces.[8] Public schools still offer a good general education, except that knowledge of the society's experience with its own reality has almost disappeared. The standard justification is that there are so many other things to learn; so much training necessary in a society having difficulty in adjusting to new economic conditions. How can there be time for history when the young need jobs? Perhaps. But how can you expect citizens to do more than wave flags and shout Yes! Yes! or No! No! unless they have a thorough understanding of the circumstances and events which have produced their society? The historic patterns tell us what has worked and what failed in our own past. Situations evolve and change, but the teaching of practical memory warns us of the pitfalls indicated by our experience. It describes the pattern which got us this far.

The situation in Quebec is no better than elsewhere in Canada, although a recent government commission of historians, under Jacques Lacoursière, has recommended a strengthened historical program in schools. Their report calculates that by the end of pre-university schooling a student in Italy will have had more than nine hundred hours of history lessons, in California seven hundred, in parts of Germany and France five hundred and in Quebec less than three hundred.[9] The other Canadian provinces are somewhere around the same level.

There is an added complication over what is to be taught. It is hard, for example, to ignore independent analyses like those of the linguist Monique Nemni, which outline in detail the simple elimination in many Quebec textbooks of most references to federalism or their concentration on the negative incidents with the rest of Canada and a presentation of Quebec as if it were more or less independent.[10] Mrs. Nemni has taken a very strong position and so has been condemned by some as being politically motivated. But whatever her motivations, her arguments have to be dealt with. My own impression from reading a number of Quebec textbooks is that it is hard to understand from them that Canada actually exists and that Quebec is part of it. The resulting picture could almost be described as an intellectual coup d'état.

On the other hand, the Lacoursière Commission has made recommendations which, if followed, could radically change the situation. It calls for "an equitable place" for the roles of the aboriginal, anglophone and other communities in the teaching of Quebec and Canadian history; new courses on international history; concentration on at least one non-western civilization; and concentration on the formation of teachers on methodology, historiography and epistemology. If all of this is put in place, a very different situation could emerge. As for the textbooks used in the anglophone provinces, there is a certain naïveté in the picture offered; an optimism based on not dealing sufficiently with what has gone wrong in the past; a tendency to replace history with anecdotal material of a local, feel-good nature. It is hardly surprising if, as a result, the citizenry in both languages have difficulty forcing their leaders to maintain a reasonably intelligent level of public debate.

In either case, the students can find their way around these deformations if they wish to. There are other sources. The real problem is the lack of teaching time and the general failure of the provinces to respond to the need for a new emphasis on education. Say what they will, everywhere the class numbers are creeping up, everywhere the amount spent per capita on students is declining and governments everywhere are attempting to replace teaching with technology. It is not inaccurate for some of the provinces to blame some of their poverty on Ottawa's cut in transfer payments. But this hardly explains the lack of will-power in Ontario, Quebec, Alberta and British Columbia. Providing education is their job. They fervently defend this power. The citizenry are dependent on education to prepare themselves for their lives as both citizens and active adults. The fact is that the provinces are not holding up their end of the federalist division of powers. They are not doing what is needed, even though this is their most important area of responsibility. If a single indicator is needed to demonstrate the provinces' failure, it is the growth in private education, which is available precisely to those corporatist élites who have no particular enthusiasm for the democratic system. The problem is the same at all levels. The recteur of Laval University quit his position in 1997, worn out by defensive battle. His ironic parting shot was: "We are administering a catastrophe."[11]

Beyond the standard explanations of why history is less important than technology, there is a strong suggestion that in a corporatist, referendum society, a questioning public is not admired by the élites. If the élites believed in practical memory they would not be so devoted to the artificial deformations of referenda.

William Lyon Mackenzie put it that "the question whether a people should be Educated is the same as whether it should be happy or miserable, liberated or oppressed."[12] That was an idea shared by Jean-Baptiste Meilleur, the first Superintendent of Education named in 1842 to Lower Canada, and Egerton Ryerson, the first Chief Superintendent of Education for Upper Canada named in 1844. Their belief was that citizens were created in schools. The experience of the referendum suggests that our élites no longer believe this.

They continually tell us that we are a profoundly democratic society, as if they wished to distract us from their undermining of the base of democracy through the weakening of the public education system, particularly those parts which build practical memories.

While public debate has been seriously damaged in this situation, the quality of the citizen's judgement so far remains intact. There are phrases to describe it, such as the collective unconscious or the genius of the civilization. These try to get at the ability of the citizenry to pass on their shared experience.

Examine the referendum and the empty though insulting campaigns run by the two camps. When the time came, the population voted with remarkable precision to humiliate both sides—a draw vote, with a few more to the side of stability. Neither side, despite their claims, could take comfort in this. As Strindberg put it, the population had expressed their "hatred against the public lie," which they sensed in the way both the Yes and the No campaigns presented their case.[13] "There is a crack in everything," Leonard Cohen wrote. "That's how the light gets in."[14]

The Referendum
Syndrome

19

GOVERNMENT-ORGANIZED REFERENDA offer the citizenry the eternally obvious answer to an eternally obvious choice. The choice is so obvious that it has often escaped our notice until it is put before us, clear and neat, a perfect package to solve our problems.

Government-organized referenda are inevitably constructed upon the naïveté of the people. Since the people are not naïve, the mechanism of a referendum is designed to create an all-embracing internal logic which, by banishing the complexities of reality, to say nothing of the outside world, imposes naïveté as if it were normal.

By running roughshod over the complexities of society, the referendum removes language as the working mechanism of democracy. The complexities of argument which have evolved to deal with the complexities of our reality are among the most important characteristics of the democratic process. Public language is intended to play a double role: to reflect reality and thus action; and to prevent the withering eye of ideological clarity from sweeping away the careful, even contradictory relationships upon which a healthy society is built.

Representative democracy in particular has evolved from a desire not to put society on a goal-oriented track. The very idea of representation tells us that our civilization is the product of larger populations living together, and inevitably they live together in the midst of contradictions and compromises. The representative system is not designed to prevent action, but to minimize the chances of those with power cutting a damaging swath of clarifying action through the non-rational patterns which citizens have arranged themselves in.

This is why the history of the referendum over the last two centuries has almost always fallen into two streams. The first has used the mechanism to destroy representative democracy, usually replacing it with Heroic false populism. The second has used the referendum as a way to structure the citizenry into doing what they would never do in the more careful, balanced context of representative democracy. There is increasingly a relationship between these two streams. For example, contemporary leaders often now try to treat general elections as if they were referenda. The Harris government in Ontario is a perfect example of this. Their approach could be summarized as, 'if you give us power, you give us the legitimacy to do whatever we want for four years.'

In a referendum society, language and argument as the central tools of democracy are swept away. They are replaced by a goal-oriented process which reduces the citizen's real participation to passive acquiescence or refusal; a participation which is expressed through one of two single-syllable words.

When a society is caught up in a referendum syndrome, the very suggestion that complexity is the basis of civilization is a disloyal act. And yet, if we play along with the illusion of the obvious answer to the obvious question, the result will require more illusion, whatever the vote.

For example, had Quebec voted Yes in October 1995, the result would not have been independence or separation or sovereignty. It would have been years of bickering and argument over how to take the country apart. By voting to leave, Quebec would have destroyed the credibility of the anglophone moderates across the country. The effect would probably have been to catapult hard-liners to the fore. Those who listened closely to what Mr. Manning was saying during the last general election will have some idea of the sort of unpleasant, brittle attitude which would have dominated. Many reasonable francophones would respond, 'But surely the rest of Canada would respect our decision.' That is the difficulty with referenda. They encourage all of us to consider our situation in isolation, seeing things only from the point of view of our own logic. The moderate anglophone voices have identified themselves since the 1840s with the anglophone–francophone pact. Moderation for anglophones means working closely together with francophones in the construction of a federal, decentralized, bicultural state. For most of the last 150 years, these moderates have held power. Some have been extraordinary, some average, some awful. But they have been moderates. A vote in Quebec which rejects that pact, whatever the reasons given, would amount to the loss of legitimacy for that long tradition of moderation. The opinions of the moderates would suddenly be worth very little. What would this actually mean? I have no idea, since I would be among the moderates who had been wrong and would therefore, for what it's worth, have been discredited. But my guess is that the endless and unpleasant negotiations would have been a struggle between two forms of extremism with no lack of opportunities for the raising of prejudice on both sides.

On the other hand, by voting No, Quebec has not given itself stability or prosperity. So long as the option of breaking up the country remains a real possibility in the identifiable future—that is, so long as it remains the policy of one of the two leading parties—the social tension will remain, as will the mesmerizing distraction from more vital and creative matters, to say nothing of the bleeding away of segments of the population both anglophone and francophone. In addition to this, the economy will continue to decline, as it has since 1976. In other words, in spite of a raft of remarkable social and redistribution policies put in place by Liberal and PQ governments over the last two decades, in spite of a strong cultural community, an innovative business sector and a population capable of dealing with new economic challenges, the basis of the economy continues to stagnate, even shrink. And it will continue to do so. The lingering presence of the 'eternally obvious choice' remains as a threat of division, bitterness and bickering whichever way the question goes in the future.

All that this tells us is that referenda are not designed to deal with reality. They are designed to serve power. They are not, as Mr. Parizeau said in the legislature, "the most fundamental expression of democracy."[1] Referenda, and referenda-style government of the sort we are now seeing in Ontario, have very little to do with democracy. After all, democracy is not primarily about voting. That is only an end-product of the system. What matters is full participation. Referenda, by replacing the complexity of reality with naïve, crystal clear either-or scenarios, eliminate the possibility of active participation. The voter is converted into a victim, whichever side she chooses.

In the aftermath of the 1995 referendum there was a great deal of satisfaction over the high turn-out. This was said to be a sign of the democratic commitment of the people, of their democratic nature. Of course most Quebecers are devoted to democracy, as are most other Canadians. Of course they voted. What else would you expect them to do? But what is interesting is not the accountants' view of democracy. Rather it is the skill with which the citizenry took hold of a process designed to enforce clarity and voted in such a way as to create confusion.

They managed to outsmart the referenda mechanism by reasserting their complexity. Ever since, the strategists and consultants— non-partisan and partisan on both sides—have been searching for tactical explanations of this referendum's failure to produce a clear answer. But what is interesting in a representative democracy is how the careful placing of votes by individuals manages to deliver a very specific message from the whole. In that sense the pattern of the votes tells you what the society wants to say.

The narrow channelling process of a referendum is designed to prevent the citizens sending a specific message of their own expression. Instead they are to respond to the dictum sent to them by the authorities. In this context, the refusal to acquiesce is the most important sign of a healthy democracy.

A referendum is little more than a "rumour of choice."[2] The idea behind the mechanism, ever since its first modern manifestations two centuries ago under Napoleon, has been to replace democracy with the sensation of democracy. That is: to replace the slow, complex, eternally unclear continuity of democracy, and all the awkwardness of citizen participation, with something clear and fast which allows those in power to impose their agenda. Through an apparently simple question with a one-syllable answer, those who ask can get a blank cheque from the citizenry; that is, if they choose their moment well and come up with a winning question or "the winning formula," as Mr. Bouchard put it.

But the democratic system, when it is working, involves a group of citizens—usually a political party—coming up with a policy and/or policies, which are then presented to the other citizens—the public. In order to present them, they need an accurate description of what they are. They hope that this language will be attractive, but since they believe in the policies, they are convinced that the most attractive formula will be the one which most clearly expresses their beliefs.

In a referendum society the process is the exact opposite. A group of citizens—usually a political party—works out its policy, but does not believe that the citizenry can be counted on to understand or embrace it. As I have said, the referendum is a product of the Napoleonic–corporatist tradition. What is required, therefore, is not language which accurately describes the policy, but language which is attractive to the public. If the public gives an affirmative vote to this formula, those in power will interpret the result as a blank cheque to do what they have always intended to do, but never clearly explained. What we are dealing with, therefore, is not language. Language is a means of communication and the referenda process is intended to prevent communication. "A winning formula" is the opposite of language. You could call it rhetoric or propaganda.

Mr. Harris found his winning formula with "the Common Sense Revolution," and once in power acted in a manner unrelated to common sense. That is, he applied an integrated ideological strategy, as if the citizens' acceptance of his vague formula provided him with the sort of blank cheque which is not supposed to exist in a representative democracy.

Preston Manning and the Reform party have demonstrated another aspect of this nullification of language through their use of the term 'reform.' This is a word which carries with it all the baggage of the humanist reforming tradition, from LaFontaine and Baldwin on. It is a term which describes the left of centre in Canadian history. It refers to a quest for increased social justice. The Reform party have engaged in what I called, in *Voltaire's Bastards*, the dictatorship of vocabulary. They have kidnapped a term, unrelated to their own policies, but which evokes a heavy and positive history running through the subconscious and the consciousness of every citizen. Not only have they tried to appropriate that positive force but, by doing it for an unrelated cause, they have made nonsense of language.

Mr. Bouchard had no trouble using the word "separatism" when in Washington in 1995. Yet no one may use it in Canada without being attacked by the PQ as being anti-Quebec. The point is that this political movement is in constant search of a winning vocabulary. The party insists that separation/independence/sovereignty is a natural inevitability. All that is lacking, apparently, is an appropriate vocabulary. Not one which describes anything clearly, but rather one which is least likely to frighten people. As each new formula is launched, the preceding one is treated as if it were banned from respectable discourse. To use it is to be discredited as a reasonable person. This use of language is thus not language, because it is related not to communicating an intent, but to rhetorical manipulation. To put it another way, the move from separatist to indépendantist to sovereigntist is the ultimate in political correctness.

This is because there is a particular state of suspended reality inside the referendum logic. There the debate is based not on language but on an illusion created by the careful choice of the right word or words. These are used as religious tokens. The situation resembles mediaeval scholastic squabbling over precisely which terms must be used in order for us to be in accordance with the wishes of our deities.

The very idea of searching for a winning question tells us every-thing about the purpose of a referendum. It is not designed to find out what the citizenry wants or even thinks, but to get them to approve a winning phrase so that those who propose it can do what they want.

Quebecers should not feel that they are alone in this situation. As the rational élites have strengthened over the last 150 years, so has false populism. These two elements were at the core of Napoleon's alternative to democracy. By the second half of the nineteenth cen-tury, this marriage of technocracy and Heroic leadership—with its constant direct relationship between power and the citizenry—had become the face of modern corporatism. All along, the referendum was used like a lightning bolt in order to fuse the populace to the leader, thus providing him not with the legitimacy of representa-tive democracy but with a blank cheque of power. The referendum became the modern instrument of that mystical, anti-democratic legitimacy, which was inherited from the days of absolute religions and monarchs.

With a growth in high levels of public education we might have expected this sort of false direct democracy to wither away. But new means of communication arrived in time to buttress the illusions of direct democracy. It was as if, in Harold Innis's terms, time were being destroyed and so "it became increasingly difficult to achieve continuity or to work for a consideration of the future."[3] With the arrival of mass communications, the complex, slow process of democracy was weakened by the authoritarian populism of corpo-ratist politics. Put another way, the referendum mechanism allows those in power to erase the factors of practical memory, including history. The lessons of experience and the sign-posts of the public interest are rendered irrelevant by the structured excitement of wiping the slate clean by choosing an all-inclusive solution.

As we have seen most recently in Ontario and Quebec, the resulting simplification of reality does not smooth the way, but instead divides the population, creating and leaving bitterness and unresolvable emotions. These emotions are all the more destructive because a referendum society encourages the citizen to chant for one side or the other but reduces him to a passive and, if possible, naïve role. In Anne Hébert's words—

> I hold my heart on my fist
> Like a blind falcon.[4]

And if that state of unnatural naïveté can be enforced, well then, society will be reduced to opposing groups. Napoleon discovered that it was Heroic populism attached to the use of referenda that would permit him to capture the abandoned forces of religious morality. The referendum permitted the framing of public questions in the context of good and evil, right versus wrong, us against them. In this context the leader became the people. They were one and the same, fused together. To criticize the leader was to criticize the people. To attack him was to do violence to the people. Laurier already understood the dangers of these tendencies at the time of the Métis crisis. "Shall we ever succeed if the bond of union is to be revenge, if we are to rake up the old scores and launch them at the heads of one another?"[5]

In other words, to seek unnatural clarity was to ensure an unnatural division of society. That's why Jacques Parizeau fell so easily, in Marc Angenot's words, into "demonizing his loss" by blaming it on specific groups.[6] That's why, when Mike Harris sees people opposing him, he immediately eliminates the possibility that they could be responsible citizens. They are interest groups or racial groups, not citizens.

In this context language loses its purpose as a means of commu-

nication. With government by referendum we are in the domain of
ideology and religion. Language is reduced to incantation. And
phrases which should have a devastating effect seem to float by
without effect. Mr. Parizeau's comment, before a dozen ambas-
sadors, that if Quebecers voted Yes they would be "lobsters in boiling water," should have destroyed his career. When our perception
of reality is functioning, nothing is more damaging to a politician
than the demonstration that he holds the citizen in contempt. Pro
forma denials were issued, which no one believed and no one was
expected to believe. Journalists made ironic or sarcastic comments,
depending on their politics, then turned to other matters. And the
words floated by, weightless.

A referendum is a spectacle unrelated to democracy. If the show
is good, democracy is reduced to the excitement of the Big Top, just
as A.M. Klein described it in the 1930s:

> Clients of Barnum, yours no even break!
> The maestroes have you, have you on the hip!
> They gloat, they hold you ready for the take:
> And you, O rube, fall smacko for the gyp.[7]

Democracy has little to do with clarity and decisive answers. It has
more to do with pursuing the complex road of the public interest.
And that has more to do with the search for not ideal but honest and
sensible choices. These are, of necessity, partial choices with little of
the excitement of an all-inclusive resolution. Since referenda treat
the populace as if they were a single indivisible body, much of the
language used resembles that of individuals caught up in romantic
dilemmas. The Yes versus No offers resolution; the drama, the emotion of final resolution. But even in our private lives we know there
is rarely resolution, and when there is it rarely is satisfactory. Here is
Alice Munro's summary of this recurrent problem. I have replaced
the name of her character with an X.

I wished that I could get my feelings about X to come together into a serviceable and dependable feeling. I have even tried writing two lists, one of things I liked about him, one of things I disliked . . . as if I hoped to prove something, to come to a conclusion one way or the other. But I gave it up when I saw that all it proved was what I already knew—that I had violent contradictions.[8]

For most of this century there has been an alternate school of referenda politics. It began around 1914 in the West, with the farmers' reform movements and the suffragette movement. They felt politics was dominated by the banks and industry. They wanted citizen-initiated referenda in order to force their governments to listen to them. This was to be a form of direct democracy; democracy from the bottom up.

At that time provincial populations were small enough—particularly in the West—that you could almost imagine the application of practical, functioning, direct democracy in the Athenian mode.

That tradition is still with us, but the population sizes have changed. Suddenly the referendum initiated from outside government has come to resemble that of the inside. It is a brittle, absolute tool in anyone's hands.

In California, where the greatest use has been made of it, anti-tax movements have managed more or less to bankrupt the state by putting severe limits on the government's ability to raise money. Needless to say, those on the outside best able to mount and run an anti-tax campaign are those most liable to pay taxes in a normal state of affairs.

The effect of these votes has been to divide the society. The state is deeply in debt, food banks are running out of money, there are forty thousand homeless in Los Angeles alone. In other words, the clarity imposed by these referenda has served narrow interests rather than the public interest.

The most recent recuperation of the 'populist' referendum has come in Alberta, where Mr. Klein has called for a province-wide vote to cap income and corporate taxes. From then on taxes could only be raised by further referenda. If this happens, a neo-conservative agenda will have effectively captured the rhetoric of direct democracy for its own purposes. In reality, Mr. Klein is trying to concentrate the voters' attention on taxes without them considering the effect on services. As in California, it is an attempt to ignore the public good in favour of self-interest, as if self-interest were a manifestation of populism.

This is why the strength of representative democracy is its ability to slow down those in power who wish to govern by blank cheque, but also those not in power who wish to yank the state about on the sole basis of their self-interest. This is why the issue-driven referendum coming from outside of power ends up resembling that of the power holders. They are both about acting, in Jacques Parizeau's words, "by and for ourselves."[9] The idea of the public interest is that we can act for what lies beyond ourselves.

This brings me back to the central referendum conundrum: it is precisely the things referenda say they can do that they cannot do. They cannot translate into reality the clarity promised by the choice. Nor do they produce the solidarity among citizens which is the intended result. The choice usually proves to be an illusion and the results either way are divisive.

In part this is because referendum politics are usually imposed on top of the politics of representative democracy, which is centred on ideas of balance, equilibrium and progress through continuity. Imposing a referendum is dependent on the ability of those in power to claim that continuity has already been broken or progress blocked. Two centuries of false populism have been based on rhetoric which blames the need for a referendum on a theoretical schism with the past, a schism which has been caused by the other side. Since continuity has already been lost, the argument goes, only a clear choice which wipes the slate clean can re-establish normalcy.

The format of this argument is so standardized that you can trace it with ease through the speeches of the first two Napoleons and the dictators of the twentieth century to the new generation of false populists or corporatists, who can be found in power in several Canadian provinces and American states.

It is their concept of the urgent need for a new beginning which Mr. Harris used to justify his omnibus bill. In a few weeks, under the rules designed for single-issue legislation, he was able to redesign much of the underpinnings of a social contract put in place through decades of debate.

He simply ignored the unwritten but nevertheless clearly understood rules of representative democracy, according to which an election is only a general and preliminary indication of the citizens' wishes.

After all, the thirty-day wide-ranging debate of an election campaign is not a decision-making process. It provides an indication of the direction to be taken, nothing more. People vote for different parties and candidates for many reasons. The result is a decantation of these factors.

For example, Mr. Harris was elected, in good part justifiably, by regions which felt ignored—the north and the outer suburbs of Toronto. Their vote seemed to indicate their desire to be included in the debate. The responsibility of the government after the election was therefore to advance their proposals one by one, so that a thorough debate could take place within the legislature and within society.

But as always with referenda-style government, an atmosphere of crisis was purposely created, of now or never, of the government on the edge of bankruptcy. In other words, the actions they proposed were put forward in a manner reminiscent of wartime. The rhetoric used to sell them was that of a military crisis; a state of emergency which justifies sweeping away normal democratic guarantees. The second wave of the government's changes so disturbed the citizenry that those in the Toronto area invented an awkward and imperfect form of plebiscite, simply to get the government's attention. This was not a referendum and had none of the characteristics of a problem-solving mechanism. It was merely an angry shout at the government to slow down and listen to the complex messages the citizens were trying to send them.

The result of these two waves of referenda-style change has been a growing level of confusion and division in the population. The more the Chamber of Commerce announces that it is pleased, the more we sense that there is no longer a shared social contract. The government may find a way to exploit this by playing further on the atmosphere of crisis and so continue down their path. But that isn't the point. Ontario has not been so divided in an apparently unresolvable manner since the disordered and tumultuous days of the 1930s.

The situation in Quebec bears all the same characteristics of referenda politics. Mr. Bouchard spoke before the 1995 vote of ". . . Quebec solidarity. And it isn't just a word. It includes all the political parties. Because, with a wave of the magic wand of a Yes, all Quebecers will be in the same camp. There will no longer be two camps. There will be the camp of all Quebecers together." But the result of such a vote has precisely the opposite effect. It leaves the scars of exclusion on the losers. One of the purposes of representational democracy is to avoid the false clarity which produces those scars.

In that same speech he spoke of voting Yes to get "a government which can take decisions. . . ."[10] By this, he repeatedly said during the campaign, was meant decisions to go in a different, more egalitarian direction than that taken by the rest of Canada. But he was no sooner premier than he called a summit of interest groups—a perfectly corporatist view of society—in order to propose policies which would cause Quebec to conform with its neighbours. Suddenly he was insisting on the need to act in the same manner as the communities with which Quebec was integrated.[11]

In fact, he went further than most of them by agreeing to a law which would limit the government's right to indebt itself. This law—which is sought everywhere by neo-conservatives—is the key to undermining the idea of the public interest. If enacted, it means that businesses and individuals may indebt themselves as they see fit, but governments, the only mechanism of power available to the citizenry, may not. To pass such a law is to shift the balance of power from the citizens to those who are able to take advantage of investment capital; that is, the large joint-stock corporations. In other words, while the referendum campaign was fought under the banner of increased democratic solidarity, the reality was a government devoted to a corporatist economic agenda.

In an atmosphere where words and reality are disassociated by the focus of the referendum mechanism, it isn't surprising that the rhetoric bears little relationship to the reality of what will be done. Thus the Yes side's strategy during the 1995 campaign was to suggest there would be gradual change, negotiations and partnerships. However, the actual legal texts empowering the government in the case of a Yes vote allowed for massive unnegotiable political change. And Mr. Parizeau was focused on the texts, not the rhetoric.

In fairness, he never hid his hand. "The lobsters in boiling water" was a clarification of intent from the very first days. And his speeches throughout the campaign were clear, and therefore in contradiction with those of his allies. Three days before the vote of October 30, 1995, he cut off all contact with Messrs. Bouchard and Dumont, cancelling all meetings, not returning calls.[12] He was preparing to act in an Heroic manner with the blank cheque of a majority Yes vote. This was reported in detail a year later. In February 1996, the contents of the speech Mr. Parizeau had taped the day of the vote was revealed. It was to be broadcast after the victory. Seven leading journalists had been allowed to see it on October 30. And yet it wasn't until May 1997 that the penny seemed to drop with the publication of Mr. Parizeau's memoirs. You knew the penny had dropped because Mr. Bouchard expressed his "stupéfaction."

I repeat this well-known sequence of events merely to illustrate the extent to which, when we are caught up in a referendum syndrome, reality is suspended. Language becomes illusion rather than a means of communication. And this state of illusion or delusion is so strong that it persists long after the searing event. We are still its prisoners. Are we to believe, for example, that only Mr. Parizeau knew how he would act the day after the vote? That Bernard Landry didn't understand? Given the complexity of government decision-making and his central role, surely that isn't possible. That Lucien Bouchard hadn't grasped it? In any case, it doesn't seem to matter, except at the unspoken level where the citizenry must digest these events. Meanwhile the pro forma denials are issued and the press focus on Mr. Parizeau without examining the role of those still in power. And the words float by, weightless.

Not only do referenda emasculate language as part of their anti-democratic process, they install an atmosphere of rigorous anti-intellectualism.

How else are we to describe the eradication of serious public communication in Ontario and Quebec? This atmosphere of false populism is not unlike that of the late-nineteenth century when lower-middle-class Protestants and Catholics became the emotional shock troops of the élites, even though by doing so they undermined their own place in the public interest. Today's situation is one which D'Alton McCarthy or, later, Maurice Duplessis would have had no trouble understanding.

The premier of Ontario in particular celebrates ignorance. When asked during Reading Week in 1997 what books he had read recently, he eventually dug up *Mr. Silly*, something read out loud to his small child. This is in the tradition of Duplessis standing up with pride in 1943 against universal education. False populism is built on the exploitation of self-loathing. But the active use of referenda make it doubly difficult to focus on this demeaning of the citizen's self-pride.

For example, one of the principal causes being celebrated and defended during the 1995 referendum was supposed to be Quebec's francophone culture. Yet it was mentioned only once in the official speeches, and then in passing as "les industries culturelles."[13] During the actual campaign, it disappeared from the arguments of the political leaders. Perhaps Mr. Bouchard had nothing to say. His memoirs contain dozens of enthusiastic references to European writers and culture. I could find only one specific reference to a Quebec writer, and that was brief and in passing.[14] As for Daniel Johnson, he was so caught up in his utilitarian arguments that the reality of culture didn't seem to occur to him, even to point out that the PQ in power had done little for creativity. The Quebec Arts Council had, in fact, been a recent Liberal creation of Lisa Frulla, perhaps the best cultural minister since Georges-Émile Lapalme. Jean Chrétien, who does, it seems, read Canadian literature, is always careful to hide the fact in public. And he didn't seize the opportunity of a campaign theoretically centred on the defence of francophone culture to talk about the central arm's-length federal role in supporting culture over the last half-century. He avoided the importance of the federal cultural institutions through which francophones have said what they were unable to say through equivalent provincial structures. This was because nationalist governments such as Duplessis's made this impossible or because PQ governments did not create the necessary institutions or indeed did not sufficiently fund those which did exist.

What I am describing here is not simply the anti-intellectualism of false populists. There is also a close relationship between referenda and ideology. What frightens ideologues about culture is that it is uncontrollable. A politician may quite naturally think of culture as something which should be in the service of the public image; therefore as something that is controllable. A more intelligent politician will realize that this isn't so. But an ideologue cannot imagine culture in any other way.

Referenda, false populism, ideology are all about control. Culture is about the exact opposite and so it frightens them. The person least likely to defend the independence and health of creativity is a rationalist who has fallen into ideology. And a referenda society is the least likely to believe that culture is a central part of our reality and must flourish beyond political control.

But then culture is tied to memory—practical, hard-edged memory which permits us to imagine the future. And referenda are dependent for their success on society losing hold of that practical memory.

One of the most curious lapses has been our inability to judge each referendum which comes upon us in the light of those which have come before. After all, the vote of 1942 over conscription divided society. It was one of the few occasions when Mackenzie King's instincts led him onto dangerous ground rather than away from it. The two referenda in 1948 in Newfoundland over Confederation have left scars in society, still identifiable long after the result has been absorbed. The vote of 1980 created bitterness and division which has never gone away. That of Charlottetown in 1992 left more a sense of unease and discomfort. Perhaps distaste is the right word.

We don't yet know how deep are the wounds of 1995—the wounds between different groups of Quebec francophones, between francophones and anglophones, Natives and francophones within the province, between those francophones and the million and a half who live outside the province, between francophone Quebecers and anglophones in the rest of the country. These wounds are not the product of the outcome. Had it gone the other way they would have still been there, probably even more so after the bruising experience which would have followed and would still be going on. The wounds are created by the referendum process, which, in a simulation of democracy, attempts to impose an absolute decision when the normal patterns of the society do not suggest that such blinding clarity is what the citizens are after. The structure of a referendum resembles not so much the complexities of a democratic exercise as the divisions of a set-piece military battle—two armies, a battlefield to be won, widespread psychic and physical damage on all sides which goes well beyond the victims and the formally identified losers.

He "felt dizzy," Alice Munro wrote of a character, "and sick with the force of things coming back to life, the chaos and emotion. It was as painful as fiery blood pushing into frozen parts of your body . . . he had to keep himself from thinking, too suddenly, about what had just missed happening."[15]

We may not even know what damage has been done to the citizens this last time before the next obvious choice with its eternally obvious answer is upon us, creating a whole new wave of division and bitterness in the name of solidarity and in aid, it goes without saying, of a sunny future.

A Natural and
Inevitable Event

20

AND YET COUNTRIES BREAK UP. THIS is natural. There are
countless examples. Groups which define themselves as a people,
nation or race become independent. It has happened so many times.
It is inevitable, as well as natural. The separation, independence,
sovereignty of Quebec is therefore natural and inevitable.

There are those in British Columbia and Alberta who use variants
on this argument to describe their own positions. However, the
immediate subject is Quebec.

This theme of natural inevitability is repeated on a daily basis by
those who seek to break up Canada. Premier Parizeau's speech
introducing the referendum question to the Quebec legislature
began with a description of "the most natural decision . . . a people
could take."[1] The formulae and logic in each of Lucien Bouchard's
referendum speeches were aimed at demonstrating the natural
inevitability of breaking up Canada and of the rest of Canada
accepting and cooperating in this kill with a well-placed blade. It
was natural, he argued, to break up a country by a vote, specifically
by a 50 per cent majority; inevitable that every group (linguistic?
regional? racial?) should and would have its own country; inevitable
that the rest of Canada would negotiate what the Quebec government wanted.

In politics—local, national or international—it is difficult to
think of anything which is natural or inevitable. The death of individuals is inevitable, usually inside one hundred years. That is a
reasonably predictable event. You can also state that individuals get
hungry on a regular basis and so on. Countries, however, do not
die for predictable or inevitable reasons.

They do come to an end, but rarely when and why people think.

If there is any identifiable rule in the politics of national longevity, it has to do with survival, not death. The longer a country lasts, the more likely it is that this is because some workable formula has been found. The longer it lasts, the longer it will continue to last.

Canada is now one of the oldest countries in the world, if you take into consideration stable borders and government attached to a peaceful and—more unusual—a democratic form. It has one of the world's oldest constitutions. It has a survival record and yet also has a talent for avoiding the levels of violence which seem to be needed to permit most countries to survive.

What about natural and inevitable ends? The Roman Empire was on its way to oblivion in AD 117 when the rise of Hadrian put it back on track for more than three hundred years. The same could be said of the Vatican early in the Reformation. Indeed death-bed regenerations are quite common. An organism loses its way, slips close to disaster, then finds the path again.

A country can lose its way in several manners. The most common is a decline in the quality, drive, commitment and conscious understanding of its élite. I am referring to the large panoply of those with responsibilities, from ministers to intellectuals and businessmen. Canada's crisis today is closely related to that problem. And the failure of the élite is equally distributed across both the country and the language communities.

This situation is neither natural nor inevitable, except in the most abstract use of those terms.

The standard way of establishing natural inevitability in public affairs is through ideology. The other way—not unrelated—is through example. This involves the use of theoretical parallels in the social science manner—that is, the false science of circumstantial evidence.

In order to explain the natural and inevitable break-up of Canada, a growing list of historical and contemporary examples is brought forward. In some way they are intended to represent models of destruction. They range from the United States, Slovakia and Catalonia to Scandinavia and Scotland. The Basques, Belgians, Corsicans, Irish and various bits of the ex–Soviet Union are rarely mentioned. Yugoslavia is sometimes brought up by those against a break-up.

But why invoke the American revolution? The simple explanation would be a continuing obsession with the United States among harder-line nationalists—an historical tradition going back to Papineau's annexation proposals.

In the enabling document that Premier Parizeau tabled in the National Assembly before the referendum, he said that Quebec's Declaration of Sovereignty would resemble the American Declaration of Independence.[2]

What would be the resemblance? The American Declaration accused the British of: the repeated dissolution of legislatures; the refusal to hold elections; maintaining standby armies without civil consent; the denial of trial by jury; imposing taxes without consent; and actual sustained violence against the people.

The principal Quebec government complaint? "To settle definitively the constitutional problem that has been confronting Quebec for several generations." To put it gently, these are not parallels or equivalents.

But take the theoretical U.S. parallel a step further. There were three central desires lurking behind the nobler language of the American text. First, there was the strong desire to solidify the legal status of slavery at a time when parliamentary opposition to it was growing in London. Second, there was a festering desire to break the barriers protecting Indian lands. London was constantly attempting to hold back the ambitious colonial population and the law-breaking frontier land speculators, George Washington among them. And third, one of the principal demands of the American colonialists was the revocation of the Quebec Act of 1774, which was considered one of Britain's "Intolerable Acts." Why?

In part because of its territorial implications. But just as important was the anger of the urban American merchant class over the granting of citizen and religious rights to the French-Canadian Catholics. The standard British religious tests would have eliminated the francophones from public life and, effectively, from the professions, leaving the territory open for recuperation by Bostonians and others. Suddenly, with the Quebec Act, francophones were back in the equation. Somehow the narrow nationalist's worship of America always forgets this detail, as it does the fundamental difference between their often justified complaints and the list of major items which brought on the revolt of 1776.

The final and the most curious of the anomalies is the PQ's desire to draw parallels with a Declaration, a constitution, a country which, from its beginning, has been determined to prevent any separation of pieces of its territory. The very idea of any breaking-away provoked a searing civil war, one of the most bloody modern wars. The American Supreme Court has consistently interpreted the original documents to represent the inviolability of territory and the supremacy of the central government. There have been some important moves towards state rights, particularly over the last two decades, as Washington has handed over programs to the lower level of government. But these have been driven by the desire of the ideological right wing to strangle social programs. By passing responsibilities to levels of government less able or willing to finance them, more open to corporatist influence and suffering from varying levels of poverty or prosperity, the neo-conservatives in Washington have hoped to bury the social progress of the previous half-century without ever having to carry such a program before the country as a whole.

Looking over the anomalies between the American Declaration and the projected Quebec declaration, the central point which sticks out is that Washington will use force to maintain the integrity of American territory. This is not a very original principle. It is an assumption present in the quasi-totality of countries. Britain and

France built themselves by force and continue to defend their internal borders by the active use of the police, the constitution or law, the courts and, if necessary, the army.

But then perhaps none of the above points were among those in the imagination of Premier Parizeau and his allies when he invoked the American example.

◄────────►

The most popular recent parallel has been drawn with Slovakia, which broke away from Czechoslovakia on January 1, 1993. This 'velvet divorce' has provoked positive television documentaries, magazine analyses and persistent references. The deputy premier of Quebec, Bernard Landry, has called on Canada to accept a process similar to that which ended Czechoslovakia. "What Canadians and Quebecers must do is to achieve an improved Czechoslovakian model."[3]

Again, it isn't terribly clear what was found to be so admirable about the process or the result. The velvet revolution was the product of back-room agreements between neo-conservative politicians in Prague and extreme-nationalist politicians in Bratislava. They were acting against the wishes of the Czech and Slovak populations. The two leaders prevented a democratic consultation which they would almost certainly have lost. The results for Slovakia (which plays the role of Quebec in these recurring projections) have been on balance unfortunate.

The scene is dominated by Prime Minister Meciar, a demagogue who plays on the negative emotions of nationalism with great skill. The result has been a steady and serious brain drain towards the Czech Republic and the rest of Europe from all sectors of society, particularly the cultural.

What are they fleeing? Prime Minister Meciar's tactics have consisted in identifying successive enemies. The Czechs were followed by the Hungarian minority. Now the enemy is freedom of speech itself. The press, he insists, are the voice of foreign enemies. Television programs which criticize the government are cancelled through the self-censorship of management or through behind-the-scenes orders or threats. Incidents in which the police interfere with those citizens who act as if they are in a free country are increasingly common. All of this is laid out in detail in the annual human-rights reports of the United Nations, the United States, the EEC and various independent bodies. Kidnappings, beatings, threats. It would seem that so long as the government believes there is even a small chance of entry into the EEC, these sorts of incidents will not be taken the next step to straight violence.

At the same time, Meciar has pushed the economy and social structures far to the right with a radical privatization program. This has produced some growth, but not enough to make up for the sharp drop of approximately 30 per cent in living standards since independence. Worse still, the atmosphere surrounding Slovakia has discouraged foreign investors. Only a tiny percentage of the money entering the region has gone their way (2.1 per cent). This both nullifies the positive effects of moderate growth and makes it impossible to fund the infrastructure investment necessary to maintain that growth.

Nor has Meciar succeeded in any sort of velvet transition to partnerships with countries to the west. His first promise, a partnership with the Czechs, fell apart within a year. With that went such things as a shared currency and any close trade agreement. His second target—entry into the European Community—seems increasingly unlikely. The Europeans are keeping their distance precisely because of Slovakia's flawed record on human rights, freedom of speech and minority rights. As a result he has had to turn, increasingly, towards Russia. This is a relationship in which Slovakia can only play the role of the weak dependant in search of help.

Although Slovakia's economic neo-conservatism has produced some growth, this is based in large part on low production costs, which are in turn the result of low standards of living and wages.

It is a classic example of a reasonably high-technology, low-wage economy.

The initial breaking-apart was rapid because of the undemocratic process. Minorities on either side of the border had neither the time nor the opportunity to voice any concerns. However, the immediate result has been to exacerbate the relations with these minorities.

It is as if the closer a country comes to aligning itself on a clear ethnic base, the more minorities become agitated. In Slovakia there are 560,000 Hungarians and relations are now so bad that there is a real threat they may unilaterally declare territorial autonomy wherever they form a majority. This growing hysteria has awakened both genuinely sympathetic and malevolent forces in Hungary proper.

There is nothing unusual in this. An ethnic focus by the majority typically unleashes ethnic nerves on all sides. The situation is less threatening but equally awkward in the Czech Republic. The greatest personal wound Vaclav Havel has so far suffered in public life came from his inability in 1993 to prevent the nationalists and neo-conservatives from dividing the two peoples. It was a profound defeat for his ethical and humanist beliefs.

"Alone at last!" one of the most interesting Czech leaders wrote ironically not long after the break-up. There is a Slovak minority, but they seem to be integrating with the Czechs as fast as possible, as if they want nothing to do with their homeland. The only remaining large distinctive minority is the Roma (that is, the Gypsy) and somehow the very Czechness of the little republic has turned the two hundred thousand Roma into a bleeding sore for both the Czechs and themselves.

In fact, whatever their nationalist sentiments, most Czechs and Slovaks seem to feel lessened or cheapened by their inability to keep the seventy-year-old union together. When you are there you find that the division is the last thing the people want to talk about. Bitterness, a sense of isolation and failure are the predominant emotions lurking just beneath the surface. The Czechs are moving towards integration with the west and entry into the European Community. But they are doing so with a dirty taste in their mouths. The Slovaks are increasingly cut off from the west, slipping under Russian dominance, frightened to use the freedom of speech theoretically available to them and caught in an economic trap worse than that which preceded the departure of the Communist party. Their parliament has adopted an anti-subversion bill which allows them to charge people for demonstrating against the government.

In 1997, five years after the split, the two republics are still wrangling over finances. The Czech Republic won't return forty-five tonnes of gold which belongs to Slovakia until Slovakia pays its outstanding debt of $1.2 billion. In March of 1997 the Slovakian government recalled their ambassador from Prague for a month. President Havel publicly said Meciar was mentally unstable and paranoid.

It is particularly strange that the PQ should be so fond of this example. After all, they insist that Quebec would be automatically admitted to NAFTA and other bodies. But the Czech–Slovak story is one which would tend to suggest the opposite. For myself, I don't know what would happen in our case. I'm just pointing out how curious the example is.

As for the celebration of the Czech Republic's success, if it seems tinged by sadness—for those who know how to look beyond Prague's status as a tourist haven—it is explained by their sense of having failed as a bicultural nation.

Catalonia is a more recent and agreeable example. The visit by the Catalonian head of government, Jordi Pujol, to Quebec in July 1996 was an opportunity to explore parallels.

The result instead was the clarification of two essential differences. One historic and the other political. The history of Catalonia is not that of a region which had had full control over education and many other powers for the last 150 years. And Catalonian has not been an official language in Spain. Rather, the language was forbidden for 250 years. Catalonians, including Mr. Pujol, served lengthy prison terms for their nationalism. In the civil war of the 1930s, Catalonia was one of Franco's principal victims. Tens of thousands died.

Mr. Pujol was made increasingly uncomfortable during his visit to Quebec by an assumption among his hosts of parallel experiences. Eventually he broke out in public with the phrase, "You don't know what a real linguistic persecution is, thank goodness for you."[4] This wasn't an unfriendly or unpleasant or unsupportive remark. Just a comment on reality. He spent the next day—under a great deal of pressure from the Quebec government—trying to reassure the press that he hadn't intended to be rude.

The political difference is that Catalonia does not, even now, have the autonomous powers which Quebec possesses and has always possessed within Canada. While Pujol seeks some of these from Madrid, his aims are carefully defined. This is for several simple reasons.

Catalonia, as part of Spain, is also part of the European Community. And the European Community, unlike the FTA and NAFTA —which the separatist movement was so central to putting in place—includes social, cultural and economic Europe-wide standards.

This concept of relatively integrated and enforceable (through the European Court) standards is at the core of what most Europeans want, particularly the minorities such as the Catalans. These enforceable standards are precisely the elements which the PQ rejects in the social, cultural and economic areas.

It is important to keep repeating that the central meaning of the FTA, and now of NAFTA, was not free trade. We already as good as had that. Rather it was the rejection of enforceable social standards in favour of a nineteenth-century—now known as neo-conservative —theory by which an invisible economic hand would regulate our lives in the manner of an all-seeing, all-powerful god. Catalonia is on the side of enforceable standards.

In addition, Barcelona is, as Montreal was for Canada, the centre of Spanish innovation and initiative. The cultural, social and economic well-being of Catalans is seen to be built on a desire to retain that role. The nationalists are therefore extremely careful not to turn Catalonia inwards lest it cause them to lose that strength. A small example: Barcelona is the centre of Spanish-language publishing, much of it run by Catalans. Education is bilingual.

Catalonian suffers from all the problems that French suffers from in a dominant anglophone atmosphere. In fact, its situation is far worse. However, Barcelona has chosen an offensive rather than defensive route. The city is aggressively bilingual; and increasingly trilingual or more. The approach is one that LaFontaine or Laurier or, dare I say it, Trudeau would have identified with.

What is perhaps most remarkable is the Catalonian ability to turn its back on the centuries of linguistic interdiction and the massacre of its people, as recently as the middle of this century, to seek a stable, middle-of-the-road approach towards Spain and Europe.

◄┄┄┄┄┄►

The Scottish example in some ways resembles the Catalonian. Conquered and oppressed over a long period of time in all of the most concrete ways, they are now in a situation of relative strength. The English massacres, which ended only a few decades before the change of regime in Canada, were followed by an English political aggression which eradicated Gaelic and centralized most powers in London. The emigration of Scots, Catholic and Protestant, to Lower and Upper Canada was in good part the result of this effective English occupation and the accompanying social crises.

Scotland was saved by the growth of a new bourgeoisie in Edinburgh. Obsessed by innovation and learning, they used the capital produced from coal reserves to take full advantage of the early industrial revolution. This brought prosperity to the Lowlands and gave it a central role in the building of the British Empire.

The Scots would be hard-pressed to argue that in the last 150 years they have been marginal to the British process. Indeed they made themselves central to the creating of the first social-democratic country. And on a per capita basis, like Quebec, they have done as well and usually better than the other regions in the redistribution of public funds. If anything, the recent rise of Scottish nationalism was provoked by the central government's move to the ideological right and the aggressive centralization of Margaret Thatcher. It was perfectly understandable. What the Scots have had in the way of powers on their own territory has been minuscule in comparison with those of the Canadian provinces. Apart from education and responsibility for law, their autonomy was reduced to a few superficial symbols, such as different images on the pound.

What most of the nationalists have sought, through decentralization, is a small part of what Canadian provinces have always had. For a start, they wanted a Scottish Assembly with basic local powers, in what had become the most centralized of the developed countries. In 1997 the conditions have been created for them to get it.

The discovery of off-shore energy and the development of the EEC system of enforceable standards gave them some protection from the worst of the relationship with London. With the creation of a Scottish Assembly, the practical conditions for sensible decentralization will be in place.

In other words, after centuries as a highly centralized country and two decades as the most centralized democracy in the world, Britain is now moving in the opposite direction, towards the Canadian model. But Scotland will still be lacking the real taxation powers which have made the Canadian federation so unusual. Perhaps these will come.

◀—————▶

Some would argue that the Scandinavians found the way to achieve exactly this by breaking up, piece by piece, into separate countries and then turning around to cooperate closely with each other. There is a certain truth in this. But the breaking-up was the product of centuries of internal violence and classic colonial occupation. It is difficult to speak about these things without appearing to denigrate the very real incidents of inequality, prejudice and even small, periodic outbreaks of violence in Canada. However, it is important not to confuse two very different experiences. That is what drove the Catalonian leader to suddenly blurt out his lesson of historical accuracy.

The Danes and Swedes, for example, fought each other with the full force of uncontrolled violence over a long period. I mention, just for colourful illustration, one small example—the Stockholm bloodbath of 1520, when the new Danish king invited the Swedish leadership to a banquet. He then executed them. In the public square onto which the Swedish Academy now looks, thirty heads of the Swedish élite were piled up in a neat pyramid.

Even the early-twentieth-century departure of Finland from Russia was followed by forty years of disorder. For example, the civil war which ended in 1918 involved the massacre of some two thousand people and the locking-up of eighty thousand men plus their families in concentration camps. Ninety-five hundred of them died of hunger and disease. The end result was independence under a Russian shadow, followed by more invasions and violence during the Second World War, followed by another half-century of delicate independence, again under the Russian wing. A relatively compliant neutrality, as well as dependence on the Russian economic market, was the price of a guarantee that Soviet troops would stay away.

Now, faced by a weakened Russia and the European Community temptation, the whole of Scandinavia is in movement. For example, the Swedes are leading an attempted reconstruction of the old Baltic league. And the Danes are aiming at influence in the southern half of Sweden, which was always the most Danish part.

But the central point in these relationships is the overwhelming history of political and military rivalry. This is not a matter of distant romantic history. Reality reasserted itself only half a century ago when Hitler's troops invaded Norway while Sweden remained neutral. The driving force in Scandinavian cooperation today is a desire—as it is between France and Germany—to turn their backs firmly on a difficult past and to solidify a shared and increasingly threatened humanist view of society.

And then there are all the parallels not mentioned.

What about Belgium? There, a French minority—the Walloons—had most of the advantages for a long time. A combination of nineteenth-century industries and the geopolitical weight of France gave them the advantage over the Dutch-speaking Flemish. The turning point in the rise of modern nationalism seems to have been World War One. Among all the other stupidities which this war provoked throughout the west, the Belgian French-speaking officers insisted on giving orders in French to Dutch-speaking soldiers. This sort of problem—involving English-speaking recruiting officers—may sound vaguely familiar to Canadians.

The eventual result was a painful, dragged-out linguistic/ethnic crisis. This was formalized through an even more painful move, from a unitary state to a federal one between 1970 and 1993. The result was a highly decentralized federal structure, in which most of the powers went to the regions. Since then the push for yet more decentralization has continued. In many ways, they are well on their way to sovereignty-association or a partenariat or some such formula.

In the meantime the French-speaking Walloons are now on the losing side and the Flemish population continues to grow stronger. The Walloons' nineteenth-century rust-belt industrial base is closing down, as it is everywhere. The Flemish, on the other hand, seem to have been placed by fate on all the key geographical axes in order to benefit from the new European trade patterns and the high-technology economy.

All of this runs parallel to the recurrent waves of decentralization. Curiously enough these have not created a great sense of well-being and emancipation. Instead, the bitterness on both sides continues to grow. For a start, in an increasing number of areas, decentralization means that there is no flexible sharing of resources between the rich and poor regions. That is, the concept of equalization payments cannot seem to exist in a sovereignty-association system—any more than it would in a Canadian partenariat. In the abstract, a nationalist will say, 'So what? We'll manage our own money. You manage yours.' In this era dominated by the shoddy economics of the Chicago School, they'll add something infantile like, 'Anyway, we'll cut down on waste caused by the duplication of services.'

However, in Belgium, the applied reality of these theories is that the Walloon French-speaking education system is now being strangled for lack of funds and the richer Flemish areas think this is just too bad. They are tasting their revenge for years of mistreatment. In fact they want more decentralization. That is, they want to divide up the social-welfare system in the same way.

The Belgian experience has been that the more power is divided along ethnic/linguistic lines, the more those communities become self-interested and thus selfish. The rich parts of the community are encouraged to think of their interests as separate from those of others, in large part because they belong to another ethnic/linguistic group. As this corporatist yet linguistic/ethnic approach to state structures grows stronger, it becomes increasingly difficult to discuss ideas or content. In other words, the public interest is strangled in the name of the group interest. Debate is reduced to mine versus yours. Or, as Jacques de Decker, the leading Belgian writer, puts it, the conflict is reduced to "intelligence versus stupidity." How can intelligence or equilibrium or humanism be applied when power is based on a voiding of ideas in favour of an abstraction called group self-interest?

This takes the practical form of political alliances based on power and completely cut off from ethics. We know that power and ethics are never ideally united in the real world. But nor need they be entirely separated; not in a normal state of affairs. In Belgium, power has been dependent for a long time now on alliances between right-wing, centre and left-wing parties constituted on ethnic/linguistic lines. Interestingly enough, this is the exact opposite of the idea-based pact between Lower and Upper Canada reformers, established by LaFontaine and Baldwin. The Belgian parties share only their desire for office, so the survival of the partnership requires the voiding of even the possibility of intelligence. Public life is therefore reduced to the occupying of positions and respect for the autonomy of the other. Human relations are, in the process, reduced to a false simplicity. This idea of political-interest groups cooperating over the structures of power on the basis of self-interest sounds very similar to Mr. Bouchard's idea of a partenariat.

The funny thing is that if you think back to Magritte, Horta, Maeterlinck, Verhaeren and the many others who made Belgium such a central force in modern western culture, you discover that it was precisely the complexity brought on by the mixing of two cultures which was their common denomination. As the journalist Jacques Frank puts it, "Les oppositions étaient propices."

Perhaps the relative absence of the Belgian example from the Canadian debate stems from the uncomfortable familiarity of this intelligence versus stupidity debate, by which is meant the stupidity of presenting group self-interest as a respectable solution to social problems. After all, even an intelligent, decent social-democrat like René Lévesque threw himself into an alliance led by the most conservative of provincial premiers. Such a fundamental internal contradiction alone guaranteed that it would end badly. Fifteen years later, premiers Harris and Klein found at the 1996 premiers' conference that their only real ally was Premier Bouchard. Ideologically they had a great deal more in common than René Lévesque with his allies. But essentially their shared interest was not a political ethic. It was a group-based concept of cutting up the pie.

The other aspect of the Belgian experience of group-based political corporatism is that it undermines the ability of the state to defend its interests abroad. Foreign policy is a necessary bore for large powers, a useful magnifying effect for those in the middle and it is essential to those on the smaller side. When population size or economic weight do not force others to pay attention, a country must work very hard in the international arena to ensure that its interests and ideas are taken into account. Belgium has been fortunate or unfortunate enough to be placed at the crux of European events. But internal group rivalry so obsesses it and eats up all its time and energy that the country has gradually disappeared from the international map.

Canada has the disadvantage of sitting on the northern margins of the west in an overly exposed position beside the United States. But it has been just large enough, when intelligently led, to defend its turf. As the internal debate has grown over the last decades, so the ability to maintain an integrated and sustained foreign policy has slipped away. Like the Belgians, we are engaged in a form of self-inflicted castration.

We can guess why the Basques, the Irish and the Corsicans are never mentioned. Seven hundred and fifty dead in France and Spain since ETA, the Basque terrorist movement, began killing thirty years ago. Several thousand dead in Ireland. And in Corsica, eight thousand bombs in the last twenty years; seventeen political assassinations in the last three. There is a solid certainty about assassination figures. However, they leave out the wounded, who usually represent a multiple of those killed. In particular there are the seriously wounded who usually represent three or four times the dead. These are the blinded, the paralyzed, those who lost limbs and, perhaps most common, those whose faces were permanently disfigured. For example, a car bomb in Bastia on July 1, 1996, killed only one. But sixteen were wounded. To my mind the wounded offer a more accurate picture of reality because they remain among us as a tangible illustration.

In each of these three minorities there is no lack of a cause or of provocation from the controlling culture. Languages were forbidden in education and government services. In Corsica this persisted until very recently. There are high levels of centralization and long-festering memories of violent domination by an outside culture.

It must be said that there is no common measure between these experiences and those in Canada. However, there are elements worth noticing. The central point is that Spain, England and France have not treated the breaking-off of any part of their hard-conquered countries as either natural or inevitable. Remember that these stories are not necessarily older than our own. France got hold of Corsica at approximately the same time England got hold of Canada, not long after the last Scottish uprisings. In the Corsican case this involved a straight invasion and the overthrowing of the Corsican government, which under Pascal Paoli was the first western democratic republic. It had been the ideal of the Enlightenment thinkers. As for the Irish saga, it is almost too well known and too depressing to be repeated.

I could work my way through dozens of other possible parallels; the ex-Soviet republics for example. To understand the battle in Chechnia, it is enough to read Tolstoy's novella "Hadji Murat." For forty-three years, from 1816 to 1859, the Russians pacified Chechnia by raiding villages, burning crops and slaughtering stock. That is, they made life impossible by following a scorched-earth policy. The revolt and war of the 1990s was merely the latest chapter in their difficult, bloody relationship.

282   What is the point of this long soliloquy on false parallels—some claimed, some denied? Perhaps it is that, one way or another, through their violent origins or their lost opportunities for reconciliation or the demeaning bickering or the reward of selfishness, these are all sad stories. Since the invention of the western nation-state, the standard approach towards bicultural or minority relations has been at best unpleasant and most commonly one of violence, cultural castration and the centralization of power. This is true of our closest friends—the United States, England and France. We cannot condemn them for this. It is an approach they have shared with almost every nation-state.

The levels of violence used by these countries to install a central mythology has required high multiples of anything unpleasant experienced in Canada. The degree of centralization and cultural interdiction has been terrifying in comparison with our own unfortunate errors and acts of ambitious, selfish stupidity. None of which excuses our treatment of the Métis or Manitoba's and Ontario's anti-French-language school regulations or Quebec's Padlock Law under Maurice Duplessis or B.C.'s Chinese head tax and internment of Japanese Canadians. But this chapter is a discussion of the theory of the natural and inevitable break-up of Canada, not of relative innocence.

Some of these stories from elsewhere are also moving. For example, the ability of the Catalans to turn their backs on such a disturbing past seems to show a strength of character which I find almost unimaginable. Or there is the determination of the Scandinavians not simply to work together and trade together, but to develop what can only be called a northern ethic, which combines internal egalitarianism with a matching view of the world.

There are, of course, literally hundreds of examples of minorities which exist within larger countries. This is a normal characteristic of the nation-state. The normal and inevitable story throughout the west is that some sort of cohabitation within state structures is necessary. In most cases, the tragedy is that this cohabitation is based on the aggressive enforcement of a monolithic national mythology.

In the parallels described above, this gross centralization has failed. In some way or other the minority has refused acquiescence. The reaction of the central authority has, in general, been violent. In some cases the result has been a modest level (by Canadian standards) of decentralization. In a few there has been massive decentralization and the result seems to have been the rise of self-destructive self-interest. Those examples represent not nationalism, but the rise of the negative aspects of nationalism.

There is another characteristic common to all of them. The minority lies as a geographical unit on one side of the nation-state. Most often they live in a frontier area added on during some expansive burst from the centre. There is the marginality of Scotland off in the north, Slovakia in the poor south; Corsica, an isolated island; the Catalonians on the distant eastern frontier of the Castilian centre; just as the Basques lie to their north in a frontier area between Spain and France; Sweden, the far northern province of Denmark; Norway and Finland, the even more marginal frontiers of Sweden and Russia; the Irish on an island off England.

It is in part geographical eccentricity which drives these movements. And in that sense, the complaints of British Columbia fit into an historical pattern. But there is no example of a minority lying at the geographical heart of a country successfully leaving it. This element of geography is particularly important when the minority has played a central role in the design and direction of the country over more than a century; in other words, when they have worked hard for the country to be shaped around many of their concerns and with their central role in mind.

In passing I should mention one more example of a break-up, because it is cited approvingly by Daniel Turp, who seems to be Mr. Bouchard's unofficial constitutional expert and is now a Bloc MP.[5] Singapore and Malaysia did indeed break up peacefully in August 1965. On the other hand, their active marriage of convenience had only been in effect for two years. In fact, Lee Kuan Yew had manoeuvred the alliance in order to rid himself of the British, then set out to so annoy the Malays that they would actually expel Singapore from the Federation. The break-up was done without democratic consultation and the process included Prime Minister Lee arresting several hundred leading opposition figures. And in case Mr. Turp hasn't looked at a map, Singapore is a small island off the extreme south coast of Malaysia. It was never an integral part of the Federation—not socially, not politically and not geographically. It played no role in building the mythology or consciousness of Malaysia. Its leaders never ran the Federation, which remained in Malay hands. Singapore was a temporary and extraneous add-on.

Repeatedly during the referendum campaign Lucien Bouchard referred to the other side of the river, in the way nineteenth-century nationalists referred to the Rhine or the Channel as a great divide. Our historical experience suggests the exact opposite. In Canada, rivers have always been the highways of communication, not of division. They have played the unifying role of movement, not the static role of division. The first great highway of French Canada ran up the St. Lawrence and the Ottawa to the Mattawa, through Lake Nipissing and down the French River to la mer Douce (Georgian Bay) and on across the country. This was Canada's principal means of internal communication for 250 years. The role of the rivers here has been that of moving waters not opposing shores.

Besides, anyone who frequents the brief Ottawa–Montreal car-shuttles or the plane-hops between Montreal and Toronto, Toronto and Ottawa, knows that this is not a great divide, but the core of national power. That centrality of Quebec and Ontario is precisely what causes discomfort in the West and the East.

Quebec does not lie on one side of Canada. Canada surrounds it on three sides. Some will argue in an age of fast communications that geography no longer matters. But that is theory. In reality there is no example of a country surviving when cut in half by great or even small distances. From an historical point of view, the departure of Quebec would mean the condemnation of what remains to further fracturing.

Those in Quebec or Ontario or the West would do well to remember that Maritimers see themselves as the primary victim of this argument between national and provincial powers. The north of Canada aside, the Maritimes have the smallest population and the most fragile economy. The national debate has dragged on and the result there has been a growth in fatalism. As the historian Margaret Conrad puts it, they see "decisions being made elsewhere over whether Quebec will leave. The Maritimes have no say." Or Rick Williams, the political economist—they are "now treated as a client-state."[6] In other words, they may receive funds from the national treasury, but their view of the effects of changes in Canada on the Maritimes, let alone their view of how the whole should evolve, is not considered.

This brings me back to the concept that the departure of a part of a country is a normal inevitability. Those with the courage to listen to the words of public debate will notice that all attempts by federalists to defend Canada are described by the other side as "excessive language and provocation" or "political radicalization." These words of Premier Bouchard at the 1996 national convention of the PQ are merely small examples of the political position which asserts that fracture is normal and coexistence a provocation. I'm not suggesting approval of the federal government's approach. Far from it. But whether their defence were intelligent or stupid, the PQ would, given the forces of natural inevitability, describe it as irresponsible.

The only reasonable observation that an interested observer can make after looking at all of these examples is that there is no case of a country's breaking-up being perceived or treated as normal or inevitable. The shape that such a process would take cannot therefore be reasonably predicted any more than the result can be discussed with any accuracy. The only sensible comment would be that, if you throw the structures, habits, ideas and rules of behaviour for coexistence up in the air, no one can expect to have predictable control over the way they come down.

In the quasi-totality of the parallels invoked or avoided by those who seek to break up Canada, the central powers have been ready to use force in order to protect their union, and the effects have been long-term unpleasantness as well as damage to one or both of the parties. Is this because the Americans or the Spanish or the French or English are lesser people than us? That would be an awkward position to defend. Is it then because these are real countries while Canada, in Premier Bouchard's words, is not?

That seems an even more peculiar argument. It would depend upon your definition of a real country. If it is exclusively limited to the description of those who have forcibly integrated their minorities through violence, language interdiction and centralization, then Premier Bouchard is right. Canada has not been rough enough to count as a real country. However, by evoking the parallels they do and invoking this very hard-edged definition of a nation, the PQ are actually saying that Canada must act like a 'real' country or cease to exist. Surely that's not what they intended. Perhaps it is. Extremes of necessity produce extremes. The eagerness with which Mr. Gilles Duceppe, leader of the Bloc québécois, has invoked the bogey of Preston Manning and vice versa would suggest that they are natural reflections of each other.

Surely, however, it is not necessary to remain the prisoner of such an old-fashioned view of the nation-state. Surely it could be broadened to include cultural complexity and a decentralized framework. But in that case Mr. Bouchard would be wrong and the 'natural inevitability' argument wouldn't stand. In other words, the comparative argument against Canada's right to survive is actually based not on comparisons, but on the rejection of an approach to nationhood which is more relaxed and decentralized than is usual; a more inclusive and humanist approach. I must say that is not an argument I would enjoy having to make.

Multiple Reconciliations

21

"It's rare to lose a country. It happened to me. I'm not talking about a state or a regime, but a country, where I was born and which was, until yesterday, my own. I loved Yugoslavia.... And yet I was not a Yugoslav nationalist."

Predrag Matvejevitch, *Le Monde* "*EX*"[1]

ON DECEMBER 14, 1995, THE president of the United States, the prime ministers of Russia and Britain, the German chancellor and others gathered in the Élysée Palace for the signing of the Yugoslav peace accord.

Stop! you say. There is no parallel between Canada and the violent mess in the Balkans. Two hundred thousand casualties. Four million displaced people.

Of course there is no parallel. But there is something else which caught my eye.

First, the government leaders in that room knew full well that the Yugoslav disaster was in part their fault. Second, they had recognized in it a magnified playing-out of the sorts of divisions and violence which had plagued most of their own countries in the nineteenth and the first half of the twentieth centuries. Third, the intelligent or reflective among them seemed to have focused their attention on the idea of reconciliation.

The Balkans have always been a logical choice for jokes about nationalism. After all, here is a place where there is no such thing as pure blood or language. Almost everyone is intermarried or to some degree the product of intermarriage. The multiple groups have always lived in mixed communities. And yet throughout the Balkans there is a low ignition level for passionate claims about religion, language and blood.

The twentieth century has been filled with the search for a Balkan *modus vivendi*. Marshal Tito, whatever his flaws, succeeded. Within each of the small ethnic groups he managed to tap those elements which believed in reconciliation. The result for almost half a century was a relatively successful country, particularly by local standards. Even in the smallest villages people of different religions and mixed cultures lived and they lived together. By local standards they were relatively free. By local standards they prospered.

Without entering into Tito's mistakes, which in the end severely weakened his creation, it is reasonable to say that he died leaving a country worth saving and capable of survival. Those who succeeded him were unable to rise to the needs of the situation. They looked after themselves, allowed a vacuum to grow and the country to drift.

When it exploded, they were blown away by the blast and the nationalist extremists were able to emerge, beat their breasts and take over the public and private agendas of the people. That is the sort of thing which tends to happen when a vacuum is created in a society.

At the signing of the peace in 1995, President Chirac said he hoped that the result would be a "unified, pluricultural, democratic" society. But that is, of course, what Yugoslavia had been. "They must live together in the respect of differences." The ex-Yugoslavs might have answered that this was not what the great powers had done in their own countries. They had pulverized their minorities. But the signatories sat quiet and humiliated while the world lectured them on ethics and respect for the other. The central lesson being delivered was that of reconciliation.

The difficulty with proffering this noble idea was that the Yugoslavs had already been reconciled for half a century. Then in the late 1980s, they slipped into a primal delusion in which political difference was added on to political difference until these seemed to be racial differences. Once launched on that tempting quicksand, they dragged one another down into a Hades of hatred and bitterness. Gradually the developed world became too embarrassed to

continue putting up with the Balkans' collective nervous breakdown. So they were to be reconciled again.

What struck me, as I listened and watched, was that the great
tragedy was not quite what it appeared to be. It wasn't the violence and the loss of lives and the waste of a civilization's time,
terrible though all of this was. These were the various products of
the tragedy. The tragedy itself was the loss of reconciliation. The
loss of the ability to cohabit. More than a tragedy, it was a human
failure, a crime of civilization. Those with power broke the pacts
which held these humans together. They accomplished this first
by doing nothing and then by exploiting despair and anger in the
basest of causes.

That the result was violence and extreme poverty is not the
point. It might have been far more benign. Still it would have been
a crime. Reconciliation is a great human quality. One of the more
important. Those with power know it can be neglected, abased,
deformed, ridiculed in the name of various emotional or financial
imperatives. Reconciliation is the most difficult of human states to
defend. It is dependent on an acceptance of the idea of the public
good. It invariably stands in the way of power, narrow self-interest
and self-righteousness.

The vacant hopeless stare of Ottawa during much of the last
national crisis, supplemented by heavy-handed warnings of a low-
level economic nature; the hyperbole and exaggeration of differences, which amounted to a raising of prejudice, coming out of
Quebec City; the increasing selfishness of provincial politics, particularly in Ontario and Alberta; all of these are the signs of an élite
prepared to abandon the idea of reconciliation, preferring instead a
vacuum of power in which they can manoeuvre.

A dispassionate observer can see the origins of reconciliation in
Canada in the Quebec Act in 1774. The constitution of 1791 was
the product of active cooperation between large parts of the newly
arrived anglophone community and the francophones, working
together on a reform agenda. The cooperation of the 1837 Lower

Canada and Upper Canada rebels and that of the reform leaders of 1840–51 confirmed what then looked like isolated events to have been a social trend. There is no lack of addenda to this reconciliation, just as there is no lack of irritants which have more or less been dealt with. And now, without the population on any side of the argument having clearly taken the initiative to break our hold on reconciliation, we stand on the brink of doing it anyway.

As I watched the peace signing at the Élysée I was filled with that sense of the horror which any conscious human must feel when faced by the possibility of a reconciliation being broken and tossed aside. And what would the result be? As the parallels laid out in the previous chapter show, the result remains a mystery until the error is made. Then it unfolds according to its own bitter, destructive logic.

But surely all the qualities of careful moderation and imagination which I described in earlier chapters would come into play. Perhaps. But the qualities of a civilization are precisely that. They are not genetic or racial qualities. They are the product of the evolution of that society. That's why I keep coming back to the importance of practical memory and to the pattern of our long experience and to the pacts struck along the way.

Our standards and our methods are in part the product of geography and political circumstance. But our reaction to place and circumstance today is the surprisingly stable result of endless small and large choices made along the road. By no means were all of these choices the right ones or even satisfactory. But they all are part of the larger pattern which I have attempted to describe. Those choices—and not our laws—are the structure of our civilization, the unwritten but understood structure of acceptable behaviour upon which democracies, more than any other form of society, survive.

The experience of other societies has been that, if you tear down that structure, then you lose your orientation. Unpleasant forces wrestled to the ground long before suddenly emerge, released and encouraged by the confusion. In other words, societies, humans, react badly to abrupt change. In most cases this takes the form of destabilization. You no longer know that if A does X, B will probably do Y or Z.

For example, Canada wrestled the worst of its nineteenth-century nationalism to the ground in the last years of the nineteenth century and the first few decades of the twentieth. The referendum of 1995 was enough to rerelease some of those forces. Suddenly, we now hear talk on all sides of violence and race. Where did it come from? How does it dare show its face? Why is it not swept away by some sort of common assent?

The response of most commentators today is to insist that public figures should respond to what are presented as essential questions. Would you be for or against partition? Force? Negotiation?

But these are not questions. They are assumptions—assumptions that, whatever happens, everything will be manageable, and therefore managed on the basis of decisions made among the élites as presently constituted. Indeed these decisions will be made among the same people who are now in positions of authority.

The democrat would ask different questions. If we do this, if we abandon the reconciliation on which we have been working now for more than two centuries, what forces will be unleashed? Or rather, will incalculable, uncontrollable forces be released? The current-affairs approach of our professional élites would be to leap immediately away from the fundamental questions and to concentrate instead on what they would see as a practical question—Well, how would we control these forces? But how can this be a practical question when you have no idea what forces will be released or how strong they might be? Again the democrat would be more likely to ask—What is a responsible act, given such unknown forces? Real questions revolve, as they always have in public affairs, around how difficult it is to create a stable, workable equilibrium which, if a great deal of effort is made, may be able to serve the public good. There is a built-in consciousness that this takes a very long time, and even then is permanently at risk. How many struggles are there along the way? What happens if you should chance to destroy that equilibrium? Forces will be unleashed. Experience tells us that they are rarely those sought by the people who wanted radical change. It is, as I said earlier, like throwing the cards in the air. That's why the citizenry cast their votes with such precise consideration.

It appears that any attempts by the federal government or anglophones or indeed francophones to talk about possible negative effects of separation, such as partition, simply anger most francophones—even many federalists—and heighten the possibility that in the future Quebec francophones might vote to go. Perhaps this is because most francophones see the issue as one of self-respect or dignity rather than of separation. Their reaction is therefore an understandable response to being threatened. And to the extent that these are threats it is probably a sensible reaction.

Put aside the complicating factor that most of us—whether francophone or anglophone—realize our moderation is being treated as of secondary importance, given that those who are organizing these sequential referenda are interested less in dignity than in political separation. Let us stay, instead, with the impact of the debate on how citizens see themselves.

The difficulty is that the possibility of breaking up the country is also a threat and can only be felt in that way by those on the receiving end. The suggestion that highly charged votes over whether to break up the country are somehow healthy exercises in self-expression, unrelated to the future of those living outside of Quebec, is a difficult argument for most to digest. After all, if such campaigns are a threat to how Quebec federalists see themselves and imagine themselves, it is equally a threat for those living out-side the province. In other words, for non-Quebecers it is a dagger aimed at the very heart of what they consider to be the national mythology.

It cannot be repeated enough that Quebec and, more precisely, francophone Canada is at the very heart of the Canadian mythol-ogy. I don't mean that it alone constitutes the heart, which is after all a complex place. But it is at the heart and no multiple set of by-pass operations could rescue that mythology if Quebec were to leave. Separation is therefore a threat of death to anglophone Canada's whole sense of itself, of its self-respect, of its role as a con-stituent part of a nation, of the nature of the relationship between citizens. From my federalist francophone friends I sense that they understand this threat in more or less the same way. And because this mythology has been gradually developing since the Quebec Act of 1774, it is lodged so deeply in the Canadian psyche that no one can imagine what would happen if it were cut away. Remem-ber, this is not a relationship born of some after-the-fact agreement between two mature nations. Its roots lie in patterns set in the 1770s and 1780s, when there were fewer than a total of 150,000 francophones and anglophones. It is therefore something which has grown and developed with the population as it has multiplied two hundred times.

The recurrent suggestions that anglophones must make as few comments as possible on the possibility and effects of Canada breaking up is meant to be a reflection of concern for the psycho-logical make-up of francophones. But it doesn't take into account the psychological make-up of anglophones.

Mr. Chrétien literally instructed the rest of the country to keep their mouths shut in the lead-up to the referendum, as if everyone should comply with the manner in which a referendum reduces the participants to temperamental children. It was only when those denied a vote saw the country on the edge of catastrophe that they reacted by pouring into the streets, not just those of Montreal, but from coast to coast. There was no time and no intellectual preparation. That these events were childlike fitted logically into a referendum atmosphere. As I said earlier, it doesn't matter whether this psychological explosion had a positive or negative effect on the vote. At the very least, it reminded everyone that anglophones, like francophones, are humans laden with mythologies, and that these are the same mythologies as those to be found among francophones, even if they are interpreted differently, that they have a sense of themselves, a sense of the *other* and an emotive force.

It also undermined the delusionary idea of officials on both sides that it was they who were in charge of the brief and would negotiate whatever was required on behalf of the citizens. The reality is that most of the federal figures would quickly have been swept away by anglophones in the case of a Yes vote. And we now know that Mr. Bouchard and his team, ready to negotiate, were in effect also to be swept away by Mr. Parizeau and a more hard-line approach.

To return to my point of departure, the question is not, therefore, whether speaking of partition angers the citizenry. The question is, in the case of a vote to break up Canada, would the sort of leaders produced by a major reconfiguration of the federation put forward partition as one of their principal policies?

I have no idea. However, history tells us that instability releases demons and encourages the extremes. Having been given a role, once the central question had been decided without them, it is difficult to see why anglophones would take a positive approach. Partition would be one of the most obvious items for the new leadership to promise. Why? Because the desire of Canadians to salvage some sort of geographical survival would demand it; because Inuit, Natives and pockets of Quebec anglophones would demand it; and because the legal position for partition is at least as strong as that of Quebec for separation.

Again, this is neither my opinion nor my desire. Daniel Turp has put forward exactly the same scenario in his writings on Native rights.

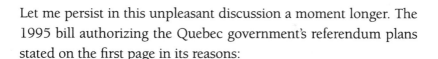
Let me persist in this unpleasant discussion a moment longer. The 1995 bill authorizing the Quebec government's referendum plans stated on the first page in its reasons:

> BECAUSE we occupy the lands outlined by our ancestors, from Abitibi to the Îles-de-la-Madeleine, from Ungava to the American frontiers. . . .—PARCE QUE nous habitons les territoires délimités par nos ancêtres de l'Abitibi aux Îles-de-la-Madeleine, de l'Ungava aux frontières américaines. . . .

But, of course, Quebec brought less than half of that into Confederation. Ottawa gave it Abitibi in 1898 and Ungava in 1912. These territories therefore do not fall within the argument that Canada is a federation of sovereign territories; an argument which theoretically permits a constituent part to leave with the guy who brung them. In addition the treaties which hold the Natives in Canada are with the central power. As Daniel Turp puts it:

> Such a right would allow the Native nations to decide their political and constitutional future as freely as the Québécois. . . . In other words, by virtue of their right to self-determination, the Native nations of Quebec could decide to attain sovereignty, to remain integrated with Canada, to stay with Quebec if it becomes sovereign or to remain within Canada even if Quebec chooses sovereignty. . . . Should the Native nations attain sovereignty or separate from Quebec to remain within Canada, there would be a problem of territorial integrity similar to that posed by the secession of Quebec from Canada. If Quebec were to object to sovereignty measures democratically approved by the Native nations, these nations could undoubtedly claim that their democratic right to self-determination and to secession had been violated.[2]

Indeed they have already made their wishes clear on two occasions by majorities so massive as to constitute virtual unanimity. Mr. Turp goes on in his 1992 published argument to discuss precisely how the province would be carved up. Needless to say, once he identified himself with the Bloc québécois, he stopped this sort of writing. And he felt himself obliged to withdraw his commitment to write a similar analysis for the Royal Commission on Native Affairs.

In any case, Mr. Bouchard keeps repeating—"The territory of Quebec has a fundamental characteristic; it is integral."[3] The sentence reminds us of his taste for nineteenth-century writers from the metropole. It has the ring about it of Charles Péguy, the romantic, conservative, Catholic French nationalist author. Like Péguy's visions of the nation, Mr. Bouchard's declarations of geographic integrity have more to do with romantic assertion than generally accepted realities.

The public place is now littered with constitutional and other lawyers ready to argue the case one way or the other. Both Ottawa and Quebec City have begun making statements to position themselves on the question. Jacques Brassard, the Quebec minister of intergovernmental affairs, stated clearly at the beginning of 1997 that Quebec would be ready to use the police to defend its territory. Mr. Manning is already tracing out an equivalent position which reflects the opposing extreme and he will increasingly press forward with it.

Jean Charest, in the one unrehearsed comment I heard him utter during the 1997 election campaign, replied to a question on his position over partition, "Once we've crossed that threshold we find ourselves in an area where there are no longer any rules."

Moderates on all sides are horrified by the drift of the debate. They rightly, but desperately, point out that separating part of Montreal would be a crazy catastrophe. They say less of the Hull area, call for calm, and if possible remain silent on the subject of the northern half of the province.

All I am doing here is describing a few elements from the maelstrom of energy-sucking arguments and emotions which could consume our lives.

I know Predrag Matvejevitch. I first met him at Zagreb University when he was running the French Department and writing his books. That was before the Yugoslav vacuum had degenerated into civil war, before he had to flee into exile. What strikes me about Predrag and my other Yugoslav friends is, again, not the scars of the violence, which they somehow disguise with an astonishing elegance of civility, but the tragedy of the lost opportunity. It is as if their lives, creative though they are, can no longer be consumed by creativity, let alone family, responsibility or pleasure. Instead, they have been taken over by the sectarian differences which have somehow, in a way which none of them can really explain to themselves, consumed their society.

That 'inexplicability,' even among the most worldly and sophisticated of thinkers, tells us everything about the forces of disorientation which can be let loose once structures which reward the qualities of moderation are torn down; in other words, once a referendum scenario has created the illusions of clarity and rebirth. The point is not whether partition is right or wrong, possible or impossible. The point is that the road away from reconciliation leads not towards resolution but into the swamps of self-destructive animosity.

22 Positive versus Negative

ONLY A FOOL WOULD DENY THE force with which emotion can drive men and women. Or believe that his own emotion or that of others can be so controlled as to effectively be replaced by something else. Or that her own emotion has greater intrinsic value than that of another.

This is one of the particular delusions of negative nationalism. The one who sees himself as victim slips easily into a defensive or exclusive position. In the process he enters an emotional state filled with internal references. The *other* and the emotions of the *other* cannot carry the same weight; often they carry no weight at all.

The attraction of the Manichean idea is that it formalizes the relationship between opposing sides. In this way we can deny the ideological pretension that one will win out and eliminate the other. That isn't what upset the third-century church. It was horrified by the theory that good and the devil had been given equal footing. But I wonder if even that wasn't a secondary point in the doctrine. Manichee was primarily trying to deal with the reality which faces every human being; that is, our impossible wait for a judgement day. The day-to-day reality of unresolvability, in which we still live, led him to design a magisterial theory of our existence. If you put the Christian particularities of that theory aside, the day-to-day reality so clearly identified in the third century remains.

Nationalism is constructed of an inescapable Manichean tension. The negative variety, like the positive, has always existed. They existed long before nationalism took on its modern form as one of the expressions of the nation-state. What's more, the existence of opposing sides doesn't mean that each is devoid of the qualities and defaults of the other. People and political parties don't divide themselves into two pure, unrelated, opposing groups. You can identify a phenomenon as essentially positive or negative only on the basis of the critical mass of its words and actions.

A chapter about positive versus negative nationalism in francophone Canada is therefore about two interrelated realities. And if you applied the same analysis to the various parts of anglophone Canada you would find the same opposing but related realities. However, I am going to limit myself in this chapter to the internal francophone tension, if only because all of us—francophone and anglophone, federalist and separatist/sovereigntist—have come to see that tension in a way which confuses positive and negative nationalism, as if they were the same thing. The result is a psychological victory for the negative, because in this atmosphere any criticism of any aspect of nationalism can automatically be presented as a criticism of francophone society, indeed of francophones. Sensible debate thus becomes impossible.

What I am suggesting here is deceptively simple. Positive nationalism is a humanist movement seeking continual reform in order to improve the life of the community. This does include economic well-being, but only as a result of the more important elements—service of the public good, aggressive responsible individualism and culture. What I mean by that is culture in the largest sense, with language at the core of it being used to further the communication of the culture. In the practical terms of everyday life, culture is not about agreement, but about questioning. In other words, culture is not about solidarity, but about discussion and disagreements.

Nationalism, the public good, individualism, culture—we rarely put these concepts together. But if nationalism is not a metaphor for strengthening the well-being of society, it is nothing at all. Or rather, it has been reduced to the exploitation of emotion. And if

300   individualism—in a democracy—is not participation as a citizen in order to affect the public good, what is it but self-indulgence?

Animals, in particular male animals, do tend to urinate around their territory in order to mark its borders. Among non-human animals this is directly and exclusively related to the well-being of their particular community. Humans tend to add ego to this equation. Suddenly, self-pride, bravado and mythologies of particularity are competing with the service of the public good.

We are more complex than other animals and so this introduction of other factors is perfectly understandable. Given a reasonable tension among the elements, the expression of our sense of ourselves—of our ego—is an essential part of the public good. But if it becomes the dominant factor, it reduces the public good and aggressive responsible individualism to subsidiary factors. These must then be subordinated to a mystic cause defined as the national good, not the public good. At that point we are dealing not with positive nationalism, but with the negative sort.

Negative nationalism usually identifies a defined national crisis as the primary problem which society must first deal with in order to save itself and thus make it possible to deal with other problems. These other problems are invariably said to be unresolvable because of the national crisis. But the national crisis is usually itself unresolvable in any real terms because it is based on abstract theories of identity or power. Negative nationalism cannot help but demote social reform to a lower level. It tends, in the normal process of political opposition, to end up as an anti-reform movement.

Indeed many of those who are attracted by an anti-reform position are in fact attracted by a public debate which avoids social reality and concentrates on abstract emotion. At its worst this is the classic position of the false populist. And many of those who are drawn to the politics of emotion—viscerally tied to fear and anger and a desire for joy—can't help but be angered by the 'pretensions' of humanists. At first glance it seems that they are angered by the humanists' belief in citizen-led social improvements. But on a day-to-day basis what bothers them is a belief that debate, uncertainty, real reforms and culture—all expressions of complexity—should be given priority over such emotional weapons as group solidarity. After all, negative nationalists tend to see life as an Heroic struggle towards the great bright day when, at last . . . ! At last! To give priority to debate and uncertainty, reform and culture is to admit that there is no overriding abstract crisis which cannot be dealt with, except by extreme measures.

Solidarity is a curious phenomenon. It seems, in the language of the negative nationalist, to be of central importance. But solidarity is not the element which replaces reform in negative nationalism. It is the precursor of the key element. And that element, one way or another, has to do with power—the accumulation of, the centralization of, the clarification of powers. The term which has most often been used in negative-nationalist arguments to denote power is autonomy. Oliver Mowat introduced it with his defence of what he felt were Ontario's rightful powers. And he then encouraged Quebec's Honoré Mercier to go down the same road.

Again, the concept of provincial autonomy is not a bad thing. Nor is the protection of constitutional rights, which it describes. They are both good and essential concepts.

But when autonomy dominates the public debate, it does so at the expense of reform. The reformers, when in power, usually defend provincial autonomy and constitutional rights in the normal course of events. But they try not to let these matters of pure or abstract power dominate their lives. Instead they have an urgent sense of what needs to be done to improve social and cultural conditions. And they have a healthy interest in encouraging the citizenry to be part of that process.

In an atmosphere of negative nationalism, this more classically democratic approach is overwhelmed by the concept of patriotic solidarity, corporatist structures and what André Laurendeau called "the need for conformity."[1] Corporatism comes naturally in this context. It is at the same time a form of passive solidarity born with the

Ultramontane movement in Europe in the early-nineteenth century, and a form of active solidarity born with the rise of technocratic methods in private industry at the end of the nineteenth century. And there is a third element: a form of passive solidarity born with the rise of public technocracies in the twentieth century. The underlying values of the Ultramontane movement were passed, almost untouched, into modern lay nationalism by the intellectual line which stretches from Abbé Groulx through the Montreal School to the intellectuals who provide the language of negative nationalism today.

But the tension between positive and negative nationalism isn't just about reform politics versus the politics of autonomy. A dozen other factors come to mind. Reformers see the past as a reality upon which you must work. The other school sees a perfect past—the dream of New France, for example. This mythology of a lost past, which is actually a mystification of reality, is something they share with all ideologues. Marx, like Brunet, believed in the little lost Eden.

Reformers tend to have the sort of self-confidence which comes with identifying reality. That's how LaFontaine was able to imagine his partnership of ideas. That's how Félix Marchand, the last Quebec premier of the nineteenth century, was able to take on the church over the question of education in a way Mercier wouldn't have dared. The negative nationalist holds a defensive position; the position of the victim who blames others, vaunts his humiliation, seeks martyrs and hates those who have self-confidence. Those are the traitors. But it is precisely those self-confident nationalists who are most often capable of taking the offensive on major social issues.

What I am describing is more than a difference in the style of leadership. Positive nationalism is most likely to encourage intelligent, complex leaders filled with contradictions. Adélard Godbout and René Lévesque are two good examples. They can be seen in contrast to the false simplicity of Heroic leaders or martyrs, such as Maurice Duplessis and Honoré Mercier.

The reformers tend to be obsessed by public education and larger cultural questions. This is a healthy obsession. Negative nationalists tend to transform these issues into a mystification of culture without content and into a corporatist, utilitarian view of education focused on the creation of élites.

The intellectual idea of the public good—of the sort the positive nationalist Georges-Émile Lapalme represented—is turned into the anti-intellectual emotions of "nous autres." Until very recently the negative-nationalist school blocked progress in the public role of women, while the major leaps forward were made thanks to people like Thérèse Casgrain, T.D. Bouchard and Adélard Godbout.

This single example of women's rights shows how deeply the negative nationalists slip into mystification. Premier Parizeau, for example, stated that "Women have always been better satisfied by the Quebec Government than that of Ottawa." What can he have been thinking about? Thanks to the opposition of the negative nationalists in Quebec City, women got the provincial vote twenty years after the federal vote and last among the provinces. What's more, most of the social programs, children's benefits, health care, pensions—all of which were central to changing the role of women—originated in Ottawa. Until the Quiet Revolution (a federalist event), provincial nationalist governments had done everything they could to block these programs. In other words, the major social reforms in Quebec came out of governments dominated by positive nationalism or out of leadership from Ottawa, where many of the francophone positive nationalists concentrated their efforts. Governments obsessed by autonomy and constitutions have more often than not been tied to social immobility and poverty.

The self-confidence of the positive nationalists allows them to look outwards and to be conscious of the *other*, while the negative nationalist is fixated on the interior. There are two exceptions to this phenomenon on the negative side. The first is a romantic, rather colonial approach towards France. The second is the mystification of an imaginary relationship with the United States. Thus those who

announce themselves most determined to defend francophone society are those most eager to entangle it deeply in the structures of
American power; the structures most uninterested, if not unsym-
pathetic, to the idea of dealing with a society which functions in
another language and culture on its borders. The annexation movement in Canada has always had two homes: first, in a part of the
anglophone business élite; second, in the francophone negative-
nationalist leadership. In the case of that anglophone élite, the desire
for annexation is the product of a classic colonial inferiority complex. In the case of that particular francophone élite, it is a more
complex form of masochism.

What I have been describing is the inclusive approach of the positive nationalists, as opposed to the exclusive approach of so many in
the negative school. If you apply these various oppositions or tensions to Quebec provincial politics, it becomes easy to identify the
great progressive governments: Félix Marchand (1897–1900),
Adélard Godbout (1940–44), Jean Lesage (1960–66) and René
Lévesque's first term (1976–81).

These are the four leaders of the four governments which took
essential and difficult steps to strengthen the distinctiveness, particularity and, in that real sense, the autonomy of francophone society. Theirs were offensive (in the military sense), not defensive, acts;
positive, not negative, initiatives. They acted not to protect the francophone fact (a loser's position), but to expand and strengthen it.

They did not make their careers by manipulating the citizens'
fears of losing their culture, all the while acting to weaken it, as so
many of the negative nationalists have. For example, they didn't
build their power by developing a sense of oppression and betrayal,
which is not so difficult to do in any minority, while at the same
time cutting education budgets or handing education off to anti-
democratic groups.

Marchand, Godbout, Lesage and Lévesque strengthened francophone self-confidence and put real tools in place which could carry that self-confidence beyond the mystifications of negative nationalism. At the opposite extreme were men like Charles Boucher de Boucherville (1874–78, 1891–92) and Maurice Duplessis (1936–39, 1944–59). The others have ranged somewhere in between. What is disturbing in this pattern—with social reform the anchor on one side and autonomy on the other—is that a man like P.J.O. Chauveau, for example, suddenly looks not so bad. And yet the dominant nationalist schools have badly mauled the reputation of Quebec's second and last superintendent of education and subsequently its first premier. On the other hand, an Heroic figure like Mercier can be seen to have reinforced the anti-reform structures in order to build his solidarity coalition. Whatever pride he may have instilled came at the cost of giving new life to the most socially and culturally damaging systems.

The history of both positive and negative nationalism begins with a single man. Papineau was the voice of democracy and justice. But he was also the leading defender of seigneurial rights and the central role of the clergy, as well as a strong advocate of American annexation.

We are constantly and rightly reminded of his radical leadership before 1837. But on his return from exile the three major contributions he made were to give respectability to conservative nationalism. "The clergé and the seigneurs are the safeguard of the country." In many ways he was the one who made it possible for Bishop Bourget and his Ultramontane friends to inherit one side of the nationalist mantle. And they would turn that mantle into the political line of negative nationalism. Papineau's persistent mystification of the United States, as the body to which Quebec should belong, anchored the idea among many reform-minded liberals that their road to 'safety' passed via annexation. Papineau never addressed how this would actually work. Perhaps because it bore no relationship to reality, this Americaphilia has had a long life and has slowly become a central element in negative nationalism. What could be more mystic and romantic than to dream of a special relationship with a great power which is totally indifferent in general to other cultures?

Finally, it was Papineau who put in place the myth of the Heroic martyrized leader. He didn't intend to do this. But it happened and it was, as it remains, necessary in the schema of negative nationalism.

Papineau was followed by a first stage of opposing nationalisms. LaFontaine and then Cartier, on the positive side, attempted to fend off the church, develop public state-administered education, consolidate democracy, and develop a solid francophone role in the civil service under the leadership of Étienne Parent (the senior Canadian public servant from 1842 to 1872). In other words they attempted to normalize the consolidation and modernization of French-Canadian society. Above all, they put the legal structures in place which gave the citizenry power to deal with the anglophone élites and francophone seigneurial élites. In a sense they were consolidating the new francophone middle class which had come into being after the departure of the French colonial power.

LaFontaine, from his Terrebonne Address on, struggled for the abolition of seigneurial rights, and therefore against his old leader. And he struggled towards a universal lay system of education. "Education is the first benefit that a government can give to a people."[2] This was something which Cartier eagerly picked up on. The first two public superintendents of education—Jean-Baptiste Meilleur and P.J.O. Chauveau—were put in place. French Canada in this middle period of the nineteenth century was a very liberal place.

However, the opposing school of negative nationalists (clericonationalists) was on the rise. Bishop Lartigue had set the Ultramontane idea in place. Bishop Bourget, on successive trips to

France, convinced order after order to install itself in Canada. Some were conservative, some more liberal, but it seems that the reactionary leadership of the movement was local.[3] In either case the effect was a political-religious movement on the rise. In Bourget's own words—"It came to him that he should find help in Europe."[4] Or, as Paul-Émile Borduas put it in *Refus global*, "without defence against all the orders of France and Navare, hungry to perpetuate in this place blessed by fear . . . the prestige and the benefits of that Catholicism so badly treated in Europe." The negative nationalists devoted themselves to the abolition of the Ministry of Public Education and ensured that after Chauveau there wouldn't be another superintendent of education for a hundred years.

The point is that the strength of the church came from its self-appointed position as the defender of the French-Canadian soul, language and culture. To assert their position they had either to remove rivals for the role or force them to compromise, thus accepting the church's leadership.

The marks of that battle can still be felt today. Chauveau floats in Quebec history as a weak, Ottawa-dominated premier. But when you look closer you find one of the apostles of educational reform. He was a flawed government leader, but he tried to stand up to the Ultramontane political forces and was destroyed. Long after he had left the premiership, they hounded him, until his life was ruined. And along the way the negative nationalists were able to eliminate the whole idea of lay education which was being established throughout the west. Instead, real power over education fell into the hands of the nationalistic church.

The next group to take on the Ultramontanes was l'Institut canadien. Young, liberal men tried to put forward the reform policies you would have expected for that time. The only peculiarity in their program was the continuing illusion that American annexation would save French Canada. In Papineau's mind the francophones were to be saved from the British. In the Institute's they were to be saved from the negative nationalists. In both cases the

Americans, for reasons which have never been given, were thought
to be the saviours.

The Institute was destroyed by the negative nationalists. It wasn't
simply Bishop Bourget who felt this was a life-and-death battle to
save French Canada. A whole Ultramontane movement of political
nationalists backed him up. Only Laurier emerged from the wreck-
age of the Institute with power. He made some compromises. But he
also understood that the best way to escape their power to block all
reform was to deal with them on a national level from Ottawa.

Theoretically, everything then changed at the provincial level. The
revolutionary event was the arrival of Honoré Mercier. But in creating
the Parti National, the first patriotic solidarity party—the Union
Nationale and the Parti Québécois followed his model—he was
forced to abandon the real questions of reform in favour of the political fight for more autonomy. His convocation of the first provincial
premiers' conference in 1887 was the formal beginning of the federal–provincial tug-of-war which we are still involved in, and was
therefore a remarkable accomplishment. In the process, however, his
promise of universal obligatory schooling was laid aside. This was
done in order to please his Ultramontane supporters. And he put the
portfolio of colonization into the hands of an Ultramontane priest.
In other words, on the two key fronts of public policy he dramatically
weakened the democratic movement. Or rather, his personal popularity was so great that he alone was in a powerful enough position to
break the church's stranglehold on education. He wasted that power
on minor issues and actually strengthened the church's role.

His concentration on the autonomy issue made him the father of
lay solidarity. He took this old religious theme and turned it into the
key new nationalist quality.

"We are divided because we have inherited the qualifications of
red or blue . . . because it is respectable to have a name and a title
under the pretext that we have principles. . . . We must stop our
fighting among brothers and unite ourselves—Cessons nos luttes
fratricides et unissons-nous!"[5]

It is an absurd phrase and the primary question remained unasked. Solidarity in what cause? The cause was the nation. But what nation? *The nation. The nation* above all. This was pure negative nationalism. Mercier's tragedy was that he was more interesting than this. His relations with Mowat, and his speeches in favour of greater independence from Britain, were signs of potential originality. But in the end he had above all solidified the model of the Heroic martyr. Two long-surviving premiers, Mercier's son-in-law, Lomer Gouin, and Louis-Alexandre Taschereau brought in minor reforms. But they governed Quebec for most of the first half of the twentieth century on little more than the memory of the martyr Mercier's stand for autonomy. "Surely," Isaiah chanted, "he has borne our griefs, and carried our sorrows. . . . he was bruised for our iniquities, the chastisement of our peace was upon him."[6] When Gouin and Taschereau were gone, Duplessis took over and concentrated on governing in a reinforced and baroque version of the Mercier manner. There are days when Mr. Bouchard seems intent on going down the same road.

The real hero, martyr and defender of French Canada would come to power six years after Mercier was driven out. Félix Marchand was a successful writer of plays, an honest man and a remarkable administrator. He used most of his personal fortune to survive in politics. And he understood that if education could not be wrenched back from the hands of the church, francophones would slip into ever-greater difficulties. The battle was remarkably unpleasant. The Archbishop of Montreal, Mgr. Bruchési, pretended to have received a telegram from the Pope against Marchand's education-reform bill. In order to get his bill through, the premier set about abolishing the second House, which was conservative and filled with financial and political interests. The strain was so great that he died in 1900 in office without completing his task.

Marchand was a martyr, but he acted like a servant of the public good, rather than a martyr married to the people. And so Mercier—who did not trouble the established retrograde order—became the symbol of the negative nationalists. And Marchand, who took on those who claimed to be the safeguard of the nation, was buried and never mentioned again.

Lomer Gouin and Alexandre Taschereau then padded down the soft path laid out by Mercier. They integrated the old liberal myth of American annexation into their essentially anti-reform politics. This was done in the twentieth-century manner by opening Quebec for business—as Brian Mulroney and Jacques Parizeau later put it. And they did so at bargain-basement prices. They began giving the province away.

Meanwhile, on the positive side, Henri Bourassa was carrying on the debate for reform. He never held real power and so could avoid the compromises that overcame public figures such as Laurier. But Bourassa lived his truth, with all its difficulties, from that moment at the turn of the century when he said to Laurier—"To govern is to have the courage, at a given moment, to risk power to save a principle."[7]

Bourassa fought endless battles over his long career. Most of the time he was on the side of reform. He was rigorously against racism of any sort. His refusal to play along with the sympathies for corporatism and anti-Semitism, which were so popular in negative-nationalist circles in the 1930s, made him an enemy of the much-sought-after national solidarity. You will find that Groulx, Séguin and Brunet have little to say about him, beyond slighting remarks. Séguin dismisses him as "l'homme d'Ottawa."[8] Why? Because he had a vision of the whole country and its role in the world. Whatever the negative-nationalist position for the francophone citizenry at large, Bourassa incarnated public decency over more than half a century. It was as if those who accept the Séguin interpretation of history have been more interested in power than in recognizing popular choices which dissatisfy them.

The temptation here would be to leap on to Maurice Duplessis, the archetype of the negative nationalist. But it is more interesting first to look at the intellectual line of negative nationalism in the twentieth century. The tendency, when this subject is raised, is for someone to protest that general conclusions are being drawn about francophones. To the contrary. I am drawing specific conclusions about a specific political movement led by a limited number of people; a movement which, along with other factors, fed directly into the creation of the PQ.

Nevertheless, Pierre-Marc Johnson, the former PQ leader, was quite right to protest in January 1996 that "Among certain anglophone political or intellectual élites, political thought had been replaced by a disconcerting facility for getting rid of the Constitutional problem by calling Quebec society racist."[9] His own career has been an illustration of how you can be a strong nationalist while taking great care over such subjects. On the other hand I'm sure he would agree that the blame should be shared. Certain anglophones have been fast to generalize, just as certain francophones have seized upon specific criticisms of specific people and chosen to interpret them, for political purposes, as if they were generalizations. One of the traps of negative nationalism is that it limits public debate by making responsible people feel they can't criticize anyone outside of their linguistic, religious or whatever group without being seen as a racist. That is the worst sort of political correctness.

So let me repeat: I am making specific comments about specific individuals and schools of thought. Maurice Séguin's *L'Idée d'indépendance au Québec* was published in 1968 with a foreword by Denis Vaugeois, a former senior PQ MNA. In his introduction, Mr. Vaugeois talks of "the authenticity of Séguin's thought—l'authenticité de sa pensée."[10] In many ways this small book is the Bible of the modern negative-nationalist movement. If you turn to the footnotes, you discover that the last seven—in other words the references which carry the idea of independence into current times—are all from Paul Bouchard and Dostaler O'Leary. They were both self-proclaimed nationalist fascists in the 1930s and 1940s. Bouchard ran a small-circulation newspaper called *La Nation*.

I myself wouldn't bother mentioning such marginal men if Séguin hadn't based his argument in favour of separation upon them; and if the arguments, phrases and chosen terms of Séguin had not become those of the contemporary separatist/sovereigntist movement. As for the period preceding Bouchard and O'Leary, Séguin covers it with quotes from *L'Action nationale*; that is, from Abbé Groulx, Georges Pelletier and Joseph Bruchard. This is Séguin's portrait of the foundations of separatism, not mine. All of the voices he chose to trace the rise of separatism were retrograde, if not reactionary.

A single representative quote will set the atmosphere. Séguin cites Paul Bouchard as refusing ". . . the right to live a hybrid life and to create a bastard people, devoid of its own personality. We want a state in which we can live integrally the plenitude of our national life à la française..." This is fairly standard negative-nationalist rhetoric. It is both romantic yet vaguely disturbing with its soft references to purity. But what is interesting is what Séguin didn't quote from the same article. For example: "[We] stand for a complete and integral re-making of our people according to a corporative and totalitarian plan."[11]

I'm not saying that the PQ proposes a totalitarian system. But what I am pointing out is an unbroken line of intellectual thought. Paul Bouchard went on to become Duplessis's election-time propagandist. He wrote books which were songs of praise to the Union Nationale, but which also created much of the modern autonomist vocabulary. "[T]he call of Abbé Groulx, who counsels us to unify ourselves on the essential problems, (and what problem could be more essential than that of autonomy!)."[12] I suppose many people might answer, 'a number of things,' particularly if constitutional questions are not endangering society, while there are high levels of poverty which are.

But the point is that from Abbé Groulx through Paul Bouchard and his friends and on through the Montreal School up to Fernand Dumont, there is an integrated argument. The phrases are the same, even the key nouns and adjectives. Most of the writers claim to belong to a highly conservative or right-wing tradition, a few to a left-wing tradition. But they are saying essentially the same thing.

They reinterpret a long history in order to convert it into one with a lost paradise at its point of origin, which is followed by suffering and a need for autonomy. Abbé Groulx sets the tone with his evacuation of social questions from the 1837 uprising. He insists that it was a racial conflict. The very existence of a second uprising, by similar middle-class people and poor farmers—who happen to be anglophones—in a nearby town called Toronto, suddenly fades away, as if irrelevant. In fact its very existence as a parallel would be seen in Groulx's context as somehow insulting: an attack on distinctiveness.

In reality Abbé Groulx was distorting history. The Patriotes of 1837 had been the enemies of the church. By placing the revolt in a new context he changed a fight for liberty, which justified positive nationalism, into a fight for national liberation, which justified the position of the right-wing negative nationalists.

Calls for one great national party reverberate through the various interventions of the Groulx–Bouchard–Séguin school, as do calls for a chef—a leader. It is an argument very much built on a marriage of the mythologies of Papineau and Mercier as Heroic martyrs. Those who doubt the links have only to look at the kindness with which Fernand Dumont treats the role of Bishop Bourget.

This is based on the firm belief that the church was the saviour of French-Canadian culture in hard times. A positive nationalist would say the opposite. In the middle of the nineteenth century, francophone Canada was on the same reform track as anglophone Canada and indeed as most of the western world. It had a remarkable middle class which produced a remarkable political leadership.

In a difficult political battle, the forces of negative nationalism gained enough power to drag the whole society off track for close to a century. In fact the church almost destroyed a healthy and vibrant society, claiming all the while that it was saving it. The damage done by the Ultramontane movement has by no means been repaired, as the continuing theories of the negative nationalists show.

This intellectual atmosphere facilitated Maurice Duplessis's rise to power and his hold on it. A single example: many francophone reformers criticized the tendency to sell off the province's resources, extremely cheaply, to American companies. But Brunet put it that such criticisms "... should be less severe and take into account the fact that our politicians have always had to act in the very best interests of their compatriots."[13] The negative-nationalist school is suffused with an atmosphere of solidarity and élitism. 'In dangerous times we must follow loyally the great party of solidarity.'

Duplessis picked up the exact arguments used by Mercier, who had abandoned political and social reforms in order to get power. Duplessis focused on the defence of constitutional powers, while working against social reform. And, as Brunet's defence of the Union Nationale's economic policy indicates, the negative nationalists once again played the card of subjecting francophone society to American protection. The years from 1944 to 1959 were filled with words like autonomy, distinct, decentralization. This classic example of the Duplessis argument comes from a 1946 speech:

> The movement of National Union is not a narrow movement.
>   It is not a class movement.
>   It is not even a partisan movement.
>   It is neither more nor less than the sincere and convinced echo of the aspirations of a people who want to live and who will live.

He attributed his return to power in 1944 to a great battle: "A question of life or death for Quebec and Confederation—the question of the respect of the rights of Quebec and of the other provinces."[14]

But in reality he was only returned to power in 1944 because the electoral map favoured his candidates. The population voted 40 per cent for Adélard Godbout as against 36 per cent for Duplessis. In fact, the population had not been particularly impressed by the argument that Godbout had betrayed Quebec's interests when he temporarily ceded some tax powers to Ottawa in wartime. His greatest error had been to go to the polls before the electoral map was updated. This is not a niggling historical rectification. For half a century it has been central to the negative-nationalist argument that francophones rejected Godbout for a weak stand over conscription and the constitution. The truth is, they did not reject him.

Godbout, who has been vilified by the negative nationalists and virtually written out of history, was the first great reforming premier of the century. In four years he enfranchised women, finally brought in obligatory schooling and free school-books, began the process of universal medical assurance, created the structures of a professional civil service, created Hydro-Québec and set fair structures in place for unions. The whole negative-nationalist structure, including the Saint-Jean-Baptiste Society, opposed obligatory schooling. Most of it opposed votes for women. When the church began to agitate publicly against him on that issue, Godbout telephoned Cardinal Villeneuve and, in a wonderful tactical move, said that as a good Catholic he would have to resign rather than act against his church. On the other hand, he would recommend that T.D. Bouchard take his place. Bouchard was a noted anti-clerical reformer and he was the senior minister in Godbout's government. The Cardinal withdrew his opposition the next morning.[15]

And while Godbout consistently opposed conscription, he also consistently and clearly condemned fascism and corporatism. The negative nationalists skirted around the edges of the latter two issues for most of the war. As the Montreal School's writings show, they continued to skirt around the issue long after the war. The key point is that Quebecers elected Godbout and re-elected him on the basis of his reforms and his principles. The long-standing theory that Quebec was a conservative society given to negative nationalism falls apart when you realize that Duplessis was re-elected not by the populace but largely by an out-of-date electoral map. Once in power he used every doubtful technique possible to stay there.

Godbout represented the beginning of the Quiet Revolution. It was very much a product of the school of the positive nationalists in their constant battle against that of negative nationalism. Had he held power after 1944, he would have completed a process which, instead, had to wait until 1960. Duplessis, once in office, was able to roll back some of the reforms, but the movement Godbout represented continued to grow. You saw it in the postwar generation of reformers, who threw themselves into battles such as the Asbestos Strike (Jean Marchand, Gérard Pelletier and Pierre Trudeau and others). You also saw it in the work of Georges-Émile Lapalme as leader of the Opposition.

There was a hint when Duplessis died and his senior minister, Paul Sauvé, took over that there might be a new and worthwhile coalition of negative and positive nationalists. But that is one of those 'what if' illusions of history. It's worth remembering, just in passing, that it was Sauvé who went out of his way to fire Borduas from his teaching job at the École du meuble when he published *Refus global*.

Finally, a flood of reforms began with the arrival in power of Jean Lesage in Quebec City and with a wave of new figures in Ottawa. Guy Favreau and Maurice Lamontagne, Trudeau, Pelletier and Marchand, reformers like Monique Bégin and Jean-Luc Pépin. The rolling-back of church power over education now seems to have been self-evident. But Paul Gérin-Lajoie had to fight the structures every inch of the way to accomplish it under Jean Lesage. René Lévesque's work on Hydro-Québec was done in the same difficult circumstances. Between them they completed a good part of God- bout's initiatives. Again, six years later, the reformers were apparently defeated by constitution-oriented conservatism. But Lesage, like Godbout, was beaten by an out-of-date electoral map, not by the people (47.2 per cent Liberal; 40.9 per cent Union Nationale). What the positive nationalists had done in six years was create a base upon which Quebecers could catch up with the rest of Canada on all fronts.

In many ways, the arrival of René Lévesque in power in 1976 was a continuation of the Lapalme/Lesage process. Much of what he did in his first four years was pure reform politics. The new strict rules on financing election campaigns is a good example.

But in order to create his party, Lévesque had gone down the Mercier–Duplessis route. He felt he had to put together the great, all-encompassing national party. That meant, once the initial fervour of the reformers in the PQ had worn down and they had gone their way, that the party would settle into a life where progressive actions were difficult, but constitutional battles easy.

The seeds of this situation lay in Lévesque's original decision to create the party in partnership with as dubious a figure as Gilles Grégoire, the former number two of the Créditistes. The Mercier– Duplessis style of name—Parti Québécois—was one of Grégoire's victories. Lévesque had wanted a party name related to reform policies, not to identify nationalism. Gradually all the old negative nationalists, from the Union Nationale and elsewhere, gravitated to the PQ. An early strange indication of just how difficult this coalition was going to be came with Lévesque's decision to allow a statue of Duplessis to be put up beside the National Assembly. The only other statue is of Mercier.

As the realization of the permanence of the PQ in a governmental or government-in-waiting role sank into the social structures, so the enormous social gains made in the 1960s began to slip away. And the reforms of 1976 paid off only very partially.

With the arrival of the PQ came yet another return of the American myth, for which Lévesque is in part to blame. The dream that the way out of the national crisis somehow still lay south of the border has had an astonishingly persistent life. After all, south of the border is precisely where, in reality, no option had ever existed.

It's curious that Lévesque missed the lessons of history. For example, the great national party syndrome has always worked against reform in Quebec; and for that matter, elsewhere in the world. It is a characteristic of ideology and negative nationalism. It plays into the hands of those devoted to form over content and emotion over the public good.

Mercier failed with an all-inclusive coalition, while Marchand came close to succeeding with a coalition based on reform policies. Godbout and Lesage set off the Quiet Revolution by appealing to the citizenry on the basis of ideas. Duplessis went down the Mercier road and accomplished exactly what he intended. But those intentions were the opposite of Lévesque's.

So it isn't surprising that a political party which attempts to legitimize itself with the mantle of *the great national union Québécois* should end up in the hands of people like Bernard Landry and Lucien Bouchard. Or that Premier Bouchard should think it an appropriate symbol to work at Maurice Duplessis's desk; appropriate for a government which has so cut health care that it ranks ninth among the provinces in per-capita spending on citizens and ninth in the percentage of its budget devoted to health.[16] Only P.E.I. spends less.

There is also something remarkably Ultramontane about a government which imposes a 6 per cent across-the-board cut to civil servants. It is the false egalitarianism which should draw the eye. After all, some public employees earn $125,000; others are secretaries, for whom 6 per cent might be the difference between being able to pay their bills or not. The clerico-nationalist concept of solidarity and suffering always had an element in it of self-inflicted pain being essential, even good for us. It is an old Christian concept. It is also a return to the idea of the citizen as victim.

For that matter it was hardly surprising to hear the premier announcing in a peremptory manner late in the 1997 federal campaign that "Si on est souverainiste, on vote Bloc!" Surely the voters' first obligation is to themselves as responsible citizens. And the citizen votes however he or she sees fit in light of the public interest.

When I heard Mr. Bouchard's phrase my mind went back to Borduas's despair over "Les murs lisses de la peur—the smooth and slippery walls of fear." It is perhaps too soon to judge a premier. He still has time to become whatever he wants. He doesn't have to continue down a road which is ever more reminiscent of the negative side of nationalism.

What is clear is that the other side—that of the positive nationalists—has gone silent. It is as if an obsession with the business of business has caused them to confuse corporatism with the public good. Certainly they have not forgotten how to look outwards, but they do so in a primarily commercial manner, thus forgetting that their primary duty is as citizens to the larger public good. Instead they also have fallen into using the mechanisms of fear.

The citizens are left with a meagre choice. They can be frightened into solidarity with a negative nationalism which increasingly has taken on the form of a religion and the content of uninspired basic politics. Or they can be frightened into conforming to economic paradigms which don't work, because they also are little more than religion without content.

This is the sort of despairing atmosphere in which the citizenry may be wheedled into emotional acts they will later regret. But it is also a time when individuals often withdraw into themselves, carefully looking out for ways to make sense of the situation, conscious of the need to rediscover the reforming strengths which have helped them in the past.

If the voice of positive nationalism is silent, that doesn't mean it no longer interests most citizens. Nor that there are no interesting

320   voices being raised. I hear them increasingly trying to find ways of
       making themselves heard. But for the moment the formal places of
       public discourse are dominated by either the negative or the utili-
       tarian. In that sense this is a period which resembles the 1830s or
       the 1930s. People are looking for a way out of an unsatisfactory sit-
       uation and their élites, instead of listening, have slipped into rhetor-
       ical choruses.

PART IV

← ─────────────────── →

APPLIED MEMORY

Quand est-ce qu'on a laissé tomber les amarres
Comment est-ce qu'on a perdu tous les chemins ...

L'ombre des absents est sans voix
Et se confond maintenant avec les murs
De la chambre vide.
Hector de Saint-Denys Garneau, *Monde irrémédiable désert*

Trying to Remember

IT IS PARTICULARLY DIFFICULT TO look at the past and its relevance when the air is filled with the excitement of revolutionary decision-making. That Canada is, above all, an extremely nuanced place is lost in the surreal clarity of referenda politics—not just those of separation, but of efficiency and trade and economics and debt, and other manifestations of corporatism.

The most peculiar and apparently seductive of those manifestations is the politics of anti-government politics. I am not referring to any particular government, but to the politics of false populism which say that democracy by its very nature is anti-government. This argument requires an interesting twist of the mind, since one of the central roles of representative democracy is to produce a responsible government.

When I say that Canada is, above all, an extremely nuanced place, I don't simply mean complicated. With experience we have found many of the carefully weighted ways of functioning which are necessary for us to be able to govern ourselves without pretending to resolve or eliminate the real, indeed the essential, complexities.

Now suddenly, the public place seems to have been swept clear of nuance and thus of memory. This artificial clarity itself represents a complex phenomenon since it is not about forgetting, but about pretending you never knew. And "so each community," as the historian Desmond Morton puts it, becomes "a prisoner of its amnesia."[1]

We have been through much of this before. Last time it took a slightly different form. Those who have a taste for black comedy

324 will get a sense of it by reading many of the popular histories written in the first half of this century. A few are honest attempts at balance. Most are baroque dithyrambs, praising the glories of the
British Empire or the purity of New France, depending on which
language they are written in. They roam haplessly through all the
possible clichés about the English race or the French race, positive
and negative. Anti-Semitism, anti-middle-Europeanism, anti-Asian,
paternalism towards Natives—it's all there. And yet this low-level
colonial rhetoric in both languages did not reflect an equivalent
level of applied policy. The attitudes existed and some of the policies. But so did attitudes and policies counterbalancing these.

Our problem today isn't simply a matter of schools teaching too
little history or of a highly politicized approach to what is taught.
Nor is it something that we share with other developed nations,
although a part of the problem is shared.

For example, there is the great uncertainty surrounding knowledge at a time of constant mutation in how we communicate. This
uncertainty can't be judged as a good or an evil. It just has to be
made sense of or we may lose the social and political contracts we
have spent so long developing.

How could satellite dishes and the Internet endanger social contracts? To the extent that they create an overwhelming sense of
immediacy—of today—combined with an ever-fragmenting
promise of tomorrow, this technology makes it difficult to dwell on
the meaning of established patterns. I'm not suggesting that these
established patterns are necessarily good or should be immutable.
Simply that they are there and represent our efforts so far. They are
what we call civilization; the agreements among people by which
they exist together. Some are conscious and visible, others unconscious and invisible. Each element is built upon the others. You
could say that they are the imprints of memory, like magnified versions of Aboriginal song-lines. To the extent that technology creates a religion of change without reference to those ongoing human
efforts, it becomes an enemy of civilization. But there is no need to

see technology in this way. After all, the governing factor is our ability to find ways of using it rather than being used.

Beyond education and technology lie other factors. There are movements and individuals which can only justify themselves if there is a need for abrupt massive change. In a nuanced society there is almost never such a need. Those whose success depends upon massive change must therefore paint a portrait of blockage, massive inflexibility, threatening international forces beyond our control, failure and, of course, betrayal, in order to make people believe there is such a need. Since this rarely reflects the reality of a developed society, and in particular of a society built on nuance, they must ignore reality by focusing attention on a mythological debate constructed of shards taken from reality. Worse still, they can only turn this into reality by causing the breakdown of the system, thus justifying their original arguments of crisis and failure. These methods are common to ideologues of all sorts and to those whose ambitions or delusions cause them to believe they have an Heroic mission.

Beyond these ideologues and Heroes there is yet another factor; this one is particularly prevalent in Canada: the persistent colonialism of much of our élites—anglophone and francophone, federalist and separatist /sovereigntist, Western and Eastern. So many of them, as they rise, find suddenly that their new vista onto the empires, current and past, fills them with insecurity. Their responsibilities give them contact with the empire élites; or at least they catch glimpses of them at close range. And they are unnerved to discover a class so sure of itself. In other words, our élites tend to be troubled by our nuanced existence. You could even say it bores them, the way colonials are always bored by their own reality.

We can imagine the effect of Harold Innis's profoundly Canadian dictum—"Most forward looking people have their heads turned sideways"—were it presented to them. In a perfect imitation of the colonial mind they ask, glancing straight ahead over the border, why can't we be just like them—bluff and clear and monolithic. "If, as I believe," René-Daniel Dubois writes, "our memory is rotting, shoved into the drawer of expensive accessories . . .," well, they would rather not remember.[2]

←   →

I could almost sympathize with their indifference when faced, as we all are, by the reduction of memory to constitutional considerations. This is not a fault of the PQ any more than it is of the Reform party. Somehow we have allowed the place in which we live to be treated as if it were no more than a clausal analysis and its purpose a search for the correct definition of adjectives and nouns. The society has been reduced to a lawyer's brief, except when it is treated as a balance sheet.

No doubt the reformulating of the constitution in 1982 upset some, pleased others, solved some problems and created others. But it is hard to embrace the argument that something someone did in that constitutional negotiation constitutes a pact-breaking act. After all, what a glance over twentieth-century western constitutional history reveals is not a pretty sight. If whatever happened in 1982 were enough to explode a country, all of western civilization would be a terrain of smouldering ruins.

Besides, even the simplest of questions over the nature of that event remain unclear. For example, did Quebec have a veto before 1982? If so, who caused her to lose it? And does she have it back again? And if so, who put it back? There alone is sufficient material for several books or political campaigns.

On Mr. Bouchard's short-list of sentences is the assertion that 1982 was a coup de force by which Quebec lost major powers in the areas of education and language. The phrase is certainly dramatic. You might even say picturesque. However, its use suggests that Mr. Bouchard has no experience of places where that term—coup de force—has practical meaning. Claude Ryan is a federalist, but most people agree that he is a severely honest man. Dourly honest. He is an expert in this area of constitutional argument and he has made a point of publicly stating that, while the process which produced the result in 1982 was unacceptable, Quebec did not actually lose any powers.

Elections, referenda, lives are spent debating the point. I myself find it difficult to reduce a country to this sort of court-room drama. Although I do understand how analytic minds can concentrate on these specific events with such reductionist pleasure.

Perhaps a more human way of looking at such a situation is to remember that what is all-consuming in the heat of the battle, with time, tends to slip into a larger context. And the larger context in a relatively open society has its own momentum—its own ongoing correctional mechanisms. For example, the force of the public good tends to gradually adjust specific wrongs until they meet its standards. In other words the wrongs are eliminated not through a second dramatic change, but through a gradual process. In a more authoritarian society, this may not happen.

Canada, being a nuanced, complex and relatively decentralized society, usually ends up finding ways of adjusting specific errors in order to deal with social dissatisfaction. The fact of being nuanced, complex and decentralized also means that these adjustments take time and come with a great deal of moaning and groaning. The Heroic is a stranger to this process. And there is nothing wrong with the moaning and groaning, which is one of the characteristics of the democratic process. All of which means that to reduce history to a permanent close-focus demonization of a single event is to risk losing track of reality. Which is not to say that the messiness and dissatisfaction produced by 1982 doesn't need to be dealt with.

The continuing theme of Canadian history is reconciliation. The recurrent underpinning is reconciliation through alliances based on principle. The recurring negative is the belief among many in the élites that alliances based on group interest will do, or that the solution is to replace the idea of reconciliation with either monolithic domination or separate monolithic groups.

The idea of reconciliation through reform began with William Lyon Mackenzie. It was at the heart of his active support of Papineau and the Patriotes.

In the aftermath of the two failed rebellions, Mackenzie's idea was picked up by the great Dr. Baldwin, father of Robert and the father-figure of the reform movement. It was in turn adopted by the bilingual Francis Hinks, who began conversations with reformers in Montreal. Finally, Robert Baldwin came to believe that this was the only way to assure a society built on ethical foundations.

At that point Louis-Hippolyte LaFontaine became convinced of the idea and laid it out for the public in his remarkable Address to the electors of Terrebonne. "Ours is a common cause," he argued. What was the cause? The strengthening and growth of the community—in this case francophone—through a permanent alliance with its true friends, the anglophone reformers of Upper Canada. In both colonies they were struggling against the class, religious and racial attitudes of the anti-reformers. The historian Allan Greer rightly points out that although present in both places at that time, "'ethnic nationalism' was much more characteristic of the anglophone Tories of Lower Canada than of the French-speaking Patriots."[3] The same could be said of the Orange Order in Upper Canada. And the reformers, both anglophone and francophone, understood—with a maturity which has seemed often to be missing in Europe until very recently—that one bit of ethnic nationalism would give birth to another through the reproduction of mirrored opposition. The only way through such a destructive mess was to understand that, beyond the narrow prejudices of conventional thought, there was in truth a common cause. And so a concept born in Toronto was taken up by a group of young Lower-Canada reformers, hardened by their terrible experiences during 1837 and 1838.

Then something unexpected happened. The balance of the creative

imagining of what Canada could be passed from the anglophones to
the francophones.

These two young men—Baldwin and LaFontaine—gave form to
the idea with their humanist pact. But they were by no means alone.
In the first Union election the reformers won large majorities in
both Upper and Lower Canada and so dominated the eighty-four-
seat legislature. Later, Cartier and Macdonald would give substance
to the next step. But in both cases the real creative force came from
LaFontaine and Cartier. What I am saying is that one of the explanations for the confusion today among many anglophones is that, if
Canada has the complex and interesting shape it has, it is largely
because the anglophones of the day adjusted themselves to a vision
which originated largely in Quebec.

I'm not suggesting that francophones had all the power. Far from
it. Often not enough. Nor that the anglophones were victims. On
the contrary. Most of the population took to the bizarre experiment
with an odd sort of pleasure which might be called cooperative
curiosity. And I can think of nothing more appropriate—more
humanist—in a democracy than that the majority should be will-
ingly led by the minority.

This imagining power did not, of course, remain in one place.
Over the last 150 years it has bounced around the country. The
West had an enormous conceptual role quite early on, with men
like Clifford Sifton, James Lougheed and J.W. Dafoe; and in a second
period with Alberta's Henry Wood and J.S. Woodsworth and even to
some extent with William Aberhart. When his time finally came,
John Diefenbaker, although an erratic prime minister, was central to
reimagining the myth of a country which existed beyond the logic
of southern, central cities. While he may not have understood the
language question, his ideas mirrored exactly those which motivate
a region like Lac Saint-Jean.

Beyond these personalities there were all the Western agrarian
and social reform movements. These were central to bringing the
national perception of the public good into the twentieth century.

330 This real leadership—that of ideas and direction—far outweighed the still-small Western population. Much of their desire for reform coalesced in the Western-dominated CCF, whose policies set the direction for Canada after the Second World War. It was an influence which culminated under Tommy Douglas's leadership. Although never more than the premier of a small-population province and leader of a smallish opposition party in Ottawa, he had more impact on the national drive to create a society based on social justice than any Liberal or Conservative Cabinet minister or any group of ministers. And the federal civil service of the sixties and seventies was dominated intellectually by Westerners like Al Johnson and Tommy Shoyama, many of them products of the Douglas school. Interestingly enough, the West's moments of greatest leadership have tended to come in cooperation with Quebec.

As Quebec slipped into the negative protectionism of the Ultramontane movement in the latter part of the nineteenth century, and then shielded itself from the meanness of the anti-French movements which the Orange Order and D'Alton McCarthy had spawned, so it lost its leadership role. But that came back again in the 1960s, as did the West's.

One of the most curious things today is that the two regions most apparently dissatisfied with the state of the country—Quebec and the West—are the two which have held the role of national conceptual leadership for much of Confederation and for most of the last thirty years. Ontario and the Maritimes have been relatively passive. In the 1960s and 1970s they did attempt to put forward ideas of economic nationalism and these were swept aside by Quebec and the West.

I am not arguing that Western alienation, tied in good part to distance, is not very real and important, or that Quebec is not faced every day by the recurring question of how a francophone minority can best live on an anglophone continent. Both of these situations have the *gravitas* of reality and will always be with us. These are much more important than solvable problems. They are a condition.

These two regions and the rest of the country must work every day in order to make that condition bearable; to take it into consideration; to shift the manner in which the other regions might act or think if they limited themselves to narrow, short-term interests. As someone from a Western family and who has lived in Alberta, Manitoba, Ontario and Quebec, I can't help but be conscious of the difficulty which the centre has in stretching itself during the day-to-day business of nationhood in order to include the full national picture in their considerations.

But what I am talking about here is the imaginative drive which shaped and is constantly reshaping the country. That drive is in many ways the product of the condition proper to these two regions. Yet no matter how successful and indeed central to the country's overall project it may be, it cannot erase the effects of the basic condition of francophones and of people in the West. So the condition and the positive reaction to the condition are like parallel tracks of mythology. Still, the result is an interesting psychological trick. A region has considerable real power on a repeated basis, but is able sincerely to dismiss the conscious acceptance of that power as if it were nothing. How? Well, for a start by the simple act of automatically dismissing its elected representatives, should they attain power—that is, assume office—as of no consequence or as the wrong kind of people.

Some of us interpret these dismissals as a clever trick—a way of being both the occupier of power and the critic of power at the same time. I would say it has more to do with our constant mistaking of a 'condition' to be lived with for a 'problem' which can be solved. So when the elected representative doesn't solve the problem, he becomes the representative of the problem; all of which is a way of denying the condition.

But this also has to do with confusing two very different phenomena. There is a perfectly justifiable regional dissatisfaction or alienation. And then there is a movement espousing a right-wing ideology. In each region the ideologues attempt to hide themselves inside the alienation. Quebec and the West have had a great deal of power. The right-wing movements of these two regions have not; that is, not at the national level. And that's because they represent a revocation of the reforming pact upon which Canada has been built. These retrograde movements have spent and continue to spend a great deal of time denying either that there ever was such a thing as a pact of two, let alone three, peoples or that such a pact has ever been workable. But at a more profound level they are denying that the pact was primarily one of reforming ideas and that Canada at its most essential is a rejection of precisely the non-cooperative, non-reconciling dogma which these right-wing movements represent. To the extent that they succeed, so Canada must fail.

For most of the last 150 years Canadians have returned national governments which attempt to reflect the complexity of the national reconciliation. It is hard to believe this at a time when a party like Reform brings back not the historic leadership of the West, but the damaging negativism of the Orange Order; and the Bloc offers the kind of sectarian arguments which LaFontaine had hoped to have rechannelled into positive participation.

I say this knowing that many citizens give these two parties their vote for perfectly valid reasons of dissatisfaction and not with a divisive or sectarian intent. The very complexity of large populations and a representative system means that there will always be a gap between what a party actually intends or promises and why a given citizen may vote for them. That's why parliamentary elections are merely intended to be indications of a general direction and not referenda-style blank cheques. That's why neo-conservative and/or false-populist governments, such as that of Mr. Harris at the provincial level, treat elections as if they were referenda conferring blank cheques. They reject the limitations on personal power which are endemic to representative democracy.

In any case, the historic fact is that at the federal level these parties of the extremes have never won enough power to gain a formal share of the national public power.

And however successful they may be at burying their particular policies inside the regional conditions of alienation, there is every reason to be grateful that they have not succeeded in their central aim, which has nothing to do with alienation and everything to do with leadership based on the exploitation of anger and fear.

24 Fragments of a Past — I

THE LEADERSHIP ROLE OF THE francophones in imagining Canada began in part as a conscious policy of the anglophone reformers to undo the damage done during the 1830s by the Château Clique and the Family Compact. They were sending an unequivocal message to the colonial authorities that they would play neither the racial nor the class game. This was an example of the force of the public good adjusting a specific situation to meet its own much higher standards. It also shows the extent to which the country was not the product of a reaction but the creation of a positive, intellectual idea. In short, Canada coalesced in the 1840s on the basis of ideas, thanks to the pact of the real reformers.

Austin Cuvillier, a well-known Quebecer, was specifically chosen as the first Speaker of the Unified Parliament of Canada to demonstrate through real power the reformers' message that the assimilation strategy was dead. Speaker, in the days before responsible government, was a crucial position. Whoever sat in the Chair was, in many ways, the formal weapon of the majority in its struggle against non-responsible government.

Remember, this was not simply the majority party. It was a coalition chosen by the electors to put the well-advertised reconciliation in place. I say well-advertised because the Address to the electors of Terrebonne was only one of many public explanations of the reform idea. LaFontaine, as I have mentioned, had lost his seat in the first Union election because the governor's gangs blocked the polls. Baldwin then gave up one of his two seats, so that his ally might enter the legislature, and wrote to his electors in the fourth riding of York explaining the situation:

The return of Mr. LaFontaine by an Upper Canada constitu-
ency will be a substantial pledge of our sympathy with our
Lower Canada friends and form the strongest bond of union
between us.[1]

In 1842 LaFontaine became the first prime minister of a responsible Canadian government. He had at first wanted an arrangement
involving the leadership of two equals, but Baldwin refused, insisting that the other take charge.

The two leading positions in the civil service went to well-known
francophones. Étienne Parent became the chief civil servant—the
greffier or what we now call Clerk of the Privy Council—a position
he went on to hold for thirty years, which included serving for the
first five years of Confederation. René-Édouard Caron became president of the Executive and Legislature Councils. The other senior
positions were fairly spread among anglophones and francophones.

This first tentative experiment with democratic government in
1842 wasn't permitted to last long. The governor died and a new
retrograde governor arrived. But on the positive side, the old parliamentary anti-reform forces which replaced LaFontaine and Baldwin in power had already begun to come to terms with the new
configuration of the country. In fact they did more than come to
terms in a Machiavellian manner. They actually seemed to understand the nature of the new experiment, or rather the normalization
of the old peculiar idea that cooperation among communities was
normal in a northern, marginal country. It was they who introduced
a law re-establishing French as one of the two official languages. All
parties supported it. The interdiction—which had never been
respected—had lasted only three years.

Still today negative nationalists in Quebec repeatedly go back to
the technical point that the intent of the union, and therefore eventually of Canada, was the assimilation of francophones. That is
incorrect. It was the calculation of the British government and
British colonial authorities that union would cause assimilation. It

was neither a Canadian idea nor a Canadian initiative. This British calculation was based on the assumption that the union would exist in an atmosphere of sectarian divisions. That is, their strategy was based on believing Lord Durham's naïve and ignorant assertion that "two nations were warring in the bosom of a single state." From the first moment of the new arrangement, the anglophone reformers sought reconciliation with the francophone reformers.

Immediately, the union was stood on its head by the citizenry— by the phenomenon of citizens serving the public good. The union therefore meant the exact opposite of that which London had intended. It became, very precisely, the central tool which would insure there was never assimilation. What's more, intelligent anglophone conservatives, who would have gone along with the assimilation strategy, almost immediately understood that everything had changed and so they scrambled to form their own reconciliations.

When a few years later Cartier and Macdonald began their long-running alliance, it was in many ways a perfect illustration of this idea of reconciliation. They each came from the extremes. Cartier had been a particularly brave young Patriote leader under Wolfred Nelson at St. Denis. And Macdonald had opposed the Rebellion Losses Bill. The experience of cooperation taught them a kind of tough moderation which would become characteristic of the Canadian conundrum.

Macdonald made only two major mistakes in his career. First, there was his handling of the Métis crisis. By then Cartier was dead and Macdonald had no first-rate francophone ministers. The political impetus in Quebec had gone over to the opposition. He was suffering from the syndrome of most long-lived governments—his ministers, whether francophone or anglophone, were more the creatures of power than the wielders of it. His mistake had to do not so much with francophone relations, as with the West and how it should be governed. In a sense he was as new to it as everyone was, understood little of the West and was more interested in fending off his troublesome supporters in Ontario than in understanding a distant cause. The West had been Cartier's great interest. He had been the one who understood it and its geopolitics. Macdonald was out of his depth. None of which excuses a major error or makes up for the tragedy. He saw it as a question of public order and somehow didn't understand the rest.

His second error was his belief that he could play D'Alton McCarthy on a line, as he had played so many other ambitious individuals and unpleasant questions, until they tired themselves out. That was his down-to-earth way of avoiding extreme explosions. But he hadn't really grasped McCarthy's puritanical edge. Nor did he understand that this was the face of the new racial nationalism which would dominate so much of the twentieth century throughout the western world. He couldn't see that the drive which appeared anti-francophone was actually a mirror image of the nationalism being introduced into Quebec.

It was nineteenth-century nationalism gradually taking on its twentieth-century face; what would eventually be called Maurrasian nationalism, after Charles Maurras, the right-wing French nationalist who combined intellectual and romantic arguments about community, blood and race. Maurras avoided the worst of the fascist arguments. He was of a more sophisticated school. His publication—*L'Action française*—influenced similar schools of thought in several countries. Abbé Groulx's magazine, at first also called *L'Action française*, and then *L'Action nationale*, was a direct imitation. In 1945 Maurras was condemned by the French courts for collaboration with the Germans and he was thrown out of the Académie française.

Maurras was the respectable, then semi-respectable, then criminal and now again surprisingly respectable intellectual face of retrograde nationalism in the west. His strange combination of intellect, romanticism and plain prejudice produced arguments which could not be dealt with in a normal debate. He had found a way to so twist the general understanding of the public good and decent human relations that it would take decades before a language to counteract him effectively could be found.

D'Alton McCarthy belonged to what might be called the founding generation of Maurrasian nationalism. In that sense it isn't surprising that Macdonald at first didn't really understand what
McCarthy represented. By 1890 the prime minister had begun to
put a face on this phenomenon—"The demon of religious animosity which I had hoped had been buried in the grave of George
Brown has been revived.... McCarthy has sown the Dragon's teeth.
I fear they may grow up to be armed men."[2]

In spite of these two running sores, Macdonald's attitudes
towards reconciliation were unchanged. For example, in that same
year, 1890, he was actively blocking the Manitoba government's
attempts to weaken French rights. "I have no accord with the desire
expressed in some quarters that by any move whatever there should
be an attempt made to oppress the one language or to render it inferior to the other; I believe that would be impossible if it were tried,
and it would be foolish and wicked if it were possible." Cartier's
biographer quite fairly says that Macdonald had been inspired by
him "with the spirit of nationhood."[3]

◀━━━━━▶

One of the factors which gave francophones such weight in the
designing of the country is that they have tended to send their best
leaders to the federal level. LaFontaine, Cartier, Laurier, Lapointe,
Trudeau; whatever you think of their politics, they were players of
the highest quality.

Curiously enough, Lucien Bouchard goes out of his way in his
memoirs to say about the Trudeau–Marchand–Pelletier commitment
to federal politics—"... for once English Canadians would see something else arrive in Ottawa than second-rate francophones with second-rate intellects, ready to trade whatever they had or didn't have in
their guts for pensions and titles."[4] Of course, every parliament
—including provincial legislatures—has its share of time-servers

from every region. There are also large quantities of modest, useful local politicians.

But the francophone leadership in Ottawa over a century and a half has most of the time been of the first level. And for much of that same time the provincial leaders have been less impressive. Some of the best—Félix Marchand, T.D. Bouchard and Adélard Godbout—because they worked against the negative nationalists of their day —have been erased from the public memory or dismissed in some way as a northern equivalent of Uncle Tom.

We all have the right to dislike or dismiss those we disagree with. But this systematic elimination from respectable consideration and often more or less from the public memory of the most successful francophone federalists creates a distortion of history which is help-ful to no one. It is particularly harmful to the francophones' sense of themselves and of their accomplishments. It can't help but be pro-foundly disturbing to the citizenry to give such strong support to remarkably active leaders only to discover that the hands which write our history eliminate these same figures the moment they leave power. It is as if democratic legitimacy were rejected by a part of the intellectual élites; as if in a paternalistic manner, they are cer-tain that they know better. The citizenry supported Pierre Trudeau for fifteen years. Yet to utter his name in Quebec in public debate in other than condemnation is to eliminate yourself from 'serious' con-sideration. It could be argued that, whatever the man's failures, what is involved here is more contempt for the citizen than for Trudeau. Since his successes are quite simply not mentioned, that contempt can only be interpreted as ideological certainty in the inquisitorial tradition. In fact the phenomenon is not primarily tied to specific events. Otherwise why would the names of LaFontaine, Laurier and Cartier be denigrated and more or less eliminated in the same way?

This rewriting of history by simply dismissing the most impor-tant figures on the other side began not so long ago. According to the historian Jean Hamelin it was "l'école paranoïaque"—the Montreal

School—which introduced this tack. "It was Brunet who reinvented LaFontaine as a traitor." Why? Because he drew Quebec into Canada. Brunet accused the reformers of being very confused and easily won over to the anglophone cause. For Séguin it was necessary to "unmask the imposter" of the LaFontaine tradition. And, as an inheritor of the Montreal School tradition, it isn't surprising to find Fernand Dumont describing the arrival of democracy in the 1840s as only "apparent." "It consecrated the failure of the social project of the Patriots."[5] All of this is based on an ethnic interpretation of the Rebellions and a denial that there was any larger, shared, social cause. It is also based on ignoring the reform legislation which the LaFontaine government enacted in a very short space of time.

Interestingly enough, the historical method in question was invented and perfected in Moscow. The cutting and pasting of group photos and documents to eliminate individuals no longer in favour was just an extreme version of this ideological cleansing of the public memory. What's more, such rewriting through erasure is almost identical to D'Alton McCarthy's approach to debating ideas. When Laurier was responding to McCarthy's anti-French bill in 1890, he mocked the manner in which Baldwin and LaFontaine were described by McCarthy as "petits politiqueurs."[6] It was exactly the manner in which Cartier would later be discarded by the negative-nationalist school as a 'railway lawyer.'

Of course Baldwin and LaFontaine were anything but small-time politicians. They were engaged in that most complex of public acts—attempting to match imaginative initiative with careful moderation. This requires a great deal more intelligence and courage than does the abrasive monotheism of a large number of the political leaders whose memory has been retained for admiration.

The key negotiations leading to Confederation took place in Quebec City in 1864. The resulting resolutions more or less became the constitution and the quasi-totality of these agreements are still in the constitution as reformulated in 1982.

The negotiations took place on the cliffs of the St. Lawrence, in a building which stood exactly where Champlain had climbed most days from his house below up to his headquarters. Negotiations are negotiations, but in 1864 they took place in a conscious belief that they were part of an historical continuity. The legislature later burnt down and there is now a park on the cliff's edge, with a statue of Cartier. I brushed away the snow last winter to read the quotations chosen for the monument.

> In a country like ours
> All rights must be protected
> All convictions respected.

It's worth noting in passing that Cartier invented the Canadian army with his militia bill and was its first minister. The structure of the country and the communication system represented a vision of the future. But the army was a victory over the past. After all, it meant that Canada's first minister of defence, or militia as it was then called, had begun his career as one of the few successful armed rebels of 1837.

◄┄┄┄┄┄►

But let me come back to this idea of Canada as a country largely imagined by francophones. One of the confusing details has been the facility with which anglophones cede power to francophones when many in the latter group say what they really want is something more like duality of power. Rather than deal with this, the anglophone tends to say, 'Well, look, you just run it.' That was what Baldwin did in the first days of the Union.

The Montreal School or a PQ minister would insist that this is just a clever way of getting a francophone to "remettre le Québec à sa place," as Jacques Parizeau puts it.[7] According to this argument, power is given to the wrong francophones; people who are creatures of the 'English.'

But, with the sole exception of Jean Chrétien, those francophone leaders have been elected with majorities in Quebec as well as strong representation elsewhere. So again the negative-nationalist argument is actually an insult to the intelligence and competence of francophone voters. In a curious attempt to distract us from this insult we are constantly told that these choices are not the result of stupidity or incompetence but of a debilitating psychological state. The voters apparently can't help themselves. Their subconscious dominates.

Fernand Dumont says that "the worst fault—défaut—of Quebec francophones is their contempt for themselves—le mépris de soi."[8] Ex-colonials often do have a problem with self-respect. In Canada, anglophones suffer from it as much as francophones. But for neither is this an all-consuming problem. It's just one of our many characteristics. And to the extent that it is a serious problem, it is that of the élites, not the citizenry in general.

It is interesting that Mr. Dumont, a noted social analyst, so easily applied to society as a whole an analysis of his own personal psyche. Had he sought about him, he might have found he shared it with others in the élites and—no doubt to his consternation—in the anglophone élites. Even in our worst characteristics there seem to be signs of a shared culture; a distressing absence of solitudes.

There are two fairly standard approaches to political power used by those who seek it. Some seek power with the assumption that the citizenry are the source of legitimacy and are to be treated with respect. Others concentrate on identifying whatever insecurities there are in the citizenry and on exploiting them. This is done by exaggerating those insecurities in order to create an atmosphere of fear.

Public figures who do this are usually precisely the individuals within society who suffer the most from a "mépris de soi." And they attempt to draw everyone else into their personal problem, as if it were a societal problem, until in fact it becomes central to the setting of public policy. This is a situation which the citizenry in general

have a great deal of trouble focusing on. It seems so odd that those
who seek power most ardently are often those most racked by insecurity. And the more assertive they are, the more this is likely to be
the case.

The tragedy for the citizen is that nothing is more harmful to
the service of the public good than a leader driven by his inferiority complex. This is one of the keys to demagoguery and to the
modern false Hero. If the leader has contempt for himself, on winning power he cannot help but have contempt for the citizen. He
assumes that the only way to lead is through emotional blackmail
and the unleashing of fear. The magic of public office turns personal insecurity not into self-confidence but into superiority, which
is an aggressive form of insecurity. But you can't serve the public
good in a democracy if you have contempt for the citizenry. At best
you can offer a noblesse oblige or corporatist version of service; in
other words, you know what the people need and you will give it
to them.

And what of dismissing people like LaFontaine, Cartier, Laurier,
Lapointe and Trudeau on the basis that they are somehow creatures
of another community than the one which produced them? It is
true that politics is complicated and requires compromise. It is also
true that to lead a large, complex country you must attempt to keep
the whole in mind and so not become the servant of one part only.
After all, the core of the original pact, which still holds true, is that
progress and the public good were best served by an alliance of
reformers across community lines. These men, by all accounts, were
particularly intelligent, extremely tough and did not suffer from a
mépris de soi. Put aside for the moment your views on their politics.
They would have been rather difficult people to push around; to
treat as your creature. My impression is that in the push-and-shove
business of politics, they pushed more than they were shoved.

But what about the question of the anglophones so often being
ready to cede power? Not all anglophones and not in all regions
and not all the time, but enough to give parliamentary majorities on

a regular basis. To suggest that there is somehow a large conscious or subconscious plot by millions of anglophone voters to elect captive francophones would suggest an astonishing contempt for that mass of citizens, to say nothing of an addiction to conspiratorial theories in the one who believes it. The continuing Montreal School view of the citizenry seems to be that the francophones are naïve and craven and waiting to be saved, while the anglophones are evil and Machiavellian and must be kept at a good distance.

Reasonable people can only ignore this and question more closely the anglophone attitude. It doesn't seem to be based on a desire for a unitary or even a centralized country. Over the last century and a half, power has slipped as you would expect, back and forth, between the two levels of government. There have been more or less four periods during which Ottawa seemed to set the course and four during which it was the provinces. We are clearly now in a period dominated by the provinces. But at no time has there been even the possibility of a centralized, let alone a unitary, state. This became clear the moment Oliver Mowat took over as premier of Ontario in 1872. And if further confirmation were needed, it came when Mowat teamed up with Honoré Mercier, premier of Quebec as of 1887, to oppose Ottawa's use of certain central powers, such as the provision for the disallowance of provincial legislation, even though the constitution clearly gave Ottawa that right.

What can be said is that most anglophones do not want a pretend country—one which is little more than a treaty between independent groups. I think that is because francophone Canada is at the core of how anglophones see the country and therefore themselves. As I said earlier, this is not because the anglophones have no core of their own. Rather, it is simply what it sounds like. Francophone Canada is at the core of how anglophone Canada sees itself and the country. This does not lessen the role of Westerners or the perception of their role in the country. It is simply a central characteristic of the nation.

Séguin, in a standard formula, insisted that "the English majority in the federal parliament will always form an all-powerful block against the French Canadian block, however solid it is."[9]

The truth is that anglophone Canada hasn't managed to form a block more than twice, in a century and a half. Francophones are usually, therefore, in a position to hold the balance of power or to be a key part of the balance of power, which is very healthy because it breaks up the idea of minority. For linguistic reasons, if for no other, the sense of being a minority continues among francophones and will continue. And a theoretically dangerous balance of power is there and always will be. But the political reality is, as I said in earlier chapters, that the anglophones also see themselves as a minority. And the regional realities mean that they are broken up into anywhere from four to six quite different voting groups.

The point is that, whoever runs it, most anglophones seem to want the country they feel they agreed to in 1841. Their fear is neither of regionalism nor of particular words like 'distinct' nor of inequality between provinces. Whatever the rhetoric, everyone knows there has never been equality and that equality in this context has nothing to do with individual rights but only with a theoretical concept of administration. Alberta would be horrified if it found its new power and influence in the federation cut back severely because it was to be in strict equality with, for example, New Brunswick. The concept of the equality of provinces is just as rhetorical and abstract as that of a distinct society. To the extent that it is a reference to a real view of Canada, equality is used to mean that the provinces should have less to do with each other and therefore have less concern, let alone responsibility, for other provinces and therefore the citizens within them. It is a concept entirely aimed at allowing richer provinces not to share with the poorer.

The underlying concern is that the agreement of the 1840s established an idea of government by shared principles, not by

346   group interests. Our experience over the last 150 years has been
that each time group interest surges, it endangers the shared principles—whether it was the expulsion of the Japanese Canadians
and the Chinese head tax in B.C., the racial problems and eugenics under Social Credit in Alberta, the language and school questions in Manitoba, the rise of the Orange Order in Ontario, the
very marginal methods used by Duplessis to stay in power in Quebec, the class exploitation in Newfoundland or the mistreatment of
Blacks in Nova Scotia. Not that the federal government has been
innocent of unprincipled action. You have only to look at the role
of the Ministry of Immigration on the Jewish question during the
1930s and 1940s.

However, the complexity of the central government offers some
hope of righting the balance sooner or later. And the tension
between the federal and the provincial governments offers another
mechanism for the protection of the public interest. Our experience
suggests that political movements which say they are seeking clarity of purpose through concepts like the equality of provinces are
often using a metaphor which disguises their group interests. The
strength of the federation is that it hampers that clarity.

Nevertheless, our attention is constantly drawn to arguments
over which level of government should exercise which power. The
rise to levels of hysterical fervour of the extremely mediocre religion of efficiency has become part of this argument. And overlap
between levels of government is condemned as inefficient, when it
is often a necessary and useful aspect of federalism. It is particularly useful to the citizen.

In these arguments, one level criticizes the other's management of
a particular responsibility—which is a healthy phenomenon—and
the other usually offers a nationalistic reply. In other words, rather
than deal with the criticism, they invoke local or national pride.
Even what criticism there is, is increasingly muted because the
growth of the technocracies has led quite naturally to discreet
behind-the-scenes negotiations and tacit agreements. This is classic

corporatism which, needless to say, leaves the citizenry out of the discussion.

But if federalism works, it is precisely because the citizen has a mechanism to look at most issues from two points of view—those of two levels of government. For federalism to work, we need the two levels criticizing each other. We need the chicanes.

Instead, we are told that these arguments are all about the battle between national unity and provincial rights. About centralization versus decentralization. So all disagreements are reduced to a curious combination of ideology and abstract management theory. We are not allowed to interpret them as real debates over content, policy and the service of the public good.

Today the federal government decentralizes in part by cutting transfer payments. In several of the largest provinces the immediate reaction has been to move away from the universality of health and social care. So the initial experience of massive decentralization actually seems to be confirming the fear that regionalism would mean the breaking of the original reform contract which created the country. And yet . . . and yet as W.L. Morton told Charles Taylor, the journalist and writer, fifteen years ago, Canada can "only survive through the recognition of legitimate regional differences."[10]

This is a conundrum of the sort which makes the country seem impossible, when it is actually complex and interesting. Our difficulty is somehow to take the time to find arrangements that work, while avoiding the false simplifications of extremists who attempt to exploit the period of gestation. That exploitation is dangerously easy because a nation caught up in full consideration and doubt can be misrepresented as merely lost in confusion.

The old Privy Council chamber in the East Block where the Cabinet used to meet has a window just behind the prime minister's chair. Since 1913, if he turned away from his ministers and looked back over his right shoulder, he could see the statue of the two friends, LaFontaine and Baldwin, standing together, up on the ridge of the Ottawa where they are visible from all directions. In historic terms they stand on the banks of the nation's oldest highway, running from the Maritimes, through Quebec and Ontario to the West.

I have always imagined that their statue was placed there to remind the prime minister, should he care to look out the window, that Canadian democracy, being particularly decentralized, complicated and open, flourishes on moderation. But it is a particular sort of moderation. You might call it stubborn moderation or idea based. The key to it is a balancing act between imaginative initiative on the one hand and a constant consideration of the community as a whole on the other.

Or it might be enough if the sight of the two reformers still together reminded the prime minister of Jacques Godbout's phrase—"You can't commit suicide if you have two heads."[11]

The Cabinet no longer meets in that room and trees have grown up, blocking the view, the way special-interest groups, lobbyists, departmental rivalries, consultants, specialist turf wars and the tactics of short-term politics have grown, blocking our view of the underlying shape of the Canadian experiment. In many ways these élites are, or act on behalf of, the Compacts and Cliques of today, smothering the government with modern courtiers and the born-dead language of briefing books and press releases. From time to time when I am in Ottawa, I go to the old Cabinet room to contemplate the view that isn't there and think about the virtues of selective forestry.

There is a Pathé newsreel of Wilfrid Laurier's state funeral—February 22, 1919. The film lasts several minutes and was edited to cover the entire event. It begins with a long shot on the Royal Victoria Museum down on Argyle Street. The building would later become the Museum of Man and is now the Museum of Nature. In 1919 it was acting as parliament's temporary quarters, fire having destroyed the centre block in 1916. You can see that it is one of those cold, white Ottawa days. All the double doors of the museum swing open at once and the ruling élite of Canada pour out onto the snow, close to two thousand of them. They follow the coffin on foot in a great procession behind the governor general in an open carriage with an enormous buffalo rug thrown over him and the widow's closed carriage, along Argyle, then right all the way up Bank, right again on Wellington past the Parliament Buildings, past the Château Laurier and left down Sussex Avenue to the Basilica, which still stands just opposite the new National Gallery. It's a long, cold walk for men who make their living with words.

The camera pans the streets. They are jammed. People must have come up from Montreal and from throughout the surrounding area. Many of them are simple people; farmers, factory workers. You can tell from their clothes. Everyone is dressed in the best they can manage, even if it is only to wait in the street. There are women wearing flowered hats in the summer style. It must be their one good hat.

A camera has been placed by the Basilica's doors. The ruling élite file in, three across. You see them all in close-up. The older men are in large fur coats. Some wear ceinture fléchée, in the nineteenth-century style, pulling the bulk of fur in around their waists. There are a good number in their seventies, perhaps eighties. They were born with the Union. A few had perhaps been born with the Rebellions. A few might have known LaFontaine, who lived on till 1864. He was only fifty-seven. Baldwin had died six years earlier, even younger at fifty-four, so racked by the death of his wife from the effects of childbirth that he left instructions in his will for the equivalent of a Caesarian operation to be carried out on his own body—which was done—and their two coffins to be chained together. Many in the procession would have seen Macdonald and Cartier in action, some would have worked with them, or with Edward Blake, or Joseph Howe, or Thomas D'Arcy McGee.

The younger men wear cloth coats with the fur hidden on the inside, only the trim showing. The modern style is more discreet, more urban, less a frank admission of the north. Abruptly Mackenzie King files by, young and plump and somehow filled with the suggestion that he will inherit the mantle.

In a few minutes of film a century of power is caught at a pivotal moment—a half-century of the past, a half-century of the future. The older men in the procession had spent much of their lives learning how to cooperate beyond their community interests, only to have that reconciliation ripped apart by the war which had just ended. Laurier almost alone of the leading figures had managed to keep himself at the level of the larger, longer-lived public interest. And now the younger men among them will have to begin pulling it all back together again. As they do, everything will begin changing around them—women getting the vote, social-democrats launching their ideas, the West pushing itself forward with new populist ideas. Only Quebec will be blocked, as the full inheritance of the Ultramontane negative nationalism comes into effect, decades after the death of Bishop Bourget and his ideologues.

But the funeral, caught on those few moments of film, is like a reconstitution of the LaFontaine–Baldwin union, around the body of the man who intellectually took the pact out of the nineteenth and into the twentieth century, and did so in spite of destructive forces roaming on all sides. He worked and acted in such a way that the ethical foundations of reconciliation and of the public good were there to be built upon, not just by Mackenzie King in Ottawa, but by the CCF and the positive nationalists, such as Georges-Émile Lapalme and the young men of the Quiet Revolution forty years later.

As I watched the newsreel the first time, it was as if I could hear a Greek chorus of disaster rhetoric rising in the background. In 1840 the chant had been that the Union would lead to the assimilation of the more than half-million francophones. In 1867 it was said again. Yet by then there were a million francophones. Laurier was criticized by some nationalists for opening the West to immigrants. The critics believed that these immigrants would drown out the French Canadians and their role in the country. But by the time of his death the francophones were almost two and half million and showing no signs of assimilation, in spite of the inadequate education system the church was permitted to administer by those same negative nationalists.

The francophone community was growing and, beyond the seemingly endless grip of the negative school, it was a strong community. Yet it wasn't growing at the same speed as the anglophone population and was slipping formally into a minority position. The stupidity and prejudice of movements like the Orange Order was partly to blame for this, as was the Ultramontane movement, which had isolated the francophones in an anti-reform social order which could only grow from within. Nevertheless the country adjusted to these changes and the community went on increasing in size.

As recently as 1982 Quebec was said to be on its knees, though no one saw any concrete signs of this, and the total francophone population in Canada was six and a half million. Today it is seven, along with a remarkable increase in semi-francophone anglophones produced by an immersion schooling system which teaches three hundred thousand students a year and continues to grow.

Many people, including many anglophones, are rightly concerned about the slow but continuing slippage in the national percentage of the francophone population. The growth, thanks to the immersion schooling system, of a large group which lies somewhere between anglophone and francophone is a partial countervailing force. It is particularly interesting because it strengthens the francophone idea across the country. And curiously enough, although the population percentage has slipped, the role of francophones in Ottawa is at a level of influence reminiscent of the days of the Union, with record levels of deputy ministers, assistant deputy ministers and the head of the civil service.

The other thought that went through my mind was just how wrong Robert Borden had been and how right Laurier. Further along on the same reel there was a short sequence of the Princess Patricias returning home, also in 1919. It had been the first regiment to go over and had been raised privately by Hammy Gault, an elegant, adventurous young Montreal millionaire. The film showed him dashing down the plank, leading his regiment off the boat. He was determined to look fit, despite having lost a leg. Thirty-five years later, he was the grand old man, the honorary colonel of his regiment which had become part of the professional army. As the son of one of his young officers, I was taken along with my family to spend a few days with him in his country place south of Montreal. He was still dashing about. If you wanted to sail with him, you had to swim out to his boat, moored in the middle of his lake. He was a frightening figure for a boy, as he unstrapped his leg and threw himself into the water. A proper hero.

But Hamilton Gault or Talbot Papineau—descendant of the rebel —who was killed serving in the same regiment, or any number of other heroes didn't make Borden right. He thought he could get the British to fight the war properly. He literally abandoned the country he had been elected to lead and tried instead to lead his army by concentrating on his role in the Imperial War Cabinet in London. We know that his strong common sense made him a great ally for British prime minister Lloyd George as they struggled with the Byzantine politics of a war which can now be seen as a largely pointless massacre organized by criminally incompetent generals.

But what power did they really have? Even Lloyd George and French prime minister Clemenceau, with their direct legal responsibility, national prestige and power within their respective parliamentary systems, weren't able to fire their own generals without risking the loss of power. The link between nationalist propaganda and the 'gallant' generals was so close in this first modern war that blame somehow fell inevitably on the politicians. You couldn't criticize the generals and continue to fight the war. They were the necessary false Heroes of blindly stupid warfare driven by the latest management methods and technology.

The emotions and unleashed violence of war almost always make it democracy's most difficult test. Put another way: democracy is not designed to fight wars. Elected representatives can't really control generals, any more than kings could, unless they were warrior kings. Fighting and killing is a very different, peculiar kind of business.

That's why, if your country is not directly involved, the best strategy is strictly to limit your participation. If you must give men, give fewer than you have so that when the inevitable call for reinforcements comes, you will have them.

Besides, the history of warfare does not turn upon the raising of ever-larger numbers of men. It is not filled with larger armies beating smaller armies. Quite the contrary. Quantity is usually a crutch for mediocre generals.

Borden allowed himself to be caught up in the excitement of the struggle—the tragedy, the tragedy of his men, the enormous Canadian army. He gave himself up to the tactics of war management which, given the power of the general staff, was scarcely influenced by politics, even if the politicians tried their hardest to act like managers. He didn't seem to understand that the responsibility of a prime minister is not war tactics but the strategy of how to get his country through the crisis of war.

Borden was so lost in the details of the military catastrophe that he hardly saw how Canada was being pulled apart. While he was standing up in London for an honourable and honest administration of the war, at home his party had slipped into the most divisive of partisan tricks, playing on differences between communities and regions and, of course, profiteering.

Empires have a great deal of difficulty drawing lessons from their military experiences. The very nature of empire is the continuity of war. The lessons they draw tend therefore to be concentrated on tactics. For smaller countries the lessons are far more straightforward and they are strategic. For those who are only indirectly involved in a conflict, the first lesson is: limit your involvement. If you don't, the maw of war and the empires, ever hungry for men, weapons and money, will draw you in and bleed you white, with consideration only for their larger needs. These are needs which you could never satisfy because they are already beyond the capacity of the empire. If not, why would they plead such dependency on the contributions of the smaller nations? If necessary, they will interfere in your home affairs in order to force you on. And when it's over they'll give you a hearty thanks and erase you from their memories and their history books.

Past wars are the glories of empires. There is no room for the shadow of junior allies. We know this from the popular media in which Americans or Englishmen are constantly winning world wars single-handedly. But historians are no different. Take British accounts of the Boer War. A popular but representative example would be Thomas Pakenham's 1979 account. You look expectantly for some mention of the drama the war created for Canadians; of Laurier putting out the fires of militaristic ardour as Canada was divided by the cries of loyalty to or betrayal of the empire; of the governor general intriguing to undermine the government. But no, all you find is one sentence referring to "colonial patriotism" and two passing references to the courage of Canadian troops; four words in total.[12]

It is argued that Canada bought its independence on the battlefields of the First World War. I doubt it. The foundations of independence were already in place, put there piece by piece from LaFontaine–Baldwin to Laurier. It was enough to have the presence of mind to exercise that independence. Besides, there were many other countries which signed the Treaty of Versailles without contributing more than half a million men and leaving sixty thousand dead on the field. There were other ways, less profligate with the blood of its citizens, less divisive, for the government to accomplish its aim, if that was its aim.

This is not such a complicated thought. Even in the crucial *Rowell–Sirois Report on Dominion–Provincial Relations*, undertaken in the late 1930s, the following paragraph appears:

> Collective action through the agency of democratic government implies a common purpose and an agreed method of achieving it. If the common endeavour is one with respect to which deep impulses in the community arouse differing conceptions, it is likely to break down and the consequent disharmony will embarrass all the common enterprises which have been entrusted to the government.[13]

Rowell, in his earlier life, had been a strong supporter of conscription and so had joined the breakaway Liberals in Borden's wartime coalition. He had chaired the federal Cabinet's war committee and was able to witness at close range the strains imposed on the country.

After his mammoth efforts, Borden retired to play golf and sit on boards of directors. Still, the experience of that war made the élite far more careful when the next one came around. In that case there actually was a cause—a great cause—although the anti-Semitic, anti-Asian attitudes of the federal and some of the provincial governments showed that they only partially understood what it was. Mackenzie King's maniacal care prevented the extremes from getting control of the national agenda, as they had during the First World War, although the conscription issue once more did damage. And again the conscriptionists were wrong. The problem was not a shortage of men, but the lack of conscious understanding of how much Canada should try to do. Our élites had still not worked out how to balance national limitations against the endless void of war.

And yet... and yet there was the cause. And this remains one of the illustrations of how difficult the negative-nationalist movement in Quebec has found it to reconcile their beliefs with the realities of history. Their effect on Quebec school textbooks has been that the

Second World War, apart from an introduction on European fascism, tends to be reduced to little more than the conscription crisis. Unless you look very closely you won't realize that tens of thousands of francophones volunteered and went to fight, alongside anglophones, indeed to die. You won't realize that the Chaudières, a francophone regiment, landed in the first wave on D-Day, let alone that that beach, one of the five, was given over to a Canadian force. I think of some of the wonderful men I met as a child, such as General Jacques Dextraze, a young hero of the Normandy campaign who went on to become perhaps the finest of Canada's postwar chiefs of staff. Their contribution to an unquestionably great cause is erased, along with that of Canada as a whole.

Again, the question at hand is not so very difficult. You can be right to oppose conscription, but wrong not to accept that there is a greater cause. And if you cannot assume the burden of that contradiction, then you will probably be unable to question why your particular cause led you into such a flawed position. In practical terms, the arguably correct position of opposing conscription has somehow made it impossible to examine the Maurrasian argument which some used to take advantage of that situation in the name of a contradictory project.

The probable explanation is that of a mythology gone wrong and thus reliant on the idea of victimization. The victim sees all events through his own prism—the prism of the wrong which he has identified as having been done to him. This is a classic characteristic not of nationalism, not of francophones, not of Quebec, but of narrow or negative nationalism. You can find it today in part of the separatist/sovereigntist movement, just as you can in part of the movement which has produced the Reform party or Mike Harris's false conservatism. In these cases the *other*, as I said in the opening pages of this book, doesn't really exist, let alone the other victim. As the one to whom things have been done, the victim has no responsibility beyond his immediate concerns. It is a form of professional innocence.

Nor, of course, is there room for non-victims among those identified as belonging to the group victimized. In the case of the Second World War, their role is erased, and with it the remarkable contribution of francophones. This approach is part of the same phenomenon which requires the dismissal or disparagement of those who succeed in the federal system.

I am not engaging in a discussion of the merits of loyalty or patriotism. The restrained feelings of Canadians in general in the period after 1945 mirrored their restraint after 1918. The fundamental distrust of Heroism translates into an unwillingness to base mythology on military triumphs or sacrifices. They knew the contribution on all sides had been far more than required. They must have felt, when they watched the German film footage of the Canadians at Dieppe, what an earlier generation seems to have felt when they saw the Group of Seven's war paintings, indeed, speaking for myself, what I feel when I look at these images today. This shale and those cracked boulders on the beach of Dieppe are bodies. These men walking calmly like everyman through history, half-dressed, barefoot, bandaged, helping each other along, were your next-door neighbours, your family. Who sent them there to risk death in that way?

It wasn't so surprising that, when the Korean War came around, leading conservative historians like Donald Creighton and even Harold Innis, who had begun as a conservative and had served in the trenches more than thirty years before, opposed any participation. The cause at hand was not clear. The hand of the empires was too obvious.

Nor was it surprising that one of the things which convinced Canadians Brian Mulroney was unsuitable for public office was the manner in which he cavalierly committed Canada to the Iraq War. Put aside the issue of the war itself and our minute contribution.

President George Bush asked Brian Mulroney to fly down urgently to discuss the Iraq crisis over dinner. Mulroney flew off, which was fine, but he returned the next day to announce Canada's commitment to American policy. Many, including Mulroney, thought that early consultation was a sign of his special relationship. He was clearly thrilled to be treated as such an important person. It was as if his personal relationship to the élites of the empire overwhelmed the possibility, even the need, of carefully considering Canada's situation and interests before making any public comments.

Consider the situation from Washington's point of view. They had just lost part of their oil supply. Much of what remained was in easy striking distance of Saddam Hussein's forces, which at that point many people thought were quite effective. A pro-American oil-producing coalition had yet to be put in place.

George Bush's military, economic, diplomatic and security advisers would have laid out for him the situation and the key relevant factors. They would have immediately reminded him: 1) that America's nearest supplementary supply of energy lay in Canada; 2) that during the previous oil crisis Canadians had begun to pull the plug on their oil exports. The president's first job, lying somewhere between tactics and strategy, was therefore to lock in the Canadian supply. He picked up the phone and invited Brian Mulroney to dine because he needed his advice on matters of international importance.

And so that vivid incarnation of self-loathing rushed down, thrilled in the manner that an eighteenth-century salt-tax collector in France—the personification of the insecure nouveau riche on the make—would have been if invited to the royal table, even if the subject at hand were the king's need of a loan. A meal and a few words were enough to secure the courtier's commitment.

The American president did his job. The prime minister was right to go. It was just that he didn't seem to be aware of even the basic lessons in geopolitics which run through the Canadian applied memory. Either that or the excitement of being included made him lay Canadian considerations aside.

What had he forgotten? Care and reticence are always the proper

reactions when invited to go to war. When the invitation comes
from an empire, be doubly careful.

By committing himself almost immediately, Mr. Mulroney made
an open debate on the subject impossible. Abruptly, to have reser-
vations was to be anti-American. With the unnerving skill of a profoundly colonial person, he had reconstituted the argument over
war exactly in the form it had taken in 1914. Was the colony to be
with or against the empire? It was a return to the attitude of Robert
Borden without Borden's circumspection and sense of duty.

In 1937, in ones and twos, in small groups, spread out over the
months, some 1,500 Canadians left Canada secretly to fight in
Spain, against fascism and for democracy. Approximately half were
killed defending the Spanish republic. The Canadians were the
seventh-largest group in the International Brigade, but they were
the third-largest on a per-capita basis, coming after the French and
the Polish/Ukrainian contingents.

They left Canada secretly because right-wing groups had pres-
sured the government to put participation by individuals in the
Spanish conflict under the Foreign Enlistment Act. Its effect would
be to make enlistment a criminal offence. After a lobbying campaign
led by Premier Duplessis, who said they were all communists, the
Act was revised in July 1937 to cover Spain. Duplessis's objection
was not surprising for someone who saw himself as leading a
nationalist Christian campaign.

Of course some of the Canadian volunteers were communists.
Others were CCFers and Liberals. Some were simply independent-
minded people who believed in the cause of democracy. The RCMP,
already launched on its anti-communist campaign, did what it
could to stop them going.

In April of 1937 many of the volunteers came together in Spain
to debate the creation of an autonomous Canadian battalion. They

decided it would be named after Mackenzie and Papineau because they believed that the two rebellions of a century before had been to all intents and purposes a single cause—not that of race but that of justice. They sent off a message to Mackenzie King, asking for his support. "We implore you from the depths of our hearts to do everything to help Spanish democracy. In so doing you are serving your own interests. We are here for the duration until fascism is defeated."[14] There was no reply.

When the war was lost and they were evacuated, the Canadian government was of no great help in seeing that they got home, but at least they did not prosecute them on arrival. They were left alone. The journalist Greg Clark waited on the quay for the boat which carried many of them into Halifax. "I don't recollect ever seeing soldiers who inspired in me so strange a mingling of reverence and humiliation and embarrassment at meeting their gaze."[15] When World War Two came, some were at first banned from volunteering, but the barriers gradually fell.

It would be difficult to think of a purer expression of idealism, whatever the politics of the men, than this group going off one by one to fight fascism three years before the rest of the world got around to it. In the years after the Second World War they asked the Canadian government to recognize them as veterans. After all, they had attacked the same enemy. They had simply done it a little faster than their nation had.

This slightly romantic request was not so much about money as recognition. The costs would even then have been small. The government ignored them, although it was only too pleased to bask in the fame of Norman Bethune—who had been in the brigade's medical corps—as his reputation grew over the years. They found Bethune's mantle particularly useful in China where he was an official martyr of the revolution. The others were forgotten.

In 1996 they were made citizens of Spain and those still alive and able went over to be officially honoured on the sixtieth anniversary of their arrival to take up arms for democracy. The French government then recognized their own ex-brigade members as full veterans of their regular army. We still haven't done it. The only gesture has been a plaque put up in the Ontario legislature during Bob Rae's short-lived government.

These small symbolic acts are just that—small and symbolic. But it is important in history formally to make note of our errors and lapses. That's how we keep ourselves more or less on track. If you look back through Canadian history in search of whom these men resemble, you do indeed fall upon the volunteers who followed Mackenzie and Papineau in a simple democratic cause. Within five years most of the young leaders of that idealistic and rebellious movement were out of prison, back from exile and members of the Union parliament. One of them, LaFontaine, was prime minister, Cartier soon would be. The leaders eventually came home and were re-elected. Even Wolfred Nelson, who had commanded at St. Denis, was soon a front-bench supporter of LaFontaine. For the government to recognize the Spanish volunteers now might have the strangely salutary effect of reminding our ministers, and perhaps us, of the origins of Canadian democracy and of the line which runs through, from the Rebellions to the late-twentieth century.

25 The Indifferent Mothers

HOW DOES A COLONY LEAVE THAT status behind? Sometimes the geopolitical situation is such that this can never be entirely accomplished. The presence on our six-thousand-kilometre-wide doorstep of the greatest empire of the century is just that sort of geopolitical reality. So to some extent is the lack of other real centres of French beyond France. But the physical and the cultural are not the only sorts of limitations a society may face. The colonial mind-set in and of itself can be just as important. This ought to be the easiest factor to deal with. Somehow it seems to be the most difficult.

Motherhood, for example, is a persistent theme in ex-colonies. This is unaffected by how mother and child came to be separated or how long ago or how successful either has become in the aftermath. Even if the imputed mother should fall on hard times and the former colony grow into the greatest nation on earth, the latter will only become more attracted with time to the idea of a womb.

In the case of Rome or the United States this psychological fetish is more a curious indulgence of power than a matter of geopolitical importance. They're powerful enough to be able to offer themselves a minor delusion.

In less powerful countries this sort of relationship can take on a neurotic aspect. But as with the greater powers, it is the élite which most maniacally harbours these obsessions. The rest of us tend to wipe away irrelevant indulgences after a few generations.

I say irrelevant because, as pointed out in an earlier chapter, there is no filial relationship. A colony is a possession, something bought and sold, something used and thrown away. There is no blame in this. It's the nature of power.

Yet still you find the anglophone and francophone élites of Canada searching desperately in Britain, France and the United States for the origins of every political and economic idea, every literary form, every confirmation of success and legitimacy. From the Shakespearean and Shavian festivals to the desperately imitative American manners of Preston Manning to the late-colonial chasing in vain of Conrad Black, apparently after a British title, to Lucien Bouchard constantly reminding us of his Parisian readings, none of this is of great importance. If we were going to examine the real contributions of the colonial powers, we might well conclude that they came down to that peculiar English belief in the superiority of white people, particularly if they speak English, and two dead-end ideas from France —the Ultramontane ideology and Maurrasian nationalism.

In a way our attitudes can be summarized through our relationship to Lord Durham. We have turned his four-month visit during 1838 into the touchstone story of the Canadian condition. All in the same breath he is treated as a great political figure from London, a radical thinker and a majestic aristocrat who came to inspire, even invent, responsible government, discover the tragedy of the solitudes ("two nations warring in the bosom of a single state") and insult anglophones and francophones alike as colonial peasants. The words aimed at francophones have been particularly retained by part of their élite as a sore to be scratched open on a regular basis.

But consider the real Durham, beyond mythology. He was neither a great figure nor a great aristocrat. He inherited money and through political activity was paid off with a title. He was of marginal junior-minister importance. He is scarcely mentioned in British histories and biographies of the period. He was sent off to Canada more or less to satisfy a few people and to get him out of the government's way. As for his great thoughts, no one but the Canadians remember them. His supposed invention of responsible government was merely (seen from his point of view) the exporting of a democratic method which had been established in Britain six years earlier. Lord

John Russell, the man who stood in the way of responsible government in Canada, was in fact the same individual who installed it in Britain. He was followed by Sir Robert Peel, another leading reformer, who again refused it to the Canadians. That this illustrates the non-existence of colonies as real places in the mind of an empire is one thing. But Russell, Peel and the others knew what the rebels of 1837 had fought for, what the moderates were asking for, what the American neighbour had given itself and what England already had. They hardly required Durham's imitative brilliance to inform them that Canada was on the road to responsible government.

His one original idea—that union of the two provinces would provoke the assimilation of the francophones—was completely wrong. Instead it formalized their nascent relationship—initiated during the Rebellions by Mackenzie and Papineau—with their natural reforming allies outside of Lower Canada and so ensured that there would be no assimilation.

Quite apart from passing a pleasant summer holiday in the colonies, Durham understood very little of what was happening. Some of those engaged to help him prepare his report listened and learnt and were probably responsible for many of the more considered elements in the report. As for Durham himself, his overdressed and overly dramatic arrival in Quebec City announced the entry of someone playing Jane Austen's Darcy, the foppish snob from London who finds himself stuck at a dowdy county dance. He doesn't really know or care who these people are or what they really mean when they speak to him. His reaction is alternately one of enforced charm and boredom—acting and not acting. And then he flounces off home in a momentary fit of pique.

This is the context in which Durham's gratuitous insults must be seen. It was just the sort of language you'd have expected from an immature graduate of Eton in the nineteenth century. Immature at forty-six? Age has nothing to do with it. The combination of personal privilege, marginal success, an unstable personality and class prejudice are enough to perpetuate this sort of juvenile wilfulness in a man who cannot engage with reality. You can almost feel his predictable logic unfolding. 'The moderate reformers are terribly middle class. The colonial élite is naturally colonial and grasping. The francophones are incomprehensible, not in linguistic terms, but in terms of the logic of racially based empires. Give them democracy, of course, but save me from these common people.'

The extent to which the *warring bosom* comment and others were superfluous can be seen in the contradictory statements made elsewhere in his report. For example, it is also argued that whatever racial differences might exist, they could not be the primary cause of the difficulties, as all the British colonies in North America were in exactly the same desperate state. The difficulties must therefore lie in the laws which were failing them.

None of this stopped Premier Parizeau, during his introduction of the referendum bill, quoting—for the how-many-thousandth time in the standard negative-nationalist rhetoric—one of Durham's humiliating insults. "Irremediable inferiority." Now there's a phrase designed to get everyone's dander up. How dare he! How dare they! But exactly who are they? I mean, beyond Durham. There's no one out there who thinks these things. Certainly not anyone with a brain or anyone who matters. There hasn't been anyone in the mainstream of Canadian history who seriously believed the Durham line since before the alliance of LaFontaine and Baldwin. There is just the ghost of little Radical Jack, or rather an old white sheet with nothing but a stick inside to agitate it along with "quelques tragédies patiemment travaillées—a few patiently polished tragedies"—to borrow a phrase of Anne Hébert.[1]

What about D'Alton McCarthy and his friends? They didn't buy Durham's line. After all, if francophone Catholics were dangerous, they couldn't very well be inferior. If they threatened to dominate, they couldn't very well be without culture or character. What about Preston Manning? He's a descendant of McCarthy, not Durham.

More to the point, during the whole lengthy period when governors and governors general mattered, Britain managed to send only two who were up to the job. Of course some were decorative, some amusing, some agreeable. Canada was treated as a nice little patronage pay-off, but not a good job. As late as the turn of the century, the mediocre Lord Minto was meddling in public affairs, trying to draw Canada deeper into empire politics and wars.

It is Durham who stands out in our mythology. We talk endlessly of him. Yet we never talk of Sir Charles Bagot who, although he was here scarcely longer than Durham (1842–43), made an important contribution. It was long enough for him to allow responsible government to function. He was an intelligent professional with a real career and he seemed to have no trouble recognizing and enjoying the society in which he lived, whether francophone or anglophone. This although he was deathly ill much of the time. He made LaFontaine his prime minister and followed his advice.

Think logically for a moment. Just over three years had gone by since Durham left. Suddenly a solid, reasonable governor with a long career at senior levels—under-secretary of state for foreign affairs, minister to France, to the United States, ambassador to Russia, negotiator of the Rush–Bagot Agreement—arrives and almost immediately understands that he is dealing with a vibrant, complex society in which anglophones and francophones wish to work together in an unusual non-monolithic relationship. Yet we choose to forget him and to quote instead in a remarkable mépris de soi the bon mot de salon of an unstable and ignorant amateur like Durham. Is there any reasonable explanation, beyond the crassly political desire in negative-nationalist circles to erase the memory of everything that has worked? The only other possible reason is a desire among our élites—francophone and anglophone, federalist and separatist—to see themselves in the self-loathing manner of spurned colonial children. If Durham is treated as our pivotal relationship with London, we can indeed imagine ourselves to be victims.

As for Lord Elgin, he is not forgotten, but his name passes by with a nod of boredom and an acknowledgment—'Yes, yes, responsible government.' He was our one truly great colonial governor.

He named LaFontaine prime minister, with Baldwin as his number two, and didn't interfere. Again, like Bagot, he was highly professional, intelligent and deeply cultured, as opposed to fashionable like Durham. For eight years (1848–54) he took enormous pleasure in the place and the society. He recognized the complexities which the anglophones and francophones were grappling with and encouraged this experimentation. Like Bagot, fluently bilingual, he lived and worked as much in French as in English, both in private and public business. And unlike Durham, with his scattiness and histrionics, Elgin demonstrated great courage and restraint.

After he was stoned in his carriage during the Montreal riots, which culminated in the burning of the Parliament Buildings, he was careful not to provoke further violence. In other words, he showed the kind of restraint which was already central to the Canadian approach. Yet for years afterwards he went to state occasions in the same carriage, with all its panels still driven in by the stoning, as if to say to the effectively neo-conservative élite which had tried to refuse responsible government, 'I remember. So watch out.'

The names Bagot and Elgin didn't cross Mr. Parizeau's lips the day he cited Durham, but in the victim's version of history these two men cannot exist. I don't suppose they have ever crossed the lips of Mr. Manning either. An analysis of our political élites in general, whatever the origins or politics, would probably betray the same masochistic tendencies towards invoking Durham.

But the colonial mind-set is more tortured than that. Durham is needed as a source of the victim psychosis. He is the required demonization figure. Bagot and Elgin are ignored, not because they were successful or positive, but because they didn't act as representatives of an all-powerful mother. They simply acted the way a Canadian might have in the circumstances. That isn't what the colonial psyche wants. It needs approval; a sense of belonging, of embrace; of love. Or it needs to be severely demeaned. That also is a sign of childlike dependency.

All of which means that we have had to assiduously ignore the general tenor of our relationship with Britain over the last hundred and fifty years. It isn't simply a matter of a string of mediocre vice-regal figures. When London did play a role in our internal affairs, it was to act almost consistently against our interests, as if we didn't matter and scarcely existed. Indeed, from their point of view, we didn't matter.

An important early example was London's disallowance of Baldwin's Secret Societies Bill of 1843, which was aimed at controlling the violent activities of the Orange Order. With proper tools in hand, the government might have been able to force the extremists out into the open and thus make their activities easier to moderate. Much of the responsibility for the momentum the Order built up was thus London's. The British, incidentally, had their own strict rules to deal with problems like that at home. The colonies were another matter.

Among reformers the sense was quite strong, even early in the nineteenth century, that London understood nothing and cared even less. "Most of them," Baldwin wrote from Britain in 1836, "seemed rarely to have had the fact of the existence of such a country present to their mind." He came home convinced, as more and more of his friends and colleagues were, that this was "my own, my native land" and that there was nothing, as a consequence, to look for over his shoulder.[2]

Such growing psychological independence in the new élite was part of the explanation for the aura which in that period came to surround Tecumseh's name. It was strange, because the aboriginal chief had been dead for more than twenty years, killed while fighting as a Canadian ally in the War of 1812–14. Gradually he became a symbol for the new generation. Every poet, including Baldwin, wrote an ode to him. Their view seemed to be that he, at least, "died fighting, while a British general retreated."[3]

Perhaps the most important sign of London's indifference, after that of its hypocrisy on the question of responsible government, surrounded the whole question of free trade. The free-traders were gradually winning ground in Britain. In the end they would get the repeal of the Corn Laws. But to do this was to condemn Canada to poverty. London had already decided where its own interest lay and it wasn't with its own colonies. This internal battle dominated Britain in the 1840s and produced constant insecurity in Canada.

In the first wave of changes, during 1842–43, a local compromise was found which saved the Canadian situation. Yet even Gladstone, the reforming president of the Board of Trade, seemed bitter about this special arrangement and issued what amounted to a threat—"If the Canadians wish to remain under our colonial system, they must submit to the application of our system fairly and properly." This meant, either accept that only London's interests count or we'll feed you to the Americans.

Just two years later London threw out the compromise and plunged Canada into economic depression. Gladstone was by then colonial secretary and still indifferent. Lord Elgin wrote to protest— "All the prosperity of which Canada is robbed is transplanted to the other side of the line [the United States], as if to make Canadians feel more bitterly how much kinder England is to the children who desert her than to those who remain faithful."[4]

With that phrase Elgin pinpointed what would become the key element in Canada's relationship with its two theoretical mothers, England and France. Above all, they weren't interested in this marginal, northern, poorish, peculiar country, because what really interested them was its neighbour to the south. Empires like to have relationships—friendly or angry—with other empires or rising empires. And once they themselves have become ex-empires, they can only validate their own status by having an intense relationship —positive or negative or both—with the empire which succeeds them. From 1914 on, both Britain and France became obsessed by the United States. This is their child, because the real inheritance in international relations is not blood or language. It is power. That's why their term for the United States quite automatically includes the whole continent—America, L'Amérique. They are always slightly embarrassed, confused, annoyed to be reminded that there is someone else there, taking up half the continent and breaking the illusion of parentship by claiming one of another sort.

The economic crisis which resulted from Britain's repeal of the Corn Laws was the second cause of the Montreal riots of 1849. The merchants, still in a fury after burning down the Parliament Buildings in April, signed the Annexation Manifesto in October of the same year. The mentality of this class was clear. If London would give them power and money (the Château Clique) they were loyal children of the mother country. If London permitted democracy and endangered their income, they wanted another mother, the most easily available being south of the border. It never struck them that through democracy they might build a different sort of economic system. It took almost half a century before Cartier and Macdonald could convince them that this might be done. But their first reaction in times of trouble remained and remains to seek the bosom of maternity, however indifferent the mother might be.

Those curious about a modern interpretation of this trauma imposed on Canada by London might look in the recent definitive biography of Gladstone, by Roy Jenkins—631 pages in which the great English reformer would surely have been given time to say something about his indifference to those in Canada, and the effects of his policies. Unfortunately Lord Jenkins didn't seem to have room for the subject.[5]

But then Britain's willingness to sacrifice its 'kin' over trade policy is tied to the obvious fact that we are not kin. Their attitude on entering the European Common Market in 1973 was a repeat of 1845. It's worth noting that when France joined the same market, albeit at an earlier stage in its creation, it negotiated tariff exceptions for its colonies and ex-colonies. This had to do with nothing other than their perception of their own best self-interest. Nevertheless, they did it.

◄———————►

Perhaps the most fascinating aspect of London's attitude was tied to its role in triangular negotiations involving disputes between Canada and the United States. In each case they have sided with the Americans, even though they were usually charged with defending Canada's interests.

The inland fisheries negotiation in 1870–71 was an early example. Macdonald didn't agree to sit on the commission in Washington because he thought he could alter London's desire to cut a deal related to Britain's desire for closer relations with the Americans. He simply hoped to compensate a bit for "Englishmen having little or no interest in Canada." He signed the resulting disastrous treaty with, in Donald Creighton's words, "cheerful cynicism." Macdonald's comments during the signing ceremony were, again according to Creighton, as follows:

> "Well," he said in a half whisper . . . as he took up his pen, "here go the fisheries."
>
> "You get a good equivalent for them," the American negotiator countered swiftly.
>
> "No, we give them away—here goes the signature!"
>
> He signed . . . and rose from the table. "They are gone," he said slowly.[6]

The fur-seal negotiations began in the same atmosphere in 1890. And in the Alaska Panhandle negotiations, which ended in 1903, Laurier was betrayed by Lord Alverstone, the Lord Chief Justice of England, who had the deciding vote. Again Britain was looking over its shoulder to Washington. The two Canadian members of the tribunal—Sir Louis Jetté and Allen Aylesworth—refused to sign the decision. They said it was a "grotesque travesty of justice." When Laurier protested to Lord Alverstone that his conclusion could not "be supported on judicial grounds," the Lord Chief Justice, who was theoretically named to the tribunal as a jurist, replied, ". . . it was our duty to take into consideration the value and importance to the parties negotiating . . ." of the land in question. In other words, London sided with the greater power.[7]

There are few lessons to be learnt here, except that the business of empires is power and business, nothing more. What many have taken to be crises in the special relationship between family members have invariably been simple questions of national self-interest. There is nothing new about this. After the rebels fled to the United States in 1837, they attracted large numbers of supporters who were ready to invade northward and were well armed. Washington made this impossible because their real interest at that time was in close relations with London.[8] Questions of principle melted away before the simple truths of geopolitics.

There is perhaps one clear lesson which we should have learnt by now. It is particularly important to concentrate on this given that NAFTA is using foreign experts to chair dispute settlement panels and the World Trade Organization is turning itself into an international court of economic arbitration. In a dispute pitting Canada against the United States, never, never agree to the British having the deciding vote. If the dispute involves Britain, never, never let the Americans get involved.

As to Britain's main interest in Canada during the twentieth century, it can be summarized in a series of attempts to push Canadians to assume part of Britain's military burden. This was never about participation, advice or partnership. It was always about payment in blood and cash.

Particular opinions about participation in these wars have nothing to do with what I am describing. During the period of the naval arms race preceding World War One, London was determined to get the dominions to pay for a good percentage of her dreadnoughts. In order to force the hand of Laurier's government, she meddled in Canadian politics, concentrating on those parts of the élites susceptible to the maternal mythology.

V.S. Naipaul described élites of this sort with great precision when writing about the establishment in Argentina, a country which has similar contradictions. They were forever setting the value of European culture against the real place in which they lived. For these individuals "... the real world is felt to be outside, everyone at home is inadequate and fraudulent."[9]

London's aim was to unleash a pro-empire sentiment which would translate into a transfer of money. Laurier more or less held them off, but it was clear that London would have happily brought the government down, if it could have been accomplished and a transfer of money been the result.

World War One was a daily exercise in pressure of the same sort, but in this case payment came in the form of men. By all the means of imperial propaganda the empire cards were played. A few decades later Mackenzie King would have great difficulty ensuring that during the Second World War the various bells and whistles of blood and motherland would not be indiscriminately yanked.

This is why Lester Pearson's intervention in the Suez Crisis was so important. For the first time we didn't simply balk before motherly interested blandishments. We actually opposed their position and suggested another in the international arena.

Although there are many explanations for the sourness and dismissive attitude towards Canada which has developed in Britain over the last forty years, one of the key elements was that decision, by a particularly mature part of the élite, to no longer even pretend that there was a family game to be played.

Suddenly, the adjectives attached to Canada were no longer 'plucky' or 'tough little' or 'valiant,' but 'whining,' 'soft' and more recently 'wet.' If this were indeed a question of family, a suitable quote might be "No greater fury..." But this is merely the awkward debris of an old business relationship which was disguised for a long time under the language of family. Empires rarely confuse personal relationships with geopolitics. But they count on smaller states, because of their psychic needs, doing it all the time.

Our experiences with France have been less frequent but no different. I wrote earlier of Paris preventing the growth of integrated production in New France in order to save the market for goods manufactured in the motherland. After 1627 the blockage put on Huguenot immigration—mainly educated and middle-class with a high level of skills—removed a factor which might have made the colony much more self-reliant.

General James Murray reported, with military precision, on what he found when he took over in 1760. "Wholesale businesses were almost exclusively in the hands of the French from the metropole, while retail was generally abandonné aux Canadiens—left for the Canadians ... Few of those with capital of any importance in France will stay in the colony."[10] The business leadership and most of the other members of the French élite simply abandoned the French Canadians to their own devices, with almost no educated leadership. After all, the metropolitan élite, which had occupied most of the positions of political and financial power, had been quite careful to limit the growth of a local élite.

In 1855 P.J.O. Chauveau's career was launched by the speech he gave at the unveiling of the monument to the dead of the two battles of Quebec—the Canadiens, the French, the British and the Huron. It was a grand speech in the Victorian style, but with tough elements in it. Reading the text, you can see why he would go on to become a very fine superintendent of education and a not very strong premier of Quebec. He described how the Canadiens had poured out in great numbers to defend the regime which would quickly abandon them and which had always kept them in poverty.

How had the loss been greeted in the metropole? "Avec une incon-cevable indifférence."[11]

And so the mother disappeared for a century, until Bishop Bour-get took the initiative of more or less importing large quantities of clerics from France, many of them reactionary and being left behind by the changes in European society. A half-century later various politicians began importing not nationalism but a Maurrasian nationalism and corporatism, the political formula which seemed often to accompany it. And finally a French president came visiting and told a crowd that he sensed an atmosphere of liberation which reminded him of his own advance on Paris in 1944.

Having written my doctorate on Charles de Gaulle and having admired his political skills, I have always been particularly enter-tained by the underlying complexity of his intervention. The ele-ments which most people concentrate on had little to do with the strategic move he was making. That it was a strategic move could be seen in the things he chose to overlook—elements which normally would have been of importance.

For example, the strand of nationalism he was supporting in Canada was precisely the sort which had generally opposed his advance on Paris. Being the good historian that he was, de Gaulle can only have decided to ignore reality. What's more, he would have been aware that the small cell within the Quai d'Orsay which was pushing the dossier of a possible Quebec separation as being to the advantage of France, belonged, as its members still do, to the right-wing Maurrasian group which survives in a minority position inside the French civil service. In other words, they belong to the anti-Gaullist tradition. In the interests of maintaining some power, they converted themselves early on into the right wing of the Gaullist movement. Finally, the general knew that in making his move he would be attacking precisely those francophones and anglophones who had advanced with him. That is the sort of choice he would make very consciously. And there is one other small detail, which would not have been forgotten in the Quai d'Orsay or the French

376   Ministry of Defence: the role of the Canadian government—and in particular Lester Pearson—in the humiliation of France during the Suez Crisis.

Lester Pearson, the Canadian prime minister in 1967, was the same man who, as minister of external affairs in 1956, had led international opposition to the Anglo-French invasion of Egypt. In many ways that was the last humiliation of the two European empires and marked the definitive arrival of American power. From the rather convoluted and paranoid European point of view, Canada had been a stalking horse for American interests, not a force for international responsibility.

Remember, it wasn't until the Iraq War of the 1990s that London and Paris got over their hatred of the United Nations' peace-keeping forces. They, after all, were Pearson's invention and his solution to the Suez Crisis. Remember also that Suez, not Algeria, was the event which announced the end of the Fourth Republic. While from a tactical point of view, de Gaulle had reason therefore to be grateful, from a strategic angle it was the Gaullist soldiers, civil servants and politicians who had encouraged aggressive military action in Suez. One of the central themes inside Gaullist foreign policy was a determination to erase the humiliation of Suez and win back a mainstream position in international strategy.

The enthusiastically naïve ignore all of this and see in the general's intervention only a sudden desire to support the concept of liberty, as well as a determination to support a francophone community. Unfortunately his actions had very little to do with either factor. On the matter of liberty, several quite different definitions of the term seemed to be in use. For example, on the basis of normal usage, the comparison to be made between France and Canada in the 1960s was not favourable to the former. French television and radio were still the absolute creatures of the government. Other forms of censorship were common, and the police had an ongoing omnipresent role of the sort which we have experienced in Canada only rarely and for very brief periods. That is why, within ten months of his Canadian pronouncement, Paris was brought to a halt by people protesting the basic lack of liberty inside France. At the same time, de Gaulle was still engaged in his long and more than justified battle against a large part of his own army. By 1967, at least the violent aspects of this division were almost over and it had been reduced to behind-the-scenes struggles.

As someone specialized in French civil–military relations, I was particularly drawn to the general's use of the concept of liberty outside of France. After all, here he was advocating the break-up of one of the world's oldest democracies—one which had avoided most of the violent pitfalls of European history. And the democracy in question, Canada, was also one of France's closest allies.

What's more, the general's intervention came at the same time that he was busy solidifying a refurbished empire of African client-states run by Paris through pliant local élites. These theoretically post-colonial leaders were commonly referred to in official Paris circles as les rois nègres. The client-states they led, with 'advisers' from Paris at every imaginable elbow, were not places where the concept of liberty was often entertained.

Paris maintained a large contingent of élite troops in strategic centres. Their job was to intervene rapidly should any real movements of liberation or positive nationalism emerge. Over the years these troops have been used repeatedly to maintain Paris's rois nègres in place.

This was a system developed by a number of old colonial hands under the leadership of Jacques Foccart in the general's office and Pierre Messner, the long-time minister of defence. In 1997 there were still close to eight thousand soldiers in the rapid intervention force stationed in Africa maintaining 'stability' in the client-states of France's discrete empire. On average, they put down eruptions of varying sizes two or three times a year. Most of these revolutions are led by groups seeking to free their country from the control of Paris.

Of course, all of these contradictions in the use of the idea of freedom might be acceptable to some people if what was at stake in Montreal in 1967 was the freeing of a francophone people. Unfortunately the meaning of the word freedom and whether French Canadians were prisoners or already free were probably not very important questions in the general's mind. What he was engaged in was yet another move in his endless chess game with the United States.

From 1958 on, he had been involved in a difficult struggle to be treated with respect by Washington. American officials had come to believe that an ally was someone who followed orders. Most of the time the general was taking perfectly justifiable positions. Two good examples are his independent action over the creation of a nuclear force and his refusal to be pushed around inside NATO.

His ongoing aim was what you would expect from a good strategist. He wanted to undermine the American position just enough to make possible the creation of a coalition in which France could play a real role. The destabilization of Canada was one of those brilliant moves aimed at rattling Washington in its own backyard. The Maurrasian nationalists in Quebec, in which he had little interest, were perfect foils in this move. And in his grand game of geopolitical strategy, Canada was perfectly expendable.

One of the disturbing aspects of Canada's lack of a long-term foreign policy—in fact its refusal to deal seriously with geopolitics—is that we have difficulty following the persistent lines followed by others. This is the worst kind of naïveté. And it is as flagrant among federalists as among separatists/sovereigntists.

As a great actor, the general always sent out signals of what he was going to do. Dramatic, theatrical signals. For example, when he landed from his battleship in Montreal, he wore his uniform. This was something he never did in France as president, except once during an attempted coup d'état by four other generals. To put on a uniform in Canada was to indicate to the Americans that he was making a strategic move.

At the same time, he was obviously having fun. De Gaulle had a very developed sense of irony, particularly international irony.

Nothing amused him more than to play out his grand politics on other people's territories. And why not, if other people, federalists and separatists alike, were willing to act as his foils? We should all laugh along with him.

If you talk with the groupuscule inside the Quai d'Orsay who continue to pursue his Quebec strategy, you will find the same indicators as in the mid-1960s. For example, it was wonderfully symbolic that the two statesmen sent in 1997 for the thirtieth anniversary of the general's intervention were Pierre Messner and Philippe Séguin: Messner, the father of the militarily maintained client-state empire in Africa, and Séguin, the leading spokesman for the sort of Maurrasian nationalism which the general had spent most of his life opposing.

◄——————►

But again, there is no reason to blame France for any of this. Most of its citizens are indifferent to Canada, whether francophone or anglophone. They know and care as little as do citizens in Britain or America, all of which is normal. They have their own concerns and problems and challenges. They have their own strategic and tactical obsessions. And most of the officials who are charged with handling Canadian affairs are of goodwill and do a professional job.

Situations such as that involving the general are of our own creation. The attitudes adopted by our élites in Paris have often been as unwise, even craven, as in London or Washington. By dragging their home problems through the Parisian halls of power, the negative nationalists have not so much embarrassed Canada as humiliated Quebec. They have turned themselves, in the eyes of the Quai d'Orsay, into just another unstable group, of the sort they deal with in their African empire, begging for imperial benediction, if not intervention.

There is always a faction in the Quai d'Orsay—as there would be in the Foreign Office or the State Department—eager to launch

380   itself into someone else's business in the vague hope that they might drag their whole country along with them. They rarely succeed in this. Sophisticated government systems have the equivalent of institutional elasticized leashes, designed to allow officials some tantalizing play on the edges of diplomatic adventure. The moment any larger national interests are put at risk, they are snapped back into line.

And there will always be a handful of députés nostalgic for empire and bored by France's democratic and institutionalized rejection of Maurrasian nationalism for itself. After all, they have rejected the old attitudes in favour of a more complex European federal approach, not unlike the Canadian model. What is no longer acceptable at home or in Europe—unless you belong to a party on the extremes—can of course be toyed with elsewhere. It's a pleasant way to let off steam. So on Monday they might rise to argue vociferously for iron-clad Europe-wide standards on social services, training, professional credentials, immigration policy and budgetary practices, then fall back into their seats, suffused with the sentiments of a good European. Then on Tuesday they might offer a sympathetic arm to a Quebec politician who has come to ask support for a theory of breaking up each of the areas I've just mentioned, in order that they might represent the particular character of particular regions.

No matter. Like the officials in the Quai d'Orsay, these députés are used to the lobbying of various central European minorities and ex-colonies in Africa. It is the destiny of empires and ex-empires to meddle in the affairs of weak countries; that is, countries which offer themselves up as weak. There is always the expectation in these cases of picking up bits and pieces from other people's disorder—some useful information, a contract, perhaps testing grounds for a missile system, a distribution monopoly and, at the very least, some regional influence. Who knows? It depends on how desperate the supplicant is. The empires have had a long experience with client-states, which is exactly the context in which the negative nationalists present Quebec.

But surely much of this is unfair. Surely we have garnered far more from London, Paris and New York than these unpleasant political experiences. What about the literatures, the ideas, the culture, the post-graduate educations, the food, the styles?

What of them? They have nothing to do with our colonial relationships. Everyone has access to them. For better and sometimes for worse, they are part of international culture.

What I am writing about is quite different. At the heart of these unsatisfactory imperial relationships lies a mythological missed rendezvous, between an expectant child and an anxious mother, waiting patiently for us to pay a visit to London, Paris or Washington. Thus, each time the mother acts in a non-maternal manner, the child becomes more expectant and troubled.

But if the mother isn't one at all, but is just another country looking after its own interests, well then, indifference is transformed into normalcy. And if the child, or more specifically, that part of the national élites which mistakes itself for an offspring, refuses to see the self-evident, well then, it will demonstrate by its actions what Fernand Dumont accurately identified as a *mépris de soi*. In order to put this in its historical context, I would call it the Lord Durham syndrome.

26 Fragments of a Past — II

WE CHOOSE OUR SYMBOLS THE way we choose pebbles on a beach. Different people are drawn to different shapes and colours. Still, Laurier's funeral was a distinctive and large stone, with a multitude of prisms. It seems not unreasonable to see this as a pivotal moment between the two centuries.

It was more than a gathering of old and young men of power in fur coats. The war was over. Half a million soldiers were coming home or were already home. In the twelve months preceding and following the funeral there would be strikes, riots, crowds fired upon, citizens shot and killed. These would be the final events needed to convince the population that there was a desperate need for new reforming policies. These new concepts would have to be grafted onto the ethical foundations of the public good—with reconciliation at its core—which Laurier had shepherded forward from the inheritance of LaFontaine and Baldwin.

By the end of 1919 it was absolutely clear that the Borden experiment had failed. What do I mean by that? The McCarthyites had never elected more than a handful of MPs, even in their glory days of the 1880s and 1890s. But Borden had governed according to the basic McCarthyite principles—as if there were only one culture in Canada and one language; as if francophones had but to conform to the majority; as if farmers were to be subject to the attitudes of the cities and, therefore, as if the West were an appendage of the East; as if a social contract were a commercial contract drawn up in a board room. He thus governed as if unaware of a need for reconciliation and ignorant of something called the public good.

That he had been able to govern in this manner for so long was largely due to the war. Without the extreme polarizations which he allowed to develop, even encouraged, it is unlikely that he would have won a second election.

The strikes and riots between 1917 and 1919 seemed at first to have separate causes; some conscription related, some labour related, some provoked by dissatisfied returning soldiers. Examined now from a distance they can all be seen to belong to a single, more general trend. The Quebec City Easter Riots of 1918 had as much to do with urban dissatisfaction as with war regulations. The troubles in Vancouver, followed by the Winnipeg General Strike in June 1919, confused the disappointed expectations of returning soldiers with those of working-class families; the frustrations of those who had fought in the war with the discontent of the rural populations who in general had been against conscription.

In the short period between the end of the war and his collapse and death, Laurier forced himself to travel about the country launching his idea of what was needed to rebuild the national reforming coalition. He was quite specific about what he meant, for example, by the democratization of industry. "[T]he workers should be represented in the management of each industry." And he who had restrained himself on the subject of the war for almost five years was now ready to argue that the state had an obligation to take care of the widows and orphans of soldiers, to ensure that the disabled were "provided with a living equal to that which they were getting before the war" and that all returning soldiers were assisted back into civilian life.

The government which had so divided the country over what it said was the true nature of patriotism now showed little interest in policies aimed at social reform, including the future of the hundreds of thousands of ex-soldiers. Patriotism was somehow seen to be a quality unrelated to the type of society in which you lived. In fact, what the government had been selling was a version of negative nationalism; a falsely romantic abstraction about belonging to a group, which might be characterized as a race or an empire, but not as a society.

Arthur Meighen is chiefly remembered as the leading advocate of conscription, a fact which made his future career as a national leader impossible. But he was also the central force in insisting that this general disquiet, which crept over the country as 1919 advanced, meant nothing. He arrived in Winnipeg on May 24 to add the central government's support to local opponents of the protest movement. "There is absolutely no justification for the general strike. . . ." He suggested it was a cloaked operation to overturn proper authority.[1]

At first the citizenry seemed frightened by the strike and so did not support it. But, as with the pivotal moment between 1837 and 1840, opinions quickly shifted. Within a year strike leaders were out of jail and being elected at all three levels of government. With the next provincial election voters turned their backs firmly on the politics of confrontation, which they attributed to the various levels of unresponsive governments, and elected the United Farmers of Manitoba. The whole approach of the UFM was one of careful reconciliation and reform and they stayed in power for two decades. In the next federal election the voters refused the Conservatives and confrontation even more decisively. They supported the Progressives and the Liberals.

The years surrounding 1919, like those between 1837 and 1840, set off a long wave of reforms. This is somehow illustrated by Tommy Douglas who, as a teenager, on June 21, 1919, stood on a roof in Winnipeg, saw the police charge, the streetcar burning, the man shot. Some forty years later he would invent Medicare; and a decade after that, stand up against the use of the War Measures Act.[2]

The twentieth century, particularly after the First World War, was not really suited to Laurier's more elegant 'sunny ways.' Instead we got Mackenzie King's careful ways. But the country had learnt from its first experiment with government under a monolithic right wing that the lesson of the 1840s was still true. Canada could not survive without reconciliation and a coalition of reformers. As for the acceptance of careful government, this was one of the lessons drawn from the Borden experience. If you want to live with complexity in an unusual, even original sort of political arrangement, which Canada clearly was, the accompanying characteristic was care.

From the election of 1921 on, the citizenry have endeavoured to choose governments at the national level which in some way were able to combine governing on the basis of reconciliation between the communities with some sort of reform impetus. Quite simply, between the two major parties, they have always chosen the one which was, in Canadian terms, to the left of the other. And if they were unconvinced by either, they created minority situations with the balance of power lying on the left, as they did in 1925, 1956, 1962, 1963 and 1965, 1972 and 1979.

When the Conservatives won power, they did so from the left of the Liberals, as R.B. Bennett did in 1930, John Diefenbaker in 1958 and Brian Mulroney in 1984.

I recently watched a film of Diefenbaker speaking in Cape Breton during the 1963 general election. He had been introduced by Robert Stanfield. It is a remarkable performance out of time and place. Not a single sentence is finished, the eyes flash, even through the bad black-and-white film. It is an almost crazy flash. Yet there is something endearing, and a terrible insecurity in the same glance, which fits with his naughty little boy smile. And if you listen to this Conservative leader, his entire speech is about opportunity and equality. And he is using equality the way LaFontaine used it and Woodsworth and King. Not in the deformed manner of D'Alton McCarthy and Preston Manning. What's more, this speech was a fair continuation of the social- and citizens'-rights issues which he introduced as prime minister. They are listening with respect in Cape Breton because he brought in the Atlantic Provinces Adjustment Grants six months after first winning power.

Watching his strange, deformed face I thought—the mind moves at the oddest angles—of Saint-Denys Garneau's poem "Le Jeu":

Nous ne sommes pas des comptables
Tout le monde peut voir une piastre de papier vert
Mais qui peut voir au travers

We are not accountants
Everyone can see a green paper buck
But who can see through it.[3]

Diefenbaker didn't speak political rhetoric. It was radical free verse, in both senses of the word radical. He was not an oddity of Red Toryism. His social theme is the sound of the mainstream of federal Canadian politics.

The great Western conservative historian W.L. Morton was near the end of his life when Charles Taylor talked to him in the late 1970s. He ruminated on the nature of real conservatism. Morton complained about bureaucratic despotism and state structures and insisted that "people are themselves of absolute value." But this was not a call for "laissez-faire economics and rugged individualism." Instead he desired the "frank and loyal acceptance of the welfare state, in order to keep it one humanely administered for people, for people who matter as people."[4]

It could be argued that even Robert Borden won his first election in 1911 on a reforming platform to the left of Laurier.

In other words, no national government has ever come to power in Canada from the right of the reigning government.

The only two disturbing elections which seem to undermine this rule involved the re-election of a government and took place in a highly confused atmosphere: 1917 and the Trade election of 1988. In both cases the citizenry quickly regretted their choice.

Mulroney's second term, like Borden's, became that of the most disliked government in a century and a half and he personally became the most detested prime minister since Mackenzie Bowell.

These patterns in Canadian politics seem to have been in place from 1867 on. While on some social issues Macdonald may have been more conservative than the Liberals, on others he was not. He offered reconciliation while the Liberals for a long time were unable to discover how to do this. And his economic policies were seen to be aimed at wider real prosperity—shared prosperity rather than an abstract theory of market-place prosperity.

Finally, if you consider the Liberals' relative failure in the election of 1997, you see the pattern continuing. The balance of power, had a few seats gone the other way or should they change through by-elections, would lie with the party which on social policy and reconciliation placed itself to the left of the government. And another party, which seeks to break up the country, still passes the test on the other issue—that of reform, and service of the public good.

While Canadians have not, given a left–right choice, chosen the right, that doesn't mean these governments have been far to the left. Often they were in the centre. Nor does it mean they were good governments. Some were mediocre, some just bad. Some did reprehensible things. Some were seriously corrupted. What I am doing here is not judging governments, but describing a long-established national pattern.

When you consider that Preston Manning's vision of "equality" has almost an identical meaning to that invoked by D'Alton McCarthy, whether regarding social relationships or community relationships, you realize that he belongs to a tradition which has never been chosen for government by the Canadian people. It is true that he has identified himself with the perfectly real condition of alienation in the West and in areas away from the southern urban

388   centres in other provinces. But beyond that, what he offers is what
McCarthy and Meighen offered—division and disturbance. Political
leaders like them can only come to power if reconciliation breaks
down and in despair or confusion the people allow themselves to
slip into the dead-end of confrontation. These are men whose
careers are built therefore on disruption, which they hasten to provoke in order to offer themselves as the solution.

But this reconciliation, will it ever be accomplished? That is the
inevitable question of the ideologues—the neo-conservatives and
the negative nationalists. Vote for them, they say, and they will
resolve all doubts by breaking the mould. They will answer all questions by destroying the essential conditions of the society. These
conditions, they argue, prevent resolution. And being ideologues,
resolution is their ideal.

Without ideology will we ever be done with reconciliation? No
more than the public good is ever accomplished or Western alienation satisfied. These are our conditions. We all live with them—
inside them and out—on a permanent basis by paying careful
attention.

How can reconciliation have been such an important part of our
long-term project when we see how francophones were evacuated
from so many of the senior jobs in the public service during the
first half of this century? This is a good question because it highlights the hard realities of living in a complex society.

The classic explanation would be that two trends collided to the
disadvantage of one. The full force of anglophone nationalism with
its desire to build, expand, grow and control came up against the
full effects of Ultramontane nationalism, now well into its defensive mode, with a high-quality but narrowed educational path.
However, it isn't accurate to say that this classical education dis-
qualified francophones from senior levels in the public service. After

all, much of the work could as easily be done with that education as another. In fact a classical education was ideal for the public service.

I think the offence–defence relationship of the two nationalisms tells you a great deal more about what happened. In spite of this, francophones were still very present in certain departments. There was also a second factor. The civil service had begun to grow in successive leaps—the First World War, the birth of the social state with the Depression, the Second World War, the next stage in the growth of the social state. Each expansion represented new administrative territory to be occupied and it isn't surprising that those on the offensive filled the space, not those on the defensive.

It's important to remember that LaFontaine, Cartier and Laurier never stopped talking about, encouraging, even berating the francophone élites to take the offensive in occupying public space. That's why these leaders were the enemies of the negative nationalism which was growing in strength. They did not suffer from the required mépris de soi. They saw no reason why any francophone should.

After the successive victories of Bishop Bourget, the trend was so much set in another direction that it would take decades to turn francophone society around. The first attempt, led by Premier Marchand at the end of the century, was defeated on the spot. The first real wave began in 1940 with Adélard Godbout's reforms. These were short-circuited by the return of the old nationalism in 1944. The second wave of reform came in the early 1960s.

And this is the key point: within four years major alterations in the role of francophones began in Ottawa. It was enough to go onto the offensive for things to change. What had been seen as institutional barriers were actually circumstantial and psychological barriers. Within a decade, francophones were back to where they had been earlier in Confederation—that is, occupying their per-capita levels in the civil service.

Needless to say this did not happen without protests from some of those who had been used to occupying most of the good positions. A great deal was made of this anglophone complaining, as if

390   it were anti-francophone behaviour. But put aside the fact that these changes were necessary, fair and overdue. Does that mean that anyone would expect people to give up space they occupy without a bit of a struggle? It would have been very odd if they had said nothing.

To which a PQ leader might reply, 'Why put up with this nonsense when you'll be a natural majority in an independent Quebec?' But that really misses the point. There was a problem. It was solved and solved quickly. In other words, the system worked. Besides, the situation is much more interesting—that is, more complex—than one involving competition between two linguistic groups.

Each department has a culture of its own and we can see how, twenty years later, some have become more francophone, others more anglophone. This creates some tension among those who are not part of the department's dominant ethic. But then tension is not an unhealthy characteristic for a civil service.

More important than this are the different ethical coalitions which exist in the bureaucracy, just as they do in society. For example, the old reforming generation, which included many Westerners, is gone. Pierre Trudeau's obsessions with rational administration pushed a first generation of modern managers to the fore. Many of them turned out to be more attached to their mechanical skills than to the public good. They in turn spawned an even more purely managerial generation. Many of these became the servants of the Mulroney regime.

None of this led to the total exclusion of other groups. And so a smaller parallel trend built on the old humanist tradition also continued. Over the last three years some departments have shown signs of swinging away from the nuts-and-bolts men and back to those with ideas about the society they serve. But so long as there is a continuation of the managerial obsessions with efficiency, client service and consultancy reports, just to name a few, it will be difficult for public servants to think every day that public service means service of the public good.

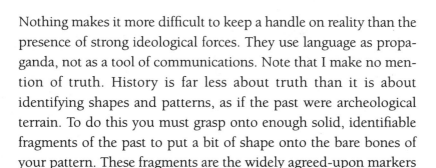

Nothing makes it more difficult to keep a handle on reality than the presence of strong ideological forces. They use language as propaganda, not as a tool of communications. Note that I make no mention of truth. History is far less about truth than it is about identifying shapes and patterns, as if the past were archeological terrain. To do this you must grasp onto enough solid, identifiable fragments of the past to put a bit of shape onto the bare bones of your pattern. These fragments are the widely agreed-upon markers of a shared existence.

This is particularly difficult when ideologies are running wild, because suddenly there are no shared ground rules about what is a fragment and what not.

For example, in October 1970 there was a crisis. Most of the players are still alive and the documentation is sufficient that we can line up the fragments before arguing about the patterns and what they mean.

And yet, mystification has enveloped this event as if there were no documentation, no film footage, no applied memory. I say all of this as someone who opposed the use of the War Measures Act (for what it was worth from a student living in Europe) and continues to believe that it was wrong and unnecessary. Just as democracies are ill-suited to fighting wars, so they are to facing internal anti-democratic movements. Everything that makes democracy strong in normal times makes it weak when the basic rules are not respected by a part of its citizenry. But that is all the more reason to act with enormous care when a crisis arrives. Care of this sort is not weakness. It is necessary because it ensures that there are no incidents which will weaken the democracy's respect for itself in the aftermath. The indiscriminate arresting of five hundred people was precisely that sort of 'incident.'

But let me go back to the identifiable fragments of the event versus the reigning mythology. It is now habitually stated that the RCMP arrested 497 citizens. They didn't. The 497 were arrested by the Quebec Provincial Police and the Montreal Police. Why is the RCMP invoked? Because it is federal and can be imagined to be anglophone. Therefore (to use the mythological terminology of the negative-nationalist movement) Quebecers did not arrest Quebecers. Canadians did it. In fact, not only was Ottawa not involved in the arrests, it had only been given in advance 70 of the names of those to be arrested.

None of which is to say that the RCMP had no role in the tragicomic behind-the-scenes manoeuvring of the late 1960s when almost-phantom revolutionary groups were pumped up by Mountie infiltration. Still, the FLQ did manage to kill seven people with its bombs and seriously wound forty-one. And it did manage to murder Pierre Laporte. For all its manipulations, the RCMP was not very effective. But the specific point here is that the mythology of 1970 is pure mystification. The Mounties were not involved in the sweeping arrest of 497 citizens.

Lucien Bouchard states in his memoirs that during the crisis "René Lévesque was the only one to stand up and incarnate, with dignity, the democratic values of Quebec."[5] This is another part of the deformed mythology. When René Lévesque stood up, Claude Ryan also stood up, right beside him. That is, Claude Ryan, editor of *Le Devoir*, future leader of the No forces in the 1980 referendum. Mr. Bouchard knows full well that Mr. Ryan was there. Why does he pretend that he doesn't? Why does he say what he knows to be untrue? He is building the hagiography of a solitary victim for the purposes of ideological mythology.

Within six lines of making his consciously incorrect statement, Mr. Bouchard concludes that this event demonstrated "l'intransigeance du Canada anglais." How he got to such a conclusion isn't very clear. But how can you even discuss that conclusion if there is no willingness to take into account the most obvious and basic events which took place?

Robert Stanfield, leader of the Official Opposition in Ottawa, also stood up against the War Measures Act. So did Tommy Douglas, leader of the NDP. For example, in Parliament on October 16, at the height of the crisis and the atmosphere of fear and panic, Douglas stated:

> We are not prepared to use the preservation of law and order as a smoke-screen to destroy the liberties and the freedom of the people of Canada. . . .

> The Government is using a sledgehammer to crack a peanut. . . .

> We cannot protect democratic freedom by restricting, limiting and destroying democratic freedom.

These same arguments were taken up by a multitude of writers and thinkers throughout anglophone Canada; and by a number of the journalists on Parliament Hill. They kept pestering the government with argumentative questions. When you look back at these clashes, you find that they went far beyond the professional questioning of journalism. The most famous involved Tim Ralfe, attempting to pin Mr. Trudeau down on the War Measures Act. Even the highly conservative Vancouver talk-show host Jack Webster can be heard giving Jean Marchand a hard time over the theory of an apprehended insurrection versus the reality. After pressing vainly for information on organizations, numbers of members, numbers of weapons, he becomes clearly annoyed—"You must have had enough information to implement the almost totalitarian War Measures Act." And when this produces nothing—"The FLQ . . . is it thirty men, is it three hundred men . . . ?"

The first and still the finest critique of the whole crisis was written within months of the events by a journalist and a lawyer from Toronto—Ron Haggart and Aubrey Golden. When *Rumours of War* was reissued in 1979, Robert Stanfield wrote the introduction, which began: "It was dramatic, it was ruthless, it was based on assertions which have never been factually supported, it involved injustice to hundreds of Canadians."[6]

Both the War Measures Act and the arrival of the army in Quebec are now presented as a Trudeau solo initiative and action. Yet we know that the constitution is quite clear on this question. A province may request the army and Ottawa cannot refuse it. That's one of the federal services available to the provinces on demand. We know that the War Measures Act itself was also requested. We know that Premier Robert Bourassa and Jean Drapeau, mayor of Montreal, were insistent. They have themselves over the years repeatedly insisted that it was their choice and their initiative.

Could Mr. Trudeau have refused? He certainly refused many things to many people during his career. It's clear that he didn't try to refuse these requests because he was in favour of the imposition of the Act. Various figures in Ottawa were pushing, along with others in Montreal and Quebec City, for its implementation. So Mr. Trudeau bears an historic responsibility in the affair. Does that mean Mr. Bourassa was merely a pawn in Mr. Trudeau's hands? Even if that were the case, the responsibility remains the same. Mr. Bourassa was the premier of Quebec. He exercised his constitutional powers by requesting the implementation of the Act and the use of the army.

Why is so little attention paid to the legal and practical responsibility of provincial leaders, in spite of their desire to assume that responsibility whenever asked? The mythology that Ottawa masterminded all actions and actually carried them out is now so strong that even anglophones tend to accept it. But why?

The quotes from Mr. Bouchard give a hint. I could have used dozens of quotes from other leaders or allied commentators of the separatist/sovereigntist group. They all draw the same portrait of the Quebec experience. It is, once you strip away the modern trimmings, the same defensive, victimized mythology of the old Ultramontane school. It moves in an unbroken line through Maurice Duplessis and the Montreal School to today. All events are presented in a simple schema placing—to use one of their formulae—Ottawa against the people of Quebec, anglophones against francophones. A francophone in Ottawa is to all intents and purposes an anglophone. That's why the concept of the traitor is used so often and with such facility. It is a word which permits the accomplishments and failures of the person in question to be swept up in the same garbage bag of betrayal.

There can therefore be no sensible weighing of pros and cons, as we might with a politician in normal circumstances. There is no examination of Pierre Trudeau as a remarkable force for social reform and a long-term protector of individual rights and indeed minority rights, including minority language rights, versus the Pierre Trudeau of the 1970 crisis and his rather mediocre economic leadership. Nor can there be any consideration of how citizens voted in the elections which followed in Montreal, Quebec and Canada. Ideology deals in a larger abstract mythology which imposes its own reality, beyond events and democratic expression. The most disturbing legacy of the October crisis is that most Canadians—both francophone and anglophone—continue to look upon the implementation of the War Measures Act as having been a right and necessary act.

In October 1990, René-Daniel Dubois wrote a remarkable essay, "8 Octobre 1990." He attempted to enunciate why it is impossible to look the crisis in the eyes and examine it. He didn't mean we should set out to identify villains and victims. Rather, we should be examining the society itself. After all, such a dramatic event cannot help but be, at some level, an expression of a great malaise. And it is highly unlikely that this malaise is the product of a structural argument pitting federalism against separatism.

"I believe that if we refuse irredeemably that which crashes up against us or attempts to crash up against us, if we consent to turn this other, whomever he may be, into the enemy, nothing is any longer possible, only slums and ruins. And I believe that the moment we have an enemy, there can only be a question of victory and yet that is not a real question. We hate in the other what we hate in ourselves. It would be better to remember. And to accept that we must take into account the memory of ourselves, the whole memory."[7]

The purpose of ideology is to prevent all reflection on our condition—that is, applied memory—by replacing consideration with assertion. I'm not referring here to the jurists' or journalists' or even the academics' consideration of the events. Nor am I making any comments on the respective rights and wrongs of the various governments, politicians, movements or police forces. It may be useful to examine what are called the facts, but that is only marginalia used as history. What I am referring to is the importance of using history to try to understand how we and our society work at some more basic level; the level of the whole memory. And it is precisely that which is prevented by ideology's need to control the surface of language and debate. With that surface under control, the citizenry are deprived of their ability to examine their own memory, let alone to express it.

←----------→

The question of trade has been surrounded by exactly the same overtones of complete mythological truth which makes impossible any reasonable examination of the patterns in which we live.

We were clearly and authoritatively told that the purpose of the FTA and then of NAFTA was to increase trade, which would produce wealth, which would translate into growth which would create prosperity for society as a whole. It was assumed by everyone, including those doing the telling, that the concept of prosperity included a job. In Mexican President Salinas's words, by "increasing our trade we will increase our standard of living."

This was a formula reiterated by Prime Minister Mulroney and picked up by Prime Minister Chrétien after his election. It was also the watchguard phrase of Messrs. Bouchard, Harris, Klein, Landry and Parizeau. It was a formula strong enough to justify a profound restructuring of our economy and—since economics was being given the leadership position in our civilization—of society as a whole.

It would appear that the first step in this formula was perfectly accurate. The agreements have either encouraged trade or at least not prevented it. Exports have moved from 24 per cent of our economy in 1990 to 37 per cent today. This represents a 50 per cent increase, which is a revolutionary success.

On the other hand, an explosion in trade has not done any of the things we were told it would. It has not produced jobs or growth or prosperity, except perhaps in a statistical dreamland which bears no relationship to people's real lives. As for wealth, to the extent that it has grown, it has tended to do so in the least useful sectors of the economy. For example, international subsidiaries have grown at the expense of Canadian-owned companies. This matters because it tends to translate into a loss of leadership positions, research and development, reinvestment in Canada, and in general of high-level jobs involving across the board responsibilities. It also translates into a drain of capital being sent overseas to the owners.

This does not mean that trade is a bad thing or even necessarily that free trade—that is, to be precise, tariff-free trade—is a bad thing. What it does mean is that trade does not have universal characteristics. Trade does not, by definition, produce wealth, growth, prosperity and jobs. It may. Or it may destroy them. That all depends on what sort of trade in what sort of conditions between which sorts of societies. In other words, if there is a place for utilitarian considerations, it is around the subject of trade. Treat it carefully, specifically, on a case-by-case basis and you'll get the best possible results. It may actually be, in some cases, that you will get more wealth, growth, prosperity, jobs through less trade. It is entirely possible if trade takes place in the wrong conditions that all of the communities involved will be losers. In economics there is not necessarily a winner and a loser. Nor do the apparently clear indicators necessarily mean what they seem to say. The United

398 States runs a large trade deficit and claims to lead the west in prosperity. Canada runs record trade surpluses and lingers in economic doldrums with high unemployment rates.

But let me go back to the original premise of this radical reorganization of our society. In the first instance we were told we were signing an agreement with the United States. Suddenly it appeared that this agreement indirectly included a large cheap-labour assembly-zone running along the American border inside Mexico. These Maquiladora zones used mid-nineteenth-century production conditions in order to reduce costs for goods which would be sold under American labels. Twelve hundred factories were involved and just under three hundred thousand workers, employed at approximately sixty-five cents an hour without any security or benefits, living in shacks without services. I remember the sequence of events clearly because I was the one who first pointed out this anomaly in the FTA during testimony to the relevant Parliamentary Committee.[8]

The government denied that it had any relevance and refused to enter into the debate. In the aftermath of 1988 they quickly began negotiations with Mexico, which suggests that they had intended to do so all along and had intentionally lied to the public during the original trade debate. This time around, many people intervened to point out that free trade was not the same thing as economic integration; and that we were negotiating economic integration treaties, not free-trade treaties; and that economic integration meant some sort of social integration, which would mean heavy downward pressures on the Canadian social system. They also pointed out that, while trade with a non-democracy was manageable and could perhaps even be helpful to the developing country, if the conditions were responsibly defined, economic integration represented serious risks for Canada and for Mexico.

At the time, writers' organizations such as PEN Canada were trying to draw to the government's attention the marginal state of free speech in Mexico and the more than twenty writers who had been killed during the first half of President Salinas's mandate—a record among Mexican presidencies. With a fury I have never seen in a Canadian government they asserted that Mexico, in the hands of President Salinas, was a new democracy in the full flood of normalization. To question Mexican standards was to insult them. The Canadian government actually denied the deaths which were admitted by the Mexican government.

In the aftermath of NAFTA and of his presidency, Mr. Salinas fled into exile to avoid questioning over the assassination of the candidate who was almost certain to replace him as the next president of Mexico. A revolt broke out in Chiapas in the south, and the army put it down, killing two thousand people in the first ten days. Most observers agree that the rebel army members had numbered only a few hundred. It was revealed that 70 per cent of the non-Asian drugs flowing into the United States came via Mexico. Between 1994 and 1996, twelve hundred senior police officers were fired for unspecified corruption. The case which keeps Mr. Salinas's brother in jail and himself in exile seems to involve a drug cartel.

Meanwhile the peso collapsed and most of Mexico's working population saw its income drop by more than 50 per cent. Unemployment stands at only 10 per cent, but another 50 per cent are considered seriously underemployed, particularly given the halving of the value of their income. That is, they are now living in deep poverty. The $52 billion borrowed from the United States to save the peso during the initial crisis was triumphantly repaid, but only because it was borrowed elsewhere on the money markets, further weighing down Mexico with high-interest-rate debt. Meanwhile there are now some seven hundred thousand workers in the Maquiladora zones, representing about 20 per cent of the independent work force.

Some people brush all of this aside. According to them, 'thanks to the new global economy... blah blah... new technology... blah blah... new communications technology... blah blah... the end of the nation-state... blah blah... it doesn't matter where cheap labour markets are situated. Parts travel happily all over the world.' Well actually, yes and no. Seven hundred thousand low-wage unsecured labourers—on their way to a million—employed on the American border in subsidiaries of large industrial concerns and thus integrated into the North American market is not the same thing as a million or ten million in China or elsewhere.

The Maquiladora are part of the North American transport system. They lie only a few hours from factories in the cheap, but not as cheap, labour states of the American south. They are at the hub of a trade system which puts constant downward pressure on established wage, environmental and social standards. Those who negotiated the original FTA were perfectly conscious that this would be the case whether the governments went on to NAFTA or not. That doesn't simply mean that they alone are to blame. In 1996 Carlos Fuentes published a book—*A New Time for Mexico*—describing the childlike manner in which his country had rushed to embrace the policies of the maternal empire next door, whatever the disastrous results.

What's more, the side agreements on environmental and social standards are generally agreed to be irrelevant to all three countries. They are, as critics of the day said, mere window-dressing. The Maquiladora in particular continue to grow as an environmental menace to those who work there and to the south-western United States. And they act as an economic pressure for lowering environmental standards elsewhere.

Of course there is more to the treaties than cheap labour. There are the dispute-settlement panels. And Canada has won a number of battles before these panels. However, the United States has tended simply to ignore the results and negotiate in the old way outside the treaty. We have seen this over softwood lumber, pork and swine, to say nothing of grain exports.

In other words, the two treaties have not done what we were told they would do. This would suggest, in a sensible, non-ideological atmosphere, that we should be discussing the pattern of economic and social events which have unfolded over the last decade. I am not making a protectionist argument. It's just a musing over the fragments of past events which can be clearly identified. We know precisely what we were told these agreements would accomplish. They have not worked out as promised. We should therefore be asking ourselves questions.

For a start, it is clear that we completely misread the political and economic structures of Mexico, as did the United States. I can understand that the politicians, diplomats, trade experts, bankers and economists responsible for such incompetence in the setting of public policy are unwilling to lead the way in re-examining our actions and their results. That was the lesson of the First World War. Modern technocrats cannot throw their own actions into question. As bad generals they attempted to cover up disastrous battles by fighting more disastrous battles. Une fuite en avant.

There are also those who are genuinely and rightly sympathetic to Mexico and its problems. They worry about upsetting Mexicans, even insulting them. But most Mexicans, including the intelligent members of its élite, are perfectly conscious that they have made a serious miscalculation. Many of them would be only too willing to re-examine the conditions and structures which have been set in place and which in some ways are part of the catastrophe they have gone through. Perhaps the heart of the problem lies not in free trade but in the Chicago school/neo-conservative idea of unregulated market-places. Perhaps we should be discussing the establishment of stricter North American standards, more along the lines of a step-by-step European social contract. That could suit the Mexican tradition, as it would ours. And it might help them, exactly in the way that their plunge into an unregulated market-place has hurt them.

In July 1997, partial elections in Mexico brought the social-democratic opposition to power in Mexico City and put the government into a minority in the national assembly. There are those who naïvely put this improvement in democratic mechanisms down to the influence of NAFTA. They are inadvertently right. It is the catastrophic effects of neo-conservative economics—including NAFTA—on Mexican society which has so undermined the reigning party that some sort of change became the only way of avoiding an explosion.

We seem unable to allow ourselves the dignity of engaging in this sort of straightforward reconsideration of our acts. After all, questioning is the great strength of democracy; the ability to doubt without losing face. Instead we charge on, chanting 'Free Trade—Prosperity' the way in 1212 on the Children's Crusade they must have chanted 'Jesus and Jerusalem!' Most were snatched up before they could reach the coast and sold into slavery or sent across the Mediterranean, again to be slaves.

The most distressing part of this situation is the way in which we go on pretending that nothing has happened. The events in Mexico are treated as interesting tidbits of current affairs. There is never any suggestion that we might take some time to consider seriously the relationship between these events and NAFTA or the effect these events might have on the validity of NAFTA as originally conceived or the relationship of these events to the assumptions we made when negotiating NAFTA.

For example, the federal Liberal party has changed sides several times on the question of what international economic relationships should look like. Their last change, in favour of NAFTA, came without any real public debate and certainly without intellectual consideration or debate inside the party. It is assumed that the right wing of the party won out over the left in Cabinet-room battles. And that those who won leaned for support on the senior neo-conservative elements in the civil service which were left in place by the Mulroney government.

After four years in office, the prime minister and his ministers can see that the trend in our trade continues to slide strongly in the same direction. We are now so dependent on a single market that it is virtually impossible for Canada to have any geopolitical thoughts. Our position is that of a classic economic colony which cannot effectively resist an American policy that affects us adversely. We have no countervailing forces to bring to the table. We have no alternate alliances which could help us in our principal relationship. What's more, the economic imbalance is so overwhelmingly lop-sided that our ability to act in non-economic areas is equally limited. We play around with a few childlike protests—such as that over Cuba—just to pretend that our situation is not hopeless.

The government's policy is to soften the edges of this reality— which is now in large part of their creation—by getting other Latin American nations into NAFTA. But the presence of Chile and a few others will have almost no effect on the real numbers and the real balance of power. What's more, in the case of a policy crisis, their dependence on Washington will cause them to side against us or simply not to get involved. Indeed the Americans have blocked this sort of expansion until they are certain that it can be done in a way which will not weaken their dominant role. And needless to say, since we have no geopolitical position, we can't even protest this blockage.

To put it bluntly, Canada has no foreign policy because in a medium-sized country a foreign policy is dependent on a long-term balancing of forces and interests. That tension or equilibrium, which makes it possible for countries such as ours to advance our ideas and interests, is impossible when you become dependent on a single power.

A foreign policy isn't about self-aggrandizement or identity. It is a central tool in a healthy democracy. If you allow your international relations to slide into such disequilibrium that you lose any use of that tool, you have also made it almost impossible for your population actually to function as a democracy.

That you have a good corps of diplomats and engage in interesting policy analysis is irrelevant. That you take hundreds of positions on hundreds of international questions is an amusing way to fill in time. In this case busy hands do little more than create deceptive window-dressing. This is the sort of activity which makes you feel as if you have an international role.

Surely even those in the Liberal party who have trouble with the realities of geopolitics can understand unemployment figures, declining research and development investment and the thinning out of the full range of senior positions in the large subsidiaries. And surely those who consider themselves free-traders have now increased their understanding of this term sufficiently to differentiate between the removal of tariffs as against wholesale economic integration. If they can manage that little intellectual step, surely they must be capable of thinking about the real implications of economic integration; particularly economic integration in an unregulated economy.

Alternately, suppose you were the minister of finance of Quebec and you had led the campaign to make the PQ a front-line supporter of the FTA. Indeed, you had gone beyond that and had played the key role in bringing Premier Bourassa on side. And that at a time when Mr. Bourassa, who supported the highly regulated social arrangements of the EEC, was tending to oppose a market-place-dominated version of free trade. And in doing this you made certain that Canada would accept the FTA arrangement, because you had got all the players on side in Quebec.

Wouldn't you, now, almost a decade later, want to look around and ask yourself whether things were working out as imagined? Trade has certainly grown. But the Quebec economy is in a catastrophic state. Of course, you can't afford to attribute any of that to political uncertainty. Everyone understands your delicate position. But then to what do you attribute the terrifyingly high unemployment levels in the industrial areas? And the drying up of industrial activity? Wouldn't it be worth at least thinking about the role of the treaty of which you are one of the principal fathers? After all, in 1987, in your gospel to Free Trade—*Commerce sans frontières*—you said: "Apparently it is the fear of the harmonization of social policies which, for progressive Canadians, is at the heart of the debate. This argument is so important that if it were pertinent and if the union analysis were correct, I would personally be ready to reverse my positions."[9]

Well, now there are dozens of studies which demonstrate exactly that. Surely you would have read, just as an example, "FTA/NAFTA, Regulatory Diversity and the Problem of Harmonization," by Robert Howse and Michael J. Trebilcock, professors of law at the University of Toronto. Failing that, there are many others to choose from. Perhaps you disagree with their demonstrations. But shouldn't there be some consideration given to these concerns?

Or suppose you were a major shareholder or chief executive officer of a Canadian-owned company. Every year you see the statistics which suggest that these treaties are working better for the large, foreign-owned transnationals than for you. And this even though your efficiency and risk-taking and product quality are unbeatable. Wouldn't you think it incumbent upon you to raise the question of whether a mistake had been made? Or whether treaty adjustments were necessary? Why would you, a practical, down-to-earth businessman, be determined to treat a theory—unregulated free trade and economic integration—as if it were more important than your annual report?

Or, to go back to the Liberal party, what if we were to put the best light on their radical policy swing in favour of these treaties? In that case we would interpret their policy change as a healthy sign indicating a non-ideological approach and a flexible mind. Surely therefore those same flexible minds must now be re-examining the facts which caused the first swing. After all, their central promise in 1993 was the creation of jobs and, whatever indicators say about technical strength in the economy, unemployment will not budge. This would suggest that a policy nine years old—the length of the two world wars put together, a long time for an experiment—has not paid off.

Nine years, soon a decade, is no longer the present. Even in the slightly broader view of current affairs, our experience with unregulated free trade is now part of the past. In order to evaluate its worth to us today we have to unearth those fragments of memory which tell us exactly what we said we were setting out to accomplish in 1988 and place them in the centre of public debate. If we are unable to do that, we are indeed running society on the principles of Alzheimer's disease.

I'm not even suggesting that these two treaties are the direct cause of our problems. Or even part of the cause. I don't know. But they are the one truly radical policy change undertaken in the last decade. Common sense alone—real common sense, not the Harris deformation—would oblige us to examine their effects on society.

And even if we can't establish a clear negative, cause-and-effect situation, we ought at least to be trying to understand why the treaties have not produced what they said they would. If the positive effects are not apparent, then what exactly is their value to society?

But there is a more compelling reason to look closely at the path we have taken. In June 1997, across the country, three million Canadians were relying on food banks. Almost one-half of them were children. In other words we are not dealing here with the politics of the right versus that of the left. Or of free-traders versus protectionists.

Democracy functions through the legitimacy delivered by the citizens. To have 10 per cent of working citizens unemployed is to undermine that legitimacy. Of course, they are still citizens. But the system as constituted is preventing them from contributing to the economy. And relegated in this way to a non-participating position, they are likely, if the situation persists, to become passive members of the community.

But to have 10 per cent of the population as a whole—in part above and beyond the unemployed—dependent for the most basic of needs, their food, on charity is quite a different matter. In a democracy, to be obliged to live off charity is to have your legitimacy as a citizen removed.

I am not describing a statistical or an accounting problem.

Ten per cent of our neighbours survive on charity. 10 per cent of Canadians eat through charity. 10 per cent. Surely if you were prime minister or minister of trade or of industry, you would wake up each day thinking that, for reasons which perhaps escape you, the central policy chosen to drive the economy is not working. It is not working because it is not meeting the needs of a democracy in which legitimacy lies with the citizenry.

Again this is not a complex idea. Almost anyone can grasp it. We will soon have had ten years of the FTA-NAFTA strategy. We have 10 per cent unemployed. And 10 per cent of the population are living off charity. Perhaps this merits some debate over possible adjustments or even changes in our direction. Just a discussion at first. Nothing too challenging. Just enough to demonstrate that we are all alive and thinking and not victims of ideology who are reduced to the one-dimensional language of press releases.

In a sensible society people discuss economic mechanisms for what they are—economic mechanisms. They stay away from financial formulae which are reminiscent of pronouncements on faith or belief or religion in general. They don't fly into hysterical tributes to global market-places and the invisible hand. At any rate they don't if they are in touch with the real world and are thus able to apply their memories to the reality at hand.

27 The Expression of Reality

"THE POETS HAVE ALWAYS PRECEDED."[1]

I hear no chorus of agreement from the managers of reality, the consecrated priests of our day who distribute truth and facts like holy wafers.

Precedes whom? With what? Certainly not with political programs or intellectual arguments. Is Robin Blaser's argument the romantic assertion of the marginal? Not really. If history is an interpretation of memory, literature is memory itself.

In spite of the deadening effect of specialist dialects, public relations and communications formulae, the poet continues to precede with language. Not language, as in one language rather than another. Nor language, as in style. Blaser is referring to language as the first expression of what lies within us—the essential communication which precedes analysis. The poet doesn't need to know what her language means; not in the sense that an intellectual is expected to police her own meaning. The poet at his best probably doesn't concern himself with conscious meaning.

But the poet does precede, as does culture. I'm not sure that—as Fernand Dumont has eloquently put it—"a nation is essentially a cultural reality." The beauty of this idea somehow eliminates the full reality of people and their lives, in favour of what Jean Paré, editor-in-chief of *L'actualité*, calls "the vague notion of culture."[2] And yet culture does precede, not so much as the ultimate reality but as the pure expression of reality.

In larger countries driven by imperial missions this expression is often used by those with power however it suits them. For their particular purposes they turn cultural reality into rhetorical mystification. Theoretically in such large societies there is room for everyone to choose their cultural position. On the other hand, the force of an imperial message tends to sweep the whole society up in its arms. Loyalty to the great cause quickly becomes a given of life inside an empire. In smaller countries, particularly those under constant pressure from the outside, the situation is somewhat different. The cultural imperative is constantly shoved to the fore of public debate. The people require the nation to defend the culture and culture to defend the nation. Yet what is shoved forward is rarely related to culture as an expression of reality. More often than not it is the illusion of culture as something utilitarian or industrial or patriotic or mystical.

The results are interminable and nonsensical arguments over the role of culture; arguments almost always devoid of cultural content. "The truth is," the poet protests, "he's not dead but only ignored." "Poète, mon enfant, tu me chantes en vain."[3]

A.M. Klein and Albert Ferland were not whining about the hard lot of the poet proper—neither about book sales nor government support. We all know about those particularities of the troubadour's life, today and always, here and elsewhere. For that matter, the precision with which public officials single out cultural budgets in debate, in order to insist that what they represent is of tertiary importance to the public good, is not what it appears to be. This isn't a matter of justifying salutary pruning or slashing. This isn't a real attempt to weight the importance of child-care versus that of public broadcasting. I'm not convinced it has anything to do with budgets. After all, the sums involved on the cultural side are peanuts in the scheme of government finance. Peanuts before slashing and peanuts after. Yet the political discourse has an *important*, disciplinarian air about it; as if a Victorian father were teaching the wilful child a necessary lesson about the harsh realities of real life.

At its more primary level this is classic false populist politics: a premier of Ontario who claims not to read; a federal minister of culture who reduces culture to flag-waving; an Alberta premier who

410   sells off cultural institutions for no particular reason; a Quebec premier whose literary references are all to 'mother country' culture, as if to humiliate the very culture he swears to defend; a public political discourse which in general falls well below the standards of classic comic-books. When you step back to examine all of this, and much, much more, all together as a single phenomenon, you realize that this superficial denigration of culture is far more than classic false populist man-talk or even than standard colonial self-loathing.

The incapacity of our élites to govern as if the society had a culture is one of the root causes of our divisions and of our often unspoken despair as citizens. As I said in earlier chapters, the Canadian political ethic, from its origins, embraced the cultural idea as central to its reality. This was a confused and uncertain assumption, but it was there and you found it across the spectrum of public discourse. The gradual growth in federal cultural policy from the 1930s on was merely a slow concretization of that assumption.

At the same time a counter-move began to gather momentum. You could find it first in William Aberhart's and particularly Ernest Manning's deformation of real Western populism, then in Maurice Duplessis's or even W.A.C. Bennett's focus of loathing on culture as somehow against the people. These anti-cultural undercurrents have slowly come to dominate the public place; that is, public political discourse. It seems to have happened through the marriage of communications technology, public relations and the technocratic and corporatist worship of power. All of these elements can't help but reject the uncontrollable nature of culture. Instead, false populism has become the standard of public debate. Whatever is claimed in short emotive phrases about 'our culture' or in long boring paragraphs about 'our cultural industries,' the painful truth is that our politics have become profoundly anti-cultural. And in the process they have become a denial of the assumptions which made Canada conceivable as a country.

Our obsession with the definition of undefinable terms—nation, distinct society, people—to say nothing of our obsession with whether you're for or against one or the other, is not just a prolongation of the paralysed deification of culture as an ideal devoid of culture. It isn't surprising that we then have so much difficulty dealing with the living complexities of who or what we are. Why do we find it impossible to digest the idea of necessary differences within communities—differences which need to be assumed, enjoyed, even accentuated in order for people really to live together?

All the lessons of psychiatry, psychology, social work, indeed culture, have taught us over the last hundred years that it is the acceptance of differences, not the search for similarities which enables people to relate to each other in their personal or family lives. This is doubly true in a country. That's why nationalism based on the assertion of love of 'the same' is a deformed marriage of the worst of nineteenth-century nationalism with the most manipulative of twentieth-century public relations.

One of the long-standing lessons of the Canadian experience has been the importance of living on several levels at once. Somehow we have found enough intelligence and developed enough curiosity to maintain this successful but uncomfortable position. Now the anti-culture culture of our élites leads them to focus on 'wasted' overlap and the virtues of power at one level or another. The whole cultural history of Canada can be traced through the growing pleasure taken by the population from living on both levels at once without regarding the complexity as a matter of waste or desperately searching for simplicity. Canadian culture could be defined as a celebration of overlap.

Recently I came across a curious little pamphlet aimed at the forty-five thousand war brides who arrived in Canada after World War Two. The preface was by the Countess of Athlone, wife of the governor general. In her pinched and arcane style she nevertheless managed to explain what would most confuse these young women coming from mono-cultures such as the English, French and Dutch. The key was Canadians' desire for complexity. "So wherever [in

412   Canada] one may make one's home one's loyalty is to Canada and one's province."[4]

Our problem in accepting this today is not one of left versus right. The left is often caught up in the administrative religion of establishing clear lines of power; the right in the market religion of clear lines of competition. Both are denials of civilization. Whatever the romantic vocabulary of contemporary nationalism, the reality behind it is one of power, control and administrative methodology. In such a context the very idea of culture as an uncontrollable and complex expression of reality is impossible to accept.

In spite of this, culture remains at the core of our actions. The manipulations of false populism may permit votes to be won. What this does not produce in the citizenry is either self-respect or respect for the public system.

There is a great deal of talk from 'responsible' people about the new forces of inevitability and the new values. But, when élites talk about inevitability, they are either incompetent or duplicitous. As for values, the Swedish writer Carl-Henning Wijkmark puts it succinctly—"[T]he sign of authentic values is that they can resist evil."[5] In other words, values are not the product of newness or change, but of careful evolution combined with the judgement of experience. That's why any sustained discussion of ethics and values automatically stretches back over 2,500 years.

And that is why, over the short period of a few centuries, the line of culture in our society is easy to follow. The women's suffrage movement rose out of language, writing and literary organizations—Nellie McClung's writing and speaking made her the leader of the advance guard. The Toronto Women's Literary Club led the way in Ontario. It was Félix Marchand, the only professional writer to become premier of Quebec, who led the revival of the lay movement against the church's control of education. His force—the force which Honoré Mercier, Lomer Gouin and Louis-Alexandre Taschereau all lacked—was a solid cultural base. As for the qualities which did exist in conservative thought earlier in the century, much of it came from the trilingual economist Stephen Leacock and the novelist, preacher, activist Ralph Connor who, among other things, chaired the Manitoba Council of Industry after the Winnipeg strike. The poet and lawyer F.R. Scott was at the core of the formalization of the socialist movement. His production of aggressive, ironic poetry and his translations of francophone poets such as Anne Hébert and Saint-Denys Garneau sit naturally alongside his two landmark Supreme Court victories against the Padlock Act and on behalf of Roncarelli against Duplessis. Both of these were victories for citizens' rights.

I talked in earlier chapters about the intellectual, even literary and creative nature of the early Canadian leadership, a tradition which gradually petered out after men like Mackenzie King and Brooke Claxton. There was a revival under Trudeau, but again it slipped away. However, the disencultured period of Canadian public life in which we are now mired at the federal and provincial levels—a period which often seems to verge on the functionally illiterate—represents only a short amount of time in the experience of a century and a half.

Laurier, in his first speech as an elected representative in 1871— he was then thirty—insisted that "In a free state, all is related and each element leads to another; legislation, commerce, industry, the arts, the sciences, letters are all part of a same body—le corps social. . . . When there is an abuse in one part, the whole social body will be more or less paralysed. . . ."[6] He was not making a corporatist argument about linked interest groups, because his point was not that of interests but of inclusiveness and interdependency.

For example, the national commission appointed in 1926 to study broadcasting was led by a bank chairman—Sir John Aird. And yet he was able to imagine himself and his responsibilities as those of a citizen, rather than of a banker. As a result he recommended the creation of what would eventually become the CBC. The national campaign to force R.B. Bennett to enact Aird's recommendations came through the Canadian Clubs, not through professional cultural interest groups. There was an almost unspoken understanding running through all parts of the social body, as described sixty years before by Laurier, that in order to carry its reality into the twentieth century, a smaller country had to give itself the new cultural mechanisms of the century.

◄——————►

Their argument was not, nor is mine, centred on technology. The central point is the role of language. It is at the core of civilization throughout the western tradition. Humanism, responsible individualism, the idea of the citizen, democracy itself all turn on the central role of language. This is an idea of civilization built entirely around the necessity of communication.

What makes the Canadian situation unusual is the unprecedented access which we give to the language of other societies. You might say that this is particularly unprecedented because these friendly cultures are also aggressive rivals. These high levels of penetration of our culture—which none of them permit in their own territories—are driven by both commercial and political agendas. They carry on a free and often destructive operation inside our borders, all the while complaining that it isn't free enough. And in the process they manage to deflect attention from their organized xenophobia at home.

This penetration is particularly strong in technologies such as film and television. It is reinforced by their use of large, complex distribution systems to shoulder aside much of local culture, quite apart from questions of quality or potential audience. As a result Canadians have tended to use language in a manner more typical of the nineteenth century. That is, books remain the central means of public discussion, while elsewhere that same discussion is more likely to take place through film or television. We use novels, essays, even poetry, to set the imaginative agenda of the society. Our writers thus tend to occupy a much larger public place than in other developed countries.

This is part of the explanation for the continuing public role of poetry, when in other developed democracies it has largely slipped into a marginal intimiste art form. I am not suggesting that large percentages of the population read poetry. But rather that poetry still lies at the core of our creativity and so reverberates out through other expressions of culture. One of the signs of this energy is the continuing role of long narrative poems; again a literary structure more associated with earlier centuries.

It's not that we use narrative poetry in the nineteenth-century form. We use it in a twentieth-century manner. It was not surprising to find Charles Mair writing "The Last Bison" or "Tecumseh" or Isabella Valancy Crawford "Malcolm's Katie" or Octave Crémazie "Colonisation" or "Les Morts." They were of their time. However, E.J. Pratt's "Towards the Last Spike," a book-length epic, is unusual for the middle of the twentieth century.

And from the 1960s on there is a sudden explosion of grandly conceived narrative poems. Pierre Morency's *Lumière des oiseaux*. bp Nichol's *Continental Trance*. Michael Ondaatje's *Coming Through Slaughter*. Emile Martel's *Pour orchestre et poète seul*. André Ricard's *Les Baigneurs de Tadoussac*, in which urban figures swim up and down in L'Anse à l'eau at Tadoussac, the first lake named by Jacques Cartier in Canada. A whole new generation of poets are carrying on this approach—Esta Spalding, for example, with *Anchoress*. There is even a sub-category delivering a narrative urban vision. Dennis Lee's *Civil Elegies* is a long examination of Toronto and is matched by George Bowering's *Kerrisdale Elegies* of Vancouver or Dany Laferrière's *Chronique de la dérive douce* on Montreal. This time the city is experienced by a Haitian immigrant:

People always believe
that the victim deserves his fate.

It is the most sinister of the little
judéo-christian jokes.[7]

The long narrative poem has also become a tool for looking at the outside world: Peter Dale Scott's *Coming to Jakarta* or Al Purdy's "In Mexico." The Canadian obsession with short stories—Alice Munro and Mavis Gallant being the most obvious great talents—could be seen as another expression of these narrative poems.

Earlier in this book I spoke of how profoundly oral Canadian civilization is. The long narration is an affirmation of the determination with which the society remains in this mode. Glenn Gould spoke of how in his orality "the Newfoundlander is, first of all, a poet."[8] In other words this characteristic stretches beyond the purely poetic. For example, Canadians seem to be returning to an old pleasure—that of public speeches, given and heard. "It was by now ten o'clock," Robertson Davies wrote in *Fifth Business*, "and even the thirst of a Canadian audience for oratory was almost slaked."[9] You sense this great taste for the force of words—seemingly oral words—in René-Daniel Dubois's *Ne blâmez jamais les Bédouins* or in Tomson Highway's *The Rez Sisters*. In both cases the words seem hardly willing to stay on the page. They require performance. It is as if the force of language in Canadian society makes it impossible for the scholastic schools of literature to develop into a viable alternative.

And yet, by coming through the political door, the scholastic has developed into some sort of false alternative. It has been unable to win any real public, but it has occupied much of the territory of public debate. And in the process it has gradually been driving culture away from the underlying political questions which determine the shape and direction of society.

You will notice, for example, that over the last twenty years the best francophone writers have gradually distanced themselves from the mainstream political debate. You could say that they now aggressively avoid it, as expressed in Pierre Morency's ironic fictional description of a "fashionable political party" which advertises in the window of its headquarters:

> Writer wanted for conceptual work, writing, correcting. We seek a talented person, with reliable ambition, filled with the desire to work for his country and wishing to live intimately with a great leader. Salary modest, but all comforts assured.[10]

The effect on creativity is important. For the first time in our history there is, as François Ricard puts it, a "rejection of subject" and a tendency to concentrate on "private happiness."[11] Among anglophones the rejection has not been so extreme. Instead, politics have been replaced with causes. But causes represent a more romantic, distilled vision of society, and in that sense there is also a "rejection of subject."

It could be said that this tendency exists throughout the west and so our writing has become increasingly like that of others. But what has happened is more complex than that. Radio and television have favoured the two extremes of communication—the regional and the international, both of which have positive implications. They remind us of what lies below and above the 'truths' of the nineteenth-century nation-state. This has been a particularly interesting release in a country with two languages. The literary critic Gilles Marcotte argues that "you could establish a link of cause and effect between the arrival of television and the renaissance of [Quebec] nationalism."[12] And, to the extent that that nationalism is tied to a real sense of the community and not to ideological abstractions, it is a healthy renaissance. Margaret Atwood puts it this way— Cultural nationalism is "merely a determination on the part of writers to stay in their own country ... and to write about what they kn[o]w and s[ee] around them, which is only what writers everywhere have always done."[13]

At the same time, a very real negative has emerged. The new means of communication have revealed an incapacity even to suggest that culture exists other than in the particular language of broadcast. And this has encouraged the exact opposite of community identification. It has reinforced the big established empires of language. Suddenly it is as if we can only communicate with the world through the mechanism of our particular language, when in fact the nature of these international empires—particularly of English and French—is not primarily communications or culture but commerce. We can applaud the internationalism, but it does create a peculiar atmosphere.

Suddenly we are meant to share our primary perceptions of society with people who happen to use the same language as us (for the arbitrary reasons of imperial history) even though they may live thousands of miles away in, for example, a non-democratic society with completely different realities. On the other hand, we are to have nothing 'cultural' to share with people who live in the same town or within a few kilometres and with whom we share and have shared all the experiences of reality. The great and complex reality of culture is thus stripped down to little more than linguistics.

In this sense culture has never been so negatively political. Why? Because the ultimate ideological expression is that of form over content. And in our current situation the positive strengths of languages are reduced to linguistic forms or prisons. These require the theoretically absolute separation of neighbouring or interwoven cultures even when the reality is one of sharing. In other words, language is being celebrated and used in the same way that religion and race were once used. This is the full expression of solitudes as a negative.

Over the last decade this ideological idea has gradually climbed up into the constitutional/economic debates over efficiency and waste caused by overlap. Suddenly, linguistic and regional concerns have become a reason to seek the separating out of regional cultures. With a quiet insistency the debate goes on as to what level of government should have what responsibility. Driven by the politics of the PQ, culture has repeatedly been put on the list of those things which might go to the provinces.

This concept contains the fascinating idea that culture should be seen as something which a constitution could assign to a government—that culture is just another administrative activity in search of efficiency and lean organization. This is the ultimate marriage of the technocratic with the ideological. The idea that culture is alive and uncontrollable is simply evacuated. That is, culture itself is evacuated. What remains is an acultural, functionally illiterate replacement of the idea of civilization by that of administrative control.

What I am describing is the means by which the rhetoric of power can make assumptions which deny the essence of democracy and humanism. What I am arguing is that culture is not—in a citizen-based society—available for technocratic assignment to one pocket or another.

It is particularly interesting that this idea of assigning the content of society to the regional structures comes at a time when the power to decide the future of those regions has been consciously moved to the international level. What is presented as a nationalistic fulfilment of destiny through decentralization is more realistically a castrating of the citizens' means of expression through globalization. As Myrna Kostash has put it, "So we (Canadians, artists) have to be diverse and decentered but they (bond traders, Disneyland) get to be monopolistic and ubiquitous."[14] Or in a slightly different way, Jacques Godbout—"We [Quebecers] are a society ready to sell ourselves body and soul to another society—the American—all the while ferociously arguing our distinctiveness from Canada."[15]

What this whole approach assumes is that, to the extent governments are involved, culture should be reliant on a single clearly defined authority, and this for both cultural and financial reasons. The history of culture and politics in Canada suggests the exact opposite. It has always been the inefficiency and duplication of a system involving three levels of government which has permitted freedom of speech and remarkable creativity.

And if we had to choose one level, it would be sensible to analyse at which one creativity has fared best. The unsatisfactory answer, but nevertheless the answer, would be the national. The complexity of a federal government, with all of its contradictory impulses, makes it difficult for culture to be used in a classically nationalistic, moral or utilitarian manner. Of course people do try, but their successes tend to be less sweeping and less effective.

Provincial governments on the other hand seem to be too exposed to the interest groups which drive those sorts of jingoistic, moralizing and utilitarian agendas. And the ability of those who create to slow them down is weaker because the system is more monolithic. Ontario, for example, after a long tradition of arts support, has abruptly taken apart much of its arts programming. That same slashing process took place in Ottawa, but it was moderated by the variety of contradictory forces in play. Since the recent creation of an arts council by its provincial Liberals, Quebec has become relatively active in supporting the arts. But this initiative is only a few years old and both its staying power and its ability to maintain a reasonable arm's-length relationship to government is as yet undemonstrated, in the sense that time is the real demonstration of political reality.

Until recently federal institutions represented the only serious sources of creative support. At the same time as the Quebec arts council has improved the situation, another important earlier creation—Radio-Québec—has been reduced to virtual irrelevancy. In fact, the federal institution of Radio-Canada remains the dominant electronic structure of francophone communications, if not the most important cultural structure of any sort. For half a century, Radio-Canada has been one of the central institutions in the development not only of culture, but of cultural independence from the political control sought by governments at all levels, but in particular the negative-nationalist governments. Where else, apart perhaps from the National Film Board, was it possible to escape the power of the church and the Union Nationale government? For all its financial fragility and administrative flaws, it remains one of the few places where the different levels of government and the private sector cannot easily get their way. The same could be said of the CBC's role in the other Canadian provinces.

There has been very little public debate about the long-term commitment of the separatist/sovereigntist movement to maintain such an expensive and relatively arm's-length structure should they succeed in their political project. The only relevant indication we have is their treatment of Radio-Québec. In that case their approach has not been far off that of the Klein government in Alberta.

The central problem of single-source public funding for the arts is that of freedom and creative energy. It is increasingly proposed as an inevitability, given that less public money will be available and more private money will be required. What this would represent is a return to the pre-democratic system of the royal patrons, under whom freedom of expression was limited and ritual humiliation obligatory. That was a world in which the less threatening domains of music and imagery prospered, while those individuals who used language as if it mattered were censored and often imprisoned.

None of which is to suggest that the federal government has done a good job on the cultural front. And certainly the quality of its policies has steadily declined over the last decade. The symbolic sign of that decline came with the renaming of the department, from Culture and Communications to Heritage. What is this concept of heritage, if not of the past cut off from the present and the future? Thus their fear of culture as an alive and uncontrollable force has pushed the ideologues and technocrats to repackage reality as if it were dead and therefore under control.

Still, to the extent that the democratic systems have encouraged freedom of expression and creativity over much of this century, the drive has come from federal institutions and most of the resistance or indifference has come from the provinces. And the more a province has been driven by regional nationalism, the more it has tended to impose a narrow, goal-oriented cultural agenda rather than encouraging the uncontrolled and uncontrollable. As a result most of the successful battles for a strong francophone culture have been carried on through the mechanisms of federal cultural institutions (CBC/Radio-Canada, the National Film Board, the Canada Council), often in direct opposition to narrow nationalist provincial governments.

Above all, it is the multi-levelled complexity of the federal-provincial-municipal system which has given so much energy to our cultural activities. The slow edging towards single-source funding has little to do with efficiency or constitutions. It is the product of the desire among technocrats and negative nationalists to control ideas.

◄——————►

One of the positive curiosities of our role in the great language empires is that we have the use of two of the leading imperial languages, without the innate imperial attitudes. Those at the centre of these languages, whatever their point of view or politics, can't help but speak and write from within those attitudes. When people try to understand the international success of Canadian literature over the last two decades, I can't help but think that our detached position is one of the key factors. Oakland Ross's *Guerilla Beach* is a classic example of this unusual approach. It brings a vision of the violence and disorder in Central America without the assumptions of any of the imperial players.

What's more, we use these languages with the curious combination of a culture both developed and developing. You could even say that we use them in a schizophrenic manner because of the aboriginal role in our mythology and—increasingly once more—in our reality. There is also the bizarre effect of western self-confidence mixed with a severe victimization complex. Robert Lepage's plays are good examples of these contradictions, as are the novels of most of our leading anglophone writers.

In fact, I'm not certain that writing in two of the great imperial languages is even a fundamental characteristic of our culture. For example, while I can think of no American or French or English book which has the tone you find in *Guerilla Beach*, I immediately think of the Swede, Sven Lindqvist, and his *Exterminate All the Brutes*.

If we were to consider these languages as our fundamental homes, then we would be agreeing in the long run that our tone and style and even our agendas should be more or less set by what dominates in that linguistic family. In both of them we are minority players and so would be accepting a self-imposed position of victimization. That is the full meaning of François Ricard's question— "What are we defending apart from language?"[16]

While making full use of the international advantages which these two languages give us, we must consciously and constantly move away from the styles, concerns and references which dominate within them. Our natural home is not in our specific language. That is an historic accident, not a cultural quality. Our natural or real home is our experience and the social, physical, political reality in which we live.

I look through the poetry of A.M. Klein and find his wonderful verse on the conscription crisis, his dramatization of Camillien Houde, his poetic condemnations of Duplessis, his ironic war poetry:

This is the man who sold the soldiers shoes—
... Now is he rated pillar of the town ...
Puffs at his pipe, is sad about the war,
And plans great honour for the boots that walk no more....[17]

In other words, some of the finest poetry which led to the Quiet Revolution was written in English in Canada. None of it was written in France. And much of the finest poetry about place, as anglophones imagine it, was written in French in Quebec. None of it was written in England.

Again, this is not to minimize the importance of the specific language. "When a language dies," Kjell Espmark wrote, "the dead die a second time."[18] Every possible effort has to be made to strengthen (not defend) French and its role in our society.

But the key to strengthening a language lies in constantly seeking to understand the experience of those who use it—that is, their culture. That—not linguistics—is the meaning of communications. The talent for that communication lies first with those who write. And so it is an obligation for as many writers as possible to master the linguistics of those their own culture is most involved with in order to be able to get at the culture.

I am particularly struck at a time when most leading Canadian politicians, civil servants, lobbyists, military officers and national journalists are bilingual; when more and more of the smart senior businessmen are also; to say nothing of people who serve in restaurants, airports, on telephone lines; that only a tiny portion of the anglophone writers have managed to grasp a second language.

These are supposed to be our intellectual class. What's their problem? Too locked up in the imperial language? It simply isn't possible for a writer of good poetry or fiction to say they don't have a talent for languages. In any case, there are obligations which come with the social status of an intellectual. The role of the intellectual has always been to increase communication. And that means a great deal more than writing in one language for one community. That may be the practical reality of most writing. And the destructive, levelling force of international commercial communications has driven many of us to concentrate on our particular communities, which is a good thing. But that is quite apart from the more basic obligation which writers have to accept—that they themselves and their words are the fundamental route of communication between communities. I'm not talking about politics or do-gooding. I am referring to the relationship between experiences and ideas and how they fit together. Stephen Leacock's simple stories were the product of a man who in public rolled around from English to French to

German as the subject required. That's what an intellectual is supposed to do. Or rather, that is one of the basic assumptions tied to the concept of the intellectual.

And although more francophones have made the necessary linguistic effort, the writers have also become increasingly dependent on ideas and styles coming from France. These shouldn't, indeed can't, be ignored.

But language in France is itself mired in a deep crisis. It suffers from a great division between the written and the oral; a sign of scholasticism's growing power on organized communications. The result is a depressingly static view of language and of society. The secondary result is a growing flight into abstraction, which is simply prolonging their crisis.

The road out of this marginalization of their own language will most likely come through their own real community—Europe— that is, through ever-increasing involvement with neighbouring cultures using other languages. For francophones in Canada, to be dependent on that process means an increasing isolation from the realities of the place in which we live.

←----------→

If the natural references for our culture do not lie in England, France and the United States, where are they to be found? We have to look at our reality to understand that.

For a start we have an obsession with communication tied to the existence of a small population in a large, difficult area. The result has been that new ideas about communication in the twentieth century have more often come from Canada than from anywhere else. We have access to the dominant imperial culture of our day and yet we live on its margins—this is what Robertson Davies once described to me as the enormous advantage of coming from the provinces, because it allowed you to write about the whole world without the curiously provincial limitations of believing you are at the centre of it. There is the astonishing strength of poetry and of new voices in poetry. There is the very unusual ability to absorb into our culture, without demanding assimilation, a whole range of immigrant voices, from Dany Laferrière and Joseph Skvorecky to Dionne Brand and Alberto Manguel. There is the constant rebalancing between regional and wider visions, between two languages, between victimization and self-confidence. There is an almost Third World aggressivity which is rarely found in the literatures of Europe and the United States.

But above all there is the sense of an uncontrollable nature running through everything from Frederick Philip Grove and Octave Crémazie to Ann-Marie MacDonald and Christian Mistral. The conclusion which I draw from all of this is that we waste a great deal of time comparing our literature with its linear neighbours in English and French.

If our fiction resembles any another, it is Russian and the other northern literatures. If our contrasting sophistication and insecurity resembles anyone's, it is that of Central Europe and Latin America. We really have very little in common with two European ex-empires and the United States, all three beneficiaries of temperate, manageable lands, dense populations and centralized mythologies.

On the other hand, if you look at Russian literature you find a certain melancholy, a celebration of the provincial—think of all those country estates on which people dream of Moscow through the pens of Turgenev or Chekhov. There is a great sense of the contrasts and differences within society, of the difficulty of change, of nature out of control. There is that curious mixture caused by living on the uncontrolled margins in a sophisticated social system.

Alice Munro, for example, in *The Progress of Love* or Monique Proulx in *Les Aurores montréales* or David Adams Richards or Mavis Gallant—in spite of their different generations and tempos—come at the world in the same cool, hard-edged way, so that what is human seems all the more real and unbearable. It is an approach you will find in Turgenev or in Gogol's *Dead Souls*. Even the dispassionate, casual descriptions of people's clothing is similar. Munro uses the

phrase "both perma press" the way Gogol uses "with some pretensions to fashion," as a summarizing conclusion after a devastating
description.[19]

As for melancholy, it runs through everything written in the
north. Robertson Davies gives it a specific edge of mythological
regret—"Like so much in Canada, its spirit was Chekhovian clothing in a present dubiously accepted, a regret for a past which had
never been."[20] Antoine Gérin-Lajoie's classic, "Un Canadien errant,"
expresses more than typical nineteenth-century romanticism.

Non, mais en expirant,
Ô mon cher Canada,
Mon regard languissant
Vers toi se portera.

You find the same melancholy tone in Gilles Vigneault or Stan
Rogers. Or, for that matter, in Wilfred Campbell or Gordon Lightfoot
or Octave Crémazie:

The fields were dead, the wind had lost its will
I'll get along, you know, I'll take tomorrow with a grin.
Sad, crying shadows,
Which in the sombre forests
In those grey, withered days.[21]

Melancholy is married to solitude in this same context. You find
it in Lermontov the way you do in Pierre Morency or in Anne
Hébert's *Les Fous de Bassan* or in George Bowering's *Kerrisdale
Elegies*—

Most of all I loved my solitude,
                              hoping another
somewhere did the same.

or the Estonian poet Jaan Kaplinski—

> I need solitude.
> The forest. For solitude is like the forest
>   or the sea. Solitude is
> space, open space.

Or Madelaine Gagnon—

> Here the
> women cry in their houses, with the men most
> often, the quays are there only for celebration...

There are strange urban solitudes in novels such as Russell Smith's *How Insensitive*, or Daniel Poliquin's *L'Écureuil noir*. There is the almost inexplicable deliberate solitude in Pasternak's *Doctor Zhivago*, with men meeting in the middle of nowhere after walking for days in opposite directions on a railway track, as if they had been following animistic song-lines. In John Steffler's *The Afterlife of George Cartwright* the hero arrives in Newfoundland and thinks—"It seemed free and aloof, preserving a secret few would be strong enough to learn."

What secret? The secret of Gilles Vigneault's "grand pays solitaire."

These ideas of melancholy and solitude are tied to that of a place which has no rational shape, nor can it be given one. It is not available for human domination. Solitude in less marginal places is often tied to escapism. In places like Canada and Russia it is part of reality. In that sense northerners seem to revel in melancholy, solitude and the uncontrollable character of the place; the marriage of "roughness and beauty," in John Steffler's words.[22] Lermontov clearly did. They accept somehow that nature will play an important role in forming the community. "White winter had set in with the cruel stillness of cloudless forests..." and so Turgenev's characters adjust themselves to a completely different life.

It is a sort of life which is marked, as it so often is in this northern fiction, by a refusal of the idea that being heroic is enough to create a hero. I talked in earlier chapters about this anti-heroic phenomenon in Canada. But that is also the message of Lermontov's *A Hero of Our Time* and of Gogol's *Dead Souls*. You find it in Dostoevsky, even in Tolstoy. "The wildly and chaotically unpredictable which formed the basis of new creation in nature must also exist in the world. In civilization," is how the Swedish novelist Kerstin Ekman puts it.[23]

Instead there is a proliferation of remarkable heroines who come as close as a developed society can to the idea of mother earth— again, a non-rational, non-European concept. Tolstoy's Natasha is perhaps the model. Blanche in Philippe Aubert de Gaspé's *Les Anciens Canadiens* has an almost identical psychological approach and plays the same role as Natasha with the men in the book, as does Hagar in Margaret Laurence's *The Stone Angel*, as does Mary Dempster in Robertson Davies's *Fifth Business*. No matter what happened she "felt no humiliation."[24] She assumed the humiliation of others and herself. In many ways these heroines are the natural product of a society which, apart from being anti-heroic, still has strong animist roots.

All of what I am describing is tied to the dominance of place; the inability to imagine place reduced to structure; to a form which humans control. In this context, I think often of something the composer Harry Freedman said to broadcaster Adrienne Clarkson— "Sibelius is a Canadian composer. Without him I could never have written music."

What makes Canadian creativity more complex than the purely Russian is the doubly marginal factor of being placed beside a great power as well as being in the north. The experiences of the Poles and Czechs with their dominant neighbour may have been far more violent than ours, but these are nevertheless the close relationships of small sophisticated societies with an unavoidable great empire. In that sense, their experience is like ours. That's why the literatures of central Europe also tell us a lot about ourselves; a great deal more than the literature of a people questioning their destiny in London, Paris and Los Angeles. George Elliott Clarke writes eloquently about the intellectual consciousness which living on the edge can produce. Talking of the revival in Toronto in the 1990s of an old American musical which dealt with black–white relations, he says that "an acceptable commodity for African-American audiences . . . was, for many African-Canadians, grimly insulting *kitsch*."[25] There is also the curious and very real mixture of western and non-western— European and Aboriginal—which links us to Latin America and to Australia. The result, again, is a literary and cultural tradition which has little to do with that suggested by simple linguistics and the false relationships produced by empires.

All of this reinforces my sense that the quality of our culture is the product of its complexity. It is the drama of that complexity which pushes us on. It was those tensions that made Montreal the centre of the first explosion of creativity in both languages. A racial and cultural mix without the depressing drive towards sameness is a great creative strength. And it is that same tension that has brought Toronto alive over the last three decades.

Complexity is not an abstract idea. Or, as George Bowering put it in two lines about winter in rural Saskatchewan,

> a farm woman clencht her buttocks,
> afraid to go out to the privy.

He then goes a bit further in his *Short Sad Book*:

> The snow covers me and I lie covered
> with snow. Is it the grasp of winter. Is
> winter my country.
> My country is not a country it is winter. . . . [26]

To remember and assemble events is the meat and potatoes of a conscious civilization. That is the most basic sort of memory; more necrophilia than history. All too often these identified remains or 'incidents' become a denial of complexity; the flagpoles of jingoism or victimization. This is particularly the case when language is treated as linguistics. Then language simply reinforces the view of history as celebratory flagpoles or cairns of humiliation.

But when language escapes from linguistics and rhetoric and propaganda, it can become the means of communicating culture and thus the means by which society expresses its reality. That reality embraces differences, but leaves behind the worship of divisions. And it reveals the interesting patterns of shared attitudes and interwoven experiences.

Robin Blaser said the poet precedes, which means that culture precedes. In this atmosphere of shared attitudes and interwoven experiences it can even precede as an expression of reality. Culture seen in this way is an expression of memory in all its complexity.

PART V

THE FRAGILE
TRIANGLE

—again time said,
"This is my birth—my deeds and handiwork
Shall be immortal." Thus and so dream on
Fool'd nations, and thus dreams their dullard sons.
Isabella Valancy Crawford, *Malcolm's Katie*

Quelques tragédies patiemment travaillées,
Sur la poitrine des rois, couchées,
En guise de bijoux
Me sont offertes
Sans larmes ni regrets.
Anne Hébert, *Le Tombeau des rois*

Nationalism

IF OUR ÉLITES TELL US THAT THE principal forces moving throughout the west are such things as global trade, the money-markets and competition, and that these are beyond anyone's control, well then, the citizen is left in an awkward position. With the ideological stroke of inevitability, we are deprived of the community powers which, particularly over the last two centuries, have permitted us to put an increasingly decent social structure in place. What does this do to the citizens' self-esteem, this return to a single absolute religion in which the forces which determine our future are as out of reach as those of an all-knowing deity? What powers does it leave us, except those old mediaeval crutches—emotion and superstition? Thanks to them, in lieu of real power, we are left free to turn in upon ourselves.

Not that nationalism in all its different manifestations has ever completely disappeared. Nor should it. Nor will it ever.

But the aggressive return of nationalism as a negative force is largely the responsibility of those élites who have embraced a higher, greater utilitarian superstition. This introverted nationalism of particular characteristics is the consolation prize offered to the losers—the citizens—when their real powers are given away.

It isn't surprising, therefore, that negative or exclusionary nationalism continues to grow. Whether in Italy, France, Austria, Germany or elsewhere, a language which marries particularity with fear is rewarded at the ballot box. In hard numbers it now hovers between a fifth and a quarter of the voters. But other, more mainstream politicians have amended their own vocabulary to fit in with this atmosphere. In Canada, Preston Manning and the premiers of

British Columbia, Alberta, Ontario and Quebec reach easily into the language of negative nationalism in order to advance their political positions.

Still, nationalism as a positive creative force continues to exist. Nationalism need not be about fear or anger. And tempting though the option is, we need not try to tie nationalism to joy. The joy of being the best. The joy of winning. Even the joy of being special.

After all, the history of nationalism tells us that joy has always been closely linked to fear and anger. Hitler, to take the most outrageous example, used fear, anger and joy as a revolving holy trinity which rolled the citizenry repeatedly and at great speed from one to the other to the other until they lost all sense of reality.

That this was negative and dangerous is now clear. And yet these are the elements and the methods used and rewarded in modern public relations, to say nothing of the business of sports and of political campaigns. And they remain at the core of negative nationalism.

But what is the positive variety made up of? What does it mean to say, for example: positive nationalism responds to the question of how humans can live together? Am I talking about a sense of community? Perhaps, yet the concept of community has also brought us great problems in the past. Look, for example, at the era of renaissance city-states. They functioned on a strong sense of civic belonging. But their devotion to their community caused them to slip into rivalries, jealousies and hatred, one for the other. If their era came to an end, creative and positive though much of it was, the reason was their inability to stop fighting each other.

A sense of place, of belonging, is central to creative nationalism, but what makes it positive is a strong sense of how society works and should work. Belonging to a community means something positive only in so far as it is attached to an idea of the public good, which is by its very nature inclusive.

Not that pride and rivalry, jealousy and competition don't have their roles in the real world. Society isn't a Sunday school and we do

have a right to reassure and distract and amuse ourselves with assertions of our qualities, just as lovers do. But this isn't nationalism; or
rather, if it is elevated to that level it quickly becomes racism or
some other dangerous characteristic.

Jean-Pierre Derriennic talks about "*civic* nationalism," which
includes all citizens, and "ethnic or *identity* nationalism," which, by
virtue of its definition of identity—language, religion or any other
criteria—"separates nationality from citizenship."[1] In other words, it
excludes people.

That is an honest and severe definition. The real situation is both
more complex and more interesting. What we have always experienced in Canada is an agreeable though challenging mess of civic
nationalism, regional nationalism and identity nationalism. And all
of this has been bound up in—or rather confused with—competing
demands for specific political powers by the federal or the provincial levels of government. There has always been a competition for
concrete responsibilities between the provinces and Ottawa. That is
a condition of federalism. Sometimes it has to do with respecting the
constitution; sometimes with an honest belief that the public good
can best be served at one level rather than the other. But most of the
time we are just witnessing banal competitions for power—politics
at its most predictable and self-interested. And as the technocracies
have grown at both federal and provincial levels, so the demands for
more powers at both levels have become automatic and alarmingly
insistent. Here we can justifiably talk about the nationalism of characteristics, even if the characteristics in question are those of a polit-
ical-administrative class rather than a mythological tribe. After all,
the innate drive of any technocracy is to increase its power. The role
left for the politicians is often little more than to provide exciting
rhetoric for a not very exciting struggle; the public entertainment
which dresses up the serious business being done in private.

If much of the ongoing federal-provincial drama is banal administrative rivalry, the way to make it exciting is to provoke the emotions of negative nationalism. Suddenly the administration of a

relatively ordinary service is transformed into an element of life or death for the national character of a province or a region or, alternately, for the nation as a whole.

◄——————►

This is further confused in a federation by the various ideas of community. After all, if there is a characteristic proper to Canada, it is that we have not rigorously set out to eliminate differences. In our more intelligent moments we have encouraged them. So our nationalism exists on a spectrum, from the impossibly generous idea that all people belong to all communities across to the exclusive and negative opposite in which each of us is limited to a single community. The latter is what Séguin approvingly called ". . . the principle of nationalities in all its rigour."[2] Now that is a phrase Colonel Sam Hughes—our disastrously Orange minister of defence during the First World War—would have liked.

This exclusive approach is our inheritance from the nineteenth-century European nation-state. European nationalism became the enclosing wall by which one type or concept of community shut its inhabitants in and all others out. That, they said, was necessary and normal, even inevitable, in a "real" nation.

What then about the impossible idea that all people belong to all communities? It could be said that this mythology is Canada's contribution to the ongoing western debate over the nature of nationalism. I am not suggesting that we have ever seriously believed in such a possibility or even acted as if we did. But for many Canadians it has been a fantasy at one end of the spectrum; a fantasy much exploited by political figures.

Our more realistic and indeed real attitude is that we all belong to several communities and do so at several levels. And we tend to see our situation as a condition which must be turned into something positive, rather than mistaking our condition for a problem which needs to be solved by eliminating differences.

The idea of belonging to multiple communities makes practical sense in a decentralized federation built upon three cultural foundations. But it has also distressed some people. For a start this is not the classic western understanding of the monolithic nation-state. And the formalization of this idea of diversity into something called multiculturalism has exacerbated the discomfort many felt.

But the social reality of our diversity—the reality we all live— has never had much to do with the formal politics of multiculturalism. I would say that both the Utopia and the bogeyman of multiculturalism are false. And the pattern of the last hundred and fifty years is relatively clear: the immigrants who come here and stay do so because in the long run they want to become something called Canadian. If you look back over that long experience, you find it has normally taken about two and a half generations for families to find their place in the larger community. If you consider the destabilizing drama of emigration and immigration, this is quite fast. If anything, it has been slowed not by the immigrants but by the exclusive attitudes of those already here.

The smoothness with which people adapt is first and foremost dependent on the quality of the public education system. This is as true for francophones as for anglophones. If you put aside some of the marginal details of Quebec's language laws, you come to the core, which relates to public education. Having got that more or less right, the provincial government found that the immigrant communities increasingly began to adjust in a way which didn't threaten francophone society.

It is interesting that the provincial governments most eager to use the monolithic European nationalist models are the same governments which have most severely cut back on public education over the last few years. Even in a rich province like British Columbia, with heavy per-capita immigration rates, the government continues to reduce per-student spending on education, as do Alberta, Ontario and Quebec. In doing this they are failing to assume their most important obligation. Instead they distract us from this central point by continually moaning about Ottawa's interference on the margins of education or in other areas and about the immigrants' supposed reluctance to fit in.

Let me restate this in a more aggressive way. The decision to admit immigrants is one made by Canadians. We have a very unusual, steady and high level of immigration. This has been, for a century and a half, a conscious policy. No matter how desperate the lives of immigrants before they come, no matter how much they may want to come here, they come because we have chosen to invite them in. If it is our decision, then we must be prepared to assume the related obligations. We cannot invite people in—particularly poor people—and then moan about their effect on our society. If their role is in some way troubling, then it is entirely our fault for not assuming our full responsibilities to smooth the difficult path of immigration. And the primary institutional responsibility is public education. You cannot have high levels of immigrants and expect them to find their way if you are not willing to spend well above the per-capita norm of western countries on education.

This is the most important provincial responsibility. These governments have the full obligation to prepare citizens for their adult lives, whether they are native-born or immigrant. By cutting back rather than increasing their education budgets at a time of high immigration, they are not, as they claim, stabilizing their economies. They are destabilizing our society. On a short-list of government failures in Canada, this stands at the top, well above the various stupidities of the federal government.

That we have seen a revival of regional nationalisms over the last quarter-century in many of the twenty-odd western countries both surprises and disturbs our élites. What's more, given the inability of these élites to accept the root causes of this phenomenon, there is every reason for nationalism to continue to grow and to do so in all its forms, from the positive through to the negative. In fact, the disconnection of the élites suggests that it is the negative variety which will dominate.

There are at least six reasons for this revival: an understandable reaction to half a century of centralization at all levels of authority, or what we might call 'normalization' to central standards; a related reaction to the growth in technocratic power and the weakening of real democratic power; a frustrated reaction to the difficulty of sustaining public debate when the élites have embraced the inevitabilities of expert answers; a reaction to globalization and the related sense of powerlessness; a delayed but hardly surprising reaction to the failure of the élites to deal with the real problems created by the factors I've just mentioned; and another related reaction to the attempts, particularly over the last century, to eliminate local differences.

If you look at Canada in the context of these six explanations, you find that, on the first point, there is a regional reaction to centralization, even if in comparison with other countries there has been very little real centralization.

There is a deep frustration with the weakening of democratic power versus that of the technocracy. This is complicated by the fact that the problem is the same at the provincial level. It is further confused by constant campaigns organized by the private-sector technocracy to attack the idea of the public good by attacking those employed to deliver it—the public technocracy.

There is a particularly exacerbated frustration with the unsustainable nature of public debate. This has always been of particular importance in Canada, given the distances, the regional differences, the linguistic complications. I argued earlier in this book that ours is an oral society. A weakening of public debate strikes at that need.

The sense of powerlessness before globalization seems to be particularly developed among anglophones, perhaps because they have been used to making the effort required every day to go on existing when there is a great empire next door using the same language. Among francophones this frustration is present, but confused by

442   the eagerness with which their élites have unanimously encouraged globalization. They have argued that language is a protection, when the opposite is more likely.

The most narrowly nationalist have argued that globalization frees Quebec from the rest of Canada. What they haven't pointed out is that most of the powers needed to create and maintain a public-private society of the sort developed across Canada, including Quebec, are gradually being abandoned in order to conform with the global model. So a sovereign or separate Quebec would have few levers left to protect or develop its social and cultural structures. What's more, those same leaders have encouraged the delusion that the United States would welcome a partnership with a more or less social-democratic French-speaking partner. This suggests that no one in Quebec knows their history. Which isn't the case. And so, sublimated though it must be, there is frustration just under the surface among francophones, just as there is among anglophones.

The sense that the élites are unable to deal with the problems at hand—high unemployment and underemployment, dropping real standards of living—is shared everywhere. The citizenry are constantly looking for ways to punish or wake up those to whom they give authority to deal with these issues.

On the final point, that of attacking local differences, Canada has taken a very different track from the other countries. When you look at how healthy the differences are here, you can't really attribute their state to the rise of regional nationalisms. If anything, the strength of French and of regional ways of life would suggest that the system works. But in the context of globalization, such simple logic makes no sense. Any sign of differences is misinterpreted as a sign that the system doesn't work. It is as if a 'real' nation is one which conforms to low-level principles of market-place theory: either harmonize or spin off the company's constituent parts.

What I draw from these six reasons for citizen discontent is that for the first time in 150 years the real power of the individual as a citizen is in decline. The mechanisms of self-interest, of interests and of technicians dominate. These are all good reasons for a revival of nationalism. The question is, will it be negative nationalism, filled with the illusive protections of self-definitions? Or will it be positive nationalism aimed at re-establishing the role of the citizen and of the public good?

The form which the gradual return of nationalism takes will depend on our ability consciously to avoid the emotions of the extremes. And because language can't help but be central to any debate over the shape of a society, a great deal will turn on our ability to identify the real meaning of words. By language, I mean here not one language or another, but our means of communication.

For example, in the language of Preston Manning you can hear the phraseology of Sir Allan MacNab, whose attempts to please the remains of the Family Compact and the Château Clique finally unleashed the riots in Montreal which ended with the burning of the Parliament Buildings and the Annexation Manifesto. I hear the same superficial respectability filled with a coded language of unacceptable behaviour. And his talent for placing the most divisive of phrases at moments guaranteed to increase division in the population is not unusual. But we have not seen someone wield such a talent at that level of influence since D'Alton McCarthy.

Mr. Manning claims to be the descendant of the early prairie reform movements. I take him at his word and read the manifestos of those movements—for example, one of the earliest, the Farmers' Manifesto. There, as elsewhere in prairie populism, you find that their concept of reform was one of justice and equality. It had nothing to do with the unleashing of personal power outside of, indeed against, a concept of the public good.

The same sort of unbalanced remarks—either unconsidered or intended to unleash uncontrolled anger—slip effortlessly from the mouths of men like Brian Tobin, Glen Clark, Jacques Ménard and Bernard Landry. You could call this cheap or lazy politics. But if you draw back, what you can hear is a growing pattern: a spreading desire to express a sense of powerlessness by taking the easy road— that of injuring people rather than dealing with reality.

In such a context negative nationalism can be seen as an almost medical condition. It resembles a violent outbreak on the human body. Societies like humans move along in as balanced a manner as possible. When something is wrong it will often build up within them like an infection, then suddenly explode in unexpected and inexplicable ways, like a fever or a boil. The unilingual movement in northern Ontario, the fighter-plane contract in Winnipeg, the sign legislation in Montreal, the air-controllers' crisis—they explode as if from nowhere. To call them crimes of passion would confer undue dignity. They are infections, which indicate deeper frustrations, and which are often related to something quite different. Each outbreak heals slowly and leaves scars.

The job of good leadership is to lance the boil before it rises. As Laurier put it in Trois-Rivières, in one of his last speeches, Borden's attitude towards conscription "was simply stupid."[3] Why? Because it didn't take into account the reality of the society. He therefore had turned his back on the public good.

Georges-Émile Lapalme quoted Eric Kierans being sensible in 1966 on the same subject—the reality of our society. "A desire for indépéndance exists in the heart of all French Canadians to a greater or lesser degree and this desire can be exacerbated as quickly by indifference as by hostility."[4] All Laurier, Lapalme and Kierans were talking about was the balance and restraint necessary in a complex society.

They were not talking of a particularity of French-Canadian society. Rather they are referring to the basic truths of such situations. Lapalme put it succinctly—"Any minority is basically nationalist."[5] The complicating factor in Canada is that everyone sees themselves as belonging to a minority. Even the Orange Order justified their position on that basis. Everyone is quick to appropriate the position of the aggrieved party or, as Margaret Atwood recently put it, "Victimization is the coveted position."[6]

This also encourages groups to seek strength through solidarity. Minorities are always told by their leaders that only by sticking together can they survive or do well. "What is nationalism?" Michel Brunet asked. "It is *simply* the manifestation of the *natural* and *spontaneous solidarity* that exists among members of a human group *sharing* a historical and cultural tradition from which the group derives its distinctive identity."[7]

This is a perfect summary of negative nationalism. At first glance his formula is heart-warming and seductive. On second glance you begin noticing and analysing those disarming terms—"simply" and "sharing." How curious to use the word sharing to mean sharing with no one else. "Natural and spontaneous"? I know of nothing in the history of nation-states, peoples, tribes, communities, families and above all democracies which is natural and spontaneous. Only ideologues claim that events or situations are natural and spontaneous. But these two words are only modifiers. The phrase is "natural and spontaneous solidarity." What happens to those who do not join in the solidarity? Do they, like Marcel Trudel and Fernand Ouellet—the historians who disagreed with the Montreal School— eventually feel that the only way to continue a reasonable career is to leave the province? Put aside whether you agree or disagree with the import of their work. What did they do which made their lives so difficult? Well, Trudel believed he was devoting his work to the principle that "history must serve no cause."[8]

Their fate is in no way a comment on francophone society. But it is a comment on those within the élites who believe they are the leaders of a natural and spontaneous solidarity, whether it be in Quebec or Alberta.

Vaclav Havel said that insiders always characterize "every attempt at open criticism as naked terrorism."[9] If you live in a minority, you can add that open criticism from the inside represents the naked terrorism of a traitor.

This explains why groups which adopt the methods of negative nationalism so often name themselves after the group in question or appropriate a term central to life in that group. This is what I described in *Voltaire's Bastards* as the dictatorship of vocabulary. It was common in the 1960s for the president of single-party nation-states to use words like freedom and democratic to name their party and/or their state. D'Alton McCarthy's movement was called the Equal Rights Association. Preston Manning's party is centred on the same two words—equality and rights. In both cases the intent was and is inequality. Mr. Manning uses the word reform to capture a central myth of Western populism, while his actual policies run counter to that whole tradition. The Parti Québécois's name is an attempt to co-opt the legitimacy of the community as a whole. Other parties may name themselves for a theory or an approach, but the PQ wraps itself in the idea of a natural solidarity. In effect, they adopted the exact arguments developed by Maurice Duplessis around the idea of a 'national union' and took them one step further. 'Which national union?' 'That of the Québécois.'

Curiously enough, minorities rarely do well through solidarity. Even to function with the strong sense that solidarity would be an advantage is damaging. Both the thing itself and the expectation of it removes the group's ability to make full and positive use of the strength of democracy; that is, of its own shared intelligence— which only dissension (les chicanes) can unlock. Solidarity encourages passivity. It is the ultimate corporatist solution.

Of course there are moments of great crisis—wars, natural disasters, extreme economic collapse, just to take a few examples —when a temporary and narrowly focused solidarity is necessary over a limited period of time. Constitutional differences and the other elements of the Canadian condition do not fall into this category of a crisis.

Society's greatest need is not for agreement but for responsibility. And in a democracy, responsibility is based on the inevitability of disagreement. Responsibility-disagreement has to do with an understanding of our obligation to society. Solidarity has to do with the artificial removal of difference. In the name of what? If you feel obligation, you cannot remove difference.

Getting power, even getting their own way, doesn't seem to remove this need felt by negative nationalists that everyone must act as one. The more nationalist movements built on the need for solidarity succeed, the more they seem to rely on calls for solidarity. The better placed they are to deliver the promised Utopia, the more that Utopia recedes and so the more the movement must make appeals to the powers of mythology deformed into mystification.

The reality of our history is that francophones have done best at both the federal and the provincial levels by avoiding the issue of loyalty to group and instead supporting coalitions built on ideas. This began with the LaFontaine–Baldwin coalition. The most creative and reforming of Quebec provincial governments have come to power and governed on the basis of ideas. The most damaging and the most mediocre Quebec governments have been attached to the idea of solidarity.

One of the outcroppings of solidarity is an inability to see the *other* as another human. This is the core of negative nationalism. The Reform party's 1997 campaign ads—"The voice for all Canadians, not just Quebec politicians"—had all the markings of this incapacity to see the *other*. As with the use of equivalent statements by the European false-populist movements of the 1920s and 1930s, Reform claimed simply to be stating facts. Dispassionate facts. Yet for the following week the Reform party had already scheduled patriotic ads with Mr. Manning talking about his love of country, while placed in front of a big flag. The two ads taken together as part of a strategy were perfect examples of the negative-nationalist trilogy: fear and anger followed by joy.

Yves Michaud, PQ stalwart and Quebec agent-general in Paris

during the 1980s, would probably also invoke the defence of dispassionate facts, if reminded of his 1964 statement on a proposed gathering of citizens—an Estates-General, which was to include only francophones—"The English, the Jews, the Americans and all the others will have no business in the Estates-General. This is an initiative that we alone can bring to good conclusion...."[10] He might add that to use such a quote against him was to insinuate something about francophones in general. Not at all. My own experience is that Quebec society in general is extremely open and relaxed about race and therefore about minorities. As in the rest of Canada there are specific groups—quite small—which burn with the anger that makes it impossible for that small group to recognize the *other* as normal. But, as elsewhere, they are indeed small groups. I sense the same fear and anger in Mr. Harris's government, which bears no relationship to the Progressive Conservatives of Bill Davis. Mr. Harris seems to have inherited part of the baggage of the old Orange Order.

The differentiations that I'm making between positive and negative nationalism all turn on the question of context. The positive nationalist is moderated by a conscious awareness of the larger real context. The negative nationalist expressly denies it. Or at least denies its relevance. The problems of the community the negative nationalist claims to represent are presented as their problems alone. Injury inevitably comes from elsewhere or from traitors within. The *other* does not exist as a human, let alone as a relevant human. Decisions are always to be made within and to be made without reference to what lies outside.

In a curious little incident after the 1995 referendum an American journalist went to Lac Saint-Jean and interviewed Lucien Bouchard's mother. She said, "I've never met an English-speaking Canadian. But I'm sure they are as nice as any other foreigners." Apparently she had been to Europe and Miami, but to no other province. I have no desire to comment on Mr. Bouchard's mother. I'm sure she is a worthy fellow-citizen of mine and of yours. On the other hand, she did comment on me as a category.

Hers was an odd statement for someone whose son says in his memoirs that many of his friends at university were members of the old and new anglophone élite: Michael Meighen and Brian Mulroney, to name just two.[11] And speaking for myself, I have often been to Lac Saint-Jean, an area I love and in which I have a number of friends (francophone). But the real point I can't help making is the oddness of her attitude. Someone might have reminded her, for example, that Quebec women had had the vote since she was five, the federal vote, and that was because of a movement begun and led by fellow-citizens of hers on the prairies. In other words, not only were they not foreigners, they had had a concrete and, in that case, positive effect on the life of Mr. Bouchard's mother. And if she has had the provincial vote in Quebec since her thirty-fifth birthday, it was the result of a victory won by a coalition of federalist francophone and anglophone women's groups. The victory had been won over the negative nationalists, who opposed women getting the vote. And if there are more than three hundred thousand young anglophones, or English-speaking Canadians, to use her phrase, in French-language schools in the rest of Canada, it isn't because they are nice foreigners. Whether she approves, disapproves, cares or doesn't, it's because they also are fellow-citizens.

None of that is to suggest that Mr. Bouchard's mother doesn't have the right to whatever her politics might be. Rather, it is to point out how a certain atmosphere erases the reality of the perfectly obvious *other*.

After all, education is not a romantic indulgence. It is the most important decision parents can make for their children. In the first years it is the parents who mark the child's life forever with their choices. Then gradually, over the years, the child assumes or alters the direction set. Again, young persons are making key choices which will set the pattern of their lives. So if hundreds of thousands of anglophone adults choose to send their children to French-language schools every year and those children choose to accept this direction in their lives, they believe they are doing something important.

450   However, negative nationalism, since it has difficulty recognizing the reality of the *other*, simply goes on insisting that all is division and that all efforts by *others* are meaningless. In the end this has an effect on many anglophones. They feel demeaned, just as many francophones have felt demeaned at various times when their reality is ignored. The important thing in any democratic situation is to be careful not to demean the other. Otherwise bp Nichol's poem takes on meaning for both sides.

> & when you have such nothing
> you love only yourself
> you fill your poems with self-love & loathing
> & it is not poetry
>   it is dead[12]

The reader can see that I am skating in these pages along the edges of the links between negative nationalism and racism. Frankly, I don't find the question of whether McCarthy or Groulx or others in British Columbia or Ontario or Nova Scotia or Quebec were or are racists is terribly useful. Nor is a checklist of who was and who wasn't. Racism was widespread, almost endemic in one form or another, from the second half of the nineteenth century to the end of the Second World War. Very few communities have reason to be proud of their attitudes, in particular during the 1930s. On the other hand, our understanding of the often tempting soft edge of racism became much clearer after 1945. Suddenly, throughout the west, most citizens and in particular most intellectuals and public personalities understood that the slightest ambiguity on the question of race could begin you on your way down a road towards disastrous actions. A new severe and unforgiving attitude thus became normal. None of which means racism went away. But it no longer had the advantage of even marginal respectability.

The real question since 1945 has been whether negative forms of nationalism cannot help but carry racism within them in the manner of a Trojan horse. There was prolonged debate, for example, over the Jean-Louis Roux affair. The well-known actor and aggressive federalist had been named lieutenant-governor of Quebec. During an interview in 1997, he used as an example of unacceptable nationalism his own participation as a student in anti-Semitic activities in the Second World War. The result of this interview was a scandal during which he resigned his office. Much of the controversy was politically driven, on both sides. In the end, Irving Abella, who wrote the definitive book on Canadian anti-Semitism (*None Is Too Many*), rightly intervened to remind everyone that this had been a Canada-wide problem, not something limited to francophones, and that it was most serious in the élites.[13]

The origin of this sickness was not simply European-inspired anti-Semitism. In Canada, it rose in part out of the nineteenth-century Protestant nationalist movements. They were vulgar, triumphalist, indifferent to the law, vigilante minded, and saw Catholicism as an evil. They sounded a bit the way Ian Paisley sounds today. From their street-gang, jaw-busting tactics in the 1830s and 1840s on behalf of the Family Compact up to their attempts to capture John A. Macdonald's agenda, they set the nationalist tone against which everyone had to react.

D'Alton McCarthy was the civilized voice of this movement and he came to prominence at the height of the Orange Order's influence. Indirectly he gave them the kind of spiritual leadership which raised the debate above their normal bully-boy tactics. He preached cultural and linguistic uniformity as the only way to build a nation. He can claim, from his grave, much of the responsibility for two language crises in the West and the tensions surrounding critically exaggerated problems such as the Jesuits' estates question, which is rightly forgotten.

On the positive side, the population never gave his movement the practical, real approval it craved. He captured no government and very few seats. What he and his friends did do was bully or destabilize successive governments into making mistakes which we are still paying for. They also created a current of intolerance which would re-emerge in the twentieth century at various moments on various issues—particularly those of minority-language education—to bedevil the more sensible wishes of what had always been a reasonably moderate society. It was a movement which would tie provincial autonomy to ethnic politics. Since provinces were usually constructed of a solid ethnic majority, those who had racial beliefs found it easier to apply them at that level of government. In British Columbia the Chinese and Natives were disenfranchised in 1874; the Japanese in 1895; the East Indians in 1907; the Mennonites and Doukhobors in 1931.[14] There were elements of the same racial politics in Ernest Manning's eugenics program in Alberta. Purity of race was a theory tied to your origins, but also to physical soundness.

This is the context in which I listen to Preston Manning's portrait of provincial rights as a means of ensuring unity of language and culture on a regional basis. These are coded attacks on francophones. But what I hear are even more coded aggressive attacks on those who, for one reason or another, find themselves stuck on the margins of society. He claims, as I mentioned earlier, a parentage to prairie populism. But there is no relationship in his policies to those movements, from the Métis through the various farmers' associations and parties to the CCF. And his is certainly not the voice of Peter Lougheed. It's just pure nineteenth-century Ontario sectarianism. In fact, it's quite amusing that he should present himself as the defender of the Western cause when what he is selling is the worst of Ontario's nineteenth-century prejudices. Perhaps there is hope that irony is not dead.

As for the Ultramontane movement, it was every bit as unpleasant as the Orange Order. Catholicism at that stage had various forms of racism buried deep within it, particularly anti-Semitism. It was also profoundly reactionary and anti-democratic. The intentions of men like Bishop Lartigue and Bishop Bourget were depressingly clear. They and their supporters were unrelenting and unforgiving within the francophone Catholic community. At first they were not so aggressive towards those on the outside of their particular world. Bourget's view was defensive and therefore somewhat limited geographically. However, the aggressive, insulting triumphalism of the Orange Order and McCarthyism—delivered with that conviction of absolute moral authority which is a sure sign of cheap prejudice—drew the Ultramontane beyond their local struggle against the democratic and liberal reformers in Quebec. The religious purity sought in this retrograde revivalist movement soon spread out into broader questions of language and culture. The endemic racism was soon expressed in ways which mirrored that of the Protestant movements.

The effect of all of this was to encourage the pride which negative nationalists on all sides could take in their ignorance. A century later, leading intellectuals could still make arch nationalist assertions without any sense of how ridiculous they sounded. For example, Michel Brunet could reduce anglophones in one of his most famous books to "monarchists, British and Protestant."[15] All the creative initiatives of the preceding hundred years were simply brushed aside. He wrote this just a few months before the Suez Crisis when, under the guidance of Lester Pearson and a group of largely anglophone senior diplomats, Canada would act as the opponent of British foreign policy.

But negative nationalism is ideology and any reference to reality is no longer necessary. Abruptly it transports us into a Manichean world where everything is equally divided between good and evil. The concept of 'equality' comes with that of expelling the *other* into an unreal space where evil and niceness have no particular meaning, because, above all, they exist far away, on the other side.

If negative nationalism is built on these elements of solidarity, uniformity, the unreal *other* and the Manichean division of good and evil, then the crowning element is the leader. We have seen in this century how a certain school of nationalism seems to require an Heroic Leader, usually a false Hero. This trend has been developing throughout the west since Napoleon. But the particularities of the modern false Hero have evolved to the point of being clearly defined.

We talk of demagogues, but we would do better to talk of martyrs. There are elements of the father figure in these men, but more accurately they are like vestal virgins, devoting their lives to the nation. Theirs is the leadership of love, so that any suggestion of any other public emotion or love offered by a citizen in another direction is a personal betrayal. The modern false Hero is married to the nation and as such fulfils Euripides' warning—

> Power and eloquence in a headstrong man spell folly; such a man is a peril to the state.[16]

Federal politics don't lend themselves easily to this formula. The country is too complex. A formula which might create an Heroic relationship with one region will probably just annoy people in the others. Prime ministers have tried and failed. With the exception of Laurier, who counterbalanced his speaking skills with a desire for consensus and a careful line of ideas, the other successful leaders have been more intellectual on their feet than eloquent. They have been survivors rather than lovers; careful balancers of competing interests while struggling to keep an eye on the main line of the public interests. And they have tended towards careful language in order to avoid creating divisions. The mistakes they have made, from LaFontaine through to Trudeau, can be catalogued, but they have tended to be errors of judgement more than a long trail of damage left by a Hero out of control. The prime ministers who are considered failures are usually those who tried to drive the citizenry onward with unrestrained, unbalanced rhetoric. Or they are people who never managed to identify the level of public good which might enable people with differences to live together. Faced with the impossibility of governing by love, they ruled instead by dividing us.

The provincial level, on the other hand, is designed for false Heroes. The greater ethnic cohesion of the populations combines with the last essential element needed for the Heroic leader—the existence of a permanent, inescapable and more powerful 'enemy.' Ottawa provides an automatic and permanent presence against which to develop the theme of victimization. And victimization is central to the emotional relationship upon which Heroic leadership is built. So our history has been peopled by men like W.A.C. Bennett, William Aberhart and Ernest Manning, Howard Ferguson and Mitch Hepburn, Honoré Mercier and Maurice Duplessis. They all, as Lapalme said of Duplessis, "had the monopoly on true patriotism."[17]

But the key element for many of these men was their wounded quality. Like the male movie star, there was/is a vulnerability about them. They had wounded eyes. L'homme blessé. If they were Catholics, they inherited the sacrificial force which was breaking loose from a weakening church. If they were Protestants, they seized hold of that same sacrificial force, which the Reformation had turned into a more aggressive weapon.

At first glance it may appear that it was the model of Christ and the Crucifixion which set the pattern of modern political victimization and Heroic leadership. But there is something singular and final about the idea of crucifixion and resurrection. The Heroic leader must suffer humiliation and sacrifice on a regular basis—monthly, weekly, sometimes daily. Politics is repetitive and the more it slips down from ideas into mystification and Heroics, the more repetitive, as opposed to linear, it is. Successful political careers go on for years and years. How often can you be crucified or make reference to an earlier event of crucifixion-like importance?

The Canadian model of Heroic leaders seems to be drawn from the less demanding model of martyred saints, in particular, St. Sebastian. Bound to a stake, pierced by a hundred arrows, still—if we are to believe the paintings—he shows signs of a survivor's wounded smile.

With time the religious origins of these political mannerisms have slipped from our consciousness. The lay version has been so often repeated throughout the western world in the twentieth century that we take for granted these are civil phenomena. Democracy itself is tarred with these characteristics of authoritarian false populism.

René Lévesque certainly had the necessary aura of vulnerability and it helped him electorally. But he was saved from exploiting it in an unacceptable manner by his democratic rigour.

Others have shown less restraint. They have played the role of the Heroic victim with great force because it is proper to the whole concept of negative nationalism, with its required humiliation and sacrifice. And so, through the vision of the Heroic martyr/leader, history becomes a line of defeats and catastrophes filled with guilty parties. The leader is constantly being humiliated by the leader of another group. An extreme language of sado-masochism accompanies these serial woundings, which are, in fact, minor martyrdoms, many of them the product of masochism not sadism.

Glen Clark is a quick learner on this front. He can scarcely open his mouth without falling into the classic language and attitudes of the martyred Hero. But Lucien Bouchard arrived in office already a champion of self-proclaimed humiliation. As his memoirs demonstrate, this is a skill which pre-dates his rise to office and his own personal tragedy. The book is filled with occasions of honour lost and honour saved, of humiliations and betrayals. He is "blessé et humilié comme jamais dans ma vie" over a little matter of expenses when he should simply have been more careful.[18] A quick survey of the volume turns up twenty occasions for humiliation or saving honour. The same air of melodrama revolving around his person has stayed in place during his short time in office. In such an emotional context other people can't help but be "irresponsables," "provocateurs," "incendiaire," "ignare," "un parfait crétin," "un imbécile." Following his example, other ministers have adopted the same sort of extreme language. Jacques Brassard: "une sorte d'opération de terrorisme politique," "M. Chrétien aime jouer au despote." Bernard Landry: "méprisant et injurieux," "une aventure scabreuse," "aberrante et absurde," Ottawa "se comporte de façon plus autoritaire, plus mesquine et plus fermée que les anciens gouvernements communistes totalitaires." I can understand someone disliking or even loathing the current federal government. But who would have thought that Mr. Chrétien was more evil than Stalin? And when anglophones question or attack Mr. Bouchard on an issue, he replies with sweeping references to "Canada anglais" as if it were a monolith. Given his belief in solidarity, perhaps it isn't surprising that he interprets any voice raised to doubt him as the sound of the collective voice of 'English Canada.'

When Laurier was under violent attack in 1886 for his courageous stand on the Riel question, he was careful not to play into the hands of ideologues or racists on the other side. He never referred to the opposing press by race or language. He concentrated instead on their party and their ideas. But then Laurier did not try to win power or to govern by self-humiliation.

I'm making two points here. The language of negative nationalism reveals an unconsciously or consciously intended display of personal insecurity. Either way it is a classic example of the victim as leader. The second point is more practical. If by chance the *other* really existed and were made up of average human beings, what would they think of this barrage of extremes? Language, I keep repeating, is about communication. Real language has a real effect on the individual who receives it, because that individual is as real as the one who delivers it. The deliverer may do so in the manner of rhetoric, but the receiver may well receive it as language, unless the receiver also slips into rhetorical rebuttals. In that case reality is abandoned on all sides and the worst becomes possible.

This raises an even more practical point: how can Mr. Bouchard expect a normalization of the atmosphere in Quebec if the government's language is more dramatic and destabilizing than that used during the last world war by the leaders of countries fighting for their lives? To be precise, in June 1997 the city of Montreal announced that almost 50 per cent of its active population was dependent on government support. This astonishing statement is difficult to make sense of, but no one questioned it. What it indicates is not an economic recession or even a depression, but a social crisis.

An economic crisis has limited and identifiable implications. It is usually accompanied by a belief in recovery; that is, a belief that in some way things will again be what they once were. A social crisis is much more destabilizing. It has unpredictable effects on society and offers much less of a hope for recovery. It is a time of unknowns, in which it is difficult to identify directions.

For example, statistics indicate that, since the arrival in power of the first PQ government in 1976, 506 head offices have left Montreal for Toronto, while 122 have gone from Toronto to Montreal. The vast majority of the large group leaving Montreal were big employers. The vast majority of the smaller group going to Montreal were small employers. We are also told that almost half the immigrant entrepreneurs admitted to Quebec in 1993–94 have already left for Ontario or B.C. and that the retention level has been dropping steadily since 1990.

I repeat, this is a social not an economic crisis. For example, the Official Languages Act, the most important formal progress made by French in Canada in this century, and one of the, if not *the*, most important formalized progress made by French in the world in the last half-century, isn't even mentioned in a large number of Quebec school textbooks. And those which do mention it tend to do so in passing or in a manner which suggests that anglophones were against it.[19] How is this related to the economic numbers? In both cases these are indicators of a destabilized society in which it is difficult to grasp onto reality.

This is the sort of atmosphere in which false populist rhetoric often prospers. But we know that if it does, it can only play a negative, manipulative role. It prospers by rolling through fear, anger and joy, guided by leaders who specialize in the emotions of public love and solidarity.

What we know from experience over the last century is that this is not the way to deal with a social crisis. I say this fully aware that Mr. Bouchard's government has its quota of good ministers and that a few of its policies—child-care, for example—are admirable and should be copied by the other provinces.

But the fundamental problem remains one of false populism in a growing crowd of false populist provincial leaders—a trend which is not balanced by any solid social leadership in Ottawa. The federal government resembles that of Louis St. Laurent's second term. A low-key, feel-good atmosphere distracts us from a general passivity before corporatist interests. A more accurate description might be complicity with corporatist interests. There appears to be little opportunity for the development of a positive nationalism which could address the social situation.

A small example: there is a slow rumble of concern outside of the political parties and the main media about an ongoing international negotiation on investment rules, or rather the removal of them. It is called the Multilateral Agreement of Investment (MAI). No one with power or a stable platform from which to communicate will engage the citizenry in a debate on the subject. When pushed, they may utter reassuring sounds.

The last decade has been filled with events of this sort; each of them representing another managerial step towards profound international restructuring. When you read the MAI texts—which as yet have no validity—it is clear that they represent an important move towards asserting the primacy of corporations or interest-based structures over citizen-based structures. And yet there is virtual silence from our elected representatives. They are, after all, the chosen leaders of the citizen-based structures.

Positive nationalism would involve the initiation of an open debate by those in positions of responsibility. Instead, the experienced citizen senses that we are now passively waiting for the initiation of a public-relations campaign designed to instruct us on the immense and inevitable good which will be done by our ceding another slice of our democratic legitimacy.

Of course, it won't be put that way. Instead there will be a chorus of received wisdom in the economic-administrative manner. This is now classic rhetoric, delivered with the assurance of religious texts.

You might ask if I am sure that the MAI will be so bad. Frankly, I have no idea. But why do I have no idea? Where is the debate which would enable me to make up my mind in a dignified adult manner? This is what I mean when I say we live in a corporatist society. Where are our elected representatives? Why do they see their role to be that of the protectors of the various interests against the citizens who elected them? In private they express a weariness with the citizens' naïveté. They, the leaders, know. Know what? The truth, of course! But how can they get the public, who understand so little, to go along with them? With this self-righteous burden on their shoulders, they dutifully do endless private polling and hire serial management consultants to advise them on how to get the public to go along with the truth they already possess.

My point is that whether or not those with power are right is actually of secondary consideration. The primary consideration is that in a democracy legitimacy lies with the citizenry. That's what makes a democracy superior to other forms of social organization. And the process which leads to important decisions is not simply supposed to include the citizen. It is supposed to use the intelligence of the society—which lies within the legitimacy of the citizen—in order to minimize the chances of making major mistakes. That is the primary characteristic of a democracy. That use of the citizenry's intelligence is what differentiates a democracy from the various sorts of dictatorships, whether direct and brutal or sophisticated and managerial in the corporatist mode.

What is most surprising about our élites is that they are unable to identify the effects of their actions. They don't see how their upcoming successful manipulation to put in place the MAI will simply increase the effect of their putting in place of the trade deals. That is, they will weaken the confidence of the citizen in the system and therefore favour the rise of negative nationalism over the positive. Perhaps most fascinating is the low level of confidence they have in the democratic process. I'm not referring to the short-term excitement of occasional elections. In effect, they identify more with the managerial idea of controlling power than the democratic idea of examining power and using it constructively. The attitudes of our elected representatives before these major questions resemble, if anything, those of senior courtiers in the eighteenth century.

In such an unstable atmosphere, a PQ premier might well be able to win a referendum to break up the country, or an Alberta premier a referendum to cripple the province's power to raise taxes—that is, to govern. They might succeed if they were to choose the right date and prepare the "winning question" with care and if they were to work on incidents which might speed everyone along through the emotions of fear, anger and joy. So long as the federalists remain mired in their unnatural position to the right of centre and continue to work on a corporatist agenda, they will play the PQ's card and indeed that of Mr. Klein. Only by occupying the great centre/left-of-centre can they demonstrate the healthy role of federalism. But that would also mean adopting the politics of positive nationalism and the public good.

Rather than deal with the realities of the public good, they are about to plunge into another round of shadow-boxing over the legalities of mythological terminology. From distinct society we are about to move on to a debate over whether or not Quebec is a nation. A great deal of time will be spent on the meaning of the word. Other words will also be proposed.

What isn't clear is where these sorts of false debates lead. After all, if you go back through the last two centuries you will find all of our leading public figures happily and frequently using such terms as nation and people to describe the French Canadians. Suddenly, late in the twentieth century, terms such as these are held up as if they were a test. Everyone is required to take a position for or against. What can that possibly mean? Isn't this a prolongation of the old character-specific view of nationalism? Are Armenians courageous? Are the Slovakian Hungarians to be considered...? Are the Russian Latvians...?

The problem is not whether these terms are accurate or appropriate. They and others are perfectly satisfactory. Why not be distinct? Why not think of yourself or others as a nation? People should call themselves whatever they want; whatever they feel is appropriate.

The only difficulty is whether such terms have any constitutional or legal meaning. To try to turn such words or equivalent phrases into legal terminology is to go down the all-consuming road of negative nationalism. Constitutions and laws are utilitarian documents dealing with specific, concrete powers and obligations. Even so, it is difficult to define terms clearly enough. That's why there are endless disagreements in most countries over the meanings of constitutions. That's why France has a high court devoted to nothing but that. That's why the United States Supreme Court is endlessly reinterpreting the concrete clauses of their constitution. And that's why real constitutions avoid abstract terms which have enormous mythological meaning, but very little legal meaning. The law is not mythology and mythology is not law. Only false populists attempt to advance one under the cover of the other.

Would it not be better to return to a more relaxed public discourse, which on a daily basis reconfirms the respect which people feel for the phenomenon of the francophone role in Canada? If francophones appear to want to be called a nation, do so. Make it part of the ongoing public discourse as it was a hundred years ago. Jean Paré has rightly pointed out that the needs of francophones to advance and solidify their position in the legal framework of the country will come in the form of increased legal clarity, not legal mystifications.[20]

Why then do we keep finding ourselves back at the stage of

attempting to legalize mythology? In part this is because we do not deal with the mystifications which pursue us like demons, dominating the public discourse. That is, we do not deal with the need to separate the mythologies and laws, upon which positive nationalism is based, from the confusing of those two elements, which is the political trick upon which negative nationalism feeds.

Séguin wrote that "to be a minority people in a federation is to be an annexed people—être un peuple minoritaire dans une fédération, c'est être un peuple annexé."[21] This is not only wrong, it is nonsense. But if we cannot express a positive nationalism and lay out how a federation works and has worked, then we will remain the victims of just such pathological mystery-plays of victimization.

29 The Belt Clingers

HOW IS IT THAT WE HAVE BEEN HERE so long—some almost 400 years, some 200, many 150 or 100—and yet our élites still struggle hopelessly with their own colonial mind-sets? Is it because we have a small population which does not therefore feel self-reliant? Or live in a poor northern place which cannot convince itself that it is at the centre of something? Certainly you'll find that same longing among Scandinavians. In their case it is directed at western Europe.

Perhaps colonial relationships, being bogus from the outset, can't help but leave suppurating sores. Perhaps the sharp contradiction between the western rational idea of civilization and the reality of a northern country is unresolvable.

One factor that does keep the colonial mind-set alive is the way in which we cling to the belt-line of our southern border. This lop-sided occupation of our territory has created a completely false mythology—a mystification—by which the vast majority of the population are able to pretend that they are a people of central North America, not of the northern half. To turn seriously towards what lies north of the belt-line—for more than a holiday—requires a difficult reconstruction of most of our lives. And yet not to do so is to become an exile in our own country; to render ourselves irrelevant to what Canada really is.

It is worth placing our endless constitutional debates in this context. Those who favour provincial autonomy (ranging from more of it to an absolute separation) have interesting, critical things to say about our current national structures. But I wonder whether most of our fundamental problems lie not between the federal government and the provinces, but inside the provinces themselves. They are too big. Most of them, on their way from the south to the north, run through three complete geographic and climatic regions.

The differences between the north of each province and its south are greater than those between the various urban souths from east to west, including Ottawa. In fact, Montreal, Toronto, Calgary, Vancouver have more in common with each other than with their northern cities and regions. We know that Toronto pays no attention to Sudbury and North Bay and that there is a schism in the province. The result is a justifiable anger in the north against the south. The same is true in Lac Saint-Jean, which feels ignored by Montreal and Quebec City. Many of the regional nationalist voting patterns have more to do with a real physical and psychological independence from the rest of the province than from the rest of Canada. You find the same patterns in Prince Rupert and Prince George. Even Edmonton and Calgary clearly belong to two separate worlds. Indeed the NDP and Reform voting patterns in Ontario and the West also have a great deal to do with the permanent condition of northern alienation. In the Western provinces, northern alienation is of increasing importance, and is slowly overtaking the traditional West versus East variety.

The utilitarians think we have too many provinces. Perhaps we have too few. It's curious, considering the enormous imaginative leaps that our early political leaders took, that they didn't see the extent to which they were deforming the country by handing these gigantic northern hinterlands over to the young southern settlements. They created a new colonial situation. After Paris and London as the centre, then Montreal, then Ottawa, suddenly all the southern cities were turned into new colonial powers. And they went on to treat the north exactly the way empires treat colonies. They bled it without great consideration for the north's own desires, interests and needs.

The creation of these enormous north–south slices drew the whole northern logic of the country down into a southern illusion.

466 And that illusion could only be filled with dissatisfaction. It encouraged laziness in the south, where much of the élite lived and still lives off the hinterland's resources without putting anything back into those areas. And so this structure also slowed the real development of the north.

It would have been far better to have created a series of northern provinces. Their focus would have been northern, gazing out from capitals like Chicoutimi, Sudbury, perhaps Prince George. Edmonton would have had its own northern logic, as would Labrador. Even Cape Breton is a strangely classical colonial appendage to an unrelated capital area. With eighteen or so provinces the internal national debate would have been drawn upwards towards the centre of the country, where the various provinces met, instead of lying flaccid on the American border. Divided up in this way it would have been possible to establish three or four francophone-dominated provinces. Riel's original idea was to maintain a limited territory in which the Métis would be a majority. The clear toughness of a province speaking from Chicoutimi would have been good for everyone. The energy level of these northern centres of government would have kept us closer to the unusual track imagined by the early élites. In other words it would have protected us from the predictable, colonial relationship proper to living along the American border.

Such a situation would have allowed us to develop an unchallenged northern sense of the sort the Norwegians and Swedes have. What is artificial in Canada is not the east–west flow, but the unnatural, forced, north–south flow within eight provinces. I insist on this, not because it is likely to change, but because it is important to focus on what doesn't work very well in our structures. Compared with the unresolvable divisions within the provinces, our federal-provincial differences are quite positive.

As the southern cities grow ever larger, so it becomes more difficult for them to feel part of the whole. Increasingly they are coming to resemble isolated city-states, cut off from their hinterland. Increasingly they act like indifferent blood-suckers of the northern resources. In part this is because of the lobbying power inside those governments of the natural-resource industries. These are the organizations which live off the hinterland, while offering back very little beyond basic jobs. Increasingly our city-state élites fall into the trap which their Argentinian equivalent have suffered from. "A collective refusal to see, to come to terms with the land: an artificial colonial, fragmented colonial society, made deficient and bogus by its myths. . . . The land that was the source of their wealth became no more than their base."[1]

V.S. Naipaul's language may seem too harsh for the Canadian situation. But, when you pay attention to our élite's reactions to the events and crises of each day, you can't help but be struck by how isolated they seem to be from the reality of this society. They show signs of having lost the solid instincts of a properly functioning élite.

"Base Canada," Louis-Edmond Hamelin asks, "can it go on dragging in its southern manner the immense North? Is it too much to think that one of the North's major problems is the South?"[2]

I would say no. It is not too much. The provincial governments, driven by the natural-resource lobbyists, tend to act with all the down sides of a national state and few of the up sides. The situation is a betrayal both of the north and of the northern idea.

30 Élites

FOR A MEMBER OF THE ÉLITE WHO wishes to take without giving back, there is no easier society to function in than a democracy. That's because power in a democracy is not intended to be linked to the concept of noblesse oblige. The obligation of the élites is therefore tied to their ability to see themselves as citizens and to act as such every day.

This suggests a modest status for men of money and power. They may find it unpleasantly modest. Indeed you can usually tell when the concepts of democracy and citizenship are weakening. There is an increase in the role of charity and in the worship of volunteerism. These represent the élite citizen's imitation of noblesse oblige; that is, of pretending to be aristocrats or oligarchs, as opposed to being citizens.

There are advantages to being an oligarch or an aristocrat in a democracy. After all, in an officially corporatist or aristocratic civilization there are real obligations attached to the concept of noblesse oblige. These may be manipulated, minimized or in some cases even ignored. And these obligations always represent a denial of the legitimacy of those who receive the largesse, while reasserting the legitimacy of those who give it. But what we would be dealing with in those societies is a type of formalized responsibility. In a democracy there are no formal class structures. Therefore there are no specific, formal obligations tied to privilege. The concept of noblesse oblige floats freely, as you would expect from something which represents a pretence of superiority among those who can afford it. The whole idea relates only to charity, which is nothing more than the goodwill and ongoing generosity of the jumped-up citizen. In other words, our pretend noblesse oblige is tied to ego not to duty.

The true obligation of the élite within a democracy has nothing to do with charity. It has to do with disinterested participation in the name of the public good. And it requires more personal, ongoing effort than any other sort of society requires from individuals.

In Canada this sort of participation comes with a particular complication. We have always been a middle-class democracy. 'Middle-class citizen' has always been the highest real rank we have to offer. There are, of course, those who pretend to be more. Everyone has the right to their personal delusion. The impression they create in the Canadian context is vaguely comic, but that is their problem. Unless, that is, they come to represent a whole class. If the élite pretend to be more than middle-class citizenry, they are betraying the idea of Canadian democracy.

On the other hand, it is unusual for anyone to pretend to be less. Look at the photos of the Winnipeg strike in 1919. These may be workers, but they are in suits. J.S. Woodsworth may be a 'dangerous' socialist leader, but he dresses and talks like a prime minister. Arthur Meighen could have done worse than to take lessons.

What makes life in the Canadian élite triply complicated is our colonial background and our current colonial status. This increases discomfort with the middle-class idea, which was never understood by the British colonial establishment. And it certainly isn't understood by the new empire to our south, which is driven by the desire to create republican aristocracies.

In spite of these complications, Canada has produced generations of élites capable of accepting and working within the middle-class reality of an atypical country. Unfortunately, these generations have been interspersed with counter-waves of élites which can only be described as colonial. From the Second World War through to approximately 1980, it seemed as if we were finally escaping this cyclical problem. The experience of the war had built on that of the

1914–18 experience and an atmosphere of growing self-confidence spread among the élites. Then, abruptly in the eighties, it seemed to evaporate; as if those with responsibility had found it too much work being in charge of a real place. Perhaps more depressing, this decline coincided with the departure from active life of the wartime generation and those closely influenced by it. It was as if the self-confidence of those anglophones and francophones had not spread beyond the particularity of their experience. All that had happened was that a new generation had come along and discovered a new empire to feel happily subservient to.

> We are an ignorant and stuttering people . . .
> We are not particularly brilliant.
> But have a great talent for appreciating

others.[1] Of course that's not the way our élite imagines itself. And if so many books and other cultural expressions are now produced and consumed, surely things are no longer as Michèle Lalonde described them. Yes and no. If you pause to concentrate on the underlying references of those who occupy the various positions of power, you discover that almost all reveal a great talent for appreciating the brilliance of what is done elsewhere.

This, they would say, is a sign of their internationalism. But again, calm observation reveals that most of their qualifying references are to a single dominant empire. And most of what is left over refers to two ex-empires in Europe. Colonial élites have always put their emotional dependence on a single foreign model down to sophisticated internationalism. Tribal leaders spoke that way of Rome; Indian rajahs that way of London; Vietnamese princes that way of Paris. In other words, the essential references of our élites indicate a strong inferiority complex.

This explains in part why the voice of positive nationalism is almost as silent among anglophones as among francophones. Oh, it is there. And it can be heard. But somehow, in both languages, it is out of sync with the structures of power. No matter how appropriate or popular or useful to the public good are the humanist ideas put forward, they seem irrelevant to what is actually decided and done. And if the policies chosen by our élites seem to be failing, that also appears to be of little importance. The structure has a life of its own and those who occupy it—as in the 1780s in France—are very pleased with themselves and have great difficulty identifying as reality the extent to which the citizenry are not pleased with them.

It's a situation not unlike that described by the Polish Nobel poet Wisława Szymborska—"He who wishes to drown himself must have an axe at hand to cut the ice."[2] Somehow, the process here is more passive than for the Poles, with Russia on their border.

It is as if our élites simply can't bring themselves to believe that this is a real place; in part because it is a non-conforming model. As so often with those who have succeeded in complex, atypical structures, they quickly lose the sense of who they are and so succumb to a desire to conform to the dominant, typical model of the day, even though this means undermining the structure upon which their success and their power are based. When Brooke Claxton retired from politics and took over a large company, he was struck by the unintellectual mental climate and the "... constant pressure right across the board towards conformity and conservatism."[3] But the problem goes much further than the traditional anti-intellectualism of managerial circles and their sudden importance in a generalized corporatist atmosphere. The playwright John Gray puts it that "Canadian leadership over the last decade has consisted of leading the bow to the inevitable. The leaders are not leaders. And when, because of this, they begin to feel desperate, they engage in symbolic acts," as if they were leading.[4]

Yet there is a long and very different élite tradition in Canada. At key moments the quality of those willing to assume responsibility has been remarkable. The defining moment in the 1840s was filled with men who knew exactly where they were and why they were doing what they were doing. Papineau, Mackenzie, Jesse Ketchum,

Dr. Baldwin, LaFontaine, Baldwin, Wolfred Nelson, Edward Blake's father, William Blake, Georges-Étienne Cartier and so on. Part of this reality was a strong contingent of reform-minded business leaders. And characteristic of them all, although most of them came from isolated, small cities and settlements, was their ability to imagine the *other*. LaFontaine and Baldwin set the standards. But one of the most imaginative, almost surreal examples was that of Cartier's relationship with British Columbia, an essentially inaccessible place.

Joseph Trutch, one of B.C.'s negotiators for entry into Confederation, described how their successful deal had come about. Cartier had from the beginning offered them generous conditions. When the government MPs in Ottawa began to balk at the costs involved, Cartier simply told the whole caucus that he and his Quebec members would vote alone for the Treaty whatever they did. "We must all remember in B.C.," Trutch wrote, "that to Sir George Cartier and his followers in Lower Canada we owe the position we are now in and especially the Canadian Pacific Railway."[5]

However, the other side of the élite's character has also been there from the beginning. The Annexation Manifesto of 1849 summarizes that position. Yes, the Montreal business élite were upset about the arrival of democracy—worse still, middle-class democracy—and yes, they were rightly upset about London's revocation of their trade preferences and by the resulting depression. But above all, you can sense in their reaction a frightening passivity. This is a colonial élite. In spite of their privileges, they feel a pathological need to belong to someone. They receive. They do not give.

Wilfrid Laurier, forty years later, put it that they were a class "famous for preaching loyalty to others... famous for being loyal, as long as it was profitable to be so." In 1849 they "... were gushing in their loyalty as long as they expected the Governor General to be disloyal to the people, but when they found the Governor General was loyal to the people, their own loyalty oozed out of their bodies and vanished into thin air."[6] In a precursor of the trade deal with the United States in the 1980s, the Annexation Manifesto brought together on the same side the extreme wing of the francophone nationalists and the reactionary business community.

Even in the 1960s this passivity and short-term interest-driven psychology could be identified by those who non-conformed. In 1963 the unfortunate John Diefenbaker gave a last speech before his government fell. In it he pointed out "the similarity between the views of the Montreal merchants in 1849 and the wealthy of Toronto and Montreal" who were ranged against him. As George Grant put it, "In neither case did they care about Canada. No small country can depend for its existence on the loyalty of its capitalists."[7]

The situation today is both worse and more complicated. Suddenly, in the panic surrounding the last referendum, the business élites became staunch federalists and patriots. The francophones among them joined in the campaign, wrote and campaigned passionately, if rather ham-handedly. The anglophone executives pushed and pulled as if, given a chance, they could have made a difference.

And yet these are the same people who tend to send their children to private schools and undergraduate colleges in the United States. When asked about this they will earnestly talk of the 'best education' the way fifty years ago parents of this sort talked of Oxbridge. Why do they do this? For the same reason colonial élites have always sent their children to be educated at the heart of the dominant power. The empire provides the best:

> . . . If they live
> in the Empire, it matters what they say.[8]

A colonial élite believes that reality exists there only; and somehow that this education will give their children an advantage when they come back home with the modern equivalent of an Oxford or Paris accent and pedigree.

And they do indeed get a fine education. Unfortunately it is usually structured for people who will live as citizens of a great empire, along with three hundred million other people. Instead they come home with skills unsuited to a northern, sparsely populated, decentralized country with a non-mono-cultural character. When given a chance, they can but apply what they know and do so with the superior inferiority complex of those educated in Rome. They either try to make their country do things unsuited to its reality—which is one of the explanations for our current problems—or they become the classic dissatisfied colonial or they leave.

I'm not suggesting that an international education is a bad thing. I'm talking about when and where it should take place. It is during the school years and those of undergraduate education that we gradually come to understand the nature of our society and how we might fit into it. In general this is a time to be home. Post-graduate education is the time to find out how other societies do things, because we are then in a position to make judgements with a context. What's more, the need of a small to medium-sized country is not to learn how the great empire does things. If you pay attention you understand that simply by living in Canada. Nor is it useful to worship at the knee of our ex-empires.

On the other hand, we could learn a great deal in countries of a similar size with similar challenges. What kind of countries? What sort of challenges? Decentralized countries. Northern countries. Countries in an awkward geopolitical position. Developed economies with small populations. Countries which are part developed, part developing. Countries with a high natural-resource dependency. Countries with awkward territories. Large territories with small populations. Countries with non-monolithic cultures. With several languages. With heavy immigration. With a mixture of western and aboriginal cultures. In countries with one or more of these characteristics we may learn something which relates to our own situation. We should therefore try to ensure that a good part of the international education we give our students happens in those places.

Even when our élite do keep their children at home for basic schooling, they tend to undermine the public-school system by fighting against the taxation levels necessary to fund it. Or they send their children through the private system. They forget or wish to forget that public education is the keystone of a middle-class democracy.

These are or may well be some of the same people who sought airline deregulation, which discourages east–west travel and travel to smaller destinations; they who have pushed north–south economic integration to such an extent that it endangers national and provincial social programs; they who, in that same way, have undermined the spreading of wealth to the poor and the poor areas; they who have turned their backs on those parts of Canada—most of it—which are not urban or are not an income source for business. Through all of these actions they have artificially turned the country away from itself and towards the south. And isn't it they who have undermined the culture of national broadcasting by starving public broadcasting and by misusing the private systems? On all occasions at all times it seems that the structures useful to the citizens as a whole must be sacrificed to their short-term profit.

And aren't these the people who have sold off such quantities of the Canadian economy that we are an unprecedented example of a developed country whose economic activity is dominated and designed from abroad? This is not a new phenomenon. Walter Gordon was already worrying about it in the 1930s. He wanted to create a large holding company to offset the trend.[9] The new francophone business élite seemed at first to resist these sell-off tendencies. During the 1960s and 1970s they seemed to identify with the Quiet Revolution going on in Quebec. But now they are cashing in their businesses at more or less the same rate as the anglophones.[10] In the name of what sort of national interest or élite responsibility are they all doing this?

The most common reply is that the question itself is old-fashioned and the concern irrelevant. Apparently in the new global economy it no longer matters who owns what. Capitalism no longer spins around the ownership of the means of production, but around the acts of trading and producing. Those who produce and trade win. Ownership is just a series of accidents in the ever-changing market-place. And that turns on how attractive a geographical location is to financial markets.

Declarations of revolutionary change in the underlying rules of the market-place always make me think of John Law and the South Sea Bubble; the two great financial 'revolutions' of the eighteenth century, both of which ended disastrously. The funny thing is that ownership has been relevant for the full history of western economics. It has also been central to that of Asian economics, which goes back further than ours. The argument therefore is that something which has been true for at least three thousand years and through dozens of fundamental technological changes has ceased to be true in the last twenty years for no particular reason. Why not? But then again, why?

The one thing I don't understand is why every bilateral, multilateral and international economic agreement we have signed over the last decade goes out of its way to prevent the citizens, through their governments, having any say in the shape of ownership. I thought ownership didn't matter.

The response to this question will perhaps be drowned out by the second answer to my original question about why everything is being sold off.

'Internationalism! Globalization!' But they can't really mean that. They can't be that naïve. No other developed country has interpreted globalization as if it meant allowing half of your economy to be directed from elsewhere. No one.

As V.S. Naipaul put it about Argentina, to be European—i.e., to be sophisticated—"was to be colonial in the most damaging way. It was to be parasitic."[11] I suppose you could see this selling off of the farm as a peculiar form of originality. But no, it isn't. It's plain laziness, passivity and a result of that inferiority complex which our business élites first revealed in 1849.

This is not a phenomenon exclusive to Upper and Lower Canada. Look at the half-dozen most important Maritime fortunes. None of these families have acted as if they were the élite of a society or even of a region. They have treated the Maritimes as if it were their back lot, to be used however they wish.[12] Or look at the Newfoundlanders who were ruled by a thinly disguised autocracy controlled by the merchants of St. John's. These were people "... who failed to provide the institutional support and politics necessary for erecting a sovereign and self-reliant economy."[13]

And, for that matter, the very obsession of the national élite with a single market to the south has undermined the more international approach which a country with two languages should quite naturally embrace. They talk endlessly of globalization and world markets. The reality is quite different. They have made us more dependent on a single market than any other developed economy. What's more, they seem frightened by other markets. A recent study showed that in ten of eleven developed countries, over half of the businessmen are expanding into new, foreign markets. In Canada the figure is only 35 per cent.[14]

In such a context it isn't surprising that the former Official Opposition in Ottawa—the Bloc—identified so closely with the United States. Or that the new Official Opposition's program is mainly aimed at harmonizing Canada in every way with the United States. The Reform party calls for elections every four years, an American-style Senate, wide-open election financing, a straight free-market economy, an end to bilingualism and the passing of balanced-budget laws. Their foreign policy turns on a single axis—seeking greater harmonization with the United States.

Any sensible person would now be thinking of the urgent geopolitical need to seek a better balance by developing relationships with other players. But the colonial élite never seeks geopolitical balance. What it wants is to suckle at the mother's teat and so feel better about its sense of inferiority. Yet geopolitics are almost entirely based on countervailing influences or powers. If a small to medium-sized country lives next to a large country, its only hope for a reasonable relationship with its big neighbour is to have other countries as allies in order to create an effective counterweight.

To sell 80 per cent of your goods to a single market represents a terrible strategic weakness. And I mean strategic in every sense. The old cliché about having all your eggs in one basket takes on new meaning with Canada and the United States, because there is something even more wrong about having all of your eggs in someone else's basket. It is worse still if that country is much larger than you and worst of all if they don't have all *their* eggs in *your* basket. This is not a relationship. It is a dependency. Canada's survival will depend largely on its ability to change that dependency back into a relationship. And one of the key factors in doing that will be the redistribution of our trade. But we can't do that if we have no politicians willing to take the lead.

So what are we to make of an élite which waxes patriotic while selling off the reality of the nation? Are they not eerily similar to negative nationalists like Maurice Duplessis, revealing an impossible divide between rhetoric and reality? We could settle for name-calling in the wonderful manner of A.M. Klein:

You elephantine ass who stolidly
Idealize idealess success,
You plutocrat of gilded emptiness.[15]

But when the rhyme is finished they'll still be there. This is, given the victory of neo-conservatism, the dominant élite of our era. And they will sell off far more than their own companies.

Hockey—a sport which combined making money with a solid relationship to the Canadian reality—has been reduced to, or rather deformed into, an American spectator sport. In order to do this, the driving forces of commerce and communications have simply removed all but the crumbs of the professional game from Canada. They accurately say this is a way to make more money and hypocritically talk about spreading the gospel of the sport. But the hypocrisy is not designed to disguise single-minded commercialism. Like so much in corporatism, money comes second.

The ownership of sports teams has always been as much about ego, or rather personal expressions of power, as it has been about making money. Since Rome, successful businessmen have often seemed to need the illusion of controlling gladiators. But that illusion was tied to a celebration of the particular and to prestige in the community. Increasingly it is now a reflection of corporate conformity and of communications theories in which sport is just another global entertainment.

Global entertainment is about interchangeable modules of distraction, all functioning in a similar way. The style of a sport can change for many reasons and can be counted on to evolve with time. But the most important factor in the case of hockey is that the vast majority of the audiences in the new NHL arenas can't skate. They are not there for the hockey *per se*. They are gathered around the ice as they might be around a boxing ring—for the thrill. And so there is little desire among the managers of the league to control violence or to encourage more than a workmanlike game, providing there are a few Heroes for the crowd to cheer.

This is a Disneylike view of a world made up of predictable factors and rounded edges. Hockey, like other sports, like adventure movies, is therefore to be packaged as a conventional, Hero-driven, goal-obsessed entertainment and sold to audiences on a 'quick-hit' basis. Audiences which are interested in the game—in a non-spectator way—actually deform and so slow the efficiency of these interchangeable modules. Hockey needed to be removed from Canada for its own good, so that it could grow through the freedom which would be produced by minimizing its particularities.

Of course the promotion of hockey to an entertainment-module theory is progress in many ways. While Canadians may be marginalized in their own game, they get the advantage of becoming marginal in American games such as baseball and basketball. But marginality is not the central advantage. The point of colonial status is hope. The hope of being noticed in Rome once our foot is in the door. I would like to use the image of the barbarians who ended up not only noticed, but in charge. However, the barbarians outnumbered the Romans even more than the Americans outnumber the Canadians. So the point is hope itself and not the hope of anything in particular happening. The colonial mind-set is just that, a mind-set, not a reality.

In the twenty-four hours leading up to the 1997 baseball All-Star game in Cleveland, the Canadian media went into a brisk fibrillation over the opportunity being offered a Canadian quartet—the McAuley Boys. They were to sing "O Canada" during the opening ceremonies and so would be heard by millions of Americans, who would certainly notice them. There was hope that someone who mattered might be listening—Ted Mack, Ed Sullivan, Johnny Carson, perhaps even *David Letterman*. The effect on their careers might well be immeasurable. The next morning there was another little fibrillation, this time filled with surprise and embarrassment. The network had run a series of ads while "O Canada" was being sung. These ended just in time for the American anthem. And why not? But the tone of the commentary was one of hope. Next time the McAuley Boys might be heard.

When Comsat, a telecommunications group, bought the Québec Nordiques, they turned the management over to its entertainment division. The president said—"Professional sports are the same business and the same culture. They're vertically integrated entertainment business." He therefore concluded that "People feel good about a winner. That's the business we're in."[16]

Of course, sports are businesses and hockey has changed since my grandfather played for Winnipeg teams like the Monarchs, in the days before the NHL existed. But I have also seen a Maple Leaf

Gardens crowd give Wayne Gretzky in his prime a standing ovation for scoring against Toronto. It was a beautiful goal. And it wasn't the goal itself they were cheering, it was the way in which it had been done. They apparently didn't think hockey was just about winning.

My point is neither romantic nor idealistic. The large and successful Canadian business élite, both the individuals and the corporations, have been virtually invisible during the hijacking of professional hockey. They might reply that the market-place has spoken. Not at all. They allowed the market-place, of which they were part, to be redefined in such a way as to virtually eliminate them and in the process make more than a marginal Canadian presence impossible. So, in business terms, they allowed themselves to be artificially eliminated from a basic Canadian business. What could be more basic than the business of the national sport? They might reply that ownership doesn't matter. Except that it clearly matters to all those businessmen south of the border who went to so much trouble to redefine professional hockey on their terms.

As for the attitude of the modulizers of hockey, it is a good parallel to the schizophrenia of the false populists and the negative nationalists. They seek to create a great movement of solidarity around the sport by removing its purpose and character.

Why go on about hockey? Because it reveals attitudes which can be found in much of the business community. For example, there is little difference between the pattern surrounding hockey and the public letter written to the prime minister on June 20, 1997, by the main Canadian business lobby group—the Business Council on National Issues. This is an organization with money and talented advisers. And yet the arguments they put forward in this major, public statement are contradictory and basely self-interested. In an attempt to distract us from this depressing reality they write as if in the national interest.

The three major economic problems facing the nation, they say, are unemployment, public debt and high taxes. Their principal suggestion for job creation is better education. What they don't mention is that the per-student expenditure on education is dropping across the country because there isn't enough public money available. And the reason there isn't enough money is because of a campaign led in good part by the BCNI to reduce government revenues. In fact, in this same letter they call for further tax cuts, which would again weaken, not strengthen, education.

Their specific tax concern is "top marginal tax rates." In other words, they can't even manage to see the economy through the eyes of their businesses or of economic theory, but only through their straight self-interest as members of the top tax-rate bracket. This is the exact opposite of an élite using their privileges to act as citizens on behalf of the public good.

It's hard to know whether the BCNI's prestigious executive committee of CEOs really read this drivel. It's hard to believe that they wouldn't be embarrassed by the low intellectual level of the arguments, the blatant contradictions and the transparent self-interest. Perhaps the blame should rest on the shoulders of the organization's chief paid courtier, Thomas d'Aquino.

Even the concept of high corporate taxes taken as a general problem doesn't stand up to any kind of examination. In 1950 almost half of Canadian income tax (46.4 per cent) was paid by corporations. This did not prevent them from enjoying a period of strong growth and high profits. In 1992 the corporations were paying only 7.6 per cent. One of the chief reasons for our public financial crisis is that the principal source of revenues is extremely lightly taxed; lightly even by western standards. The BCNI letter makes the point that our top marginal tax rates put us at a disadvantage against the Americans. As with their contradiction between education and taxation, so with the Canada–U.S. differentials. They don't bother to explain just how lower taxes will permit us to "provide more efficient delivery of services to citizens," which they also call for. They spend some time on the political crisis and Quebec and talk about making our "social union work." But that social union is, precisely, made up of social programs which are not harmonized with those in the United States. If you remove our tax differentials, you effectively starve the government and so close down one of the key characteristics of Canadian society—its social programs.

Perhaps I'm naïve to try to take Mr. d'Aquino seriously or to treat his letter to the prime minister as a real argument. Perhaps it's meant to be treated as PR bumph. But I can't help thinking of the 1929 Depression and the Kidd Report commissioned by the B.C. government in 1931. Twenty-two organizations (corporations in the Mussolinian sense) were involved. All the interest groups: the Canadian Manufacturers Associations, the Chambers of Commerce. They concluded that taxation couldn't be raised, expenditure had to be cut by about 22 per cent, education cut by one-third, free tuition limited even at the public-school level, the number of teachers cut, public funding for universities ended, funding for social services frozen.

Fortunately an election followed, the government was defeated and the report shelved. But proposals such as that of the BCNI present themselves as new thinking, when they are just the tired, self-interested arguments which the interest groups have been trotting out for almost seventy years. At their core lies the failure of large sections of the élite to rise to their obligations as citizens. They hide this close-focus selfishness behind the rhetoric of neo-conservative economics. But that's what neo-conservative thinking offers—short-term self-interested self-gratification. The BCNI wants the government to deal with the nation's political crisis, but calls for policies which would make it explode. It's worth going back once more to the crisis which led to the burning of the Parliament Buildings in Montreal in 1849. In the debate which preceded the rioting, Edward Blake's father, William Blake, the Solicitor General West and one of the great reforming parliamentarians of the day, intervened to chastise the anti-reform party—the BCNI of the day:

There are two sorts of rebellions. You can rebel against your country or you can rebel against your king. You gentlemen, for fifty years you have trampled on the interests of the people, you have laughed off their complaints, you have mocked their demands, you have rebelled against their most legitimate desires. It is you who are the real rebels.[17]

I repeat, this was the voice of the solicitor general in the defining Canadian government; the great coalition, which brought us democracy. Blake's was an argument which Laurier would rework forty years later during the Riel crisis and J.S. Woodsworth another thirty-five years later during the Winnipeg strike.

The point is that a part of the business community has always made a strong argument against the public interest. They have gone so far as to burn down parliament. And they have been answered and stood up to on a regular basis by the political mainstream. That's why these citations are not gratuitous insults. They are the meat and potatoes of Canadian legitimacy. The self-interested argue that "poverty makes virtue flower—la pauvreté fait fleurir les vertus."[18] And the mainstream, from Blake Sr. on, reply severely. What we are missing today in our politics is the vigorous echo of that reply.

The first step is to stop taking seriously what are in reality mediocre and predictable bits of propaganda. For example Mr. d'Aquino, in a puff piece published on the opinion pages of *The Globe and Mail*, enthused in 1997 that the "Outlook for social progress [was] bright." "History shows us quite clearly that trade and direct investment are powerful catalysts for economic liberalization, democratization and the improvement of domestic social conditions."[19]

Well actually, no it doesn't. History is full of examples of trade taking societies in all sorts of contradictory directions or, more often, being used in a measured manner by various societies. What do I mean by a measured manner? Well, for example, a pure trade-based society kept a comfortable dictatorship going for centuries in

Venice. Today trade is consciously used to reinforce a severe dicta-torship in China and to solidify a strict dictatorship in Singapore. On the other hand, in some places these same economic factors have been carefully harnessed by democratic forces and made to fit in. So trade, like economics in general, is primarily a tool to be used and not a cause in itself. As for "technical superiority," it does not exist, as the Swedish writer Sven Lindquist put it, to provide "a nat-ural right to annihilate the enemy even when he is defenseless."[20] The point holds, whether taken literally or figuratively.

That's why Harold Innis was such an important economist. He kept arguing in favour of "an economics which derived its laws from the history of the place, rather than deriving the place from a set of all-purpose laws formulated in Britain."[21] Or, now, in Chicago.

I am not making a negative-nationalist statement. It is almost pure positivism. That is, I am treating economics as a practical busi-ness, no matter how global the forces at work. The question which I am raising is: why are governments such as ours signing broad abstract trade agreements which relate to unprovable theories and negate the physical reality in which economics takes place? Part of the answer is that we have given leadership within our élites to busi-ness managers who tend to have a narrow view of their own self-interest and no view at all of the public good.

And so there they are, in the largest province, redesigning it as if there were no particularity, as if Ontario were just an extension of western corporatist theory and of American neo-corporatism.

Our parliamentary system is only very partially based on law. Much of it is the daily result of unwritten conventions. The system depends on all sectors respecting those conventions. Instead, the provincial government began by passing an omnibus bill which transgressed the most fundamental conventions of democratic process. This was done behind a false populist façade of saving money in a crisis (described as if it were worse than any world war). What is fascinating is the Barnum and Bailey revivalist, born-again moralizing which accompanies this cutting process; as if something unprecedented and evil had taken place and needed to be cut out of our lives like a cancerous growth.

But overspending is among the most common characteristics of human organizations, whether governmental, business or personal. It comes in cycles as it has for thousands of years. It is as common as debt cycles or love-handles. From time to time a serious government has to act with some severity to rectify the cycle. But there is no reason for this to be a matter of moralizing. It has to do with administrative standards, not policy, and should not distract politicians or the public from what a government actually stands for.

If a government presents cut-backs as if they were essential policy, indeed a moral obligation, then they are probably trying to distract us from their central policy intentions. The attack on overspending, while perhaps to some extent necessary, is then fundamentally a tactical distraction.

Indeed, Mr. Harris's advisers—who are a mix of downtown ideologues and Bay Street conventional thinkers—have organized a cutting program filled with extremely specific patterns. For example, there is a concentration on removing both the observers, investigators and enforcers from programs which protect the public interest, and the powers which allow this monitoring. The pesticide-residue inspectors are mostly gone. Water-pollution regulations are to be eased. Environmental assessment programs have been moved almost under the minister's discretion. Great Lakes pollution research and monitoring is cut heavily. Spending on the judiciary is cut, while that on prisons goes up.

None of this has to do with money. The amounts involved are peanuts. What it does have to do with is removing the mechanisms which permit the citizenry to understand what is happening inside their society. There is nothing abstract or theoretical going on here. This is an attack on applied democratic practice; a conscious and persistent removal of the citizens' right to know. More importantly, it is a denial of their need to know. After all, they are the source of social legitimacy. Informing the citizens of social practices is not about indulging their curiosity. They need to know in order to be able to do their job as citizens.

Like all false populism, that of the Harris government is based on contempt for the intelligence of the citizen. In classic terms, they are engaged in organized and conscious censorship. In rather more mundane terms, it is all about acceding to the demands of corporate lobbyists.

And beneath all of this we are continuing to play out a self-inflicted struggle which goes far beyond Ontario and Canada. Ever since the democratic systems permitted their various courts to give corporations the status of persons, the individual as citizen has been on the defensive. How could it be otherwise? If you are a person before the law and EXXON or Ford is also a person, it is clear that the concept of democratic legitimacy lying with the individual has been mortally wounded. It is also clear that our élite, in allowing the continual solidification of this aberrant concept, have given in to their role as beneficiaries and/or prisoners of corporatism. At the same time, they have betrayed their most profound responsibilities as citizens. I find it difficult to imagine how democracy can prosper, so long as corporations maintain their artificial status as persons.

A very simple illustration of the extent to which our under-standing of our democratic obligations has been deformed can be found in the lack of reaction to Mr. Harris's decision to reduce the number of MPPs by twenty-seven. His argument is a continuation of the moral need to save the taxpayers money. But these members are the only link between the citizen and the government. They are the citizen's only practical way into the democratic process. If Ontario is a presidential-corporatist society, he has done the right thing. If it is a parliamentary democracy, he has transgressed the underlying principle of representation.

That this removal of an important percentage of the representatives hasn't received much attention is in itself a sign that false populism is well advanced. After all, much of the citizenry have been convinced that it was a democratic victory to get rid of their representatives.

What I am describing is not only a society dominated by corporatist structures, but by the received wisdom of a corporatist atmosphere: one in which the élites are interest-driven, whatever their jobs. And so the society is gradually being redrawn to suit this ethic-free system. I go to the Canadian figure-skating championships and discover that they are now the Royal Bank Canadian Figure Skating Championships. One public building after another is financed up to 90 per cent by the taxpayer and then named after the corporation or father of the president of the corporation which gives the last 5 or 10 per cent. In July 1990, there is a disastrous flood in the Saguenay and Premier Bouchard immediately announces that "It seems to me obvious there is no blame to assign. It's a phenomenon that happens once every 10,000 years." His minister of the environment, David Cliche, repeats this. Why? Why this instinctive, automatic, immediate defence of constituted authority, whether public or private?

What do these two individuals actually know about dams and floods? What did they know about the specific actions and inactions of the private corporations and the public service in the Saguenay? Nothing. It isn't even their job to know. In the end, the sensible public protest forced the provincial government to name a commission of enquiry. And the commissioners found out that there was a great deal of blame to assign and therefore systems to be reformed.

So whatever the flood was, it wasn't an act of God. At most it may have been a test by God. And the various constituted authorities and structures failed the test.

The point here is, why did an intelligent provincial premier and an intelligent minister of the environment instinctively blame everything on God in order to avoid even raising the possibility that those responsible on a rather more day-to-day level might need to be

questioned? The answer is that they operate within a perfectly corporatist and therefore anti-democratic mind-set. They automatically
see their job as that of protecting the corporations, whether public
or private.

The Somalia Enquiry report is published in July 1997, and the
profoundly mediocre Art Eggleton, having been minister of defence
for three weeks, immediately, instinctively, automatically defends
his staff officers. But he knows nothing about the military. He wasn't
involved in either the scandal or the enquiry process. He doesn't
even have personal experience which might be helpful in evaluating
the situation. Is it his job immediately to defend his staff, as if there
were something to hide? Only in a corporatist society.

Premier McKenna goes to the Olympics in Atlanta. He is the
guest of IBM. In other words the head of government is given a
handsome present. Public protest eventually causes him to assume
the costs. The premiers meet in Alberta. Their conference is literally
sponsored by various companies. They pose in jackets bearing
private-industry logos. The Ontario Securities Commission, the
most important in the country, has been so starved that it has hardly
any investigators. It's close to becoming a joke. The government of
Quebec farms out part of its foreign representation to a bank. The
federal minister of state for finance admits that bank lobbying forced
the government to water down its review of the financial services
sector. And so on.

Were I describing a functioning democracy, this litany of wrongdoing would have been accompanied by a continual and impossible-
to-ignore outcry from elected representatives. Instead we might as
well be living in pre-revolutionary Russia. There the élites acted as
if they had—in Tolstoy's words—"no conception of life without
authority and submission."[22] Men and women, theoretically
entrusted with great power, plead inevitability and stare curiously at
us with "... the pure smiling eyes trained only for Form."[23]

Suddenly all of this seems normal. I am struck by the curious
reflection that if everything is inevitable, as our élites tell us, well

then we don't really need them. After all, this is the biggest and most expensive élite in history. Either they should do their job or make way.

Instead they wield the tools of defensive silence and insidious fear with increasing expertise. As a result, we find ourselves believing that government fails at everything; that public programs are ineffective and expensive; that a disinterested structure is probably a mess; that only self-interest works; that the public interest is a romantic dream and probably part of an outdated theory of left-wing paternalism.

I step back from this panicked atmosphere and look around. Most of the public services seem to work if they are properly funded, reasonably transparent and open to questioning. I notice in passing that Algonquin Park was set up in 1893 to control lumbering and stop settlement. This wasn't a socialist creation. It was a mainstream public-interest idea. Now, for the first time, the administration of these parks is being thrown into doubt. Profit-motivated services may be used. But the system in place hasn't failed, isn't expensive and is part of a mainstream, public-interest method of running public institutions.

The problem lies then not with a bogus utilitarian comparison between the public service and private interests, but with our élites, who have slipped into corporatist conformity. They survive by spreading fear as much as they suffer from it.

There will always be, in any élite, a percentage driven only by self-interest. Now it seems that that relatively small percentage has infected the thinking of the élite in general, no matter how intelligent many individuals may be or how devoted to their particular role. Much of the problem lies in the conversion of our public sector from an ethic, centred on the strengthening of the public good, to an abstract managerial religion.

That in turn has facilitated the massive penetration of the public sector by business interests. The shift in the income-tax burden, which I mentioned earlier, illustrates this reality. But our crisis is not primarily about tax avoidance, or about money. Nor am I making an argument against either business or the market-place. They have their essential role in every society, including a democracy, and the citizenry have everything to gain by helping in the success of the private sector. We do this best through regulations which are simple, clear and strict.

However, private interests are now so integrated into the functioning of the public good that our practical sense of the latter has been erased. It is difficult even to identify this corruption of the public place, except in the less important, blatant cases. The corruption that really matters has been normalized and renamed, as if it were a useful part of the democratic process.

Central to this normalization has been the gradual rise of lobbyists and their sophisticated conversion into the profession of consultants. Slowly but surely over the last twelve years, the arm's-length public institutions of social, economic and scientific research have been shut down, along with the investigatory and enforcement arms of government. The argument given for their destruction was budgetary, yet the costs these bodies represented were minimal.

The aim has been to blind government. Having removed the arm's-length vision of the citizenry, the interest groups could then substitute their own eyes. What began with the destruction of the Economic Council of Canada and the Science Council was followed by that of dozens and dozens of lesser-known but important mechanisms. This lobotomization of the public mind continues today with, for example in 1997, the closing of the federal Bureau of Drug Research.

Even the minister of finance now uses consultants to develop policy. The minister of finance! Of course they are not presented publicly in that way.

In 1963 Walter Gordon's first budget was destroyed when it was found out that he had brought in four financial experts he knew and trusted to complete some work. He was not asking for creative input. He had clearly set the parameters and the purpose in advance. During the election campaign, a budget had been promised within sixty days. Without these four experts, who understood the new policies, the work was not going to be completed in time. Today the minister happily uses consultants on a regular basis to develop policy. In other words, the interest groups are formally invited in to help define, if not actually to define, the very core of public policy.

In 1992 a Conservative Cabinet minister, Harvie Andre, arrived from his modest house in Ottawa at a party given by Harry Near, head of the smoothest of consultancy groups, Earnscliffe, in his ever-growing Rockcliffe mansion. Looking around with awe the minister mused, "Why is it better to know Harvie Andre, than to be Harvie Andre?"[24] Was this an unconscious parody of the young Louis XIV, arriving for a party at Vaux-Le-Vicomte, the splendid new palace of his chief adviser, Fouquet? Perhaps it was conscious. The king looked around, drew the obvious conclusions, imprisoned his consultant and seized the property. As for Mr. Andre, he simply went away perplexed. And Mr. Near, along with the hundreds of other courtiers, continued to prosper.

No one is doing the calculation, but this new, anti-democratic system, which exchanges public-service salaries for consultants' fees in the name of financial efficiency, is probably costing the taxpayer much more, not less. Consultants are expensive and they are everywhere, feeding upon each other in both Ottawa and the provincial capitals, doing government's thinking for it at hundreds of thousands of dollars a pop. We elect our representatives to work out what lies beyond self-interest. Instead they hire interest groups which redefine the public interest as a mere extension of the market-place; that is, of self-interest.

The result is the institutionalization of simplistic, romantic and ideological received wisdom. More precisely, it is the canonization of anti-thought. The core sentence for which the taxpayer pays in thick report after thick report goes as follows:

On the issue of public interest, an important consideration in assessing the impact on employment of any merger is the rapid globalization and increasing competitiveness of the industry. Canada is not an island unto itself and . . .[25]

Which industry? It doesn't really matter. This is religious dogma, not analysis. It happens, in this case, to have been offered as the justification for more or less deregulating the financial sector. Just think of it. We are paying people a great deal of money to tell us we are not an island unto ourselves.

Much of this facile material has its origins in what passes today for independent opinion-making, as produced by organizations such as the Howe Institute and the Fraser Institute. These are little more than the extended and somewhat abstracted tentacles of their funders. Their purpose is not thought or inquiry, but rhetoric and propaganda. They simulate intellectual activity to produce corporatist and interest-based messages, which are in clear contradiction with the ideas which have created and built Canada.

The citizenry are rightfully relieved, at least at the federal level, that we have left the coarse corruption of the Mulroney years behind us. On the other hand, that was only the icing on a cake which has layer upon layer of highly accessible rich cream baked right into it. We are well beyond the straightforward and sensible instructions of Lester Pearson to his Cabinet. He told them they could accept any present they and their wives could consume in one day. A bottle of whisky? Two bottles of champagne? A tin of caviar?

The individuals may drink less, but the state itself now gratefully receives presents from the corporate sector. The premier of Ontario poses in front of piles of prominently labelled breakfast cereals which are to be donated to schools by the manufacturers. He seems to have forgotten that the rise of democracy was driven by the citizens' desire to escape from the paternalistic and arbitrary charity of those with money. They accomplished this by replacing charity with a fair, balanced, arm's-length system of public obligation.

494   The principal tool of that obligation was taxation. I spoke earlier of the distortions created by allowing corporations to become 'persons.' The conundrum is that the more they become 'persons' the more they seem successfully to avoid the obligations of the person as a citizen.

The real threat in all of this is the normalization of the corporatist mind-set in public debate and in the public sector. So long as that exists we will find it impossible to have any sort of serious debate about the public good. Petty corruption has always existed and always will. But a democracy cannot function if its internal structures are co-opted by interest groups. That is endemic corruption. Until the citizenry deal with it, they will not be able to recuperate their role as the source of political legitimacy.

There is an urgent need to rebuild the whole arm's-length sector of research, monitoring and enforcement. Yet this democratic system is still being taken apart by the ideologues, who insist it is old-fashioned in our age of "rapid globalization and increasing competitiveness." To rebuild such systems, they say, would mean a return to big, paternalistic government.

This is nonsense. Flawed though it has always been, the arm's-length principle is one of the key inventions of modern democracy. It has nothing to do with big or small government. And it is under attack simply because there is a corporatist assault on the public good. As for paternalism, the only paternalistic retrograde policies on the table are those now being enforced. They are dragging us back towards the self-serving systems of the late-nineteenth century.

What we find disconcerting is that all of this is being done with highly sophisticated-looking consultancy reports written by sophisticated-sounding men. Once you realize that they are nothing more than courtiers providing rhetoric for a demolition of the public interest, the situation becomes much clearer. People like this have always existed, as have their reports. Go back to the eighteenth century. You'll find the corridors of royal palaces filled with them.

"What we must fight against at this moment," Laurier said in 1881, "is our destructive tendency to take only personal interest into account, which leads to venality, to the flattening of consciences, to all these infamies that we see around us..."[26]

To escape from the distracting, draining impression that all of this is inevitable, we must imagine the logic of Canada. That has never been about clinging either to the border or to narrowly defined self-interest. The country is simply too marginal to survive as an anti-intellectual profit centre. Beyond the logic of the country we have to try to understand the geopolitics which dominate the continent. Above all, there is an obligation for those who are weaker or fewer in number to try to be faster, better informed, more agile and more strategically sophisticated than the larger party. As Bernard le Calloc'h puts it, when talking of Finland, "The great Finnish politicians have had a profound understanding of the Russians."[27] It was once taken for granted that the best Canadian politicians would have the same sort of understanding of the United States. Somehow we have still not recovered from the Brian Mulroney/Allan Gotlieb naïve and colonial approach, which so weakened our position by acting as if personal friendships and bravado could replace understanding.

The ways of ideology and absolute answers are filled with bravado. Countries of Canada's relative size, internal complexity and difficult geographical positioning can't afford ideology or bravado. We do best through a very aggressive use of our smartest and most committed élites. It would be naïve to suggest that only disinterest is central to this, but it must at least be consciously present. In a corporatist society the very idea of disinterested criticism is extremely difficult. Those who maintain it find that their reputations are enhanced in a manner which cuts them off from practical power and therefore, in the end, from social reality.

Confederation came about for several reasons and thanks to a variety of personal drives. But one of the key factors was Thomas D'Arcy McGee's role. And that was because, as Macdonald put it after the assassination, among McGee's chief characteristics was "his personal disinterestedness..."[28]

That stance was difficult enough for McGee. It made him the most respected but also the poorest of the important Fathers of Confederation. As the various players consolidated their power after 1867, he was gradually squeezed towards the sidelines. He was, in a sense, too good to be successful. What was difficult for McGee in the nineteenth century is much tougher for the citizenry today. How are they to impose themselves on the role of the market, of self-interest, on the large public bureaucracies? That's why ongoing participation in political questions and public service are key to any success. That's why the neo-conservatives, corporatists and false populists so rigorously remove the enforcement mechanisms from as many public services as possible. It is enforcement which makes it possible for the citizen to have a disinterested role.

But there is also a matter of examples being set by those who have power; not because power implies superiority, but because, in a democracy, particularly a middle-class democracy, power is meant to be the servant of humility.

In August 1996, Monique Bégin, the former minister of health, wrote to the Krever Enquiry on tainted blood to state that she would assume responsibility for her role, whatever that might turn out to be. This was a rare example in a corporatist society of someone volunteering to accept responsibility.

In her letter, Mme. Bégin stated that she felt obliged to write, "as a matter of personal morality and integrity."[29] That she did this was particularly important because the Health Ministry and Medicare have become symbols for the humanist idea of society which Canadians keep insisting they want. They see this not, I think, as a privilege or a right, but as a working example of what a decent society can do. That Medicare exists and works is daily proof that the public good means something and that legitimacy can still lie with the citizenry. There is a direct line from Dr. Baldwin's York Dispensary, offering free medicine in 1832, to Mme. Bégin acting in exactly the manner, I imagine, that Dr. Baldwin would have acted had he been active in 1996. It was an illustration of the old humanist pact struck by the younger Baldwin and LaFontaine, because it showed that a public figure can still act on the basis of principles. And the principle in this case is the well-being of the citizen.

Gabrielle Roy, in her autobiography, described in detail the discussions between the family doctor and her mother over an urgent children's operation which the family couldn't afford. When you read this scene, which would have been repeated in millions of lives, Roy makes you understand with perfect minimalism that health care is not a question of privilege but a matter of dignity.[30]

That's why the citizenry insist and insist and insist that they are proud of the Medicare system and that they want it to work. They continually send instructions to this effect to their governments. They do so in every imaginable way. And yet, day by day, the governments and the bureaucracies chip away at the system as if in the hope that, by opening holes in it and creating a new ineffectiveness, the citizenry will drop their commitment to it.

The silent, ongoing, committee-room manoeuvring against Medicare has become a great test for the citizens, for the élites and the citizenry as a whole. Will a sufficient percentage of the élites respond honestly to the citizens' desires? Will the citizens find the ways to ensure that they are obeyed by those to whom they have given responsibility?

The citizenry have now had some experience of the methodical, silent refusal to listen of the constituted élites, and so are becoming better at fighting back. But the message from this struggle between the public good and short-term corporatist self-interest has been that corporatism is strong and smart. And democracy, in

498   the form of Medicare as a practical illustration of the public good, has still not found out how to make the structures of corporatism work on its behalf.

This tells us, on a superficial level, that corporatism dominates. But in a more serious way, it tells us that the élites to whom we have entrusted our democratic system are refusing to do their jobs in a responsible manner.

The Sensibility
of an Idea

HISTORY FUNCTIONS AS HISTORY when it embraces a broad sweep of functioning memory. It is not about converting our condition into solutions. Yet many Canadians have come to the astonishing conclusion that if there is a problem in the system and it cannot be solved, well then, the system should be destroyed. That this problem may actually be the central condition of the civilization—and therefore its strength—escapes notice. Such an approach converts our functioning memories into little more than sequential sitcoms with clearly stated problems followed by clearly stated resolutions.

None of this would be of great consequence if there were not such a crisis within our élites and we were not so confused about the nature of nationalism. For example: Why do we have so much difficulty recognizing the difference between positive and negative nationalism? In part because the essential Canadian debate—that which pits the school of reconciliation and reform against the anti-reformers—has been obscured behind a secondary argument over which level of government should have which power.

All argument over the nature of our social contract has been buried beneath an abstract theoretical debate over constitutional powers and administrative ambitions. In the process, Canada as a coalition of ideas based on an assumption of the public good is being transformed into little more than an alliance of powers and interests.

Of course there is also a perfectly valid, ongoing argument to be had over the balance of powers between the national government and the provinces. In the right circumstances there is every reason to favour or at least to consider decentralization—in some areas, massive decentralization—providing that the public interest is the core consideration. But today decentralization is being used largely to institutionalize corporatism and negative nationalism. Decentralization, as we are approaching it, is destroying the reforming ideas and the force of the reforming coalition on which Canada is built. What we are taking part in is the final undoing of the work of LaFontaine and Baldwin and the victory of a revamped version of the Family Compact–Château Clique. It has only taken those forces 150 years to work out how to get their way. In historical terms that is not an unreasonably long wait.

Such a statement may sound apocalyptic. But realism isn't pessimism. And though the anti-reform interests have won an unconscionable number of battles over the last decade, the war is by no means over.

When the public interest is reduced to self-interest everyone's attention span is gradually shrunk until it is narrowly focused on gaining powers. Control over specific powers are the chips in what is little more than a corporatist poker game.

We live in a world of constitutions and laws. What was once the privilege of the king to bestow is now a matter of legal and back-room jockeying. Suddenly, powers are spoken of as if they were sacred objects. This is the ultimate abstraction of negative nationalism.

But what are powers if not for the most part utilitarian, administrative tools? The real question should be not who has what power, but in what administrative configuration is the citizen's idea of her society best served. That can only be established through a debate. Not a debate about configurations, but about the public interest. Yet we act as if that sort of discussion were virtually impossible.

Canada has spent more time on constitutional questions, according to Peter Russell, than any other country, and has done so more intensively and passionately. Yet this effort has led nowhere except to draining "the creative energy of the leaders."[1] Why? Because no matter how much beautiful language is stuck on, constitutions remain rather low-level organization charts. And because our constitutional debate is never about which structures can serve the reforming tradition versus those which serve self-interest. It therefore has very little democratic purpose.

The result has been a continual drift towards decentralization. The citizenry have difficulty identifying this trend because it is the product of intergovernmental negotiations taking place out of the public eye. Most of the public rhetoric denies that anything of consequence is happening. Ottawa goes on blustering about a strong and united Canada, whatever that is, and the provinces go on wailing that Ottawa is intransigent.

Those very provinces which complain most of duplication and overlap now talk of creating a third level of government to coordinate the powers they control. Being intergovernmental and administrative, this structure would remain invisible to the citizenry and inaccessible to any sort of practical democratic control. Curiously enough, it resembles the Quebec premier's proposal of a partenariat. It is also typical of a corporatist society: you insert successive levels of executive or administrative government in between the voting public and actual policy-making. The effect is to water down, even remove, the citizen's real role.

Again, the problem is not decentralization, but the absence of debate about the content or real intent of decentralization. For example, over 150 years, with very few exceptions, decentralization has favoured the promotion of individual self-interest as against the public interest. That is, it has favoured social inequalities. Just as it has, almost without exception, been accompanied by the mistreatment of linguistic minorities. Remember, the Manitoba School Question was primarily about provincial rights. Not just provincial rights versus federal rights, but provincial rights versus reconciliation and the public good.

The added problem today is the impossibility of regional governments financing complex, universal programs when the real financial levers needed to raise money now lie somewhere between national governments and the international market-place.

We erase our conscious sense of these realities by concentrating on the abstract debate over powers and the very real sense of alienation which a number of provinces feel. Yet the confusion between equality real and false, alienation real and mystified, and for that matter between corporatism and the public good, is exactly what requires real debate. What does each of these elements mean? What are their actual functioning relationships? What should they be? This debate ought to be going on in both the federal parliament and the provincial legislatures. Instead it takes place in a purely structural manner in invisible intergovernmental committees.

This is a process which appears complex to the citizenry, dominated as they are by the dialects and methodologies of the technocracies, public and private. We are forced to observe power through the intellectualization of administration. Public debate is reduced to a curious mixture of inaccessibility and glibness, the tools of executive government.

This exclusionary system is deceiving. After all, complexity is not necessarily a sign of intellectual content or of ideas. Indeed executive politics are profoundly anti-intellectual. They are a denial of Canada's strength as an idea of a country. They relegate progress through ideas to the margins of unprofessionalism. Instead we are dragged away from our originality and down into the banal predictability of courtierism and managerial in-fighting.

Perhaps I am creating the impression that our problems stem from a lack of ideas, indeed a lack of policies. Not at all. We are drowning in policy ideas and policy analysts and policy studies.

A sensible strategy to drive the diversification of our trade policy
is there for the asking. A complex but nevertheless integrated, long-
term foreign policy would not take a great deal of creative effort.
We have good thinkers inside and outside of government. There is
absolutely no reason why we have to deal with the mid-life crisis of
our social policies by putting a bullet through their heads. There
are dozens of ways in which they could be strengthened to work for
yet another quarter-century—a long time in political policy. There
is no need to open up gaping holes in the safety net, as we now are
doing. Indeed, the whole immobilizing confidence trick of neo-
conservative economics can easily be seen for the superficial, regres-
sive romanticism it really is. The reintegration of the aboriginal
community into the centre of our society is actually well on its way.
What lies ahead could be the easy part, if we wanted it to be. No
doubt the question of francophone–anglophone relations is politically the most complex that we face. Yet again, it is not so difficult
to conceive of positive approaches, especially given the very real
and creative changes of the last half-century. In particular there is
the remarkable progress made over language inside Quebec and
New Brunswick, at the national level and in the other provinces.
I'm not suggesting this could or should eliminate the nationalist
movement. We are all in need of it. But we could, much more easily than we think, establish the extent to which the school of negative nationalism is retrograde—in fact, bizarrely retro—and so
rehabilitate the ideas of positive nationalism.

Our problem is not a lack of policy, but rather an inability to
believe that such a thing as long-term, integrated policy could still
have a place in Canada; particularly policy which responds to the
particularities of the place. We seem unable to believe that power
could be anything more than self-interested manoeuvring obscured
by false-populist bombast.

What is it which so impresses or depresses us? After all, if you step
back from the arid rhetoric of the interest groups and the negative

nationalists, they suddenly come into focus, as if metamorphosed. Abruptly, Sir Allan MacNab, Monsignor Bourget, D'Alton McCarthy, Maurice Duplessis and a little crowd of their historical doubles stand before us. As if with the flick of a magic wand you can see how essentially destructive they are for a society which believes in the public good; how essentially comic are the BCNI, the C.D. Howe Institute, buffoons like Messrs. Harris, Klein and Landry.

What is it that frightens us out of believing that original or non-conforming action is possible, if not the rhetoric of our corporatist élites? They in turn are mimicked by many of our public figures, who seem reassured by their own *ad nauseam* repetition of the sort of received wisdom which transfers their personal sense of being victimized onto the public. They convince themselves that there is no need to act in an original manner when the big picture is so effectively controlled by globalization and other clichés. Responsibility, they murmur with false sophistication, consists of tacking tightly to keep some small part of the ship of state afloat in this unprecedented storm of change. The whole idea of the public good recedes, as if it were an old-fashioned ideal rendered obsolete by the horizonless complexity of the new ways.

History is reality. But it is also the product of how we imagine reality. In a successful society this is a creative process and the result is a mythology on which the community can continue to build. When a society becomes fixated by a few ideological truths, it loses the ability to see the reality of its own history, let alone to imagine its shape. Then it falls easily into a negative approach full of blame, bravura and promises of salvation. An aura of mystification replaces mythology and the result is a generalized sense of inescapable immobility. It is that sense of being victimized by one force or another which frightens us out of believing that original and non-conforming action is possible.

Yet our experience tells us that the opposite is true. The series of original and unexpected actions which made the idea of Canada practical in the first place came during particularly difficult times. It is a conceit of each generation that the new erases the old and that their changes and crises are the like of which no one has ever before seen.

The truth is that LaFontaine and Baldwin brought about their revolutionary reforms while surrounded by general disorder. Society was weighed down by a major economic depression, caused by London's free-trade policies. There was social turmoil because of the massive immigration brought on by the Irish famine. The Orange Order and the Toronto Tories, frightened by the unrest in Europe, were repeatedly rioting. There was serious industrial unrest involving railway employees and sailors. There were riots going on in rural French Canada against Meilleur's new education system.[2]

It is precisely in times of difficulty and confusion that the public good needs most to be asserted and imposed by the citizenry and their representatives. What this requires is a belief in the long-term cause of reform—the unbroken line from Mackenzie and Papineau, LaFontaine and Baldwin. This is not a romantic view of history. The recognition of our past actions is a central part of our ongoing, unfinished experiment. As for the received wisdom of our day, what conclusions are we to draw from élites which shower inevitability upon us, except that they are failing to do their jobs?

How do we so easily forget that reconciliation and reform are at the heart of the country's creation and survival? The explanation lies perhaps in our ongoing confusion over the nature of equality.

The Canadian experience has shaped individualism to mean some sort of balance between equality of opportunity and equality of results. This is the attempted equilibrium of a middle-class society, eager for freedom on the one hand and the stability that comes of minimizing extremes on the other.

As the century wears on, so a very different American view penetrates ever deeper into our society, thanks to their domination—direct and indirect—of every imaginable means of communication.

506   By their definition, individualism is limited to equality of opportunity, the result being real inequality.

Our own practical counterweight to this siren call has been the physical reminder, all around us, of a more balanced equality, created and maintained by a reasonably effective social-democratic system. But now our élites are carefully removing that structure, indirect step by indirect step, never facing the electorate clearly on the question. In fact they keep insisting that they are not doing what any fool can see they are doing. And so our practical reminders of balanced equality gradually fade, ceding the public place to a more ideological, abstract American view.

There is another, more complex confusion surrounding the idea of equality. This is part of the tension between our two levels of government and between the different regions. Quebec rightly claims a particular or special or unusual or separate status, all of which in practical fact it already has. Other provinces talk of the equality of provinces when what they actually mean is a generalization of what Quebec means—that is, special status. It is gradually becoming clear that the concept of equal provinces actually means the rich provinces get to keep their riches and the poor their poverty.

As for real equality, it consists of a constant rebalancing act—one which the federation carries out through the participation of both the national and the provincial governments. That act is centred on the redistribution of both money and services. And those services have as much to do with culture as they do with our physical well-being. It was our commitment to this sort of equality which lay at the centre of Canada's evolution. That was the meaning of the Mackenzie–Papineau cooperation, as it was of LaFontaine and Baldwin's belief in their "absolute necessity not to be found lacking." Their sense of "obligation" led to the idea of a country built on the conception of ongoing reform. The railway was a redistribution device, just as public broadcasting has been over the last sixty years, just as Medicare and transfer payments have been over the last quarter-century. The service of the public good in such a complex federation is based on the unending application of ever-evolving methods of redistribution. That is the meaning of reconciliation and reform. It isn't just financial. It may be linguistic and cultural or social and political. That is why, whatever you think of the 1982 constitutional revision process, one of its true accomplishments was the guaranteeing of minority language rights.

Our rush to decentralization has carried us away from the delicate balance in which equality refers to the public good. Instead it refers to special status all around. As you would expect when individualism is based only on opportunity, no one asks what happens to those who have neither the financial nor the political clout to exercise their tiny portion of that opportunity.

The question must surely be whether the problems, which people sought to address through this theoretical equality of provinces, have been addressed. Or has the increasing decentralization of powers actually aggravated the old problems and created new ones? And if it has, what is the reason? Is it that this decentralization has been taking place without the question of content being seriously addressed?

To a dispassionate observer it would seem that increasing decentralization has led to or been accompanied in both anglophone and francophone Canada by the growing dominance of American models and thus of America. The greater endemic poverty of the Maritimes and Quebec in comparison with the other regions has been accentuated rather than reduced. The Canadian idea of a balanced society has been weakened. The social instability into which we are moving seems to have had the effect of driving us away from our mythologies and back into the ancient mystifications of victimization.

I am not making in any way an argument for centralization. Rather I am describing the need for a continuation of the Canadian idea of reasonable balance. The struggles between the various levels of government over which should have which power are always rich material for the animation of current affairs. And, for that matter, they

508   often involve questions of great importance. But if such battles take place outside of the essential context of reconciliation and reform, and thus outside of our solid mythological context, then they are no more than self-indulgent posturing. A country which is an idea of a country is not a theoretical or utopian ideal.

The Inuit quality of *isuma* summarizes that essential context. It has as much to do with positive nationalism as with the public good. *Isuma*—intelligence that consists of the knowledge of our responsibilities towards our society. It is a characteristic which grows with time. If you choose to look, you can find it at the core of events through the long line of the Canadian experience. It is an intelligence, the Inuit say, which grows because it is nurtured.

Notes

P A R T   I

1. Victims of Mythology

1 Charles Sangster, "Song for Canada," *Canadian Songs and Poems* (London: Walter Scott, 1892), 25. François-Xavier Garneau, *Histoire du Canada* (Quebec: 1845–1848), 1:24.

2 Hector de Saint-Denys Garneau, "Monde irrémédiable désert," *Regards et Jeux dans l'espace* (Bibliothèque québécoise, 1993), 144. Originally published 1949. bp Nichol, "Familiar," *An H in the Heart: a reader* (Toronto: McClelland & Stewart, 1994), 10.

3 Monique Proulx, *Les Aurores montréales* (Montreal: Boréal, 1996), 109.

4 Kjell Espmark, *L'Oubli* (Paris: Gallimard, 1987), 58.

5 *Debates of the Legislature Assembly of United Canada* (Montreal: Presses de l'École des Hautes Études commerciales, 1971), vol. 2, 40 and 43. Speeches of 13 September 1842.

6 Paul-Émile Borduas, *Refus global*, second paragraph. From André-G. Bourassa and Gilles Lapointe, *Refus global et ses environs* (Montreal: l'Hexagone, 1988), 51.

7 Jacques Godbout, *Les Têtes à Papineau* (Paris: Seuil, 1981).

2. The Mythology of the Victim

1 "So in spite": Réjean Ducharme, *L'Hiver de force* (Paris: Folio, 1973), 15. The opening line of the novel. "it is fear moves": bp Nichol, "late night summer poem," *Canadian Poetry* ed. Jack David and Robert Lecker (Toronto: Stoddart, 1982), vol. 2, 270. "It was a country": Jean-Guy Pilon, "L'Étranger d'ici," *The Oxford Book of Canadian Verse* ed. A.J.M. Smith (Toronto: Oxford University Press, 1965), 407.

2 Roger Gibbins and Sonia Arrian, *Western Visions: Perspectives on the West in Canada* (Peterborough, Ont.: Broadview Press, 1995), 9.

3 Michel Brunet, *Canadians et Canadiens* (Montreal: Fides, 1954), 86. Maurice Séguin, *L'Idée d'indépendance au Québec—genèse et historique* (Montreal: Boréal, 1968), 37.

510   4 "Papineau's former": Brunet, *Canadians*, 99. "the pseudo-leaders": Brunet,
         110. "Once again": Brunet, 91.
      5 *Papineau* comp. Fernand Ouellet (Quebec: Les Presses Universitaires
         Laval, 1958), 55. Speech of 27 February 1834. Philippe Aubert de Gaspé,
         Les Anciens Canadiens (Montreal: Bibliothèque Nationale du Québec,
         1988).
      6 *Papineau*, 55.
      7 See Allan Greer's analysis in Allan Greer, *The People of New France*
         (Toronto: University of Toronto Press, 1997), Chapter VIII, "Epilogue:
         The Fall of New France."
      8 Fernand Dumont, *Genèse de la société québécoise* (Montreal: Boréal, 1993),
         331, 333.
      9 *Wilfrid Laurier à la Tribune, 1871–1890* (Quebec: Ulric Barthe, 1890), 384.
         His first public speech as Liberal leader, 1887, at an enormous picnic in
         Somerset (Megantie).
     10 Gibbins, Arrian, *Western Visions*, 87. (My italics)
     11 Séguin, *L'Idée*, 16, 35.
     12 Donald Creighton, *Dominion of the North, A History of Canada* (Toronto:
         Macmillan of Canada, 1957), 289.
     13 "Canada was built": Brunet, *Canadians*, 49. "In order to save": Séguin,
         L'Idée, 37.
     14 Ernest Renan, "Qu'est-ce qu'une Nation?" *Conférence faite en Sorbonne, le
         11 mars 1882.*
     15 Charles Taylor, *What Is a Nation?* (Toronto: Tapir, 1996), 4.
     16 Joy Kogawa, *Obasan* (Toronto: Penguin Books, 1983), 111.
     17 Jean-Pierre Derriennic, *Nationalisme et démocratie* (Montreal: Boréal,
         1995), 31.
     18 Arthur Buies, *Lettres sur le Canada* (Montreal: l'Étincelle, 1978), 53. Lettre
         #3. L.M. Montgomery, *The Blue Castle* (Toronto: McClelland & Stewart,
         1989), 118. Originally published 1926. Bruce Hutchinson, *The Unknown
         Country* (New York: Coward-McCann, 1942), 4. Margaret Atwood,
         "Marrying the Hangman," *Two-headed Poems* (Toronto: Oxford University
         Press, 1978). Milton Acorn, "I've Tasted My Blood," *I've Tasted My Blood*
         (Toronto: McGraw-Hill Ryerson Ltd., 1969).
     19 Harold Innis, "Minerva's Owl" in *The Bias of Communication* (Toronto:
         University of Toronto Press, 1991), 31. Originally published 1951.

3. Imaginary Options

1 Jean Barman, *The West Beyond the West* (Toronto: University of Toronto Press, 1995), 359.

2 Alan Artibise, "Cascadian Adventures: Shared visions, strategic alliances, and ingrained barriers in a trans-border region." Unpublished paper, 1996, 2.

3 *Exhibition of Canadian West Coast Art—Native and Modern*, December 1927, The National Gallery of Canada. *Primitivism in Twentieth Century Art—Affinity of the Tribal and the Modern*, The Museum of Modern Art, New York, 1984. Denis Reid, *A Concise History of Canadian Painting* (Toronto: Oxford University Press, 1988), 54.

4 Emily Carr, *Hundreds and Thousands: The Journals of Emily Carr* (Toronto: Clarke, Irwin, 1966), 6.

5 Gerald Friesen, *River Road—Essays on Manitoba—and Prairie History* (Winnipeg: University of Manitoba Press, 1996). See in particular the chapters on La Vérendrye and on bilingualism in Manitoba.

6 Friesen, *River Road*, 16.

7 W.L. Morton, "The Bias of Prairie Politics," in Donald Swainson, *Historical Essays on the Prairie Provinces* (Toronto: McClelland & Stewart, 1970), the Carleton Library series, No. 53, 290.

8 Morton, "The Bias," 289.

9 Lucien Bouchard, speech to the nation, 22 October 1995.

10 Lucien Bouchard, speeches: "As for me": 14 October 1995, Saint-Justin, Rosemont. "That won't be done": 9 October 1995, Mont-Royal. "We will have solidarity": 15 October 1995, Montreal.

11 Lucien Bouchard, speeches: "The beauty of": 11 October 1995, Montreal. "But, if they agree": 7 October 1995, Montreal.

12 Lucien Bouchard, speech, 27 October 1995, Centre St-Pierre.

13 Lucien Bouchard, speech, 25 October 1995, Verdun.

14 Morton, "The Bias," 291.

15 René-Daniel Dubois, "8 Octobre 1990." Unpublished essay.

4. The Quality of Solitude

1 Gatien Lapointe, "Ode au Saint-Laurent," *La Poésie québécoise* ed. Laurent Mailhot and Pierre Nepveu (Quebec: l'Hexagone, 1990), 359. Glenn Gould, "The Latecomers." Drama/concerts on Newfoundland. CBC Radio, 1969. Pierre Morency, *Lumière des oiseaux* (Montreal: Boréal, 1992), 46.

512

2 Brian Fawcett, "The Hand," *The New Oxford Book of Canadian Verse* ed. Margaret Atwood (Toronto: Oxford University Press, 1982), 418.

3 Isabella Valancy Crawford, "Malcolm's Katie," *Collected Poems* (Toronto: University of Toronto Press, 1972), 213. Reprint of 1905 edition.

4 Leonard Cohen, "A Deep Happiness," *Stranger Music* (Toronto: McClelland & Stewart, 1993), 398.

5 *Le Devoir*, 4 June 1996, 1.

6 *La Presse*, 4 June 1996, B7.

7 Mikhail Lermontov, *A Hero of Our Time* (New York: Doubleday, 1958), 2. Originally published 1840.

8 *Papineau* comp. Fernand Ouellet (Quebec: Les Presses Universitaires Laval, 1958), 72. *La Minerve*, 17 March 1836.

9 Colin Read and Ronald Stagg, *The Rebellion of 1837 in Upper Canada* (Toronto: The Champlain Society, 1985), 62. From the Declaration of the Reformers of the City of Toronto to their fellow-Reformers in Upper Canada.

10 *Papineau*, 82. Letter of 12 February 1838. For a clear and brief analysis of the relationship between the two rebellions, see Allan Greer, "1837–38 Rebellion Reconsidered," *Canadian Historical Review*, vol. LXXVII, no.1 (March 1995).

11 *The Globe and Mail*, 8 February 1997, B6. Agropur purchased the Ontario fluid-milk operations of Ault Foods Ltd.

12 Quoted in Pontus Hulten, *Littératures de Finlande* (Paris: Massives, 1996), 13.

13 Louis Fréchette, "La Découverte du Mississippi," *Les Fleurs boréales* (Quebec: Darveau, 1879). E.J. Pratt, "Towards the Last Spike," *Complete Poems, Part 2* (Toronto: University of Toronto Press, 1989), 228.

14 Eli Mandel, "Envoi," *The New Oxford Book of Canadian Verse* ed. Margaret Atwood (Toronto: Oxford University Press, 1982), 229.

15 Anne Hébert and Frank Scott, *Dialogue sur la traduction* (Montreal: Éditions HMH, 1970).

16 Émile Nelligan, "Le Vaisseau d'or," *Poésies complètes (1896–1899)* (Montreal: Fides, 1952).

> Ce fut un Vaisseau d'or, dont les flancs diaphanes
> Révélaient des trésors que les marins profanes,
> Dégoût, Haine et Névrose, entre eux ont disputés.
>
> Que reste-t-il de lui dans la tempête brève?
> Qu'est devenu mon coeur, navire déserté?
> Hélas! Il a sombré dans l'abîme du Rêve!

17 Renaud Longchamps, "Primaire," *Miguasha* (Montreal: VLB Éditeur, 1983).

5. A Triangular Reality

1 Glenn Gould, "The Latecomers." Drama/concerts on Newfoundland. CBC Radio, 1969.

2 Peter H. Russell, *Constitutional Odyssey* (Toronto: University of Toronto Press, 1992), 49–51.

3 Fernand Dumont, *Genèse de la société québécoise* (Montreal: Boréal, 1993), 335.

4 R.M. Baldwin and J. Baldwin, *The Baldwins and the Great Experiment* (Toronto: Longman's, 1969), 151.

5 Baldwin, *The Baldwins*, 190.

6 J.W. Dafoe, speech, 11 June 1941, Kingston, on the fiftieth anniversary of Sir John A. Macdonald's death. Tape recording, National Archives.

7 House of Commons, *Debates*, 6 April 1868, 471.

8 George Grant, *Lament for a Nation* (Toronto: McClelland & Stewart, 1970), 46 and x. Originally published 1965.

9 Quoted in Stan Dragland, *Floating Voice* (Toronto: House of Anansi Press, 1994), 7.

10 Gerald Friesen, *River Road—Essays on Manitoba—and Prairie History* (Winnipeg: The University of Manitoba Press, 1996), 11.

11 Abbé Lionel Groulx, *Notre maître le passé* (Montreal: Granger Frères, 1936), 258.

12 Quoted in John Kelly, "We are all in the Ojibway Circle," *From Ink Lake,* comp. Michael Ondaatje (Toronto: Vintage Canada, 1995).

13 Dragland, *Floating Voice*, 10.

14 Roger Gibbins and Sonia Arrian, *Western Visions: Perspectives on the West in Canada* (Peterborough, Ont.: Broadview Press, 1995), 14.

15 *The Atlantic Region to Confederation* ed. Phillip Buckner and John Reid (Toronto: University of Toronto Press, 1994), 29.

16 Lesley Choyce, *Nova Scotia* (Toronto: Viking, 1996), 19.

17 See especially Robert Allen, *His Majesty's Indian Allies: British Indian Policy in The Defence of Canada, 1774–1815* (Toronto: Dundurn Press, 1993).

18 George Woodcock, *Gabriel Dumont* (Edmonton: Hurtig Publishers, 1976).

19 Gerald Friesen, *The Canadian Prairies* (Toronto: University of Toronto Press, 1987), 165.

20 Rudy Wiebe, *The Temptations of Big Bear* (Toronto: McClelland & Stewart, 1995), 381.

21 Gabriel Dumont, *Gabriel Dumont Speaks* tr. Michael Barnholden
(Vancouver: Talonbooks, 1993), 13–14.

22 As argued by Buckner and Reid, *The Atlantic Region*, 38.

23 Robert Baldwin, "The Death of Tecumsee," written in 1819–20.
Contained in a collection compiled by James Hunter Samson in 1820.
File L6, section II, Robert Baldwin Papers, Metropolitan Toronto
Reference Library.

24 Quoted in Helen Caister Robinson, *Joseph Brant—A Man for His People*
(Toronto: Dundurn Press, 1986), 169–70.

25 John Kelly, "We are all in the Ojibway Circle," *From Ink Lake*, 585.

6. The North American Nation

1 James Thomas Flexner, *Mohawk Baronet* (New York: Harper's, 1959), 312.

2 Allan Greer, "Historical Roots of Canadian Democracy." 1996 Porter
Lecture, Canadian Sociology and Anthropology Association.

3 George Grant, *Lament for a Nation* (Toronto: McClelland & Stewart,
1970), x.

4 "protector and wet nurse": Maurice Séguin, *L'Idée d'indépendance au
Québec—genèse et historique* (Montreal: Boréal, 1968), 12. "humanized":
Michel Brunet, *Canadians et Canadiens* (Montreal: Fides, 1954), 12.
"stood behind": Séguin, *L'Idée*, 10–11.

5 Brunet, *Canadians*, 51.

6 L.H. LaFontaine, *L'Aurore des Canadas*, 28 August 1840, 1. R.M. Baldwin
and J. Baldwin, *The Baldwins and the Great Experiment* (Toronto:
Longman's, 1969), 168. *The Examiner*, 8 September 1841, 7. "To the Free
and Independent Electors of the Fourth Riding of the County of York,"
Debates of Legislative Assembly, 13 September 1842.

7 Kevin McMahon, *Arctic Twilight* (Toronto: James Lorimer & Co.,
1988), 20.

8 Nellie McClung, *In Times Like These* (Toronto: University of Toronto Press,
1972), 97. Originally published 1915.

9 Quoted in W.L. Morton, *The Progressive Party in Canada* (Toronto:
University of Toronto Press, 1967), 237. Originally published 1950.

10 Leo Tolstoy, *Master and Man and Other Stories* (Harmondsworth: Penguin
Books, 1977), 33.

11 Alfred D. de Celles, *LaFontaine et son temps* (Montreal: Beauchemin,
1907), 183.

12 Graeme Patterson, *History and Communications—Harold Innis, Marshall*

McLuhan, the Interpretation of History (Toronto: University of Toronto Press, 1990), 34. All of Parts I and II help to understand this theme.

13 Jacques Godbout, *Les Têtes à Papineau* (Paris: Seuil, 1981), 21.

PART II

7. Ideas over Facts

1 Patricia Smart and Dorothy Howard, comps. and trans., *The Diary of André Laurendeau: 1964–67* (Toronto: Lorimer, 1991), 95.

2 Monique Proulx, *Les Aurores montréales* (Montreal: Boréal, 1996), 132.

8. A Country of Minorities

1 *Eyeing the North Star: Directions in African Canadian Literature* ed. George Elliott Clarke (Toronto: McClelland & Stewart, 1997), 12, 18, 24.

2 Lawrence Wright, "Double Mystery," *The New Yorker*, 7 August 1995, 46.

9. Poverty

1 L.H. LaFontaine, "Address to the Electors of Terrebonne."

2 Louis-Philippe Audet, *Histoire l'enseignement au Québec, 1840–1971* (Montreal: Holt, Rinehart and Winston, 1971), vol. 2, 63.

3 Gerald Friesen, *The Canadian Prairies* (Toronto: University of Toronto Press, 1987), 248.

4 Emily Carr, *The Book of Small* (Toronto: Clarke, Irwin, 1942), 116.

5 All of these numbers are from Robert Bothwell, Ian Drummond, John English, *Canada 1900–1945* (Toronto: University of Toronto Press, 1987), 188, 193.

6 Gerald Friesen, *River Road—Essays on Manitoba—and Prairie History* (Winnipeg: University of Manitoba Press, 1996), 193–94.

7 Harold Innis, *The Bias of Communication* (Toronto: University of Toronto Press, 1991), 82.

10. Anti-Heroism

1 George Bowering, *A Short Sad Book* (Vancouver: Talon Books, 1977), 75.

2 George Woodcock, *Gabriel Dumont* (Edmonton: Hurtig Publishers, 1976), 10.

3 Arthur Buies, *Lettres sur le Canada* (Montreal: l'Étincelle, 1978), 20.

4 Hugh MacLennan, *The Watch That Ends the Night* (Toronto: Macmillan of Canada, 1958), 167. Leo Tolstoy, *War and Peace* tr. Rosemary Edmonds (Harmondsworth: Penguin Books, 1982), 484–87. Robertson Davies, *Fifth Business* (Toronto: Penguin Books, 1970), 6. Jacques Brault, "Suite fraternelle," *La Poésie québécoise* (Montreal: l'Hexagone, 1986), 368. Nellie McClung, *In Times Like These* (Toronto: University of Toronto Press, 1972), 26. Charles C. Hill, *The Group of Seven: Art for a Nation* (Toronto: McClelland & Stewart, 1996), 65. Emily Carr, *Hundreds and Thousands: The Journals of Emily Carr* (Toronto: Clarke, Irwin, 1966), 80.

5 George Frederick Cameron, "My Political Faith," *The Penguin Book of Canadian Verse* ed. Ralph Gustafson (Harmondsworth: Penguin Books, 1958), 54.

11. The Coureur de bois–Habitant Tension

1 Oliver Goldsmith, "The Rising Village," *The New Oxford Book of Canadian Verse* ed. Margaret Atwood (Toronto: Oxford University Press, 1982), 5. *Projet de Loi sur l'avenir du Québec, Préambule, Déclaration de souveraineté.* Éditeur officiel du Québec, 1995, 7.

2 Stan Rogers, *North West Passage* (Halifax: Fogarty's Cove Music, 1981). Quotes from "The Field Behind the Plow" and "North West Passage."

3 E.J. Pratt, "Towards the Last Spike," *Complete Poems, Part 2* (Toronto: University of Toronto Press, 1989), 209, 219, 232.

4 Alfred DesRochers, "Le Cycle des bois et des champs," *La Poésie québécoise* ed. Laurent Mailhot and Pierre Nepveu (Quebec: l'Hexagone, 1990), 181. From *A l'Ombre de l'Orford (1929)*.

5 Don McKay, "Accidental, Exotics and Escapes," *Birding, or desire* (Toronto: McClelland & Stewart, 1983), 26.

6 *From Ink Lake* ed. Michael Ondaatje (Toronto: Vintage Canada, 1995), xvii.

7 Laurence Kelly, *Lermontov* (New York: George Braziller, 1978), 38.

12. East–West

1 Paul Painchaud, of the Laval International Institute for Environmental Strategies and Security, quoted in the *Report of the House of Commons Standing Committee on Foreign Affairs and International Trade on Canada and the Circumpolar World*, April 1997, 23. Chair: Bill Graham.

2 *The Ottawa Citizen*, 17 April 1997, 1.
3 Donald G. Creighton, *The Decline and Fall of the Empire of the St. Lawrence: Towards the Discovery of Canada* (Toronto: Macmillan of Canada, 1972), 160.
4 Gerald Friesen, *River Road—Essays on Manitoba—and Prairie History* (Winnipeg: University of Manitoba Press, 1996), 16.
5 Figures cited in an exhibit at the New York Historical Society, January 1996.
6 Alaska, Iowa, Maine, Massachusetts, Michigan, Minnesota, North Dakota, Rhode Island, Vermont, Wisconsin. The other three are Hawaii (again an exception to the North American rule), D.C. and West Virginia.
7 Stan Rogers, "Free in the Harbour," *North West Passage* (Halifax: Fogarty's Cove Music, 1981).
8 Gerald Friesen, "Western Canada and the Pacific Rim." Paper presented to Vienna University. Association for the Promotion of North American Studies, 1992.
9 Friesen, "Western Canada."
10 "Do National Borders Matter for Quebec's Trade?" Draft paper for presentation at the Annual Meetings of the Canadian Economics Association, Université du Québec à Montréal, 1995.
11 For a discussion of this, see Graeme Patterson, *History and Communications—Harold Innis, Marshall McLuhan, the Interpretation of History* (Toronto: University of Toronto Press, 1990), especially Chapters 1 and 2.
12 Marshall McLuhan, "The Later Innis," *Queen's Quarterly* 60 (1953), 385.

13. Practical Metaphysics

1 For example, see J. Murray Beck, *Joseph Howe* (Kingston: McGill-Queen's University Press, 1982), vol.1, 141.
2 Graeme Patterson, *History and Communications—Harold Innis, Marshall McLuhan, the Interpretation of History* (Toronto: University of Toronto Press, 1990), 12.
3 Alastair Sweeny, *Georges-Étienne Cartier* (Toronto: McClelland & Stewart, 1976), 239.
4 *The Globe and Mail*, 16 July 1996, A4. Statement by Jacques Brassard.
5 Address by the Right Hon. Sir Wilfrid Laurier, The Eastern Ontario Liberal Association, 14 January 1919, Ottawa. Booklet.
6 Clément Marchand, "Les Prolétaires," *Les Soirs rouges* (Montreal: Stanké, 1986). Originally published 1932.

7 Georges-Émile Lapalme, *Le Bruit des choses réveillées* (Montreal: Leméac, 1969), vol. 1, 238.

8 Lapalme, *Le Bruit*, 304.

14. Animism

1 Gerald Friesen, *River Road—Essays on Manitoba—and Prairie History* (Winnipeg: The University of Manitoba Press, 1996), 168. "Environmentalism need not become determinism": Friesen discusses the tendency of Canadian scholars to balance environment and human endeavour.

2 E.B.Tylor, *Primitive Cultures* (London: J. Murray, 1871), vol. 1, 414 and 502. See also William McDougall, *Body and Mind, A History and a Defence of Animism* (London: Methuen, 1911).

3 Henry David Thoreau, *Walden* (New York: Everyman's Library, 1910), 3, 188, 199, 102. Originally published 1854. His retreat lasted from 1845 to 1847.

4 Jaan Kaplinski, *Through the Forest* (London: The Harvill Press, 1991), 40, 42, 43.

5 August Strindberg, *By the Open Sea* (Harmondsworth: Penguin Books, 1984), 3. George Bowering, *A Short Sad Book* (Vancouver: Talon Books, 1977), 42. Joy Kogawa, *Obasan* (Toronto: Penguin Books, 1983), 111. Kaplinski, *Through the Forest*, 12. Anne Hébert, "Je suis la terre et l'eau," *Poèmes* (Paris: Seuil, 1960). Al Purdy, *Purdy Selected* (Toronto: McClelland & Stewart, 1972), 21. Gatien Lapointe, "Ode au Saint-Laurent," *Les Poètes du jour* (Éditions du Jour, 1963). Gwendolyn MacEwen, "Dark Pines Under Water," *Magic Animals: Collected Poems Old and New* (Toronto: Macmillan of Canada, 1979).

6 Kjell Espmark, *L'Oubli* (Paris: Gallimard, 1987), 86.

7 Rudy Wiebe, "The Elusive Meaning of North," *Canadian Geographic*, January–February 1996.

8 Louis-Edmond Hamelin, *Canadian Nordicity* (Quebec: Hurtubise, 1980), 77. See also Hamelin's definition of nordicity in *The Canadian Encyclopedia* (Edmonton: Hurtig, 1988).

9 The poet Dan McKay, quoted in Stan Dragland, *Floating Voice* (Toronto: House of Anansi Press, 1994), 18.

10 Stan Dragland, *Floating Voice*, 46.

11 Diamond Jenness, *The Faith of a Coast Salish Indian* (Victoria: British Columbia Provincial Museum, 1955). *Anthropology in British Columbia*, Memoirs, Nos. 2, 3.

12 Jenness, *The Faith*, 41.

13 Stephen Inglis, conversation with author, 18 June 1996, Canadian Museum of Civilization, Hull.

14 George Grant, *Technology and Empire* (Toronto: House of Anansi Press, 1969), 17.

15 "no self-deceiving": Robertson Davies, *World of Wonders* (Toronto: Penguin Books, 1977), 313. Robertson Davies, *Fifth Business* (Toronto: Penguin Books, 1970), 59. Hugh MacLennan, *The Watch That Ends the Night* (Toronto: Macmillan of Canada, 1958), 361. Pierre Morency, *Lumière des oiseaux* (Montreal: Boréal, 1992), 50. Don McKay, "The Great Blue Heron," *Birding, or desire* (Toronto: McClelland & Stewart, 1983), 32. Paul Quarrington, *King Leary* (Toronto: Seal Books, 1988), 53. Marian Engel, *Bear* (Toronto: McClelland & Stewart, 1976). Claude Gauvreau, "La Jeune fille et la Lune," *La Poèsie québécoise* ed. Laurent Mailhot and Pierre Nepveu (Montreal: l'Hexagone, 1990), 258. Kerstin Ekman, *Blackwater* (New York: Vintage, 1996), 10, 31. "geographical animism": *The Oxford Book of Canadian Verse* ed. A.J.M. Smith (Toronto: Oxford University Press, 1960), xxx. Isabella Valancy Crawford, "The Lily Bed," *Collected Poems* (Toronto: University of Toronto Press, 1972), 169.

16 Rudy Wiebe, *The Temptations of Big Bear* (Toronto: McClelland & Stewart, 1995), 28.

17 Kevin McMahon, *Arctic Twilight* (Toronto: James Lorimer & Co., 1988), 114.

18 Sharon Butala, *The Perfection of the Morning* (Toronto: HarperCollins, 1994), 130. David Young, *Inexpressible Island*. 1997 workshop production, du Maurier Theatre, Toronto.

15. The Animistic Image

1 Marius Barbeau, quoted in Charles C. Hill, *The Group of Seven: Art for a Nation* (Toronto: McClelland & Stewart, 1996), 192.

2 Roald Nasgaard, *The Mystic North: Symbolist Landscape Painting in Northern Europe and North America, 1890–1940* (Toronto: University of Toronto Press, 1984), 8.

3 Nasgaard, *The Mystic North*, 9 and 38. Richard Bergh on Karl Nordström, writing at the end of the seventeenth century.

4 Nasgaard, *The Mystic North*, 36.

5 Hill, *The Group of Seven: Art for a Nation*, 71.

6 Préfontaine, quoted in Hill, *Art for a Nation*, 31.

7 François-Marc Gagnon, *Paul-Émile Borduas* (Montreal: Fides, 1978), 304.

8 A.J.M. Smith, "The Lonely Land," *The Oxford Book of Canadian Verse*, ed. A.J.M. Smith (Toronto: Oxford University Press, 1960), 98.

9 Michael Ondaatje, introduction to *Paterson Ewen* (Toronto: Douglas and McIntyre, 1996), 3, 4.

16. Oral over Written

1 Charles C. Hill, *The Group of Seven: Art for a Nation* (Toronto: McClelland & Stewart, 1996), 79.

2 Stan Dragland, *Floating Voice* (Toronto: House of Anansi Press, 1994), 7.

3 George Woodcock, *Gabriel Dumont* (Edmonton: Hurtig Publishers, 1976), 11.

4 Honoré Mercier and Wilfrid Laurier, speeches, in Robert Rumilly, *Histoire de la province de Québec* (Montreal: Éditions Bernard Valiquette, 1940), vol. 5, 117–25.

5 House of Commons, *Debates*, 16 March 1886. *Wilfird Laurier à la Tribune, 1871–1890* (Quebec: Ulric Barthe, 1890), 270–321. "Rebellion is always... What is hateful": 292. "Loyalty must be... Have the government": 298. "Had they taken": 319. "Our prisons": 320.

6 Oscar Douglas Skelton, *Life and Letters of Sir Wilfrid Laurier* (Toronto: Oxford University Press, 1921), vol.1, 328–31. *Wilfrid Laurier à la Tribune*, 363. Toronto, 10 December 1886.

7 William Kilbourn, *The Firebrand* (Toronto: Clarke, Irwin, 1956), 19, 68, 23.

8 Kilbourn, *The Firebrand*.

9 Woodcock, *Gabriel Dumont*, 18.

17. An Idea of Balance

1 Seymour Martin Lipset, *American Exceptionalism* (New York: Norton, 1977).

PART III
18. An Existential Moment

1 A.M. Klein, *Complete Poems, Part 2* ed. Zailig Pollock (Toronto: University of Toronto Press, 1990), 466.

2 Wilfrid Laurier, speech, 10 December 1886, Toronto.

3 Lucien Bouchard, press conference, 27 October 1997.

4 Gordon Lightfoot, "Back Here on Earth," LP (UAS 6672, 1968).

5 Wilfrid Laurier, "Le libéralisme politique," speech, 26 June 1877, Quebec, 83.
6 "Welfare Incomes, 1995." A report by the National Council of Welfare, Winter 1996–97. Minister of Supply and Services Canada, 1997. Page 15, Table 2. "Estimated Welfare Income, by type of Household, 1995." Based on: Basic Social Assistance, Additional Benefits, Child Tax Benefit, Provincial Child Benefits, GST Credit, Provincial Tax Credits.

The calculation in this table is for a couple with two children:

North-West Territories	25,264
Yukon	22,413
Ontario	21,070
Manitoba	19,422
P.E.I.	18,511
B.C.	17,906
Saskatchewan	17,451
Alberta	17,367
Quebec	16,104
Nova Scotia	15,120
Newfoundland	14,834
New Brunswick	13,256

Note also (page 25) Welfare Income as a percentage of the poverty line, again for a couple with two children. The lower the percentage, the farther the family falls below the poverty line. As the table shows, even those at the top of the list live in deep poverty. What isn't shown is the growing percentage of families who are excluded from welfare and have no calculable income.

P.E.I.	69
Ontario	67
Saskatchewan	63
Manitoba	62
B.C.	57
Alberta	55
Nova Scotia	55
Newfoundland	54
Quebec	51
New Brunswick	48

7 *Projet de Loi sur l'avenir du Québec, Préambule, Déclaration de souveraineté.*
   Éditeur officiel du Québec, 1995, 8.

8 For example, see Ken Osborne: "Democratic Citizenship and the Teaching
   of History," *The Journal of the Citizenship Foundation.* "Citizenship, Heritage
   and Community: The Place of History in Canadian Schools." Paper
   delivered to the Association of Manitoba Museums and Heritage Canada
   Conference, Winnipeg, Manitoba, October 1995. "Teaching Heritage in
   the Classroom." Symposium on The Place of Memory.

9 *Se souvenir et devenir: Rapport du groupe de travail sur l'enseignement de
   l'histoire* (Quebec: Gouvernement du Québec, 1996), 36. See also its
   recommendations, pages 73–76.

10 For example, see Monique Nemni: "L'école québécoise au service des
   nationalistes," *Cité Libre,* November–December 1994. "Comment on
   abrutit nos enfants," *Cité Libre,* November–December 1994. "Le
   nationalisme dans l'enseignement de l'histoire au Québec," paper
   presenteed at ACFAS, May 1996. "Les histoires qu'on raconte sur Pierre
   Elliott Trudeau," *Cité Libre,* March–April 1997. "Bienvenue au Québec! Le
   Canada, connais pas," *Cité Libre,* March–April, 1997.

11 Michel Gervais quoted in *La Presse,* 9 April 1997, p. 34.

12 William Kilbourn, *The Firebrand* (Toronto: Clarke, Irwin, 1956), 115.

13 August Strindberg, quoted in Olof Lagercrantz, *August Strindberg*
   (London: Faber and Faber, 1984), 141.

14 Leonard Cohen, *Stranger Music* (Toronto: McClelland & Stewart,
   1993), 374.

19. The Referendum Syndrome

1 *Débats de l'Assemblée nationale,* 11 September 1995, 4751.

2 Renaud Longchamps, "Primaire," *Miguasha* (Montreal: VLB Éditeur, 1983).

3 Harold Innis, *The Bias of Communication* (Toronto: University of Toronto
   Press, 1991), 83.

4 Anne Hébert and Frank Scott, *Dialogue sur la traduction* (Montreal:
   Éditions HMH, 1970), 105.

5 House of Commons, *Debates,* 16 March 1886. *Wilfrid Laurier à la Tribune,
   1871–1890* (Quebec: Ulric Barthe, 1890).

6 Marc Angenot, quoted in *L'actualité,* 1 June 1996, 18.

7 A.M. Klein, *Complete Poems, Part 2* ed. Zailig Pollock (Toronto: University
   of Toronto Press, 1990), 465.

8 Alice Munro, "Miles City, Montana," *The Progress of Love* (Toronto:
   Penguin Books, 1986), 123.

9 Parizeau, *Débats de l'Assemblée nationale*, 11 September 1995, 4751.
10 Lucien Bouchard, speech, 10 October 1995, Chateaugay.
11 See the analysis by Michel Venne in *Le Devoir*, 12 March 1996, 6.
12 *The Globe and Mail*, 29 October 1996, 1.
13 Parizeau, *Débats*, 4757.
14 Lucien Bouchard, *A visage découvert* (Montreal: Boréal, 1992), 351. A curiously inaccurate reference to Jacques Godbout's *Les Têtes à Papineau*.
15 Munro, "Monsieur les Deux Chapeaux," *Progress of Love*, 112.

20. A Natural and Inevitable Event

1 *Débats de l'Assemblée nationale*, 11 September 1995, 4751.
2 My comments are based on David Cameron's lengthy discussion in *The University of Toronto Bulletin*, 9 January 1995.
3 Bernard Landry, *The Globe and Mail*, 8 January 1996, P1.
4 *Le Devoir*, 11 July 1996.
5 Daniel Turp, "Quebec's Democratic Right to Self-Determination," *Tangled Web* (Toronto: C.D. Howe Institute, 1992), 101.
6 Conversation between author and a group of Maritimes social historians, including Rick Williams, Colin Howell, Margaret Conrad and Jim Sharpe, 26 June 1996, Halifax.

21. Multiple Reconciliations

1 Pedrag Matvejevitch, *Le Monde "EX"—Confessions* (Paris: Fayard, 1996).
2 Daniel Turp, "Quebec's Democratic Right to Self-Determination," *Tangled Web* (Toronto: C.D. Howe Institute, 1992), 118–19.
3 *La Presse*, May 1977, B5.

22. Positive versus Negative

1 Patricia Smart and Dorothy Howard, comps. and trans., *The Diary of André Laurendeau: 1964–67* (Toronto: Lorimer, 1991), 91.
2 L.H. LaFontaine, *L'Aurore des Canadas*, 28 August 1840. "Address to the Electors of Terrebonne."
3 Brian Young, conversation with author, 20 March 1996.
4 Léon Pouliot, *Monseigneur Bourget et son Temps* (Montreal: Bellarmin, 1977), vol. 2, 80.
5 Honoré Mercier, speech, 24 June 1889.
6 Isaiah, 53: 4–5.

7   Joseph Schull, *Laurier* (Toronto: Macmillan of Canada, 1965), 384.

8   Maurice Séguin, *L'Idée d'indépendance au Québec—genèse et historique* (Montreal: Boréal, 1968), 56.

9   *La Presse*, 27 January 1996.

10 Séguin, *L'Idée*, Preface, 7.

11 Séguin, *L'Idée*, 60. Footnote 131. Paul Bouchard, *La Nation*, 7 May 1936.

12 Paul Bouchard, "L'Union Nationale et l'Autonomie," speech, 5 May 1948, Club Renaissance. See also: Paul Bouchard, *La Province de Québec sous l'Union Nationale* (Quebec, 1956). André-J. Bélanger, *L'Apolitisme des idéologues québécois* (Quebec: Les Presses de l'Université Laval, 1974). Michael Oliver, *The Passionate Debate* (Montreal: Véhicule Press, 1991). Fernand Dumont, Jean Hamelin and Jean-Paul Montminy, *Idéologies au Canada français* (Quebec: Les Presses de l'Université Laval, 1978).

13 Michel Brunet, *Canadians et Canadiens* (Montreal: Fides, 1954), 115.

14 Maurice Duplessis, speech, 1946, at the Windsor Hotel.

15 Jean-Guy Genest, *Godbout* (Montreal: Septention, 1996), 153.

16 *The Gazette*, 11 June 1997, A9. $1,228 per man, woman, child and 22 per cent of the budget. At the top, B.C. spends $1,814 and 34 per cent of its budget.

PART IV

23. Trying to Remember

1   *Le Devoir*, 25 March 1996, B1.

2   Harold Innis, quoted by Donald Wright in "The Innis Research Bulletin," Toronto, December 1995, Issue 3. René-Daniel Dubois, "8 Octobre 1990." Unpublished essay.

3   Allan Greer, *The People of New France* (Toronto: University of Toronto Press, 1997), 19.

24. Fragments of a Past — I

1   Robert Baldwin, writing in *The Examiner*, 18 September 1844.

2   Quoted in Ramsay Cook, "Founding Peoples or Sovereign Nations?" *The Beaver*, June–July 1996.

3   Macdonald to Robert Gowan, 10 July 1980. Quoted by Larry Kulisek in the entry on D'Alton McCarthy, *Dictionary of Canadian Biography* (Toronto: University of Toronto Press, 1990), vol. XII, 583. Alastair Sweeny, *Georges-Étienne Cartier* (Toronto: McClelland & Stewart, 1976), 102.

4 Lucien Bouchard, *A visage découvert* (Montreal: Boréal, 1992), 80.

5 Jean Hamelin, conversation with author, January 1996, Quebec City. Michel Brunet, *Canadians et Canadiens* (Montreal: Fides, 1955), 21. "unmasked the imposter": Maurice Séguin, *L'Idée d'indépendance au Québec—genèse et historique* (Montreal: Boréal, 1968), 65. "consecrated the failure": Fernand Dumont, Jean Hamelin and Jean-Paul Montminy, *Idéologies au Canada français* (Quebec: Les Presses de l'Université Laval, 1978), 328.

6 Wilfrid Laurier, speech, "Contre Le Bill McCarthy," House of Commons, *Debates*, 17 February 1890, 595.

7 *Le Devoir*, 27 May 1997, 1.

8 *Le Devoir*, 29 May 1994, 8. "Le pire défaut des Québécois francophones, c'est le mépris de soi."

9 Séguin, *L'Idée*, 63.

10 Charles Taylor, *Radical Tories* (Toronto: House of Anansi Press, 1982), 54.

11 Jacques Godbout, *Les Têtes à Papineau* (Paris: Seuil, 1981), 95.

12 Thomas Pakenham, *The Boer War* (London: Weidenfeld and Nicolson, 1979), 136, 215.

13 *The Rowell–Sirois Report on Dominion–Provincial Relations* (Toronto: Macmillan of Canada, 1978), 4.

14 William C. Beeching, *Canadian Volunteers, Spain—1936–1939* (Regina: Canadian Plains Research Centre, 1989), Duplessis, 6–9; message to King, 56.

15 Victor Howard and Mac Reynolds, *The Mackenzie–Papineau Battalion* (Ottawa: Carleton University Press, 1986), 240.

25. The Indifferent Mothers

1 Anne Hébert, "Le Tombeau des rois," *Œuvre poétique* (Montreal: Boréal, 1994).

2 R.M. Baldwin and J. Baldwin, *The Baldwins and the Great Experiment* (Toronto: Longman's, 1969), 56, 146, 152.

3 Herbert C.W. Goltz, "Tecumseh," in *Dictionary of Canadian Biography* (Toronto: University of Toronto Press, 1983), vol. V, 800.

4 Bernard Holland, *The Fall of Protection: 1840–1850* (London: Edward Arnold, 1913). See 117–29 and 291–321.

5 Roy Jenkins, *Gladstone* (London: Macmillan, 1995).

6 Donald Creighton, *John A. Macdonald, The Old Chieftain* (Toronto: Macmillan of Canada, 1955), 80, 102.

7 Oscar D. Skelton, *The Day of Sir Wilfrid Laurier* (Toronto: Chronicles of

Canada, 1915), 215. Oscar D. Skelton, *Life and Letters of Sir Wilfrid Laurier* (Toronto: Oxford University Press, 1921), 157.

8 See Allan Greer, "1837–38 Rebellion Reconsidered," *Canadian Historical Review*, vol. LXXVI, no.1 (March 1995), 15.

9 V.S. Naipaul, *The Return of Eva Peron* (New York: Vintage, 1981), 124.

10 *Les Deux Canadas: 1760–1810—L'Histoire canadienne à travers le document* (Montreal: Guérin, 1978), 117.

11 *L'Honorable P.J.D. Chauveau* (Montreal: George Desbarats, 1872), 27, 31.

26. Fragments of a Past—II

1 Wilfrid Laurier, speech, 14 January 1919, Ottawa (Liberal party pamphlet). Donald Swainson, "J.S. Woodsworth and a Political Party for Labour," *Historical Essays on the Prairie Provinces* (Toronto: McClelland & Stewart, 1970), 243.

2 Doris French Shackleton, *Tommy Douglas* (Toronto: McClelland & Stewart, 1975), 37–40, 25.

3 Hector de Saint-Denys Garneau, "Le Jeu," *Regards et jeux dans l'espace* (Montreal: Bibliothèque québécoise, 1993), 24. Originally published 1949.

4 Charles Taylor, *Radical Tories* (Toronto: House of Anansi Press, 1982), 74.

5 Lucien Bouchard, *A visage découvert* (Montreal: Boréal, 1992), 85.

6 "You must have had": John Saywell, *Quebec 70* (Toronto: University of Toronto Press, 1971). Ron Haggart and Aubrey Golden, *Rumours of War* (Toronto: James Lorimer, 1979), 1. Originally published 1971.

7 René-Daniel Dubois, "8 Octobre 1990." Unpublished essay.

8 It was clear from the confused reaction of the government members of the committee that the Mexican aspect had not been taken into account. Either that or the government had gone out of its way not to inform its own members.

9 Bernard Landry, *Commerce sans frontières* (Montreal: Québec/Amérique, 1987), 154.

27. The Expression of Reality

1 Robin Blaser, *The Holy Forest* (Toronto: Coach House Press, 1993), 275.

2 "a nation is essentially": *L'actualité*, 15 September 1996. "vague notions": *L'actualité*, January 1992.

3 A.M. Klein, *Complete Poems, Part 2* ed. Zailig Pollock (Toronto: University of Toronto Press, 1990), 635. Albert Ferland, "La patrie au poète,"

Poètes du Québec ed. Jacques Cotnam (Quebec: Bibliothèque Québécoise, 1992), 40.

4 Countess of Athlone, foreword to pamphlet *Welcome to War Brides.*

5 Carl-Henning Wijkmark, *Da Capo* (Paris: Belfond, 1996), 116.

6 Wilfrid Laurier, *Discours sur l'adresse en réponse au discours du Trône*, 10 November 1871.

7 Dany Laferrière, *Chronique de la dérive douce* (Montreal: VLB Éditeur, 1994), 91.

8 Glenn Gould, "The Latecomers." Drama/concerts on Newfoundland. CBC Radio, 1969.

9 Robertson Davies, *Fifth Business* (Toronto: Penguin Books, 1970), 98.

10 Pierre Morency, "Voyage à partir d'une carafe," 1995. Unpublished paper.

11 François Ricard, conversation with author, 25 March 1996.

12 Quoted in *L'actualité*, 15 September 1996.

13 Margaret Atwood, *The New Oxford Book of Canadian Verse* ed. Margaret Atwood (Toronto: Oxford University Press, 1982), xxxvii.

14 Myrna Kostash, "Imagination, Representation and Culture." Paper presented at The Encounter Canada Conference, York University, 6 March 1997.

15 *Le Devoir*, 12 February 1996.

16 François Ricard, conversation with author, 25 March 1996.

17 "Camillien Houde": A.M. Klein, "Political Meeting," *Complete Poems, Part 2*, 657. "This is the man": "Blueprint for a Monument of War," *Complete Poems, Part 2*, 453.

18 Kjell Espmark, *Route tournante* (London: Forest Books, 1993), 4.

19 Alice Munro, *Friend of My Youth* (Toronto: McClelland & Stewart, 1990), 137. Nikolai Gogol, *Dead Souls* tr. David Magarshack (Harmondsworth: Penguin Books, 1961), 17.

20 Robertson Davies, *The Cunning Man* (Toronto: McClelland & Stewart, 1994), 107.

21 "The fields" "In those grey": Wilfrid Campbell, "How One Winter Came In the Lake Region," *The New Oxford Book of Canadian Verse*, 41. "I'll get along": Gordon Lightfoot, "Rosanna." "Sad, crying": Octave Crémazie, *Les Morts.*

22 George Bowering, *Kerrisdale Elegies* (Toronto: Coach House Press, 1984), 6. Jaan Kaplinski, *Through the Forest* (London: The Harvill Press, 1991), 41. Madeleine Gagnon, "Archéologie," *La Poésie québécoise* ed. Laurent Mailhot and Pierre Nepveu (Montreal: l'Hexagone, 1986), 404. John Steffler, *The Afterlife of George Cartwright* (Toronto: McClelland & Stewart, 1992), 93. Gilles Vigneault, "Mon Pays." John Steffler, "Explosions," *Writing Home: A PEN Canada Anthology* (Toronto: McClelland & Stewart, 1997), 332.

23 Ivan Turgenev, *Fathers and Sons* (Harmondsworth: Penguin Books, 1984), 290. Kerstin Ekman, *Blackwater* (New York: Vintage, 1996), 185.

24 Robertson Davies, *Fifth Business* (Toronto: Penguin Books, 1970), 52.

25 *Eyeing the North Star: Directions in African Canadian Literature*, ed. George Elliott Clarke (Toronto: McClelland & Stewart, 1997), xx.

26 George Bowering, *A Short Sad Book* (Vancouver: Talon Books, 1977), 52.

PART V

28. Nationalism

1 Jean-Pierre Derriennic, *Nationalisme et Démocratie* (Montreal: Boréal, 1995), 18.

2 Maurice Séguin, *L'Idée d'indépendance au Québec—genèse et historique* (Montreal: Boréal, 1968), 9.

3 Wilfrid Laurier, speech, 15 August 1918, Trois-Rivières.

4 Georges-Émile Lapalme, *Le Bruit des choses réveillées* (Montreal: Leméac, 1969), vol. 1, 149.

5 Lapalme, *Le Bruit*, 146.

6 Margaret Atwood, conversation with author, 24 June 1997, Toronto.

7 Michel Brunet, "The French Canadians' Search for a *Fatherland*," *Nationalism in Canada* (Toronto: McGraw-Hill, 1966), 47. (My italics)

8 Marcel Trudel, quoted in *L'actualité*, 16 June 1997.

9 Vaclav Havel, "On Evasive Thinking," speech to the Union of Czechoslovak Writers' Conference, 9 June 1965. Translated by Paul Wilson.

10 *The Montreal Gazette*, 20 April 1964.

11 Lucien Bouchard, *A visage découvert* (Montreal: Boréal, 1992), 51.

12 bp Nichol, "late night summer poem," *Canadian Poetry* ed. Jack David and Robert Lecker (Toronto: Stoddart, 1982), vol. 2, 271.

13 *The Globe and Mail*, 21 November 1996, A9.

14 Jean Barman, *The West Beyond the West* (Toronto: University of Toronto Press, 1995), Table 6.

15 Michel Brunet, *Nationalism in Canada* (Toronto: McGraw-Hill, 1966), 29.

16 Euripides, *The Bacchae* tr. Philip Vellacott (Harmondsworth: Penguin Classics, 1954), 200.

17 Lapalme, *Le Bruit*, 315.

18 Bouchard, *Visage*, 135.

19 "almost 50 per cent": *La Presse*, 11 June 1997, A1. "head offices": *The Globe and Mail*, 21 November 1996, B7. "Official Languages Act": *La*

Presse, 4 March 1996, A1. Monique Nemni, "Les histoires qu'on raconte
sur Pierre Elliott Trudeau," *Cité Libre*, March–April 1997.
20 *L'actualité*, January 1992.
21 Séguin, *L'Idée*, 9.

29. The Belt Clingers

1 V.S. Naipaul, *The Return of Eva Peron* (New York: Vintage, 1981), 123.
2 Louis-Edmond Hamelin, *Canadian Nordicity* (Quebec: Hurtubise, 1980), 12.

30. Élites

1 Michèle Lalonde, "Speak White," *Speak White* (Montreal: l'Hexagone, 1974).
2 Wisława Szymborska, "Vocabulary," *View With a Grain of Sand* (New York: Harcourt, Brace, 1995), 17.
3 David Bercuson, *True Patriot* (Toronto: University of Toronto Press, 1993), 273.
4 John Gray, speech at annual meeting of the Canadian Museum Association, 17 June 1996.
5 Alastair Sweeny, *Georges-Étienne Cartier* (Toronto: McClelland & Stewart, 1976), 227.
6 Wilfrid Laurier, House of Commons, *Debates*, 16 March 1886.
7 George Grant, *Lament for a Nation* (Toronto: McClelland & Stewart, 1970), 69.
8 John Newlove, "America," *The New Oxford Book of Canadian Verse* ed. Margaret Atwood (Toronto: Oxford University Press, 1982), 344.
9 Walter L. Gordon, *A Political Memoir* (Halifax: Goodread Biographies, 1997), 25.
10 *L'actualité*, 1 March 1996.
11 V.S. Naipaul, *The Return of Eva Peron* (New York: Vintage, 1981), 123.
12 Rick Williams, conversation with author, 1996, Halifax.
13 Stephen Tomblin, *Ottawa and the Outer Provinces* (Toronto: James Lorimer, 1995), 70.
14 *The Toronto Star*, 1 November 1994, D5.
15 A.M. Klein, "The Poet to the Big Business Man," *Complete Poems, Part 2* (Toronto: University of Toronto Press, 1990), vol. 1, 117.
16 *The Globe and Mail*, 10 June 1996, A11.

17 Alfred D. de Celles, *LaFontaine et son temps* (Montreal: Beauchemin, 1907), 123.

18 Joseph-Arthur Lapointe, "Les Pauvres," *The Oxford Book of Canadian Verse* ed. A.J.M. Smith (Toronto: Oxford University Press, 1960), 123.

19 *The Globe and Mail*, 30 January 1997, B2.

20 Sven Lindquist, *Exterminate All the Brutes* (New York: The New Press, 1996), 65.

21 Quoted by Donald Wright in "The Innis Research Bulletin," Toronto Issue, December 1995, 3.

22 Leo Tolstoy, "Hadji Murat," *Master and Man* (Harmondsworth: Penguin Books, 1977), 176.

23 Leonard Cohen, "Kerensky," *Selected Poems, 1956–68* (Toronto: McClelland & Stewart, 1975), 176.

24 Charlotte Gray, "Lobby Horse," *Saturday Night*, July–August 1992.

25 Newspaper interpretation of the Interim Report of the Federal Task Force on Financial Institutions. *The Toronto Star*, 12 July 1997, C1.

26 Laurier, 29 May 1881. Banquet for Edward Blake in Montreal.

27 Bernard le Calloc'h, quoted in *Littératures de Finlande* (Paris: Massives, 1996), 13.

28 John A. Macdonald, House of Commons, *Debates*, 17 April 1868.

29 *The Toronto Star*, 24 August 1996, 1.

30 Gabrielle Roy, *La Détresse et l'Enchantement* (Montreal: Boréal, 1988), 19, 23, 34.

31. The Sensibility of an Idea

1 Peter H. Russell, *Constitutional Odyssey* (Toronto: University of Toronto Press, 1992), 193.

2 See the remarkable essay on Robert Baldwin by Michael S. Cross and Robert Lochiel Fraser in *Dictionary of Canadian Biography* (Toronto: University of Toronto Press, 1985), vol. VIII, 54.

Acknowledgments

This book was written with the constant help of friends and people I hadn't previously met, drawing on them almost daily, often for the sort of background which wouldn't be mentioned but would give me the confidence to make my own arguments.

First I must acknowledge Jacques Godbout and Alastair Sweeny for their earlier use of the concept of Siamese twins.

And Andrew Staples, for his inventive research, along with Jean-François Garneau, who volunteered so much help. My thanks to Donya Peroff, who dealt wonderfully with a more than complex situation. Laura Roebuck, who again made so much possible. Mary Adachi for her care and knowledge.

Professional historians in particular were open and generous with their thoughts, indications and warnings. Among them were Gerald Friesen, Desmond Morton, Gilles Gallichan, Jean Hamelin, Brian Young, Margaret Conrad, Colin Howell, Allan Greer, Ramsay Cook, Fernand Ouellet, Jacques Lacoursière.

Of course, more than historians can be helpful and generous with their time. I am grateful to a group of professors of political science, economics, geography, literature, law and others. Rick Williams, the political economist, and John Dickson, the civil-liberties activist, were particularly helpful; as were François Ricard, Doug Myers, Jim Sharpe, Alan Artibise, Jim Harding, Paul-André Bourgue, Mel Watkins, Meric Gertler, John Kayes, Daniel Perrault, Patrick Mackelin.

My thanks to the librarians at the Library of Parliament, Donald Curtin in particular; at the Bibliothèque de l'Assemblée Nationale, Jean-Luc Fortin and the other librarians, as well as Maïté Le Goff and David Côtes.

532   To Stephen Inglis at the Canadian Museum of Civilization; Michael Kew and Jennifer Web at the Museum of Anthropology in Vancouver; Robert Janes and Dennis Slater at the Glenbow Museum in Calgary; Charles Hill and Denise Leclerc at the National Gallery.

In Sweden, Heidi von Born, Håkan and Marianne Berggren, Kjell Espmark, Carl-Henning Wijkmark, William and Ellie Clarke, Lucette Nobell. In Finland, Charlotte Airas and Pierre Legué. In Belgium, Jacques de Decker and Jacques Frank.

Also Bill Toye, Bill Glassco, André and Marie Ricard, Brian Fawcett, John Gray, Rob Hillyard, David Silcox, Greg Selinger, Mary Sparling, Paul Corriveau and Josst Bakker.

If this long and difficult project has been possible at all, it is thanks to the wonderful support from my publishers: Cynthia Good and everyone at Penguin; Pascal Assathiany and Jean Bernier, and everyone at Boréal. And to Adrienne, with her perceptions, sharp eye and memory.

Index